Stalking The Average Man
(Volume 1)

The teacher arrives when the student is ready.
She did.
I wasn't.

Library and Archives Canada Cataloguing in Publication

Axelson, John, 1951-
Stalking The Average Man : based on a true story / by John Axelson.

ISBN 978-0986879500

1. Spiritual life. 2. Canada—Biography. 3. Title.

BL624.A94 2011   204   C2011-904908-2

Cover design / photograph © Geri Nolan Hilfiker

Editorial assistance Cote Copyediting

Original Printing by SIPS Publishing, Victoria, B.C. Canada

Visit www.axelson.ca for background pictures, video clips, Large Print format orders, international orders, and pre-orders of the next two volumes.

Contents

Contents

Based on a true story:

The absurd theatre in which I was an unwitting participant is based on an intricate teaching construct that unfolded in a manner unsuited to established storytelling formats. By design, my teacher's nonlinear presentations forced me to extract the elements of the first scheme, or gathering phase, and conform them to a chronology that did not distort otherwise true events. Her goal was to have me claim as my own knowledge the efficacy and necessity of her procedures as if my life depended on them, because it did.

Acknowledgments:

This work would not have been possible without the four decades of overt friendship and surreptitious guardianship that Ed Koenig provided, and the many forms of support that Britta Young and Brenda MacPherson offered. It is dedicated to JBM, the loving memories of Eric and Mary Lee Axelson, and Michael Monty, each of whom left this place better off than they found it.

Special thanks to Lia Avalos for her contributions to editing, and design suggestions, and Geri Nolan for all of the above.

I gratefully acknowledge my former close associations with cameramen Robert Whyte and David Wilson, with whom I shared much of the world's misery, and correspondent Brian Stewart with whom I worked in El Salvador, Nicaragua, Brazil, Chile, Ethiopia, and Mozambique – all hard stuff for me that this gentleman of deep consideration made tolerable.

I also thank Jim Shutsa of CITY TV, a college friend and boss of great skill and integrity, Ann Medina (ABC, CBC) whose often brazen and delightful verbal assaults of Middle Eastern leaders lessened the tension of a rookie, Gavin Hewitt (BBC) for the intangibles that working with a man of heart brings to the table, and Tony Burman, (CBC, Al Jazeera - English, who was relentless in the pursuit of the truth as he understood it.

Foreword

Three hours off the plane from working my first war, I was telling tales in the Cellar Blues Bar in an effort to come to terms with what I had seen; my mouth ran freely from fresh scents of death and obscene scenery for hours.

As colleagues fell silent, and subdued barmaids quietly served us, I began borrowing from 'bang-bang' folklore to create the sense of pending danger and revulsion that I had yet to realize isolated me from their world. And when an otherwise indifferent beauty finally embraced the idea that I was a fascinating man, the template for my post traumatic behaviour was set.

Ironically, maybe inevitably, by my sixth sojourn into man's dark side, I was enduring real incidents I had previously borrowed from now familiar international crews, and had talked about at the Cellar as if they were my experiences. Then I had a déjà vu event: I was so familiar with what was happening around me that I had no doubt about an outcome that had no influence my decisions. As a free spirit in the officially staid business of television news, it did not cross my mind that I had become far too familiar with irrational circumstances. To the contrary, I thought I was becoming uncommonly wise.

My twelfth foray into the madness became my last, when the winds of change blew a tornado across my path in the form of British immigration authorities denying my work visa renewal. This unexpected event caused me to fly to Vancouver, Canada, to see my best friend, Ed, and to check out the freelance market for soundmen.

During this stay, my polished tales of crappy ways to live and die enthralled his friend, Tom, an executive at a post-production company who subsequently offered me contact numbers in the film and television industry. He also suggested my experiences would make an excellent screenplay, an observation I received as schmoozing from a shameless visionary seeding new business.

Ultimately, I stuffed my worldly possessions into three nylon sail bags, and carrying an electronic typewriter, boarded a flight to my hometown, Toronto, only because I knew more people in the industry there. This reasoning turned out to be problematic because events had changed me, and sixteen months later I was again considering moving to Vancouver.

By this time, I had stopped writing a book about what it was like to cover wars to script an innocuous screenplay about helicopter pilots

[6]

working in bush country: on the suggestion of a good friend and mentor, I had applied for and been awarded a New Screenwriters Development Grant, which tipped the scales for me.

I landed in Vancouver with a fifty percent advance toward expenses, six months to complete my project, and nothing standing in my way except my penchant to follow 'insightful' flashes that invariably led me away from developing established elements of my plot. As a result, I lost valuable time trying to make these flashes relevant to my climatic surprise—which, as it turned out, was on me. With only three weeks to go, elements of insights I had individually coaxed into my story over the months merged to allude to a better climax than I had been crafting.

I was not as concerned about getting the balance of the money as I felt gutted by the sputtering fizzle of an ending that screwed up the potential references offered by the review committee. This meant I had to consign my first professional credit to silence, and because I had no track record, start over.

Ed saw that I was troubled, by what he didn't ask, and on his dime he invited me to join him, Tom, and two others at the Avalon Gentleman's Club to help me find a broader view of life than my own colon was currently providing.

Fortuitously, nearing the end of this evening, Tom made a double entendre comment intended to have me speak about my version of the bang-bang and I told him about an incident in a place I called Goodbye. Because it involved helicopters, this tale led me to explaining the problem I had with my screenplay, to which Tom dedicated brief seconds before saying I should upgrade one of my helicopters. In two sentences, he explained how I could fuse my unintended implication to a slightly reworked climax, then offering me a business card on which he had scribbled a phone number, he said, "A friend needs help converting her book into a screenplay format. She's a looker," he said seriously.

"Maybe later," I said, to not seem unappreciative; I had a lot to do.

"That's perfect," he replied, sliding the card between my fingers. "Bonnie is expecting to hear from you tonight...shit!" he exclaimed, looking at his watch as if it had bit him. Dropping cash on the table, he left to meet his girlfriend.

Later at home, fuelled by unnecessary nightcaps and thoughts of lacy undergarments, I made the call that would lead to the doom of everything I believed about free spirits, the winds of change, and how much baggage I really had brought with me.

Chapter One
The Fourth Estate

Early the next morning, I inserted a floppy disk into my Atari 64 computer and called up files from my book in progress: Bonnie had hinted that we should exchange samples of our work to see if we were creatively compatible, and as a courtesy act of trust, by revealing ideas that were not copyrighted. Confidently pleased over the clever ease and causal humour we had shared in our first conversation, I read the best of my potential offerings without feeling I had to commit to it.

Axelson   You Taught Me Well   Page 42
Chapter 03 –The Good Guys: Pt 1

"Axe!" LeBlanc barked as he wobbled into my eye line through the after work crowd at Julie's Mansion; Illona casually reached sideways from her overstuffed chair and grabbed his belt to steady him.

"Couple loose cartons and lots of pins," he said, expelling a lung and a half of steely grey smoke into an unsuspecting room. "No ball caps," he added, waving a fickle path with his index finger. "The fuckers'll steal'em on the way in." Abruptly, he turned to leave and Illona released him into a lurch, which Robbie twisted into the pivot of an afterthought by swinging his arm to tap the side of his substantial nose. Rolling her eyes, Illona leaned forward to again steady him, as he sagely said, "Rio," meaning bring lots of toilet paper, as if I would forget projectile shitting in one of the most beautiful places on earth.

"No sweat. I've still got some Canadian flag collar pins, as well," I said, re-establishing eye contact with the leggy woman who had been checking me out. Thirtyish, subtly painted, no ring on the kill-joy finger. Even if...

"You're gonna know sweat," Robbie muttered toward the carpet, apparently willing his feet to move through the tangle of boots, coats, and purses that had ensnared him. Pausing for an intellectually tedious drag on his cigarette, a solution made its way through the internal haze, Rob wiggled his toes to locate his own shoes, then he leaned toward the exit.

Illona released him into God's hands a day sooner than was scheduled on The Nationals' assignment board.

"The flight to Rochester leaves at ten," I said to his back. "Meet you at customs at eight."

[8]

"Anything else he should know?" Percy, a pretentious technician who occasionally worked with him said.

LeBlanc stopped short, swaying under the influence of combined poisons while the four women on the love seats next to ours snatched quick sips in preparation for another rutted pilgrimage into the remnants of his mind.

"When we hit the ground," Robbie replied, turning to locate Percy's face, "Axe will say nothing he doesn't want every fuckin' one to know, and if the state plumber says shit runs uphill, he'll stand on his head to fart. S'not simple," he opined with a questioning glance at our table. An independent thought inserted itself, and he reached into his pocket to pull out a wad of crisp travel money. A twenty fluttered toward the floor.

Rob's contemplative expression quickly resolved that retrieving the bill was too risky, as Percy said, "I got everything up to how snot is simple." He glanced toward the petite brunette sitting next to Legs.

Refocusing, LeBlanc jabbed a nicotine-stained finger toward Percy's smug face and emphasized, "I'm telling him to act like a dumb-fuck, who can't find a shithouse without a producer booking the hole. If anybody talks to him, he's not gonna whine about his pay scale humping heavy shit through mined fields because his second wife is getting nastier by the pound, and dying quick is better than word by nagging fuckin' word." Standing studiously erect, he carefully peeled a hundred dollar bill from the stack in his hand, and said, "S'not simple *learning* how to be an asshole." He set the bill beside the hundred he had forgotten he had already put there.

"R.J., buddy," I said, tapping my wrist where a watch would have been if I gave a shit about time.

Satisfied with a parting shot that was less than his full capabilities, Rob left to pack for a three week road trip.

Percy dismissed the exchange with a pitiful shake of his head, glancing toward the brunette to gage whether she had learned of his marital status, while the busty brunette sitting close to Doug leaned unnecessarily far to ask him what misfortune had befallen Rochester, New York.

"They're working a story on cable TV programming," he said blandly.

"Then they're going to El Salvador," Illona said, picking the twenty off the floor. With a wink my way, she took the extra hundred from the table and handing me the money said just loudly enough, 'If Legs doesn't do you, come and see me for your last one."

"Whom and what was the mad fornicator about?" Legs interjected, pronouncing 'for-neh-kay-tor' conscientiously.

"That depends; do you work for a credit card company?" I said as Percy mouthed 'whom?' toward the brunette.

Without hesitation, in crisp sentences, Katerina placed her life in time and space before closing her monologue with what I interpreted

[9]

as sultry syllables insinuating a satin sheet ride if I was forthcoming. Setting my crystal glass aside, I cleared my throat in preparation of explaining the paradox that was Robbie (R.J.) LeBlanc.

I first told Katie that he was a senior network news cameraman who worked and drank like an obsessive-compulsive never quite getting it right, and that correspondents from Washington to Hong Kong joked about his rare moments of lucidity with a confused respect for nature having compensated him with uncanny instincts and a brilliant professional eye. I admitted that I hadn't paid attention to his gifts during a year of constant embarrassment, as world events tortuously constructed our personal history, because it took all of my physical energy to keep up with a man fifteen years my senior and all of my intellect to decipher his transmissions to Earth.

No-one-calls-me-Katie asked me how I had come to recognize his genius.

I told Kathy that I had not realised his ramblings were veins of professional gold until an encounter in the London Press Club. As a part of the introduction ritual, a producer from France's O.R.T.F. asked me who I worked with, and without thinking I said "Leblanc" as if his name was De Gaulle. Overhearing me, an Australian television cameraman passing by with fists full of beer stutter-stepped and expertly tilted the mugs so that only foam breached the rims as he said, "Fuckin'-ell–didn't 'ee go missin' in Biafra? Bin sixteen years since the-bugger-an-me knocked some back."

"He's missing wherever he is," Cliff, the CBC bureau chief would have said with affection, had Robbie's expense reports never required his signature.

"Shoots crackin' stuff, though. You with 'im?" the cameraman said, motioning a pint my way.

"Ya–John," I said, mindlessly stretching my arm across the table.

"Tim," he said, placing a pint in my hand instead of setting it down. "Tell 'im the Aussie is at the Imperial."

"Will do, but Robbie has a hard time remembering last Saturday."

"No worries, mate. Nam," he said turning away.

I explained that no one forgets a combat assignment, and that abbreviating locations is not slang, but earned and respected as such.

"No matter how hard they live afterwards?" Kathy-is-a-chatty-doll replied.

"There may be some gaps," I said, failing to appreciate her insight.

I next told Kate that in the respectful silence acknowledging the slaughter of illusions that followed the utterance of 'Nam', we overheard Tim say, "You'll never guess 'oose in town," to which a cohort immediately replied, "Must be LeBlanc if he took me fuckin' beer already."

[10]

"Recognition like that," I said, to the woman who was now eyeballing me like a diabetic at a dessert buffet, "is the highest non-posthumous accolade you can get in this business. I paid attention to everything he said after that."

"How did you learn to understand him?" Katerina-or-nothing said, with a playful shake of her head.

I told her that R.J. established contexts through historical events and geographical references like normal people would use Waterloo to reference a defeat. However, there were rarely more than three people on the continent who understood his waypoints—all of them colleagues who were familiar with his assignments. Even then, Robbie conjufuckgated so many disparate elements of his travels that even close friends were often obliged to intuit his meaning.

"Now that we've shared enough experiences to have evolved our own Waterfuckin'loos," I said, taking a sip of scotch, "there's a beautiful irony about translating his version of reality for local reporters who consider working with him a trial by fire while internationally vetted journalists fight over his time."

Staring, as though I'd vanish if she took her eyes off me, Katerina asked me why I called him different names—or was it a quirk of all television crews, she quipped blandly.

"Usually, it's about circumstance," I explained. "Robbie and Rob are off duty names. Leblanc kind of addresses the legend, and R.J. is a code. He can't see anything to his right when we're shooting, so if I see something he needs to know about, I call him R.J., and he does whatever I say without asking why."

"There's a lot more to you than you've shown in this place," Kat purred provocatively.

Sadly, this is all I remember about my last truly naïve night on the planet. The morning shoot in New York was also lost to a thumping, dehydration blur that mercifully gave way to an antihistamine induced coma during the late afternoon flight to the place I would earn the right to call Salvador in press clubs around the world. And in the wee hours, hope the flashbacks would be in black and white.

I thought the profanity worked in the context of a scene that implied terrible things past and to soon come again, but I questioned the wisdom of offering a sexploit in the first material Bonnie might read, so I didn't print it. Show and tell could wait; we had gotten along too well for it to matter.

Chapter Two
Contexts

Finished writing for the day, I went for a three kilometre shuffle I would euphemistically call jogging until it was true, then I took a shower as the rare cloudless blue outside of my window bowed to a tawny dusk. Still half an hour early for our appointment, I walked four blocks down Pendrell Street and across Denman to the English Bay Café where I expected a double dram of Scottish bog would add sparkle to my personality. I was still a bit dull from the night before.

Passing through the tandem glass doors, I nodded toward the back bar and said to the hostess, "Waiting for someone."

"Aren't we all," she replied laconically, as I passed by.

With a quick glance back, I saw her sardonic grin abruptly change to fright, and I barely managed to side step a striking woman in a sea-green summer dress. Quickly regaining my balance, I assembled a boyishly crooked smile to apologize when she exclaimed, "You must be John!" announcing our circumstance to the entire dining area.

Figuratively off balance, the spontaneous cleverness that having no tact had forced me to develop over the years abandoned me like sincerity in a confessional, and I tardily squawked, "You must be Bonnie!" like an elderly parrot on Valium.

Laughing as if I had intended to be funny, Bonnie tugged my sleeve, leading us to a table as if we were a couple playing a familiar game.

Soon seated with drinks on the way, our exchange of approval pleasantries flowed like the patter of old friends meeting after years apart, including finishing each other's sentences and chuckling at the same unspoken ideas. Ironically, I was thinking this was too good to be true, like our phone call had been, when she did something that made me think I might be right: Bonnie interrupted my lead line about traveling to England, as a prelude to a battle tale, to say she had made a decision that had irrevocably altered her life as well. I hadn't said anything like that, but I couldn't deny that it was true, so I dutifully asked her what it was about.

[12]

"Oh—I'm sorry; it's too soon for that," she said sheepishly, then suddenly pitching forward with misplaced ardour, she asked, "Why did you go to England? Why did you leave, for that matter?"

I first thought our rapid-fire exchange might have caused a slip of her tongue, which made little sense because we had been bottom-dealing nuances since my stunned Polly impression, then I noticed her emerald eyes illuminating mischief lines in her expression.

"I went to England to freelance, and I left by invitation," I said as if no time had passed.

"Were you standing around the palace when a guard told you to move along, and you didn't think to ask how far?"

"A work visa problem moved me along. Didn't Tom mention that?"

"He said something about a deportation to enhance my interest in you," she said, with a discerning grin. "Why did you end up leaving Toronto to come here—the freelance world not as good as you thought it would be?"

"It was time to go."

"What happened?" she said eagerly.

"Nothing big," I said, unsure if she was mocking me for some reason.

"It was big enough to bring you here?" she said innocently.

"I guess stuff just added up until it made sense to leave," I said, cutting short a peppery sip of Caesar.

"Can I assume you're ashamed of that stuff, so I'll stop asking you about it?"

"Not at all." I shrugged to hide my surprise. "I hit the wall writing a book, and a friend suggested I enter a short story contest to clear my head. I was fiddling with…"

"What was it about?"

"A guy gets a letter from a friend who's then killed while working in conflicts. Still wondering what could have gone wrong, because the old pro had taught the young guy how to work in that world, he makes a call to the network to fill the vacancy."

Bonnie stared as if I had farted.

"It's called, '*You Taught Me Well,*' as in he won't make the same mistake," I explained.

"Ahhhh," she said, stretching a breath, "which is exactly what he's about to do. Clever. Can I read it?"

"Huh? Ya, sure. Anyway, I was working on that when I heard about development grants; I mentioned that last night."

She nodded for me to carry on.

[13]

"I had just finished an interesting job in Northern Ontario, a story filled my head, and I thought what the hell? Maybe four months later..."

"A story just filled your head?" She snapped her fingers.

"Writing the proposal was more like copying than creating. Anyway," I shrugged again, "about four months later, the short story came in the money at the same time a core client and I weren't getting along. After that..."

"You saw the inevitable heading your way," she interjected, bobbing her head in recognition of a familiar experience.

"After that, my grant was approved on the same day that I got an offer to teach at my old college."

"When it rains..." Bonnie said, "but I haven't heard anything that would cause you to move three thousand miles into unemployment."

"I haven't gotten to that part, for some reason." I said wryly.

"Please continue," she said demurely.

"Thank you, madam. Freelancing in Toronto wasn't looking good in the long term, and the teaching offer evolved into something I wasn't interested in." I picked up my glass. "I talked to Ed, and he offered to underwrite my career change if I moved here. Like I said, little stuff added up."

"Giving up the sure thing was gutsy. Do you know how you actually made up your mind to come here?"

Having no idea what she meant, I grinned and said, "How many ways are there?"

"Four," she replied easily, then glancing at the ceiling, she amended her statement. "No—five common ways," she said confidently.

"Don't let me interrupt."

With a curious nod to imply challenging her claim was uncalled for, Bonnie said, "We all have an internal dialogue that follows different processes depending on our perceived circumstance." Counting on her fingers, into my less amused expression, she said, "If timing isn't important, we can boil down some situations into simple arithmetic and play the odds, or we can grind answers out of our experiences if it's a close call. If timing matters, we might react from necessity, or our egos might take over the ship. Anything familiar yet?" she grinned.

"They all fit to some degree," I said evasively.

"Was your move here a life-altering decision?" she persisted.

"Any move could be thought of in that way," I deflected.

"Yet you didn't assess the very moment of making that important decision?"

"I told you, twice actually, that a bunch of little stuff added up."

"But you didn't say what influenced that moment of significance," she replied, raising her brow.

"How would I know that after seven months?" I chuckled awkwardly. "And what does it matter now?" I shrugged.

"Do you mean it?"

"Mean what?"

"Do you want to know what influenced you, and why it matters?"

"Sure, go ahead," I said puzzled.

"Let's look at what just passed between us, as a framework to investigating your decision making process."

"Let's do that," I said, looking for our server.

With a crisp grin she probably thought I hadn't seen, she said, "You thought I was kidding about the ways there are to assess a decision, then you felt put on the spot by me asking specifically about one experience. Your ego took over to 'twice actually' put me in my place," she mimed quotation marks, "instead of your brain grinding out an answer you didn't realize was available to you because it's rare that anyone properly assesses any moment." She pitched forward to touch my hand. "I speak about these kind of personal evaluations only to special people, because everyone else takes offense so easily." Bonnie painted the word 'easily' with a hint of exasperation.

"I can see how that might be," I said studiously.

She settled back in her chair.

Reaching for her drink, Bonnie said, "Good, so let's go through the processes: what did you feel in the moment you decided to come to Vancouver?"

Pausing to try to recall that moment, I honestly said, "I felt a mixed sense of loss and relief, like when you realize the end of something is certain, but there's nothing you can do about it. Or maybe there's nothing you want to do about it."

"That's the moment we recognize the demise of a circumstance which frees us to create a better one. What thought drove the idea of moving here?"

"It's a beautiful place, and Ed lives here."

"Go back to Toronto in your mind."

I wanted to argue the unreasonableness of expecting me to pinpoint this moment, if not the accuracy of my recall, but my mind shifted focus as if it had been whisked there on her command, and I suddenly understood what she was after. "None of my options looked good," I said confidently.

[15]

"The arithmetic method seems to be how you made up your mind, so why did you call Ed?"

Hearing this question somehow took me past that phone call to the moment of actually making my decision; Ed's presence in Vancouver and his generous offer were certainly influences, but they were not the deciding factor. Enjoying this odd moment of reflective clarity, I said, "This may sound too simple, but I think it's what you're after."

"Don't ever worry about what I think," she said softly.

"Ultimately, by which I mean I *know* this was my deciding factor, I didn't feel there was anything wrong with coming here."

"Excellent. That's the fifth option; you did it as an act of faith."

"Pardon me?"

"You trusted that things would work out, even though you focused on the negative to discover how you really felt," she said, with a tiny shrug.

"Faith had nothing to do with it," I said coolly. "I've seen people pray for a battle to pass by their homes instead of leaving with us because they didn't believe a softening up bombardment is an oxy-moron. Faith is a sucker punch," I explained into her baffled expression.

Scholastically, Bonnie said, "Your intensity mourns its loss con-cerning the rest of the universe, but your actions say that something inside you knew what to do, and when you stopped fretting over peripheral circumstances your choice became clear." She waved her statement aside as if it had been embarrassingly obvious. Offhandedly, she then said, "You can tell me what happened when you're ready. The same applies to your screenplay, by the way."

"The same what?"

"If you were happy with your screenplay, you would have brought some scenes to impress me." Wearing a playful expression to diffuse my affront, she shrugged another miniscule affair. "You also wouldn't have fired a salvo at me if your faith in anything other than yourself hadn't been damaged. As I said, whenever you're ready is fine. Or not."

Puzzled by her warm, yet indelicate approach to sizing me up, I felt trapped into explaining at least one of the issues she had mentioned, so I told her about my diluted screenplay plot to explain why I had arrived empty-handed.

"Quality barbershop quartets can create the illusion of a fifth voice called a ringing chord," she said when I was finished. "It's very difficult to do."

[16]

"Hmm." I nodded as if I had a clue what she meant.

Chuckling, she said, "You created the illusion of outside influences being in play without directly referring to them. You should run with it—it sounds like a gift waiting to be opened." She looked at me expectantly.

"My deadline is too close for that. Besides, Tom came up with a practical solution. Still..." I said, indicating that I wasn't out of trouble.

"You're experienced enough to know that expedience is everything it's cracked up to be."

"Six months of six day weeks speaks to that," I agreed.

"But now you're letting a deadline potentially ruin your story after all of that hard work. Who's to say following that outside influence isn't the way to go?" She sipped her drink.

"Following peripheral issues is what put me in this bind, not that it hasn't worked before," I quickly added, lest she think I was unimaginative. "You are a curious one," I deflected ambiguously.

Pushing her drink to one side, Bonnie left me a sentence behind by dealing with my idle comment as a personally important topic.

"It takes time to get to know people in the best of circumstances, but in superficial surroundings like these, it can be more work than it's worth." A bolt of cynicism creased her academic expression, the influence departed with the memory of whoever he was, and she continued casually. "I don't mean some people aren't worth knowing. I'm saying there's no point in trying to penetrate their social mask, unless they're ready to look at themselves like you did a minute ago." She rested a hand on mine. "I cut to the chase with special people, but it can still unnerve them."

"Is that why you hold their hands down?"

An electric interlude passed between us before she slid her hand away, leaving them both flat on the table as if lying in wait. Whether she did this in anticipation of comforting me or protecting herself was unclear.

"It sounds more like you study people than interact honestly with them," I said, my casual tone belying an accusation of deception.

"We all do that in our own way." Bonnie reached across the table, and tapping twice on the top of my hand with her finger, said, "Learning what makes a person tick is as critical to my work as understanding the details of combat situations had to be for you. At their core, they're the same thing."

[17]

"Where's the threat in here?" I said, relieved that she had revealed the reason for her game playing, not that I understood the need for it with me

"Almost everybody in here is in conflict with themselves in some way, and I'm not going to become a casualty of their internal disputes." She leaned forward. "The world is dangerous enough without my help. Speaking of which, Tom tells me you've lived quite an adventure so far: scuba diving, flying planes, parachuting, covering combat?"

The candle casting curious shadows around the pucker of her bust line made me a heartbeat slow at dismissing my splendour before I said, "All past tense."

"You drive a donor cycle at an age when you should know better," Bonnie replied, dragging a finger across the tablecloth coyly.

"I'm thirty-five and the motorcycle is an economic necessity," I said, answering both queries.

"Some people might think your activities are evidence of a death wish," she said. Her grin belied the accusation.

"Some people think backgammon is exciting," I said, nodding towards a game underway at the corner of the bar, "when anything..."

"You did it for the excitement?" she interrupted me.

"....when anything you do can create the wrong impression for people who haven't rolled those particular dice."

"In what way?"

"The further away an event is from everyday activities, the more you have to explain its context. Even then, as you know, it's a waste of time."

"Why do you think I know that?"

"Because you thought better of explaining your life-changing decision until you were reasonably sure I won't judge it or you."

"Which means you know things you won't tell to just anyone, as well."

"Only to special people," I deadpanned.

"Such as?" she said without hesitation.

"Few people understand what living for the day is really about," I replied as quickly.

"A lot of them would claim they do." Bonnie nodded toward a gaggle of animated singles at the chrome and smoked-glass bar.

I flashed a peace sign toward our server at the same moment Bonnie circled her finger for another round. We shared a smile over our like-mindedness and the elevation in her status to 'special', as I said, "Intellectually, they know they could drop dead before the next round

[18]

arrives, but it's not real to them unless their sense of immortality has been blown out of the proverbial nest. I was thirty before that defining moment happened to me, and you know I'm not shy about doing things other people just talk about." I looked away and eruditely said, "An end-of-the-world cataclysm aside, they have a decade to go if the umbrellas in their drinks mean anything."

"What happened?" Bonnie gushed, grasping my forearm tightly.

Still unsure whether she was playing with me, although now I knew why she might, I reached for a cloth napkin so that she had to let go of my arm. Taking off my glasses, I breathed a spicy fog onto one lens and rubbing slowly, said, "It was late April of eighty-one, at four thirty in the morning when our producer called my room ..."

"You weren't kidding about defining a moment," she tittered.

"I have a garbage dump for a mind," I said truthfully, somehow failing to mention that I had reviewed that section of my book hours earlier. "Anyway, our driver called our producer to tip him off to a slaughter going on in Mexicanos—that's the suburb where the revolution began." I fogged the other lens and began rubbing it. "The shoot-to-kill curfew didn't end until five, so I took my time getting ready... just not enough of it." I sniffle-chuckled as I put my glasses on, and explained, "We turned onto the street a Death Squad was just turning off a block away, on the stroke of five, so we waited to see if they would circle back."

"Why would you do that? Why would they, for that matter?"

"Death Squads usually drove around the scene of their crimes to discourage witnesses from coming forward. No one ever did." I sipped my drink, swallowed and said, "Including us."

"You mean they would shoot them, as well?" Bonnie said incredulously.

"Maybe. Eventually. Hard to tell."

"So why would you wait? I mean, wouldn't they shoot you?"

"It was getting light, and it was too public a place to kill us as long as we stayed put." I cleared my throat to explain the way things were in that place. "If they came back, and we were out in the open, they would take our IDs as a threat that never went away, but our driver and his family would have to vanish as soon as the morning traffic picked up." Into Bonnie's puzzled expression, I said, "The Death Squad could have been waiting to take us out on the empty highway if we had been spooked into running from the scene of their murders. They would have claimed the killers were reported to have been in a car with Prensa logos all over it—like all press cars did—which would also

[19]

explain why we dared to travel before the curfew was lifted and had been mistakenly killed as the murders leaving the scene of their crime."

"Hold on a minute," she said, taking a deep breath as if she had been trotting to keep up with me. Resting her palms on the table, she said, "Knowing what might happen around the next corner, you stayed in the car where the worst that could happen would be learning that your driver had to go on the run because nothing would happen to you beyond the threat of authorities having your names?"

"Correct, except the threat was real."

"And this situation existed because it was five-o-one?"

"Right, again."

"Okaaaay," she said as a conclusion filled her mind. "This means the time you personally took to get ready at the hotel wasn't a bit short; it was precisely enough to allow you to see what you saw and live to talk about it." She leaned in with keen anticipation, of what escaped me.

"Sure, I guess."

She pinched in closer to the table. "Seriously, you're not going to tell me that you haven't thought about what might have happened if you had left the hotel sooner?"

"Correct, I'm not going to tell you that," I said straight-faced.

Poised like Mona Lisa, Bonnie awaited an explanation for my dire lack of curiosity about a potentially life ending event.

"Looking back," I said, trying not to sound condescending, "was a dangerous distraction from assessing the potentials in front of us."

"Such as?" she asked quietly.

"Soldiers played with us by detaining crews outside of town around curfew time, so that we might run into other soldiers or the guerrillas on the way back. This meant we always had to be aware of where we were, in terms of travel time to a safer place. San Salvador is in the middle of nowhere, so we did our best to time our work to be no more than half an hour away before curfew. If we were delayed for any reason, we needed to know how far we were from Santa Ana and the Guatemala border to the north or San Miguel and Honduras to the east. We also had to be sure we had enough water to spend the night in the jungle, if it came to that, which was a bigger deal than you might think. A single person could easily go through two gallons a day, but the biggest thing to get right was making sure someone knew where we were going and when we said we'd be back. If we were even a minute late, and I mean that literally, someone called the press liaison office to say the next call was going to the American Ambassador. That call would kick-start an immediate radio search for the missing crew because America was spending a billion dollars to support the government, and even the common soldier knew it would be easy to track our movements. The bottom line was that their Death Squads might pay their own soldiers a visit for risking their finances. That said," I grinned ruefully, "we couldn't count on that beautiful irony, so a group of reporters designed photo ID cards with Salvadorian emblems, had them signed by the Press Liaison office, and then laminated them like an officially issued card. Taking the idea as his own, the Liaison Officer made registering with the Salvadorian Press Corp Association mandatory, which created a legitimate safeguard because many soldiers were illiterate."

Bonnie raised her brow.

"Any official looking document was deemed to be permission to be where ever we were, and flashing the S.P.C.A. card left a trail. The downside of it," I said, snickering," was the general population sometimes thought we were working for the government and they literally ran from us."

Bonnie's expression briefly betrayed appreciation for the acronym, before she anxiously said, "That applied to the guerrillas, as well?"

"It wasn't a perfect solution," I admitted.

"No kidding," she quipped, then studiously, "Is your sense of humour based on soldiers being more at risk than you guys because they just wanted to intimidate you, but you could get them killed?"

"Not at all, three or four Dutch journalists—I can look it up—wrote about government death squads after being warned not to. General Garcia's men kidnapped and killed them."

"Where can you look up that information?"

"I have a pay diary and newspaper clippings to keep things realistic."

"Realistic? Why are you writing fiction?"

"Official history changes with every coup. I'm not trying to correct the past."

"What are you trying to do?"

"I'm trying to explain a context for adopting the philosophy of living for the day," I said evenly.

Shaking her head self-consciously, Bonnie said, "I gather the death squad didn't come back to check out the area?"

"Correct." I paused to conspicuously allow Bonnie time to interrupt me, a gesture that did not go over her head as I continued my tale.

I told her that we crossed an ominously quiet street, before walking through the front door of a tiny bungalow that had been left open as a mark of contempt, and a reminder to witnesses that soldiers weren't accountable to anyone.

The first four bodies were stacked in the middle of the small living room. Flies buzzed in clustered clouds around their wounds, and the still pooling blood on the plank flooring. Three children, ranging from about four to ten years old, were on the bottom. After watching them die, their mother was shot in the head and draped across the top of the pile. Grandma lay sprawled on the kitchen floor a few feet away, pieces of her brain dripping off the wall above the ancient wood stove behind her corpse. We found the husband in one of the two closet-sized bedrooms. His throat had been slit, tongue pulled through the opening, and his severed penis stuffed into his mouth.

"The Salvadorian Necktie," I explained to the now wan beauty sitting across from me, "was about the insult and indignity of imagining their death pose as they bled out, while they suffocated. Curb side mastectomies," I said, picking up my drink, "were common for the women who pissed off soldiers, so I don't know why they shot the mother. Maybe they were tired."

"Jeee-zuus," Bonnie whooshed, in disgust.

"Nowhere to be found," I said around the rim of my glass.

A suspended moment of incomprehension passed through her eyes then she quietly said, "Living like that would have pushed me off the edge."

"You've almost got it."

She cocked her head.

"My context of living for the day was born in a place that was all edge, all of the time, which is why I don't tell just anyone about it. Or at least expect to be understood, when I do."

"It must have taken courage to just leave the hotel in the morning."

"Everyone was scared most of the time."

"You overcame it," she said.

"Nope." I said, glancing toward the bar and a naïve-as-a-turd young thing twirling a miniature teal, yellow, and cobalt coloured umbrella over her red drink.

Tracking my gaze, a fledgling grin twitched Bonnie's lips as she made the connection between her comment and my reality.

"Combat changes how you think about a lot of things," I said, dissolving that correlation into a harmless glance.

"Is combat the source of all your secrets; you know, the ones you only share with special people?"

[22]

"They're not secrets. People who understand that situation don't talk about it for the same reason you stopped short earlier."

"Which you think is what?"

"Tell me the funniest joke you've ever heard."

"Pardon me?" she said confused, which was satisfying before she understood my point—you had to have been there.

Chuckling her appreciation of my illustration, she said, "Maybe you can only defend your philosophy within the context of conflict, so you don't speak about it when that context does not apply?"

"I've got nothing to defend. Before Salvador, I thought you had to be brave to cover combat, then I learned there was just a fine difference between courage and stupidity."

"The difference being?"

"It's about knowing what you can and can't do before you have to do anything, which means bravery usually isn't what you might think and heroes usually aren't, at least not in the way most people think of them. The bottom line is, before that morning my life was an adventure that should end according to how I lived, and hopefully it would still come as a surprise. After that day, I knew that we all live within easy range of someone's whim and that if there is a God, He's ambivalent about us." I shrugged. "There's really nothing to be concerned about, other than trying not to damage things too badly while we're on the way to our own long-pine stare."

"Oh," Bonnie whispered, which was the shape of her mouth for a poignant moment as excess moisture came into her eyes. Clearing her throat, she gently said, "Circumstances dictated that you think this to survive emotionally. In fact," she switched topics before I could comment, "it's the politics of the time that dictate how we think."

"By which you mean all circumstances are political?" I replied, relieved that she hadn't tried to justify the dubious existence of a deity to a man who had seen the underside of creation, be that of His design or a random act.

Leaving the bodies behind seemed to suit Bonnie, as she categorically stated, "We are all political in the sense that we negotiate our way through everything in life, until we learn how to create positive circumstances responsibly. After that, there's almost nothing to negotiate other than the appearance of negotiation to smooth our way. Thanks Allisha," she said as our server set down a fresh round of drinks. "For example," Bonnie leaned forward, taking full command of the less disturbing topic, "throughout history the typical artist couldn't pursue their goals without a benefactor. Essentially, they had nothing to

[23]

lose or nothing they weren't willing to lose." She leaned back. "This circumstance demands that they become a work in progress, as well."

"As in developing character, sure."

"It's more than that." She looked at the singles chatting at the bar then back to me. "An actor dedicated to learning a character's heart discovers things about himself that his daily personality wouldn't otherwise allow him to see. Writers do the same thing with their character development, by drawing from inner resources they didn't know were available to them until they made the initial effort." She leaned into a pose of emphasis. "It's little different from you assessing a key decision for its underlying process a few minutes ago. You discovered something about yourself that you can now more consciously trust in other circumstances, which is why it mattered, by the way." She smiled at the fulfillment of her promise.

"Thanks," I said, "I didn't see that." And still didn't: she had talked me through the entire process.

Bonnie continued. "A dedicated creative process always changes the creator of the process faster than people who don't look inside themselves as the creator of their own processes." She tittered. "Which is why it can look like we're not all there." She tapped her temple.

"You seem okay to me," I quipped. Kind of.

"You're not doing badly yourself," she said. "Speaking of which, what specifically did you have to do to get the grant?" She fluttered her eyelids.

Thinking I must have given her only an overview the night before, because it was less important than my scotch-driven tales, I gave Bonnie a detailed accounting of the application process, adding as an afterthought that the idea of writing a screenplay had been seeded by our mutual acquaintance, and was I correct in assuming Tom had been a catalyst for hers?

"It was certainly fortuitous," she said vaguely. "By the way, he told me about you before you left for Toronto, but the time wasn't right for us to meet." She waved away the thought. "Is there any reason why we couldn't get a grant to do my project?"

"Not that I know of—what was wrong with the timing?"

"You didn't know you had nothing to lose until you lost it all, and we needed that in common in order to work together," she said, with surprising candour.

"Assuming that's true," I said evenly, "why would we need that in common?"

[24]

Bonnie addressed my caveat first. "It's only logical that you finally came here when there was nothing worth saving in Toronto, which is essentially what you told me last night—between the lines." Big smile. "Common experiences create common assumptions which simplify what others might otherwise view as complex understandings. If we start out on the same page, working together can be as easy as our conversation was last night."

"Makes sense."

"Tell me then," she said, pitching forward again, "what process did you use to determine why you should stop working wars? That must have been a... a hefty moment," she said, looking dissatisfied with the word, but there it was.

Unable to recall all of the ways she had listed, I decided to tell her about a particularly difficult day from which she could then draw her own conclusions. "In Lebanon, we were working a volunteer job in a town we called Goodbye..." was all I managed to say before Tom slapped me on the back.

"This is a good one!" he exclaimed, as I wiped Caesar dribble from my beard. Leaning over us in a hover, he said, "I had a few minutes, so I thought I'd drop in and see how things are going between you two." He glanced from me to Bonnie and back again.

"Sit, sit!" she gushed. "Glad you could make it."

My telling delay to also invite him prompted Tom to suddenly appear torn between a personal desire and sacrificing himself to an unnamed responsibility; invoking a short squall of social fluff, he pivoted smartly and disappeared like a ghost in the wind.

Bonnie and I exchanged amused glances as if to confirm that we had both actually seen him, then dismissing the interruption as an app-arition anyway, she said, "Volunteer job, as in delivering food or medical supplies?"

"No, a job that was too dangerous to legitimately assign," I said uncomfortably.

"How did you decide what constituted a volunteer job, and how did you decide whether to go?"

"Outright bang-bang was volunteer work. If it sounded too risky, I didn't do it."

"How often did that happen?"

"Technically never," I said, realizing this for the first time.

Bonnie chuckled as I explained what I meant by technically.

"A cameraman I worked with, literally for a few minutes in Lebanon, later asked me to work a documentary on the Camere Rouge

[25]

in Cambodia. I couldn't go because I was already booked." I shrugged off the sin of omission—I could have easily replaced myself for a minor job. "That said, they were the bloodiest army of modern times, I would have been traveling through the most mined country in all of history with a cameraman who had been wounded seven times, and dealing with a language and culture I couldn't fathom." I left it to Bonnie to draw her own conclusion.

"It took that much to cause you to feel a job was too dangerous?" she said sceptically.

"Obviously, in the beginning I didn't know better, but it became easier to scope out the potential of crappy things happening."

"And dismissing the ones you were used to, sure … by scope out do you mean intuit?" she said with a twinkle in her eye.

"Sometimes things felt wrong, or an empty street shouted at us, sure."

"Why did you say a town you called Goodbye?"

"Why do you care so much about that little stuff?"

"You know why; the big stuff rests on it." She cocked her head.

"Uh-huh. Anyway, western ears tend to have trouble with Arabic, so we simplified place names to avoid confusion about where we were talking about. Anyway, we were holed up in a crawl space below the basement of our hotel during an all-night shelling…"

Back on track, I captivated Bonnie with a brief version of the events that might have led me to quitting working wars, after which she asked me to describe the very moment I had avoided talking about. Because I had never categorically thought it was time to quit, I was at a loss for an explanation when a forgotten event overrode all else in my mind. Chuckling at how acute my memory could be on this evening, yet how hollow this explanation was going to sound, I said, "We were in an armoured personnel carrier that was under fire, and I was about to ask a soldier to close the hatch, when I just knew that I would be okay. I think that moment planted the idea of quitting, but I went to two more wars to cover other issues after that."

Bonnie looked at me intently. "Why did you think you would be okay?"

"I guess because earlier events hadn't killed me." I shrugged.

"Did you think you would be safe in terms of a prophetic certainty?"

Pondering the question only long enough to placate her intensity, I said, "I probably realised my bucket of luck had sprung a leak, and it started me thinking."

"You counted on luck to keep you safe?"

[26]

"I worked with some of the best people in the business. We were good and lucky and lucky because we were good," I said crisply.

"I know they go hand in hand," Bonnie said, raising her hands in mock surrender.

"What's with the interrogation?" I smiled solicitously.

"You had faith in yourself," was all she said, which I interpreted to mean she was looking for the moment when I had lost faith in all else.

On alert for the subtle sanctimony of a closet bible thumper, I said, "Maybe you're confusing faith with confidence, especially the penetrating kind that comes from getting everyday stuff right in places where the unusual was so usual that you couldn't count on much of anything—usually. If that makes sense," I grinned.

"That depends on what your days were like in the Middle East," she replied slyly. "Were there long stretches of boredom broken by seconds of terror?"

"Veteran crews rarely got bored or became terrified. They lived in between caution and surprise... without much surprise," I amended my statement.

Bonnie lifted her chin.

Searching for the proper words because she had been right, I had never assessed anything about my past precisely because it was behind me, I said, "In a way, working in the Middle East was the opposite of Central America. There was so much history and politics in play that we lived as if there was always something about to happen, which didn't necessarily mean it was ass-pucker tense, like it was in Salvador. We took in everything our experiences had taught us to be aware of, so there wasn't much that could catch us off guard. I don't mean we didn't flinch when the shooting started, just that we knew what to do because, for the most part, fighters on all sides had rules." I snickered. "It wasn't unusual for them to stop shooting to have a morning coffee, and any crews that had been caught out in the open would surrender to one side or the other, have coffee with them and get on with their day. The fighters in Salvador were all sadistic fuckers. Pardon me."

"Maybe explaining a typical day in Lebanon would clear things up for me."

"Typical?" I said, choking on a pepper-cooling sip of ice water.

Bonnie waited patiently for my recovery.

Becoming amused by this in-depth audition just to do Tom a favour, I told her about a youthful martyr's final expression and literal spreading of beliefs by blowing himself up in the midst of those who did not share them. I then assaulted her open expression with a series

[27]

of anecdotes that took her imagination on a slick tour of malice and idiocy, the totality of which went far beyond a typical day's events, although their impact on Bonnie seemed to be about right for a crappy day. Three drinks and dim lighting notwithstanding, by nine o'clock I thought she was perceiving a better looking man than the Barbie and Ken couple could see when they glanced our way and evidently wondered, why him?

Chapter Three
The Nature of Events

Pausing to sip our Caesars amid my bloody images, it crossed my mind that, fascinating as I clearly was, I had been dominating our conversation. Dismissing the option of suddenly developing an interest in her job selling advertising space for the Yellow Pages, or more transparently asking about the trials of raising two teenagers alone, I said, "Tom tells me that with a little advice you're heading to the academy awards."

"Actually," Bonnie said as deep lines of reluctance creased her brow, "I've since realised l need a full-time partner to do it properly."

"Screenplays aren't that difficult to format. Tell me about a scene, and we'll convert it now."

Brushing my request aside, like a maître d clearing offensive crumbs from freshly laundered table linen, she said, "My key characters operated at a level of assumptions you would need to experience or recognize you have already experienced before you could script scenes properly."

"Script? I thought you needed help with technical descriptions and basic formatting?"

"That will certainly be helpful, but some aspects of a special character's development are... tricky," she said hesitantly. "I need a second point of view but not just anyone's."

"Obviously, someone special," I quipped lightly.

"Exactly," she replied seriously.

"Tom couldn't help you with that?"

"He's got other things on his mind," she said vaguely, but I knew what it was because it was certainly on mine.

"Okay, I've got all night to unravel whatever seems tricky."

Her minimalist grin acknowledged my innuendo before vanishing like Hoffa, as she said, "I'm not talking about understanding foreign cultures, as I'm sure you can do better than most people. I'm talking about assumptions that are foreign to every culture's way of thinking, not unlike how we just looked beneath your physical circumstances to assess the nature of your decision making... which was interesting, don't you think?"

[29]

"Uh-uh."

She cleared her throat and carried on. "My difficulty is that key characters thought this way all of the time, so keeping my audience in step with a plot that develops based on their advanced way of thinking demands that I explain the steps they have taken to view things the way they do."

"Why is that a problem? You walked me through it in five minutes." *And if I had been paying attention I would probably be able to do it again*, I thought.

"I walked you through your own experiences to discover something you knew; you just didn't know that you knew it." She leaned toward me. "This is much different; I have to lead a character away from how he currently views events , all events including his own experiences, by first placing them in a different context—in the context of their true nature. When he catches on, this context will irrevocably alter how he views the key experiences that shaped his world view. The audience will then better understand why he embraced that old view, and why he's leaving it behind." She leaned back a few microns. "I've never observed that process, I just know the steps."

"You must have been through it, so what's the problem?"

Sheepishly, she said, "I learned about this other way of thinking in a different manner, but I thought projecting my understanding on my character's struggles would work." She shrugged. "It's one hundred percent accurate but it doesn't ring true because it wasn't my experience, and credibility is everything in my work."

She waved her comment aside, indicating that she was not going to tell me what her particular experience had been.

"It seems to me," I softened my certainty. "your characters' daily interactions and dialogue will explain their different way of thinking. I mean, your audience doesn't need to have the actual experience, do they?"

"No, but if I get it right some of them will." She shrugged. "But maybe you're right," she said without enthusiasm.

"It's happened before," I joked, but Bonnie managed only a polite grin.

"Maybe you're just standing too close to it," I said, "and voicing how you set up the two trains of thought in your work would make things clearer in your own mind. I do that with intricate dialogue all of the time and changes I struggled with for days have become embarrassingly obvious."

[30]

A brief look of intrigue passed through her expression before she said with anticipation, "Like you and I playing the roles of a teacher and student to see how it sounds?"

No. "Sure. Go ahead. What's the background of the scene?"

Tentatively she said, "I begin separating the two ways of thinking by having an elder explain to a newcomer why their commune's justice system isn't based on the presumption of innocence like it is in the nearby city-state."

"What's wrong with presuming innocence?"

"Enshrining any supposition as a fact inevitably generates contradictions that undermine the purpose of the assumption," she said, with a subtly raised brow.

"Are you talking about cops violating a suspect's rights in some way that's unrelated to their crime," I said, unravelling her point, "but the bad guy gets away with it anyway?"

"Yes."

"As I understand it," I said, avoiding a declaration, "presuming innocence protects people from things like thin circumstantial evidence and malicious prosecution."

"That's how I understand it, as well," she said agreeably.

Looking over the rim of my glasses, I politely spelled it out. "How does your elder rationalize his society not having those safeguards?"

"*Her* society," Bonnie corrected me, "would say it's the other way around; the newcomer's society rationalizes the precaution to protect the majority at the inevitable expense of allowing some criminals to continue to harm the few."

"Technically, they're not criminals, and the point is to protect the majority."

"Do you think it's logical for a technicality to overrule reality, regardless of the numbers involved?"

"What I think isn't the point. Superior thinkers and centuries of experience have made it clear that it's not a perfect system, but it's better than subverting everyone's right to a fair trial."

"Actually, what you think *is* the point," she said, evenly.

"Right—right. Sorry, go ahead."

With a half-nod needlessly punctuating that we had an arrangement, she said, "The concept of fairness happened to be the stranger's concern as well, so we're already on the same page." She smiled. "The elder started him off with a basic example of their different ways of thinking," Bonnie stated, clearly enjoying herself. "In their time, some societies reasoned capital punishment to be a fair penalty for specific

[31]

deeds and a deterrent for those who might rethink doing similar crimes. My elder's culture said hanging a man was murder." She held out her arms like the scales of justice and raising one said, "Fair, as reasoned by one society," then lowering it and raising the other hand, "murder, as determined by the nature of the act." She placed her hands on opposite sides of the table. "That's how far apart the two ways of thinking can be on an identical circumstance. It's scary, if you think about it. Really scary."

"Some political systems take their moral cues from …"

"I'll stop you there to avoid confusion."

"That ship might have sailed."

"I doubt it," she chortled. "You just want to see if I know my stuff."

I shrugged to imply I was that clever and appreciated her cleverness in seeing through me.

Bonnie continued academically.

"Those who embraced the elder's way of thinking dealt with the essence of any act as a core assumption of evaluation; their view was without mitigating circumstances so it was knowledge untainted by beliefs." She searched the ceiling for an example. "You can spin a brick to blur its edges, but it's still a brick," she said, seemingly unsatisfied with the example.

"Statistically, that law works..."

"Again," she said, holding open a palm like a stop sign, "lawmakers create their own continuity of justification. The fact that cop-killing statistics go down in some of these places, if it is a fact, doesn't change the nature of the event regardless of how you arrange your so-called facts to suit a particular social circumstance. With me so far?"

"You mean any circumstance?"

"Yes." She leaned toward me as if clarity was relative to the distance between us, and continued, "Our culture's assessment of events is based on an ever-evolving set of consensus beliefs, including app-earances and codes of morality, which affect our emotions and adjust our prejudices. This means we translate our experiences so that they align with mass assumptions that are essentially an entanglement of current and historical opinions about the way things should be in this time and place. Still with me? You don't have to agree." She grinned and snickered, "That rhymes."

"I get the drift."

"Specifically," she said seriously, "we define fairness as honestly fulfilling reasonable expectations and contractual obligations entered into with informed consent. The concept is also wrapped within

[32]

commonly understood moral and ethical considerations that have evolved over time, based on their impact on the greatest number of people. I will add to this, again, that our assumptions are based on how we are conformed to the way we are told things should be. It follows that if any one of these requirements is not present, then we deem the circumstance to somehow be unfair, or with caveats. Do you agree?"

"I wouldn't change anything," I said, beginning to feel like a dyslexic adrift on a sea of Greek calculus.

"Is there anything you would add?"

"No, you've got it smo—covered."

Speaking succinctly, as if she was trying to hide an accent, Bonnie said, "People like Plato and Nietzsche wrote versions of, 'the mind-set that creates a problem cannot solve it,' which means our assumptions can lead our reason astray until the convolutions they create *become* our resolution." She waited for me to acknowledge that I was still in the library, if not exactly on the same page.

"Maybe an example of that would help," I said.

Bonnie cocked her head slightly as if asking, "Are you sure?" then before I could respond, she said, "To justify your successful risk taking, you claimed your intellect kept you safe, then you qualified that, adding sensing things, preparation, experience, and other people's expertise contributing to you having confidence in a place where the unusual was usual. You also used luck as a buffer between these conditions to fill in any holes in your reasoned explanation. The underlying nature of your reasoning was that you had no clue how you made it through some days, so you arranged what you considered to be facts to suit various scenarios, also as you interpreted these to suit your reason, you then dismissed anything that either didn't fit or you couldn't explain. The result was a convolution you embraced as a resolution."

An intrusive comprehension displaced, maybe erased is a better description, my annoyance at her presumptive explanation allowing me to reluctantly grasp her point. To avoid sounding as if I was surprised by having a relevant thought, I casually said, "You're saying I created a continuity of justification to explain how I survived—right?"

"You're this close," she said, holding her thumb and forefinger together, "to experiencing that other level of understanding we're after."

"Your fingers are touching."

[33]

"Touching upon a view isn't grasping it. You created a convoluted continuity of clarification because you were *unable* to explain how you survived."

"Okay, so how would your elder explain it—my survival, that is?"

With a stifled chuckle, which I interpreted to mean, "What the hell, why not?" Bonnie said, "To have seen the things you saw close-up and generally survive unscathed in high risk situations would have shouted to her that you were on a special journey. You might say that regardless of your interpretation of events, that feeling of deep security you experienced at the core of your being was the Universe whispering it had plans for you."

"Uh huh - as convoluted as my explanation sounded," I chuckled, "it actually *was* an explanation. In fact," I said leaning forward to scrub the sting out my statement, "I think what you called convoluted is an appropriate description of how we synthesize events into reasonable explanations. Like The Band sang, 'take what you need and leave the rest.'"

"Words that perfectly demonstrate my point about our inherent confusion. We are so mired in the myths of our enlightenment that we knowingly build fatal flaws into our social order then self-righteously hang our heads for those we sacrifice in the name of the greater good."

Leaning outside of the invisible ring of Bonnie's personal space, and amused by imagining a pulpit in front of her, I said, "What are the myths of our enlightenment?"

"Things like our version of historical evolution, honour, duty, and especially the greater good." She shrugged a delicate affair.

"Are you saying your elder didn't believe in any of them?"

"I'm saying my peo—her people didn't believe in anything they hadn't historically experienced and properly assessed for its true nature, in which case it wasn't information or opinion. It was knowledge." She cleared her throat. "My elder explains to the newcomer how her people developed core assumptions from this knowledge, about how to live properly based on experiencing logical, and interwoven rules about handling energy. Bear with me," she said, briefly lining up her ducks, before she continued her explanation: "students of this way of life had to learn to see past the curtain of common behaviours and presumed good intentions, to evaluate the true nature of events, while also learning that all events have an energy equivalent based on that nature. Positive acts generated positive energy waves, regardless of any appearances to the contrary, by which I mean a given event may not be recognized as being positive by everyone,

[34]

depending on their beliefs and expectations. Distil this idea, and you can see that the concept of behaviour was itself an aberration to their way of thinking because all behaviours are based on interpretations of circumstances—the blur of the spinning brick—not the brick." She mimed the scales of justice scene, again.

"If I'm a test case, you're pretty much screwed," I said, now feeling like I was holding a broken toilet handle and the Pope was knocking on the door. "If all behaviours are crappy, what did your people do—stand there?"

"You're missing the critical difference."

"Also not for the first time."

"Our social conformation is based entirely on institutionalized continuities of justification," she said, smirking at my comment, "which through the relentless pressure of daily example surreptitiously taught us all the same reasoning process. In other words, our society acts on their beliefs *about* circumstances—the cultural spin. My teachers acted on the true nature of an event—the brick." She took a quick drink and continued as if her point was now clear to me. "To learn how to see what's in front of their eyes, without imposing any interpretations on their vision, my teachers purposefully guided children through practical situations that proved the principles of energy-efficient living. Simplistically, from a young age they understood that if you hang around bullies at a bus stop, you will eventually get a bloody nose because that's the nature of the energy they would be sharing in that space. They weren't fooled if the bully," she said, leaning back to raise my eye-line, "was genuinely funny in his contrived confrontations with weaker people because they would recognize that his humour is derived from intimidation and domination."

"Where does fairness enter into this?"

"If a bus hit a mother of three children, we'd say it wasn't fair."

"You're not saying it would be fair if the bullies were hurt?" I interrupted her.

"Correct, I'm trying to say that it wouldn't be fair or unfair for anybody to be hit—let me finish," she said, raising a finger toward my lips. Choosing her words carefully, she continued her explanation, "My people understood the nature of the energy of where they were standing, so staying there was a conscious choice, like you purpose-fully looking for a battle to film." She brushed the top of my hand as if this would erase my puzzlement. "I'm saying that what you may view as an innocent bystander being unfairly hit by a bus, my teachers saw

[35]

as a matter of having the energy to recognize their situation because gathering energy is a choice. If they had enough of it, they could chose to distance themselves from the gang, whose energy was negative, and miss the next bus for no apparent reason other than they felt like it, no different from you choosing not to go to Cambodia."

We had another one of those brief stare-offs then I said, "Apparently, I'm missing something simple."

She opened her palms and plaintively said, "It's all about awareness, and awareness is about gathering energy, which is a choice."

"If you know about it, sure," I said, feeling silly voicing the glaring flaw in her advanced people's thinking.

"And now you do. It's a great day!" she said excitedly, as if pi had suddenly run its numerical course.

"I appreciate the advantage, but what about everyone else in here?"

"What about them?" Bonnie said innocently.

"Wouldn't your elder think they deserve to know, as well?" I said, waving my arm toward the bar area.

"Nowhere in our definition of fairness did we mention the attendant belief of deserving, and as a man with a steel trap mind will recall, I asked you if there was anything you wanted to add."

She looked at me casually. I stared back disbelievingly. She stared harder, a grin beginning to seep through her gaze.

I got the point, but it was too simple to be real: "Are you telling me that the concept of fairness is moot to your people, because they didn't believe in it?"

"I'm saying the concept of fairness comes from evaluating circumstances and behaviours which are themselves biased evaluations based on consensus thinking, and that the concept has no energy equivalent. To deserve is a perspective that has no relevancy to the nature of a circumstance. It's the spin—not the substance." She pitched forward. "There was nothing fair or unfair about you sensing which road to take, literally or metaphorically, nor would it have been fair or unfair for the mother to be at the bus stop at a dangerous time. Your choices were based on the awareness that energy provided to you both, where energy is tied directly to evolutionary development." She tittered. "Use our assessment of your decision making process as an example, then imagine what my people's full examination of a legal circumstance would be like, and tell me which judicial system you'd rather be under."

"Depends on whether I'm guilty," I jested.

[36]

"Exactly!" she exclaimed, then calming, "A master of the art of assessment could grill you about your actions and whereabouts back to the very moment of you deciding them, so lies couldn't hide. They would all scream, 'Here I am!' As would the truth, so there was no need to presume anything."

"That's not true: they are presuming people will remember events long past."

'You did."

"I mean really long past."

"With a little guidance, you can do that, as well."

"Not ever... did your people have any rights?" I said, avoiding the newest gaping hole in her logic.

"Such as?"

"The right to privacy, for instance," I said, offhandedly.

"They didn't legislate courtesy, if that's what you're thinking." Bonnie looked at me strangely.

I explained my point of view. "I'm thinking that a system with no starting point would need virtually unlimited investigative authority, and that most people would have a problem with cops breaking down doors to find evidence or suspects just because they felt like it."

"Their system's staring point was teaching children how to assume responsibility for all of their actions; it followed that refusing to co-operate was socially irresponsible and tantamount to declaring you had something to hide." Bonnie pitched forward into my favourite view. "My people's knowledge about the underlying nature of events translated directly into social responsibility, which precluded inter-fering with the authorities whose job it was to safeguard society. It wouldn't have crossed their minds to feel inconvenienced, let alone invaded." She leaned back, grinned sardonically, and said, "Unless, of course, they were guilty." She twitched a shrug. "Privacy is an issue to us only because we'd rather maintain an image of a free society than fulfill the responsibilities that would actually safeguard our freedoms." She reached for her drink. "The same reasoning applies to your wars."

"In what way?"

"A peaceful society would fulfill the responsibilities of maintaining peace, not endlessly fund the means for war."

"Responsibilities of peace being what?"

"Now you're playing with me."

"I know what they'd be if I had my own country."

"In this moment, you do."

[37]

"Okay, health, education, a level playing field in opportunity, free beer, and then an army to protect the brewery."

"We're almost on the same page," she said, apparently enjoying something other than my comment.

"What would your people do about aggressors?" I said, evenly.

"I didn't say my people wouldn't fight if they had to, but they'd first have aggressors look at focusing on peace."

This gaping hole silenced me.

Chapter Four
Spending Energy

Bonnie took a short sip, and gently clearing her throat said, "If you tell me about the circumstances you needed to know for your survival, I can tell you what my people would think of them. The point," she continued, heading off my question, "is to extend your understanding of my people's way of looking at things energetically. Good job so far, by the way. Not many people get this far without feeling frustrated," she chuckled, "as if I'm intentionally trying to annoy them." She chuckled again.

"I don't mind giving it a shot, but there's a lot of background stuff," I managed to say as if I weren't frustrated or annoyed.

"As you said, we have all night." Bonnie settled back in her chair.

Cautioning her that I was offering information in the context of my daily activities, not historical accuracy, I began with what I had learned on my first few days in Lebanon: the Christian Lebanese government had invited the Syrians to send in their army to help stabilize Lebanese society when a civil war erupted in 1976. The Syrian's relatively inert, when not covert, presence during endless civil violence effectively declared them an occupying force, and when the dust finally settled, Syria would have strong influence with the new government. This meant the official referee was heavily invested in the outcome, a deep interest that showed through who they assassinated, and with whom they shared intelligence.

In 1982, Israel invaded Lebanon, not the Lebanese, to oust the Palestine Liberation Army who had been shelling Kibbutz's with relative impunity from across the border for over a year. I once had the dubious pleasure of being on the incoming side before I crossed the border and met the guys who were shelling me. Nothing personal, they said.

Bonnie didn't care about this.

For political and practical purposes, the Israelis invited the Americans to help keep at bay the Moslem factions who were generally too busy fighting the Lebanese Christians to officially hassle the Israeli Defence Forces, but you never knew. Upon their arrival, the Americans discovered that it wasn't prudent to shoot just anyone because they had no idea who they were related to, and their official rules of engagement changed at the direct expense of their safety. In terms of the Middle Eastern psyche, the barracks bombing that killed 283 of their sons and daughters was an unfathomable embarrassment to the American army because it caused political America to circle their military wagons around the airport perimeter. This literally became the outer ring of a kilometre wide target with soldiers as the bull's-eye, thereby leaving the Israeli's more on their own than they'd like to be, spy satellites, and other sources of intelligence notwithstanding.

This change in tactics, or lack thereof, caused the Israeli Defence Forces to embrace their American brethren with more cordiality than respect because their wealthy cousins from across the sea had been neutered by one big bang in a place where a weak relative is a niece. Generally unaware of local politics and specifically ignorant about the Palestinian / Israeli history of tick-tock terrorism by which their leaders come and go, the average American soldier arrived naïve, and went home disillusioned or died confused.

My point in telling Bonnie this was that traveling near Israelis or Americans was as dangerous as traveling known "terrorist" turf because both armies were target practice for kids with time on their hands. We also regularly worked the wire at the airport perimeter on the coast road to Damour and an extremely delicate section of town crews called the Perch. Sufficient to say that it was a mistake to think there were any friendlies in my working day, with the possible exception of the Mafia. But that was another story.

Unofficially, but not a secret, Syria funded the P.L.O. and their hard-liners who had shot UN, Israeli, and American forces because in their world an enemy's friend is an enemy. It followed that Syrian and American troops avoided each other for the safety of both, as did we avoid positioning ourselves between them lest we be mistaken for one or the other on a quarter moon night after either side had been at the bottle or pipe.

Speaking of positioning, I told Bonnie that Syrian forces and the Israeli Defence Forces literally avoided eye contact, generally because Syria had their ass handed to them in previous conflicts with Israel and specifically because Israel still occupied their Golan Heights. As a result, Israelis motored through Syrian checkpoints as if they weren't there. Reciprocally, seeing the large blue and white flags waving from the back of approaching Israeli vehicles, Syrian soldiers turned their backs as they drove by. The mood on both sides, whose twitchy fingers rested inside the trigger guards, was something the press corps always needed to consider.

Where the Syrians treated the P.L.O. like their little nephew Abdul, and the I.D.F. treated Americans like Cousin Nancy, the P.L.O. were overtly indifferent to the Lebanese Army and their breakaway faction of the Christian Phalange. They could afford to be because if push came to shove, their Hezbollah brothers could rally enough temporary support from all Palestinian factions to smack the Christians back into the Bronze Age. Practically speaking, this was unlikely because it would give America reason to come out of their trenches when Israel rushed to the aid of their de facto allies, the Lebanese regular army, whose alignment with Israeli forces was an unavoidable affront to the P.L.O., who also distinguished a friend from an enemy by the company they kept.

That said, taking on the Lebanese army would be to, in effect, invade the country that wasn't officially giving the P.L.O. sanctuary, which would have been unconscionably poor form in a culture where manners are practiced as an art. This is also what made the P.L.O.'s indifference so insulting to the Lebanese regulars, an attitude that applied to the Christian Phalange for a while, but how that changed into acidic hate was a story for another time. It was enough for Bonnie to know that a click of the tongue from a commander could put into play a scrupulously designed misunderstanding between factions, which would be accepted as a reasonable mistake within the convoluted nature of relationships in the area.

"That's the overview," I said when I felt I was finished. "Do you want to know specifics like how to deal with roadblocks or firefights?"

"It's not necessary. My people wouldn't change their view, regardless of having that knowledge."

"Which is what?" I said, settling back for the long haul.

"They wouldn't have been drawn into that cauldron of destruction."

"Pardon me?"

"My people would have seen how a number of countries had passed the point of change where logic could prevail, so they would let them battle it out until they came to understand what they were doing."

"You're a harsh woman."

"Not at all," she replied seriously. "You can't make anyone believe anything they don't want to believe until they're ready to see it," she explained, "and my people knew that doing anything else could only delay the combatants moment of understanding. My teachers employed

[41]

the same principle of using their student's own standard of behaviour as the most effective way to teach them anything important."

"You're really saying they would do nothing if they were neighbours, trading partners or even the Red Cross?" I said incredulously.

"I'm saying they would do nothing as a proactive choice. Every circumstance you described would not have camouflaged the nature of those events."

"Which is what?"

"We just talked about it—murder. Mass murder, actually."

I took a lengthy sip to help me swallow the idea that she had summarily dismissed the circumstances I had toiled to list so well. Cautiously, lest I somehow be hallucinating her surreal reply, I said, "This would include no press coverage?"

"To what purpose?"

"You know as well as I do that accurate information allows people to make better choices."

"It certainly does, but I think you don't appreciate how the *nature* of information guides people to making their choices, and the media are instrumental in ways they might not realise."

"Pardon me?"

"The blanket assumption that accurate information allows people to make better choices masks the underlying nature of your actions and those of the media in general."

"Which you think is what?"

"Something you will discover as we go along."

"I'd settle for what's on the energetic plate right now."

"Fair enough," she said, grinning broadly. "You risked yourself for years to be able to speak intelligently for five minutes about ten years of war that killed thousands of people. I spoke for five seconds on the same subject, and nobody died. Our conversation is a metaphor for spending energy efficiently."

"Sure—if you believe in the things you said," I said chuckling.

"I thought you understood; my people didn't believe anything—they knew."

"They knew about an intelligent universe?" I scoffed.

"Yes, but we're not there yet."

No shit. "Uh huh."

Chapter Five
The Magic of Mankind

"It seems to me that you have an agenda beyond making a living?" I said, more casually than I was feeling about her work.

"I do," she replied agreeably. Counting on one finger, she said, "Over time, my characters peel back layers of common assumptions to reveal aspects of the human condition that are crippling our development now. When they subdue these behaviours with the disciplines they developed to mirror the rules of handling energy," she pulled down a second finger, "my audience will see that by changing our view of ourselves we can change the world."

"Your agenda is to change the world?" I snickered.

Bonnie waited tranquilly for me to say something more mature.

"Okay, so how much time are you talking about?" I said pushing through the awkwardness of the moment with what I thought was an irrelevancy.

"Immediately after the opening scenes," she replied looking pleased, "I introduce an ancient Egyptian culture as the base setting from which other time frames will reveal the destructive progression of our common beliefs and the effectiveness of my people's assumptions at turning things around."

"Time frames, as in flashbacks?" I said warily; she was smarter than this.

"I place my teachers throughout time and have them reappear to keep their lessons on track until it's time for them to reveal themselves and their agenda." On no cue that I could see, Bonnie lunged into a myriad of descriptions of architectural designs. I had no idea what she was getting at, but the respite from mental jousting was more than welcome: I nodded like a dashboard doll crossing railway tracks, alternately meeting her gaze at points she indicated I should acknowledge, between peeks at her cleavage under the guise of introspection.

Five minutes passed before she paused to sip her drink, and I wryly interjected, "You're certainly not short on details; that's great for the Art Director."

"My settings are as integral to my story as warfare is to yours, along with learning what makes people tick."

My studious "Hummf", representing the sum of my socioarchitectural knowledge, prompted Bonnie to explain why her settings were crucial.

"From sporting arenas through burial customs, every culture creates monuments to their self-interests. The pyramids, for example, are of such elegantly precise dimensions and celestial orientation that how and why they were built remains a mystery to this day, but there's no doubt their builders were miles ahead of us socially, as well as technologically."

"You don't believe the slaves and tombs version?"

"It doesn't make sense that a society capable of building those magnificent structures would enslave generations of people for the purpose of aggrandizing a cruel ruler."

"What makes sense to you?"

"Those structures are a metaphor for a society dealing with ponderous issues with the precision and elegance of moving millions of tons of stone."

"I've been to places with high technology and remarkable architecture surrounded by filth you can't imagine. How would you explain that?"

"There's no incongruity; the businessmen and politicians' belief in their comfort and accouterments of power superseded the needs of the people."

"Uh huh, so how do you explain the bodies?"

"The pyramids became tombs after their original purpose was lost to social upheaval."

"Their original purpose being what?"

"Also a topic for another time. Really," she said apologetically, slowing the pace of our exchange, "it would interfere with you fully experiencing another level of perception tonight."

"Okay, so what's the third time frame?"

"The time of Jesus."

Somehow, I was not surprised to hear this.

"If I understand you," I said, hiding my concern about her flawed logic, "you reincarnate teachers so they can continue their own lessons, but how do they know what their original teachings were?"

"It's a process." Bonnie chuckled at a private thought, composed herself, and said, "In an early scene, I have two archaeologists independently experience visions while working at an Egyptian dig site. When

[44]

they talk about these events, they realize they've collectively received directions to a chamber buried deep within the base of a pyramid. This isn't enough to make them act until they have identical visions about artefacts inside the chamber."

"They find those things, then what?" I hazard a reasonable guess.

With a quick nod, she said, "They discover inscriptions written by a man-God named Osiris." Setting her glass aside, Bonnie gathered her breath and explained, "Sections of the hieroglyphs claim that man-kind's cycles of birth and death are carefully chosen by the individual so that their experiences address specific challenges of personal evolution. Eventually, individuals have enough energy to knowingly tackle these, and then other massive challenges, head on. Osiris wrote that his message is specifically meant for two individuals living in the archaeologist's time who have evolved to this level. He also charac-terizes other times in terms of his own, by writing things like, 'People live in the sky,' to describe high rise buildings. This allows me to shift the point of view to Osiris dictating his message about a quest that defies logic, to show his culture to my audience, and switch between time frames to portray the development of beliefs described in the glyphs. I also personalize characters with subtle gestures or a quirk of phrasing that's designed to awaken deep memories–energy memories, if you will." Her upper lip quivered with anticipation. "Osiris wrote detailed descriptions of the two archaeologist's lives, so there's no doubt about to whom the messages are meant."

"What's the quest?"

"They have to learn that in measured steps because it's too ridiculous to contemplate without preparation."

"In that case, you'll need to tell your audience what it is so they can grasp the elders' approach to teaching, and have something to hang onto as you reveal the pieces."

She looked at me with enlightened gratitude, as if I had invented the wheel to solve her personal transportation problem, then she said, "Of course, of course! That's beautiful. I'll add that after my opening scene prepares them for the scale of the plot," she grasped my arm, "but it doesn't give away the farm because the steps the archaeologists will take to understand how to achieve their goal will become the audience's journey as well." Bonnie lurched forward and discarding our topic as if it had been inconsequential, she said, "I'm having trouble portraying Maria and Kristoffer's mental and emotional struggles because the very nature of their existence is being assaulted by events they can't simply dismiss as coincidence." She edged back in

[45]

her seat. "I need to create an ineffable sense of enchantment because they're stuck with a miracle to explain their visions. What's funny about that?"

Sniffing back a snicker in the face of her Border Collie stare, I said, "*You're* stuck with a miracle to explain that scene."

"I explain it and many more," she said matter-of-factly. "I said I'm having trouble portraying an ineffable sense of enchantment."

"Maybe that's why it's called ineffable. How many gimmicks does your audience have to deal with?"

Clasping her hands, Bonnie added a layer of justification: "Osiris designed the process of preparation to pass through common aspects of mankind's magic, which most people don't realize they've already encountered because they had no reasonable explanation for those kinds of events. So they're not gimmicks, they're just overlooked or misinterpreted events like the moment you had in Lebanon. That kind of experience, but much more in-depth, will reduce what seems like an outrageous quest into a series of manageable challenges."

"Does everything take place in their minds?" I guessed.

"That suspicion will certainly plague them."

"Because they're being brain-washed by the lessons?"

"Did events brainwash you into making up your experience at Goodbye?"

"No, but..." I had nowhere to go with this idea.

"Strictly speaking," Bonnie said, letting me off the hook, "they're flushing their minds to see things clearly. Eventually," she interjected into her own thoughts, "Osiris will inform them that to continue their lessons will break them free from the world they know and strand them with others of like mind because there's no going back."

"Teasing them with power—got it," I nodded.

Bonnie sat up. Her pinched expression conveyed that she was taking note of my comment even as she said, "Osiris wrote that ideas exist independently of the mind within their own parameters of reality. In effect, our brain translates ideas into physically related data that we comprehend according to how our circumstances and experiences colour them. Tarot cards, for example, work as a focusing agent, but we need relevant background knowledge to support the ideas a card reader can access. I dabble with them, by the way."

"What kind of background information are you talking about?" I said attentively to hide my newest concern over exceptions to complexities that were already shredding her plot. Working with her wasn't looking good, but she certainly did.

[46]

"If two people psychically accessed the idea of a chair," Bonnie said professorially, "the one with the bad back would say it was a firm construction while the couch potato would see a cushioned lounger. If you went to their respective homes, you would find these ideas faithfully represented in three dimensional reality, which is how we can determine a society's beliefs from their physical surroundings."

"What background knowledge would a Tarot card reader need about a chair?"

"If I were a small invertebrate visiting Earth from Cassiopeia, I wouldn't understand the structure because I came from a place without chairs. To me, it would be a hieroglyph."

"What about when there is no point of focus?"

"What about it?"

"I mean, how does a mother suddenly sense her child is in danger, and she runs two blocks to save him from thin ice?"

"Did that happen?" she said, excited by my first metaphysical morsel.

"It was part of a story I worked."

A flash of disappointment crossed her face as she replied, "My Tarot scenario deals with physical translations of beliefs. Yours is about the mother's concern for her children attracting specific information about them. She tapped into a probability that had actualized."

"What would that mean in English?"

"There's some background you need to know." She grinned.

"Shoot."

"The glyphs state that our spiritual essence is an idea-identity and that all ideas transcend time in the same way dreams carry on without regard for physical rules. It then makes sense that we can travel outside of time, to choose our next experience after we die, or before we travel into another time as a three dimensional representation of our idea-self. From this level of perception, we can see that the ramifications of our acts had many potential outcomes that all manifested to the degree of the energy we put behind them." She sipped her water, and said, "The mother's natural concern for the safety of her child drew her focus to a probable event that had crossed a point of change beyond which it became inevitable. You do know that this kind of event is common?"

"I do, but it sounds…. actually, it sounds like the makings of good stuff, if you're careful with it." I said this hesitantly because pieces of her presentation were clearer to me in that moment; something inside me had been tweaked by the terms she had used to differentiate between events. Then the moment passed.

[47]

"You'll have to be careful about leaving even a little gap in any of your premises because audiences will turn those into canyons of discredit in a heartbeat," I said as Allisha came back to our table. "Trust me; it's a long way back if you leave them behind. Doubles please, Allie," I said, looking up.

Allisha looked at Bonnie for confirmation, and they exchanged the type of glance that wise men ignore because nothing would change in the unlikely event that we cared about the explanation.

"Of the same," Bonnie said, tapping the rim of her glass, then she looked at me pleasantly and said, "Do I have reason not to trust you?"

"Does it matter if you don't believe in reason?" I said, sipping the last of my drink. Bonnie cocked her head as I said, "I mentioned the potential problem because any abstraction will cost you a piece of the audience's attention, you seem to have a lot of them, and they all require more explanations than your movie will have time for." I sat up. "Your book format seems to be the way to go, so I'm not sure why you're doing this. I know Tom is convincing, but...."

Nodding her thanks to Allisha, Bonnie ignored my statement and said instead, "I will demonstrate a rudimentary version of our magical abilities, which will apply to everyone, so I won't be leaving people behind."

"What kind of demonstration?"

"At some point in your life, you were unable to recall information that was familiar, like a name, then later in the day it popped into your mind, correct?"

"Sure."

"The effort to find this information is akin to sending a messenger to retrieve it, and with practice you can access a lot more than the name of an old acquaintance." She leaned back. "Most people in the audience will have already experienced this, while others will feel compelled to try it, and it will work—maybe not in the moment, but eventually. Can you imagine what's possible if you had access to your entire evolutionary history this way?"

"Please tell me that's not how you expect your audience to understand your premises?"

"That's not how I expect my audience to understand all of my premises," she deadpanned.

"Then what? Ouija boards?"

Instantly enthusiastic, Bonnie told me about a Ouija board experience she had shared with a high school friend. Far too excited about the pubescent information she was 'revealing', Bonnie dragged this tale through why average dead people didn't respond from the other side, but spirit guides did.

Allisha brought us fresh concoctions as Bonnie concluded her admittedly well-organized rant by saying highly evolved teaching identities were the executors of the knowledge her characters had received in their visions and, in part, this was how knowledge of their past was brought forward.

I assumed her anticipatory gaze was somehow related to her statement and me, but the connection eluded me like the popularity of Abba.

"If you're worried about credibility," I managed to say casually, "how can you have spirits talking to people?"

"As I said, understanding these things is a process." Squaring her shoulders, she said, "If you think about it, we're all a process—works in progress."

"How's that?" I said, obligingly taking this detour.

"Being happy, for example, is an art that takes years of practice to achieve."

I could not imagine how one would practice happiness, but briefly trying to imagine it brought me to another insight: with our uncommon comfort level acting as a safety net, my blunt manner had probably left Bonnie no room to imbue my practical expertise with her creative spin. This would explain the crisper moments, even implied threats in her tone. In fact, she probably agreed with me about the pitfalls of gimmicks, but I had cornered her so she couldn't help but think I was taking shots at her labour of love.

"It must be," I said amicably, "because there aren't many people who are good at it."

"You liked your television work, correct?"

"Sure."

"You weren't really out to save the world from ignorance?" she grinned solicitously.

"There was a time when I liked the idea that our work might influence people toward making better decisions, but I had a couple of beers, and the idea went away."

"You can do better than that."

"It wasn't my job, but it would take all night to explain why," I said crisply.

"I'm looking forward to that night." There was no crinkle at the bridge of her nose or creased lip-line to undermine her sincerity. "After reaching that realization," she said, "did you still like your work?"

[49]

"Why do you ask?"

"Taking risks made you happy, you practiced it, and you became good at it?"

"That's something else I haven't given much thought to, but you're probably right. Is that a crime to your people?" I jested.

"It can be—depending." She sipped her drink.

I didn't ask.

We next had a light exchange about our school days, friendships, parents, potato chips and fizzy pop; I would have been happy spending the rest of the evening in this casual way, especially not taking a detour after every innocent comment I made, but Bonnie had other plans.

Regularly injecting the word magic into our conversation, always without qualification, became so annoying that when she eventually used the word to blithely describe all of human existence I almost lost it. My intention was to satirize a New Ager on recreational pharmaceuticals when I asked Bonnie to define the term, but my exasperation bloomed into the embarrassing sarcasm of an adolescent. Nonplussed, Bonnie asked me what I found so troubling about the idea.

Relieved for the reprieve and cued by the flickering candle, I said, "A cave man staring at fire could only explain the heat and light as magic. Time-shift him into your book, and he'd bow to the God Biclighters by virtue of a billion miracles a day."

"Can't there be magic in fire even after its science is understood?" Her eyes glowed with a beguiling mixture of mischief and delight.

"Maybe if I knew what it was."

"You are magic," she said, covering both of my hands with hers.

Ingeniously, I maintained an endearingly stupid expression, thereby leaving it up to Bonnie to explain her comment.

Instead, she pushed back from the table and said, "It's strange to meet two truly interesting men in one week, when years went by without meeting anyone. I'll be right back."

"Boggling," I muttered, signalling Allie for the bill, which she somehow had at the ready and placed on our table moments later.

My fuzzy scrutiny of our tab revealed that Bonnie had been drinking Virgin Caesars for most of the night. Nevertheless, when she returned, Bonnie insisted on going Dutch while doubling my tip before handing the leather presenter to Allisha. This exchange happened so quickly that I could not protest Bonnie's obvious gesture aimed at demonstrating that she was more generous of spirit than some points in our conversation had otherwise indicated. I knew I was "in" with her after this, but I didn't appreciate just how much until we parted company

[50]

outside of the restaurant, and she kissed me gently. With our lips still touching she said, "Be sure to call me tomorrow."

"Steel trap," I said, tapping my temple, which she found hilarious like only the smitten can.

Chapter Six
Approaching The Bridge of Reason

The next evening, I worked a job in North Vancouver recording the recovery efforts of firemen responding to a child's fall from the Capilano River bluffs.

"In the summer," the petite paramedic said to our reporter off the record, "high school kids full of booze or smoke jump into the swirls because they look deep." Gillian pointed to an outcropping surrounded by dead drops across the gorge. "Maybe a child losing her footing on the moss will play on their minds a few months from now," she lamented, searching for something redeeming in her day.

"Appreciate the background," Natalie said.

"No sweat," the paramedic replied, with a dismissive gesture.

Natalie signalled a thigh-high micro-slash for Matt to stop his surreptitious recording, and in a thickening silence they watched Gillian re-join her own kind.

"I won't use her," Natalie explained when she was out of earshot. "I like to get details and the mood on tape when the air date is…"

"Shhhit," Matt hissed as the crown of a helmet bobbed over the crest of the road from the riverbed gully.

"New tape. Risk setting up wide and nothing else. This is a budget and bunny huggers piece," Natalie ordered succinctly.

The risk she had acknowledged was of Matt missing the moment when the rim of the wire Stokes basket appeared because it offered endless "final journey" scripting possibilities. "Nothing else," directed him to avoid making visual statements that raised an audience's sorrow to fear, the catch twenty-two being that the framing of a picture is inherently editorial: the firemen's lack of haste, exaggerated in a static wide shot, would be enough to cause parents to forbid Sara, Sam, Ben, and Paige access to the free world for a while. Still, Steve would climb cliffs because they were there, and Damon worshipped him.

Matt pushed the eject button, and as the tape unspooled we trotted to a vantage point that would remain outside of the firemen's personal space. Switching tapes the moment the tripod legs touched ground, I

[52]

counted to three while it threaded before pushing the record button. "Rolling," I said as Matt centred the level bubble. Seconds later, we recorded four brawny men taking baby steps to raise a tiny girl's body in a plastic covered basket. To most of our audience, they would appear cautious lest they slip and fracture a bone, but their brothers and sisters in the business of mankind's folly would know the foursome were engaged in the first ceremony of calamity—gentility—lest something else break.

Natalie moved beside me as I finished scribbling, "EMT's standing around + firemen #2 on the label, then I handed her the box. Deciphering my surgeon's scrawl, she nodded her approval at my concept of a shot list.

"Touchy-feely?" Matt said in a neutral tone.

"No, just like we see it," Natalie confirmed her original directive.

Understanding her purpose, Matt stayed medium-wide on the yellow-clad pallbearers cresting the rise, their slow walk and careful shifting of the body from her cradle onto a padded gurney and the tender touch of the blanket from firemen with children. He did not push in on the line of hairy knuckles grasping the cold aluminum rim nor did he tilt to catch the aging Pulitzer face trickling a tear into a regulation moustache. Matt's only camera movement was one the audience wouldn't likely notice, a dirge-paced pan to a line of red and gold vehicles, one of which slowly moved away, roof lights off, just like we saw it.

"Follow up for Nightside?" Matt said when the rear lights of the ambulance merged into a single dot in his viewfinder.

"They don't care about parks and recreation," Natalie said, intentionally missing the point as she checked her Swatch. "Get them packing up, then it's a wrap... but pack your stuff carefully," she said with a sniffle.

Matt grunted his approval of the new domestic affairs correspondent. Her instructions meant we weren't going to haunt the parents with questions that required a ladder to approach ludicrous, take shaky footage of grieving relatives on their way to the morgue or do an asinine location stand-up to imply the network's omnipresent guardianship of the community they served. Local reporters would have no competition for the moronic ambush clip of the year award from Natalie. This was a grown-up piece. I liked her, too.

Ten minutes was all we could legitimately waste without a case of beer or act of God intervening, neither of which appeared before we loaded the van as if we were shipping Ming vases across the Rockies by Palsy Express. Our pace effectively consumed all of the time that a local producer might have used to screen our raw footage for a hot roll to air—footage that wouldn't be mentioned if no one asked, nor be easily found on the generically labelled cassettes until the family had time to barricade themselves against the parasitic faction of journalists.

Overall, it was a good shoot. Matt's clipped queries had informed Natalie that he knew what he was doing without questioning whether she knew what she was doing, when she had called for that wallpaper shot. She would probably recommend hiring him again. Matt and I, also strangers until this day, understood what needed to be done to feed the machine without either of us having to delineate craft from responsibilities. He would hire me again.

It was after nine o'clock when I phoned Bonnie.

Instantly excited at hearing my voice, I apologized for the late hour, which she dismissed, and riding the coattails of her "don't be silly," I said I had worked a job at the gorge, and I needed...

"That was long a day," she said, before I could pitch a nightcap with her. "You should get some rest, and we can meet at Nolan's on Davie Street in the morning. Is nine too early?"

Embraced and dismissed in two short bursts, I knew there was no point in telling her I wasn't tired because I hadn't begun work until after five; it was clear to me that the other 'interesting' fellow was at her house, a few seconds away from asking Bonnie what had made her gush.

"Nine is good."

Up early the next morning, as always, I first worked on my screenplay, then on my book before showering and heading to the cafe. Rounding the corner of the West End's hooker high-rise haven from Pendrell onto Davie street, I saw Bonnie getting out of a metallic brown, Honda Civic across from Nolan's, four doors away. She saw me at the same instant, waved with exuberant guilt over having stonewalled me the night before, and then she trotted across the street to greet me. With a quick hello and peck on the cheek, she led us inside toward a window booth—the window booth—from which I looked around the cozy cafe to find a server—the server.

Six red leatherette booths hugged three eggshell white walls with additional seating for two couples in the centre of the former Irish pub. A chalkboard on the back wall, hung between posters of a mist-enshrouded Boris Karloff in medieval drag and James Dean dragging on a smoke, listed the soup and sandwich special. To my right was a

[54]

commercial display cooler of fresh cakes and pastries behind which stood a stout man of jowled mileage affably doing a brisk takeout business of caffeine and cholesterol, the aromas of which were Pavlovian from a block away.

To my practiced ear, the newest immigrant owner was from a Baltic state, his accent endearing because it reminded me of Paul, Ed's father, who had met his wife, Elizabeth, while they were escaping Poland and Lithuania, respectively. They had taken me in when I left the navy; Ed had the foresight to tell them I was landing the next day and living with them. Good people, the Koenigs.

Above him, a dour Bogie stared truculently at Bacal whom, with preoccupied indifference, surveyed the inscribed musings of teenagers in heat preserved for posterity by layers of shellac on the solid wood tables from the nineteen fifties. I identified with the feel of the place. I was a scribe, scarred, from the fifties, and in heat.

Taking off her sweater, Bonnie's disposition then shifted to caution as she retrieved a thin manila envelope from her Aztec imprint cloth sack. "Tell me what you think," she said, sliding it across the table.

To avoid appearing too eager, I made small talk until Bréta, the owner's grand-daughter, came for and returned with our orders. Bonnie sipped her latté, trying to look casually out of the window, while I read ten double-spaced pages of an untitled chapter that began on page twenty-six.

The narrative's point of view was of an elderly man recounting a journey of rescue, from what was not stated, but it must have been a spectacular disaster: the scale of the operation was so immense that comprehending its intricacies required specialized training, without which his true tale would sound like a fantasy. In fact, the full scope of the mission was kept from student rescuers for this very reason, until they were ready to hear it.

The narrator also advised the reader that he would defer to other characters' recollections, after which he would return to take the reader to the next stage in the operation.

"The story of preparation begins with the gathering of Aleena," he said.

Aleena's scene was told from her point of view as an elder, of what specifically Bonnie didn't say, reminiscing on a cloudless fall morning as she contentedly looked across a timber bridge which spanned a sliver of river that would remain shallow until the spring rains came. In the distance, Falconers were exercising their birds from the grassy slopes at the edge of the flood plain.

Aleena had identified with potential prey straying into the falcon's territory when, years earlier, she had first crossed the bridge to enter a horseshoe shaped, open-air market that operated in the mornings, every other day. Fresh products and scrupulously honest weights and measures ensured its success equally with the merchant's antics entertaining customers.

The market's short hours aside, the one drawback to shopping here was the merchant's 'no haggling' policy in a land where bartering had been the essence of contracts since men began differentiating grunts. As a result, new customers could not help but feel they were paying too much, in spite of likely having priced similar items as they passed through the town centre market. On the rare occasion that a townie insisted on haggling, the merchant explained that she (typically) was paying for the commune's meticulous efforts and expertise, as were reflected in the quality of the products, and these were non-negotiable standards. If this customer did not understand what their work ethic had to do with the price of pears, they could easily find themselves bartering for their own self-worth, as this was the only basis upon which one would argue against the evidence all could freely examine. That said, the merchants were realists, so to compensate for some of their customer's conditioning they occasionally added product to purchases after payment had been made or made small errors in the customer's favour when giving them change.

By page six, I was familiar enough with Bonnie's style to appreciate the irony of the merchant's rule, which explained the secret pleasure they took in simple conversation and utter delight in a debate: Anyone who could convince a customer that the purchase of fruit entailed a virtuous principle, the breaking of which would irrevocably diminish the value of both their lives, could have sent a happy customer home with a peach pit in their palm and not a penny in their pocket. In other words, their bartering rule protected the buyer, the majority of whom corrected the calculating errors and went home feeling righteous.

Regular shoppers who had become sensibly confident in the value of their transactions ascribed these merchant's errors and otherwise odd behaviours to a communal affliction. Slow poisoning from the well water in their isolated commune was the chief suspect, primarily, although illogically, based on the fishmonger being the most odd among a generally peculiar people. That the gentle octogenarian, or so people guessed, did not fish in the community well, did nothing to undermine accepted lore. Water and fish went together like birds in the air, and Leith, pronounced "life" in his native Scandinavian dialect, often told his customer's children that the sea whispered stories to him. It was definitely in the water.

Sipping my cooling coffee, I said, "This is dense stuff, and nothing has happened."

"Glad you like it," Bonnie replied.

I continued reading, hoping for some action.

The young, ill-dressed Aleena was drawn to a baker's effusive disposition, and she joined a loose line in a position that allowed her to witness two street urchins at work. One of the ragged boys distracted the merchant by bumping into his display, and when they both bent over to pick up dislodged loaves his partner cut through the front of the queue to pilfer from the cart in passing. Aleena wasn't certain, but she thought the baker noticed the loss while he was thanking the expansively apologetic boy for assuming responsibility for his clumsiness. Nevertheless, he gave him a sweet pastry of which there was one less than a moment ago. It was a tense moment.

Avoiding the baker's stare, the boy thanked him as he turned into Aleena's shadow and glare; a conundrum locked his knees as the merchant reached across the cart to tug on the shoulder of his tunic. Believing the baker had figured things out, the boy steeled himself for blows he considered a cost of doing business. It helped that the baker was scrawny, and the boy had seen him coddle his hands on cool mornings.

"There are so few like you. What is your name?" the merchant said, cocking his head deferentially as if recognizing a prince slumming as a pauper.

"Mihaleh of...Mihaleh," he said, cutting short his place of birth and lineage.

"I am Tartuu, and I will remember you, Mihaleh of Mihaleh". Gushing, the baker said, "That rhymes!" and he handed the anxious boy another tart.

In Aleena's mind, the little beggar's vigilance should have declared his guilt, but Tartuu seemed oblivious to the boy's apprehension, as were the women in front of Aleena too occupied sharing their affront over an ill-mannered brat bumping them to notice the sky was on fire, should that have been the case.

In due course, the women went on their way without mentioning the incident to the baker, if they had seen it, and Aleena stepped forward absently poking potential choices, as she pondered the circumstance.

"As fresh as a new beginning!" Tartuu announced to the crowded market as he gathered the three loaves Aleena had touched. "Will that be all?" he said.

"Oh—yes, I guess," she said, opening her cloth sack to receive two more than she needed.

"Then it may not be everything?" Tartuu said, placing the bread inside.

"No, no. It's more than enough." Embarrassed, Aleena pivoted to leave but managed only a single step before curiosity turned her around. "Why did you let them get away with it?" she said, without preamble.

"Why do you ask?" the baker replied, apparently puzzled.

"It costs you money," she explained the obvious to him without judgement, having heard about the communal affliction.

"Though what you say is certainly true, this isn't what I asked of you." The baker's eyes crinkled roguishly as he then said, "Does it really interest you?"

Intrigued by the potential of any intellectual conversation after months of self-imposed isolation in a new land, Aleena hung her satchel on the edge of the cart to engage the merchant in a friendly verbal waltz. There was flare without fire, grace without pretence, and passion without possession as they grammatically swirled in a refreshingly rhythmic discussion. Aleena could not help but feel curiously close to the little gnome who acknowledged her mental dexterity with pained expressions whenever one of her views apparently pierced the heart of one of his.

Not coincidentally, she was absorbed in a fresh flush of one such acknowledgement when the misfortune apparently struck Tartuu: for no apparent reason, he forcefully said that curiosity is a good thing when applied properly but a crime to pretend, and so pillage another's time to comfort one's self-interest.

Perplexed over the change in his demeanour, the compassionate young women indulged the wandering introspection of the man of indeterminate age, certainly no less than sixty years, agreeing with everything he seemed to be massaging from a misspent youth.

Having thusly lulled Aleena, the merchant boldly stated that adolescent male behaviour had caused her to comment on the theft.

Startled by his candour, Aleena lifted her nose and stalked away.

Tartuu allowed her three paces before he said, "Your bread."

A dignified retreat out of the question, she returned to pick up her satchel, and instead of cutting her losses, she sternly said, "Only a gossip would say anything about me, and by your own measure, that crime is a theft of time." She mimicked his refrained expression, over the rhyme, and could have left it at that, but unspoken events demanded that she take her revenge for being made to feel foolish. Cradling her purchases over her breasts, Aleena awaited Tartu's defence.

Looking around his cart furtively, the baker lowered his voice and said, "I hear many things. If I wasted time separating the truth from the chatter, I would lose sight of the matter. That rhymes!" he declared to the market place.

Aleena was not side tracked by the showman who had passed on an earlier opportunity to demonstrate his mental imbalance. "What matters to you?" she said icily.

"What matters is what I learn by asking the dreaded question." He bowed toward her and whispered, "Why?" in a comically threatening tone.

"What does that have to do with you commenting on the life a stranger?" she said, shifting her weight to her back foot.

"What has it got to do with anyone? Absolutely everything, dear girl!" he declared loudly.

"Everything!" the vegetable seller at the next cart shouted, startling Aleena.

"Absolutely!" the potter on the other side of him declared a milli-second later.

"Dear girl!" little Evie shouted with glee, because she was known as one.

Confusion froze Aleena's expression as if she had missed a step in a ladder, while an elderly voice, from across the semi-circle, queried into the sudden and rare silence, "Whom may I serve?"

"Serve us!" ten out of eleven children shouted in unison because Evie was still tittering over her own cleverness.

Tartuu tapped Aleena on the shoulder, startling her out of her trance.

On his toes, he leaned across the cart, so that his face was uncomfortably close to hers as he said with a sly grin, "You saw the boys steal, but you didn't tell me until it was too late to deal. I have practiced asking the why of so many acts that I can see the answers before words cloud the facts. So with all respect that is your due, I saw that you resent how a man treated you." Leaning back, with patriarchal compassion, he added, "However, a wiser part of you knows you are also responsible for that mistreatment. I'm right, aren't I? No—don't tell me. I know when I'm right, and I am right. Aren't I?" he settled on his heels, blathering incompetently.

"Wh-wh..." Aleena stuttered, torn between dealing with the idiot, the logician, or stomping away if she could only engage her legs.

"To resolve the conundrum of punishing your man without having him think ill of you," Tartuu settled the matter, "you hurt him in absentia by telling on boys you don't know. However, by not speaking at the appropriate time, you punished me. It's a clever ruse," the baker said, shaking his head appreciatively, "but it is one you played on yourself."

"It was you who let him get away with it," she said, planting her feet.

"You didn't know what I knew, and you chose to pass on the opportunity to assume responsibility like you're doing now," the baker admonished her gently.

[59]

"What I knew has noth..." Aleena stopped speaking as the scythe of truth disembowelled her protest. "What about you?" she tried to demand, but the urge to return his broadening grin dissolved her accusation into a warble.

"Fortunately," Tartuu said, "the theft has presented us both with wonderful opportunities that I," he shouted, "will not squander!" He burst into a fit of private laughter.

"Well woven!" the weaver shouted, and his customers laughed at the pun they didn't understand, but he was a good man and an excellent tailor.

"A tight weave does not assure a catch," Leith cautioned his sizable audience of children. "Whichhhh," he stretched the word dramatically, "brings us to a verrrry fresh wind blowing east from Graedon." Focusing his mercurial attention on his audience, he said, "How fresh was the wind?"

"Verrrry fresh!" they recited to the ancient man.

"It was a day like none I'd ever seen," the elder of endless stories said sombrely, "and like none I will ever see, again."

"Why Master Leith?" little Shan-ah shouted because she knew he would forget his way if they let him pause too long.

"I cannot leave my responsibilities; there are none who are prepared to replace me."

"No, Master Leith—how bad was it?" the boy called K.T., aka Khol the Tireless or the Terrible depending on the day, said on behalf of them all.

"There is no bad. There are waters that are unsuitable for passage, and there are people who are not suited to the water." He lowered his voice. "The surf boiled beneath a pitch-thick sky that came tum-tum-tumbling across the horizon."

The children mimicked the tum-tum tumble as best their soprano voices could while laughing at their own efforts. Leith enjoyed this interlude before becoming absorbed by a space about an arm's length in front of his nose.

"Poor man nearly dies when he even thinks of the sea," one mother said from behind her brood.

"It won't be long now," her neighbour replied prophetically.

"He'll be better off," the first woman commiserated, looking despondently at the man who had entertained her when her mother came to this market, and her mother before her.

"Your opportunity is this," Tartuu said to Aleena, who stared at the bizarre goings on around her. "You didn't know that vitriol mires you in the swamp of self-serving redemption, but now that you know how you use people you can guard against it. It's a great day!" he shouted, backing her up a step and a half of surprise.

"A great day!" the tanner said.

[60]

"A great day!" two children regurgitated, and their mother's ex-changed glances confirmed that the day wasn't as difficult as it could have been without the old fisherman.

Aleena could not voice what was happening to her, but this oddly jubilant scene stripped her of concern, and a blameless conviction settled in her mind. The baker somehow knew this, and that her path would be full of bumps—he would make sure of that—but she had conquered a pitfall that swallowed people of lesser conviction.

"A great day," Tartuu said quietly, in the direction of the fishmonger, who could not possibly have heard him above the din of rambunctious commerce. Nevertheless, Leith paused to smile before he said to his captive audience with dread, "The flying desert of fine, red sand blowing from the west caused the sky to boil like a cauldron of blood pudding..."

"East!" the children objected as a choir, lest the master monger begin a different tale. "They were from the east of Graedon!"

Leith raised a bony finger. "The mid-summer winds twist before they rise to join the northern currents," the old man said, covering his contrived mistake smoothly. Slanting his head as though to share a secret, he said, "Remember this if nothing else from today; if the wind is westerly and the morning star golden, two titans scour the shallows, and you must not feel emboldened. Go north of the pillars so their might passes beneath you, and stay until the light fades to a yellowish hue." He waved an arm, and the children could not help but look at the sky in expectation, even though the old man's caution was equally old news: generations of children had consumed relevant oceanographic, geographic, and celestial information because the sea of life was the canvas upon which the masterful teller of tales had constructed a playground for their imaginations.

Feeling an unusual calm, Aleena said, "Did you not squander your opportunity? Will they not return and steal from the others?"

"There are none here who do not know hunger," Tartuu replied.

"You let them get away with it—all of you?" she waved an arm to encompass the entire market area.

"There are times when ..." he began to explain, when a single cloud cast a cool shadow on his forehead. "But this is not one of them." Standing to his full height, which still came short of Aleena's nose, the baker officiously said, "Dress appropriately for our next appointment." He turned abruptly to greet a woman who was unaware that she was his next customer.

Puzzled by the curt dismissal, Aleena didn't return for days, not that she had to, and when she did come back dressed in similar attire, she found only the baker's apprentice.

"Will it be the same today?" Eirik said.

[61]

"I suppose," Aleena said absently, looking around the market. "I came to see Tartuu. We started talking, and I forgot to pay him."

"The same today!" the apprentice shouted, scaring her onto another footing.

"The same?" the butcher queried the sky sadly, and his customers looked away while he recovered. So young, so unfair, they thought.

"The same it is," the apprentice said, handing Aleena two more loaves than she needed. "Don't worry about payment. No one can buy what he offers."

"Well?" Bonnie said, taking the pages from my hand.

"It's good as far as it goes," I said diplomatically.

"What would you have done if you were the baker?"

"Pardon me?"

"What...would...you...have...done?" she said as if I had a hearing problem.

"Nothing," I shrugged, "a third kid was probably waiting for the baker to chase either of the first two."

Baffled by my suggestion of a triple whammy, Bonnie processed the idea, and I presumed mentally tried it out before saying, "Did you think he was clever?"

"With Mihaleh or Aleena?"

"Both."

"He wasn't too bright letting the boy go." I shrugged, "I don't have a clue what he's up to with Aleena."

"He's offering to teach them both the source of life's trials. I'll begin to show you how tomorrow." Bonnie slid her work into the envelope with a crisp precision that had the effect of closing our conversation.

"Why not just tell me?"

"Because it wouldn't help me research your development of a new way of thinking." She shifted in her seat and leaned toward me. "My merchants were all teachers who led people to discover their own conclusions because that process inherently dealt with the laziness of most people who demand to know what would be functionally useless information if it was just handed to them." She looked me in the eyes mischievously.

"You think I'm lazy?" I said in disbelief.

"No, because you are this close," she touched her finger and thumb, "to embracing a new assumption."

"I'll have to trust you on that."

"Have I given you reason not to trust me?"

"It's an expression," I said peevishly. "Were everyone's comments aimed at distracting Aleena?" I asked to move things along.

"Actually, it was the other way around. The merchants were shutting down her internal dialogue by overloading it so that she could process the only event that was important in the moment, Tartuu's words." She grinned. "It'll make more sense later on."

"Fair enough. Why did the baker pretend not to notice what happened?"

"He effectively told the kids that he knew what had gone on by giving the boy a second tart for his silent partner. The next time they come around, he'll set aside some easily stolen items so his cart and customers won't be upset. These contrivances will create an opportunity for the baker to explain how they're playing a dangerous game they can stop; he'll offer to take them in."

"To work off their debt?"

Bonnie looked at me distastefully. "He's going to offer them the chance to change their lives when they trust him enough to consider it an option."

"It's a good idea, but for clarification, offering food to the starving isn't an incentive. It's extortion."

"Offering the irresistible is a principle of an art called How to Teach, in my society; it's also immensely energy efficient, which is crucial for boys who are at the end of their options. Left alone," she explained, "they would become permanent prisoners of their society or of themselves, so Tartuu used the strongest lure he had. If things go according to plan, the boys will abandon their old ways as he teaches them how to live properly."

"Maybe you should have Tartuu explain his scheme to Eirik, so readers will know what he's up to?"

"Hmmm," Bonnie cocked her head in consideration. "I like it...now that I know my audience won't wait to hear it." She chuckled.

"Glad I could help. Will knowing life's trials clear up the contradiction in your haggling rule?"

"What contradiction is that?" she said, placing the envelope safely into her carryall.

"You say it's like a law, but they kick-back money or pretend to have shorted customers and add to their purchase, right?"

"Correct."

"Both of these things add value to their customer's experience. In effect, they're teasing them into coming back, which is bartering with their expectations." I shrugged. "It's not that big a deal, but if they're

[63]

not overtly haggling, they're being haggled, and once you've got your audience thinking in terms of abstractions you could lose credibility to the ones who might not make the distinction you do."

"This is one of those situations where doing the right thing for the right reason looks like something it's not." Bonnie settled into the corner of the booth. "My merchants believed that beneath the surface of almost everything the average person does lies a predilection to make ourselves feel better. Because of this, they helped their customers express a natural impulse that left everyone feeling better."

"So you admit that your guys were bartering?"

"I admit that my customers got more than they bargained for." She sipped her coffee and still holding the cup near her lips said, "Teachers know that the *nature* of everything we do comes back to us. In part, this is why they didn't allow customers to leverage either their personal position or purchasing power against them. Haggling would have allowed customers to act to their own detriment, essentially deceiving themselves into thinking deception was an acceptable behaviour in places other than the market." Bonnie waved an arm around the café. "We deceive ourselves to our detriment every day, so what's the problem if it takes a little coercion to deliver a gift of knowledge?"

"No problem, except no one got it."

"Opening these kinds of gifts takes time and the willingness to unwrap ourselves."Abruptly raising her brow, she said, "Are you objecting to generosity or the specific influence of a full stomach?"

"Neither and you know that."

"Just as well as you know that capitulating to the truth is a personal victory; it's the idea of them being tricked that must offend you."

"I've never been tricked into something good, but I'm not offended by there circumstance."

"There's a first time for everything."

I chuckled on some phlegm. It was better than words.

"It's time for the park," Bonnie said, signalling for the bill.

We split the tab in silence, left the café, and headed toward the English Bay entrance to Stanley Park amid streaks of sunlight that intermittently raised our hope for a dry day.

Setting a casual pace, Bonnie said, "Someone fell into the river last night? I cut you off—sorry."

"You were busy."

Four steps of penalty time later, I explained that the story was about public access and safety versus the prosperity of the flora and fauna in parks. The incident would lead to a coroner's inquest determining

[64]

death by misadventure, followed by residents demanding miles of fence that five-year-olds could climb. Their position would be countered by artists arguing against a fence for aesthetic reasons, and the renowned environmental activist, Dr. David Suzuki, explaining how a fence could create an artificial island habitat for a species we didn't realize had to be mobile to survive.

Bonnie hum hum-ed over aspects of my story until, without comment, a fine drizzle simultaneously turned us around. Setting a time to meet the next day at the same café, we parted company amicably.

That night, I had a vivid dream I could clearly recall in the morning. This wasn't a particularly strange event for me, because I had a pocketful of dreams I still remembered from different times in my life, the most recent of which was of a convict escaping from an island detention facility near Horseshoe Bay, British Columbia. I had no knowledge of such a place when I first had the dream, on my sailboat in the Mediterranean, but the vivid sequence had regularly drawn my attention westward. Other dreams I still recalled in detail were from when I was a kid and between nightmares after working in El Salvador.

***

Zzzzz: Innocuous soft tones over Thunder Bay, ozone crackle, a voice devoid of concern prepared us for some harsh minutes as we belatedly skirted a chaotic mass of farmer's delight. Earphones plugged into my empty pocket forced the fellow sitting in 12b to tap the pages in my hand, before pointing to the seat belt sign. I nodded my thanks as the plane bucked tomato juice onto the woman's lap in 14C; her shrill scream lit the fuse for unescorted ten year old girls sitting across the aisle. A male flight attendant flashed by them to rescue the woman's cashmere ensemble. A second attendant made her way to the sister twins, whose faith had been forfeited to a bottle of seltzer and a shaker of salt. They were inconsolable. Three rows back, a handsomely scruffy twenty-something fellow retrieved a mandolin from the over-head storage bin and ignoring the attendants' objections, nodded for the businessman sitting next to the children to switch seats, which he was happy to do. Two men and a woman similar in common physical appeal, youthful age, and rural clothing changed seats with passengers in front and behind the children, as a tattooed Neanderthal carrying drumsticks stooped to whisper in the tomato juice woman's ear. Abruptly silent, spittle dribbled from the corner of her mouth as the

[65]

giant turned to sit on her armrest. Leaning across the aisle, he sang, "Ahhh aa ahhh ah," sticks tap-tap-tapping lightly on the nearest girl's arm. Confusion from the incongruity of a gentle voice emanating from such a physical powerhouse chased her fear away, and envy quieted her sister until the drummer's brothers crooned, "Ohh ha ohh." Their cousin blended a feathering, "Ahhh–ohh-ayyoh," while his pixie-like sister overdubbed, "Ayya-yaa, aay-yaa," a cappella that at times sounded like two voices, surrounding the children with a haunting prelude to an abruptly jaunty tale about fishing off the Grand Banks. As a hundred tons of technology twisted through the unfriendly skies, I found myself chuckling at the irony of the Newfoundlanders restoring peace to the passengers who didn't know how many men had died there.

That's what woke me up just after four a.m. - chuckling.

Chapter Seven
Positioning

Short of breath, Bonnie came into Nolan's two minutes late, according to the Coca Cola wall clock, and before the door had finished closing, she explained, "A newspaper page caught on my wiper."

"Shit, were you hurt?" I said from our window booth.

"Let me finish," she said, sliding into the seat across from me. "When I pulled over to take it off, I saw a picture of crumpled cars beside a story about insurance rates. Naturally," she said with a huff, putting her carryall and jacket next to the wall, "I had to find a place to park and walk here."

"Naturally." I nodded at the manila envelope sticking out of her cloth bag. "What puzzle have you got for me today?"

Finding nothing in my expression that I could be convicted of, Bonnie opened the envelope and handing me the pages mouthed, "Latté, please," toward Bréta as she turned to face our table. Then back to me, "There are two scenes; the first is the opening to my screenplay, so far, and the second is a continuation of the last scene you read; they don't appear back to back."

"Got it," I said, and I began reading.

(PORTENTIA or TIME, AGAIN?)
SCENE ONE

SILENT: FADE IN SPATIAL INFINITY
View of the galaxy with thousands of points of light, as seen from a distance that only hints from its size that our planetary system is minutely present in screen quadrant D –lower right. Swirling energies of all colours and consistency cross the screen. Some are cloud-like, others like gentle mists of rain. In their apparently random movement there exists a complex order of motion. The

[67]

largest cloud swirls to the centre occupying one half of the screen.

FADE IN: MUSIC

Far away and lilting, the esoteric quality of a large choir is joyful. Slow riffs are eerie but calming.

FX: ENERGY CLOUD FORMS

(All happens in C-2, the circular middle third of the screen) The centre cloud forms into a pink rose, then petal by petal they slowly open like a lens aperture to reach out and (eventually) transparently fill full screen. C3 (circular centre third screen) is the highest density of colour. From C3, a bubble of translucent, bluish light forms.

MUSIC: Is now sweetened with the addition of an instrument representative of an Egyptian culture, then another from an Asian culture, and another from an African culture, all following a slightly different pattern but in sync and harmony with the base layer. The choir and music now resonate with a multi-cultural tone and complex back-beat.

FX: ZOOM IN:

As the central petals of the rose grow to fill C2 and C3, the bluish light streaks from our solar system creating a ripple as it approaches the aperture that snaps shut immediately behind the light's passage. The bluish light slows and takes on form to shape an astral body of a floating male entity. KHA-LI's white robe shimmers with a blue aura. His hair is white, curly, and shoulder length. His features are strong and angular. He is barefoot, a scar on the right foot shimmers as he walks toward screen left, creating underfoot a translucent stone path that grows five times the length of every stride, reaching toward a distant energy construction of a pyramid.

"It's good so far," I said, tapping the pages, "and I have no doubt that your book is meticulously researched, but the cost of period sets and special effects for ethereal scenes can be a problem. I gather there's more of this to come?"

"Words are free," she said miming typing, ignoring my comment.

"They're also without value if they don't translate into a reasonable budget," I said, pitching forward like she so often did, but to lighten the moment, not emphasize my point "An agent told me that beginners confuse artistic values with practical considerations that can screw up the sale of a property, like over-pricing production values written by someone with no track record." Having reminded her that I had actually written a screenplay—kind of, I leaned back. "It's better to hone the hell out of the dialogue in visually sketchy scenes, and allow the producers to make it their own work."

"To change it?" Bonnie said coolly.

"Just how to film it. I'm saying that while it's still a work in progress, you shouldn't script expensive scenes because you could be spending the opportunity to sell the words." I shuffled the pages below the next scene and shrugged. "It's just my first impression."

"I appreciate it, really. Go ahead," she said, nodding at the scene written in standard prose format. "I'll be right back," Bonnie said, standing to go the washroom.

The setting was a bustling forenoon marketplace in which a soft breeze swirled mixed scents and children's sounds around the women who were circling potential purchases. Aleena was wearing a single piece mauve tunic with matching head scarf and new sandals with a subtle pattern of the infinity symbol burned into the ankle backs; as I read this, I realised this was the tattoo on my dream drummer's forearm. No matter, Aleena's footwear was secured by knee-high straps of a thickness that accented her shapely legs.

She greeted Tartuu enthusiastically with small talk about the beautiful day. Instantly engrossed, as if she were talking about his late mother, the baker effusively tabled everything he knew about the weather's effects on fishing and farming before switching to the human landscape. Interpreting his excessive play as relief because she had come to see him dressed as he had requested, Aleena augmented his observations with some of her own. Delighted by her agile frolicking, Tartuu offered her lead lines until Aleena's mouth ran unchecked: he covered his goods with a thin cloth to give her his undivided attention.

The encounter felt so good to Aleena that it took a while for her to realize the baker's rapt attention had slid into the mental meandering peculiar to many of the commune's residents. To coerce him back into her world, she admonished him as a parent would tell a child that it was not the time to play because he had work to do. Nodding in agreement, Tartuu casually accused her of indulging in her intellect to make herself feel smarter than most people, which she was, therefore safer than the witless, which she wasn't, because her ego would inevitably lead her into traps tailored to intelligent pampering as long as she felt out of place.

Aleena had not quite gathered enough spit to object when Tartuu chided her, "I asked you to wear good clothing to a common market as a way to bring your insecurity to your attention, which you did by over-

[69]

compensating to the point of costing me business. You're getting expensive to know, young lady."

"I was playing, like you were," she said, defensively.

"Do you do everything other people do to fit in?"

"I did what you asked of me." Planting her feet in a wrestler's stance, she added, "I do not deserve a scolding."

Chuckling dryly, Tartuu said, "The first physical step we take is a stand for our independence. After that, the world relentlessly tells us where to go and how to get there as if these are our own choices. We are not meant to become a product of other's beliefs, so we rebel, only to be beaten back by the keepers of custom until we agree to impersonate our culture. With no safe place to go, a revolutionary heart must protect itself to the degree that our inner actor forgets it is playing a roll, and as our full potential suffocates we begin to steal breath from everyone we meet."

"I have stolen nothing," Aleena said obstinately. "I have brought payment for everything."

Looking patiently over the top of his nose, Tartuu continued his thought. "Inevitably, the actor creates a secret he keeps from himself, about himself, which feeds a self-image that reason demands he maintain in ever-changing circumstances. To endure this endless circumstance of compromise he must embrace flexible beliefs from a contradictory world that has trapped all who came before him within cycles of justification that ultimately crushed their essence. Having nothing to hide, my dear," he said, standing as tall as he could, "means you are not encumbered, there is nothing blocking your view, and everyone's obligations are clear."

"Obligations—in a market?"

"There are only two choices in life: you can live and die stupidly, or you can learn the hard way because there is no easy way. Logic dictates that you are obliged to learn where ever you are." He winked. "Today's lesson is that you are smart enough to keep your self-interests a secret from most people, but you do not take into account that you are not going to live forever so you waste time nurturing your sense of belonging to places you have outgrown. Make that single change in your thinking, and your child will grow up free."

"How—how did you know?"

Ignoring her question, the merchant said, "It will take time to free your revolutionary heart from the shackles of custom, but you have achieved a noteworthy feat by coming back to face yourself today."

Written in an abruptly poetic manner, i.e.: sparrow soared, terror-turning, frantic flight... Bonnie then wrote that a bird wandered into the falconer's training area, sensed its error, and beat a hasty escape directly between the baker and the girl. The flash of grey and the fuph-

fuph-fuph staccato beat of wings sent Aleena back a step. Tartuu, lips pursed in brief ponder, withdrew the cloth.

That was it.

"It suits your other piece," I said, sliding the pages across the table to Bonnie.

"But?"

"Same observation as before; you've got to be careful about beating the audience over the head with even little abstractions, ahead of extending your story line, so they have a context for them."

"Great, thanks," she said. As she scribbled notes on the front page of her work, she said to herself, "I need to punch up the opening scene about comprehending the intricacies of the rescue, so it doesn't sound like pure fantasy."

"I don't think I said that."

"It's the nature of your comment that matters," she said finishing her note then looking up. "If a smart fellow like you is already impatient, well..." She shrugged as she slid the pages inside the envelope, then the envelope inside her carryall from which she snatched a five-dollar bill and put it on the table. Sliding out of the booth and standing, Bonnie said, "Let's go for a walk," as she turned away putting on her coat.

Hurriedly, I left my share of the bill on the table, and just caught the closing door behind her. I said nothing, waiting for her to get over her disappointment as we walked along.

Steering us toward freshly furrowed rows, where thousands of yellow daffodils would soon line the park entrance, Bonnie indirectly justified her manner of presentation by saying, "I'm leading the audience to an ancient principle of learning: watching the world for guidance is a metaphysical practicality when you know how to inter-pret the answer, like you interpreted Tartuu's cue as a shadow of doubt. Thank you for that. It's more important than you know."

"You're welcome. I assume you expect the same from your audience?"

"Tartuu will tell his apprentice—thanks for that suggestion—that the bird wasn't paying attention to its direction in life, and it carelessly discovered that the long way around was the prudent way to avoid a deadly encounter." She grinned. "The rewards of expediency."

"The shadow was a sign that Aleena wasn't paying attention?"

"More than that; it wasn't time for her to hear the whole truth because, with few exceptions, students need to circle that from a safe distance before they can face their death head on."

[71]

"They have to face death to make them ready to learn about the mission? No wonder you don't tell them about it right away." I snickered.

"The death is symbolic, about illusions, and it's nothing to laugh at," she said sternly. "It's the most difficult thing they will every do. After that, accomplishing the mission is almost a *fait accompli*."

"Good to know," as I causally looked across the bay at a distant fog bank lazily rolling toward the inner harbour. "Couple of things. Why did you use a falcon to represent the truth?"

Bonnie praised my insight with a half-grin that collapsed as fast as it had materialized as she explained, "A falcon is what it is, a hunter that strikes from out of the blue; it has no extraneous concerns, and the wayward path of its prey reminded Tartuu of his first encounter with Aleena, when she realised self-pity was stalking her happiness. He knew that without changing her core beliefs she would remain committed to playing the role of a victim until it killed her."

"Symbolically?"

"It could also be literally, if she didn't change her ways; a person of great energy who acts without direction is a monumental idiot waiting to be hit by the proverbial bus. If she did change her ways, the death of who she thinks she is arrives when she recognizes the essence of her actions for what they are." She turned toward me. "Didn't it strike you as odd that no one but Aleena saw what happened the first time around, and not even one customer in a busy market came by while they were talking afterwards?"

"Actually," I said, stretching my arms, "parts of your dialogue made me feel like a kid eavesdropping on an adult conversation, so I didn't notice that. But you can make the point by scripting wide shots to imply people are walking around an invisible fence." I grinned and shrugged, "Then you'll have to explain what that's about, as well."

"To keep us on the same page," Bonnie said, apparently preparing her explanation through a vacant stare, "my people understood that the energy of an impeccable Will inherently aligns with the momentum of their life-force's intent. At my teacher's level of evolution, these energies were a rolling force of unstoppable potential, so they had to be extremely careful, literally, about what they thought. Another reper-cussion of the coalition of these energies was that the events the teacher needed to further their student's development had an uncanny way of happening as a matter of course." She leaned back. "You could say that my teacher's energy was an ocean liner and the waves of its wake are the events that happen when it passes." She tittered to herself.

[72]

"From the student's perspective, strange events often rocked their boat, especially when they were with their teacher, so being left alone to deliver a lesson is just a small demonstration of their energy's influence."

"Why was it more pronounced when they were with a teacher?"

"You'll have to take this at face value, for now," she said apologetically: teachers lend students energy, so they can experience specific events while they're in a safe place, and the teacher can explain things. Some of these events are subtle and external, like no one bothering them, while others can fall like an anvil of enlightenment. You said you were having trouble with my dialogue?"

"It's more with your style. Sometimes your dialogue is more formal than real people would speak, and the scenes you've shown me are all leading to other things. I mean, it looks like you're building a good story, but I can't tell if you've left something out or if it's just me." I smirked as a wave of fatigue ran through me. Taking a deeper breath than usual, I said, "You might not have considered that most of your audience will have parked blocks away from a ten dollar seat, be half way through a bag of five dollar popcorn and a three dollar cup of brown ice by the time the lights dim. They'll want some payback for your teasing pretty fast. All of this thinking is wearing me out," I said.

Looking pleased for no reason that she cared to explain, Bonnie took my elbow in her hand and aimed us at a nearby park bench.

"You don't think my archaeologist's scene, without defining their quest, will intrigue them?"

"For a short time."

"Why is that?"

"Honestly?"

"What purpose would there be in lying?"

"We both know I meant you might not like what I could say."

"Apparently, only one of us knows that can't matter if we're going to be on the same page." We sat down.

I suddenly had no energy to argue, especially silly crap, so I paused to gather my thoughts, which for a man feeling he was about to enter a coma was surprisingly easy.

Lacking the energy to contrive delicacy, I said, "So far, you've ignored action fans, threatened or alienated everyone who knows anything about mental or emotional distress, your kids are thieves, and your adults play verbal chess with people who at best think in terms of checkers. On the upside, the Baker's Union will love it. I really need to know the big picture if I'm going to help you," I said.

[73]

"Are you trying to back out because learning my people's way of thinking is more difficult than you bargained for?" she teased.

"I didn't bargain for anything," I said flatly, which is what I felt my electrocardiogram would have looked like in that moment.

"By your own rules," she said cheerfully, "we exchanged and agreed upon our expectations after I said I needed a full-time partner to do it properly. I also demonstrated how my people's way of thinking is outside of our culture's considerations, and you agreed to put in the time it takes to have an experience at their level of understanding if I agreed to try to create one for you." She titled her head. "I also asked you to remember that you asked for this." Bonnie squinted flirtatiously, and the spectre of an elf or leprechaun, whichever one is a pain-in-the-ass, slipped through the aperture of her gaze. In that peculiarly dense moment, as if I was encased in concrete, I clearly understood that within our entire dialogue she had elicited my agreement to be her partner, the subterfuge notwithstanding, and that it was her experiment to conduct as she saw fit.

"You know I can't tell you the big picture," she said coincidentally, as I concluded my internal thoughts.

"I do, but I find it strange that you put out so much energy establishing that I am an average person in thought, while you're tailoring scenes according to how someone special, in your character's terms, reacts to them?"

"Couple of things," she grinned. "You could only say that if you think we are in a competition of some kind. Otherwise, there's no incongruity in my approach; you are not an average person, you're just acting like one." She switched modes, more than moods, and speaking as if I wasn't there said enigmatically, "How a student reacts to a lesson affects the next lesson, which is why I am researching scenes with someone who knows what it's like to know things they can't express, someone who made that knowledge a secret influence in their life, but it's not their only secret influence." Regaining her customary manner, she looked me in the eye and said, "I can tell you that my characters are working on a plan of biblical proportions."

"You said religion has nothing to do with training your characters?"

"I said my characters weren't religious, not that religion isn't a part of my story."

The Point Atkinson horn blared a warning to mariners that there was a continent nearby, effectively robbing me of my moment to respond because I had already taken that breath and expelled it.

[74]

As the horn's resonance bounced off the water and faded into the forested mountains, Bonnie said, "What do you think my audience will assume so far, and I mean everything that comes to your mind?"

Still feeling physically dull and emotionally uninhibited, I blandly said, "You've implied there's a lost love, and you mentioned over-sized clothing and caring about what people think. From that, I thought Aleena was pregnant before Tartuu said anything, and meeting a baker who's really a teacher implies that she needs some kind of internal sustenance or maybe saving of some kind?" I raised my brow.

"Maybe it would help to know that my teachers' culture is against all forms of religion, so you can let that go."

"Nothing I've read tells your audience that they're not a sect of some other kind, and now you're objecting to the impression you created. Maybe you've worked so hard at setting up complex inter-actions that you expect me to see what you think is in plain sight. We're not going to get far if you're going to escort me to the conclusions you want."

"You are correct. Please carry on."

Vindicated, I casually said, "These scenes seemed to happen in the Egyptian time frame, in an arid coastal climate. The market setting suits a Mediterranean or Red Sea trading port and the diversity of your merchant's names suggests they're refugees who formed a commune. This implies they could have been running from a war or famine, but I like the idea that persecution drove them away; Islam is probably their common bond."

"Why is that?" Bonnie said noncommittally.

"There are no important women in your story."

"You like that?"

"I meant your characters' roles favour that idea. You know that, as well."

Smiling briefly, she said, "My teachers knew their students' words were sign-posts to their underlying beliefs. If their grammar was inconsistent with their stated intentions, chances were good that their beliefs weren't what they thought them to be, as well. This means teachers had to interpret their student's assumptions and negotiate shared meanings to ensure they were as much on the same page as they could be. So I'm not criticizing your manner of expression or grammar, I'm minimizing the possibility of misinterpretation as we discuss our story, and there's no time like the moment of expression to explore a relevant point." She grinned.

[75]

"Where's our negotiation?" I joked. "You just beat me up with my average thinking, again."

"Teachers and students need to share specific experiences from which they can build common assumptions. This requires positioning the student for an accurate interpretation of these experiences, and that can often look like a beating, when it's really a kindness. That said, similar experiences don't necessarily generate the same assumptions in different people, so a negotiation of understandings is often required to arrive at a single point of view assumption... which is ultimately the teachers." She cocked her head teasingly.

I understood her without taking offence, and said, "Fair enough. Can I continue?"

Bonnie nodded graciously.

"Taking religion out of it, your commune would be based on other commonalities, like metaphysical beliefs, but how they shared these over great distances and then managed to gather in one place would take an extraordinary explanation. Even then, your main characters seem to be coercing specific individuals into joining their way of life, and helping the kids to grow up safely is probably a metaphor for the rescue mission."

"Thanks for that. I'm on track, and we're on the same page."

"You're welcome. Would it make sense to bring you up to speed on some film terms and production methods so we don't get our wires crossed about those? I mean, at least I can contribute something today."

"Fire away," she said easily.

My intrusive fatigue lifted as suddenly as it had arrived, while I explained visual and aural insinuation through manipulating tempo and layering, camera movement, implying emotional interplay between characters, as well as reviewing post production techniques Tom had probably already spoken about. Bonnie learned quickly, her insightful queries reflecting a solid grasp on how to tweak expansive imaginings with inexpensive sounds and how to use camera motion as nuance.

Eventually, not surprisingly, she asked me how I would portray ineffable insights on the screen. This caused me to draw from personal experience—having often sensed things without apparent cues—and trying to link these to a physical expression of some kind. My attempts were archetypical, which is to say poorly representative of the moment, and which, I finally said, is why they call it ineffable.

"What happened?" she said.

"What do you mean?"

"I saw a change in you when you were struggling with language."

[76]

"Sure—I was struggling," I said.

"I told you, you can trust me."

"It doesn't make sense," I relented. "And it doesn't apply here."

"We both know there was more going on than a search for symbols. What was it about—a teacher would need to know these things?"

Tentatively, I said, "I went back to a moment when it felt like I was at the end of something, that's all."

But it wasn't all; I had felt, in this present time, like I was walking away from viewing a massacre, but unlike the original experience that had been imbued with the sense that I had nowhere to go, that any direction would do because all directions were 'away,' I felt the ineffable loss of my past.

"You didn't recognize the sign posts," she said softly.

It took me a moment to realize she had addressed my thoughts, by which time she was saying in her normal tone, "It's a rare person who can allow a feeling to overrule their intellect. Let's head back." She stood up and began walking toward the park entrance.

Catching up to her, it crossed my mind that her statement was the point of the exercise—confirming to me that I was not average, so that I wouldn't automatically interpret her intellectual bashing as declaring me otherwise. Not appreciating her back door approach to stomping on a point already stated, if not yet believed by me, I said, "Feeling knots in the stomach was pretty much a way of life for us, and lots of people turned around for no other apparent reason. So, wouldn't it be accurate to say we were all average within our group?"

"That may be, but I suspect you sometimes knew what was going to happen, beyond thinking about potential events when you weren't in danger."

Memories of my portentous bar-talk flashed warmly on my forehead, as Bonnie suddenly turned on me as much as toward me, and for a fractured second, her face appeared old, not just older. The illusion faded, and she said, "What do you think fate had in store if you hadn't paid attention to your knots?" Under the imminent threat of tripping over her own feet, she steadied herself with a hand on my arm, and what I had heard as a challenge became an inquiry.

"I wasn't where I would've been, so there's no way to know what destiny had in store," I temporized.

"I use the term fate to mean a better path offered but not taken, in which case a destiny may not be realised. Consider this: your fate would have been to die if you had ignored the omens that led you to safety."

[77]

"You've also implied that me being here was a design of destiny, when I made thousands of decisions before coming here."

"As you should have. Destiny is a decision-making process."

"Fate isn't?"

Fate is about making decisions that fly in the face of the evidence or not making them until your choices have evaporated, which you earlier defined as stupidity. You also said you didn't have to come to Vancouver, correct?"

"I had options, and I still don't know that coming here was the best thing to do," I said, floating that implication between us. "Where to?"

We had reached the intersection of Denman and Davie Street, and I was essentially asking her if we were done for the day, part of me hoping we were because I was feeling strangely vulnerable.

Bonnie stared at me like Einstein on the brink of understanding the nature of time, and there we stood, unblinkingly experiencing its passage.

"Take charge!" she suddenly exclaimed.

The force of her comical demand caused me to step back, then to cover my surprise I converted my motion into an exaggerated sniffing effort, as if searching for a scent to follow. I first tilted my head toward a young couple lazing under a tree; their muffled animation conveyed the pitching of premature promises that one of them would eventually call lies. Turning to the right, I thought of veering toward the beach, but I nixed the idea because walking in sand would be an effort on my sore legs. The Denman Street hill straight ahead was a better choice, and we would have to pass the hotel near the corner—the Point Atkinson horn blared an invitation to nervous mariners as the fog blanketed the western shore. Taking the hint, I sought shelter in a glass of wine at Checkers.

With that pleasantry twice behind us, Bonnie led the way out and again waited for me to decide on our course or to call it a day. On an impulse, I crossed Denman Street to the bicycle path that followed Beach Avenue, in the strip park that paralleled False Creek.

Walking a wayward course around youths beginning the ten kilo-metre skate around Stanley Park, we chatted about things promptly forgotten, to put a patina on the bonds I may have scratched earlier in the day. Ten minutes later, we came to the Burrard Street underpass where we could have turned around, continued into the city, or turned up a slope to Pacific Avenue and headed back to Nolan's. Option three seemed to be the lesser evil, and we leaned into the task.

[78]

Reaching the top of the slope with a huff, Bonnie said, "Same time tomorrow?"

"What—sure—why?" I said confused.

She pointed toward her Civic parked fifty feet away, and said, "I had options, but I knew coming here this morning was the best thing to do, even if I didn't know why." She brushed my arm. "Call me later." Without a backwards glance, Bonnie walked to her car and drove toward the city centre without first offering me a ride home.

***

Zzzz: From an impersonal distance, I watched a young Robbie LeBlanc struggling to be heard, baffled that people did not understand the world this strangely endearing man saw so clearly. The contrast ratio of the black and white image paled and the shadow of a thief come to rob him of wonder melded into toxic tales about Vietnam: jungle green images erupted into patches of boiling black-orange blasts that resolved into Ski sitting in the comfortable shade of his wife's common sense and earthy humour. Their forms intertwined to become a corkscrew depositing experiences at the bottom of a carousel. Wizichinski in Rhodesia turned to Leblanc in Biafra, turned to me in Argentina.

The growing pile of experiences needed to be sorted before they jammed the machine, but when I bent down I found myself staring at the tire of a midnight blue Mercedes, the custom hub cap reflecting the cedar-covered mountains of southern Lebanon. Instinctually, I checked my pockets: I had cash for daily expenses in local currency in the right front for easy access, and additional local currency in the lower left pocket in case I had to grease a palm. Larger amounts of bribe money in British pounds and American dollars were in an internal slot on my recorder pouch. Official press passes, militia permission slips, and doctored pictures of me with various politicians and clerics were stacked according to the likelihood of encountering their factions. Maronite, Christian, Sunni, Shi'ite, and Druse groups lined my back pockets.

Behind my recorder were passes from the Palestine Liberation Organization, the Popular Front for the Liberation of Palestine, the Popular Palestinian Liberation Front, the Palestine Liberation Army - popularity not designated, and a crumpled document emblazoned with all of their official stamps. Technically, I was ready to deal with anyone I met. Practically, I was too overburdened to run from any of them.

Wizichinski honked the horn.

[79]

I couldn't leave because my passport was in the hotel safe.
Ski said I was safe, my passport was always with me.
The carousel melted into a brook. The babbling was soothing.
I stepped into the clear water. It was over my head.

Gulping breaths awakened me between the reaper's favourite hours of three and four a.m.

Chapter Eight
Uninformed Consent

Toying with another thin envelope, Bonnie began our next meeting at Nolan's by criticizing junk mail, primed by her son jokingly asking her before she left the house to pick up his free gift on the way home.

"Placing a monetary value on a gift implies an expectation of reciprocity," she said distastefully, "notwithstanding the redundancy of free and gift."

"Greed drains the brain," I said, with a nod toward the pages she was idly tapping.

"Intelligence has little to do with it," she said, ignoring my gesture. "If companies can tease us into thinking we're taking advantage of them or pick our pockets by pandering to our fears of having less in some way, we're at their mercy. And we both know they don't have any."

"MacDonald's and Mattel are secretly taking over the world?"

"I'm serious. If we spend money on things we don't need, we risk displacing a responsibility."

"We pay for gratification all of the time. It's built into the cost of a free society."

"Excellent." Bonnie opened the envelope and fanned the pages. "Our merchants understood how to manipulate semantics and nuance to stalk students into discovering their own detrimental assumptions. From here, they could embrace new understandings that inspire the imagination to go outside of their experiences and claim knowledge of entire concepts."

"Meaning they don't really understand them?" Like me, in that moment.

"To claim knowledge in this context is to understand the entire spectrum of cause and effect in a particular arena. It's a mental hologram within which you can instantly reference any point to every point because you understand the roll of each and its influence on the whole."

[81]

"Duane Allman could play guitar like that."

"Like what?"

"Roam the fret board: he could take you to undefined places, without drugs," I added, but not categorically.

"Good, so you do understand. Now imagine our social indoctrination in terms of political parties and corporations roaming their threat boards to create public assumptions that obscure the fact that they're plucking our strings."

"I get your point, but a free gift is an outright lie; everyone knows you have to buy something."

"And they do because the indoctrination has become an insidious influence."

"How is a free side of fries insidious?"

"I know you're capable of deeper thought."

"I don't want to use it all up this morning." I nodded at the envelope. "I might need some for that."

"Overall," Bonnie said, placing her palms on the table, "we are so clouded by rhetoric that we can't imagine the harm we cause through seemingly innocent acts. My teachers understood this influence, so they relentlessly taught their students clarity of mind as an art to be practiced like scales and played like a symphony." She looked at me, the pages on the table, then back at me. "Bear that in mind as you read about Tartuu: he knew the townies would have punished the kids for being hungry, that they were exhausted by their daily routine, ready to be played by cruel people, and the damage to their spirits could take lifetimes to heal if he didn't intervene."

"Isn't he playing them, as well?"

"Yes, and if all goes well, he'll teach them how to heal themselves."

"From what?"

"They believe in nothing and trust no one. They would be empty without fear and suspicion to keep them going. Tartuu knew they couldn't last much longer because they were sent to him." Bonnie handed me the pages as she slid sideways on the bench seat.

"Don't you mean chased to him?"

"No, I mean that as literally as the Universe gets. When it wants someone to be helped, it sends them where they need to go. It doesn't matter what the route looks like, but it's helpful to recognize it during their rehabilitation." She smiled a secretive affair and said. "Read between the lines. See if it makes more sense to you." Bonnie left the table and headed for the washroom.

[82]

Her latest offering, which began on page 229 of an untitled chapter, was awkward and stilted. I understood why she had to set up the scene and why she left me alone with it.

A boy of ten years brought a weary traveler to a communal gathering, where they shared their food and drink while comfortably conversing as if he were a neighbour dropping by. All of them seemed to be oblivious to a girl who was leaning against a nearby tree, rhythmically moving to music in her mind while her lute lay silent by her side. Close by, two young boys were engaged in a staring contest at a shrub, when well into the meal an old man asked the traveler what circumstances had brought him to their table on this fine autumn day. The stranger responded glibly, essentially saying that he had become bored with the same routines, quickly adding that he meant no disrespect to those who thrived on routines. They just weren't for him.

To his chagrin, his comment launched an in-depth analysis of the cause and effect of glibness between two elderly men, until a woman of middle age interrupted the skirmish to say she had lost the point. Looking for the stranger to reorient her, she asked him again what circumstances had brought him to their table. The traveler answered honestly this time, if sketchily about his situation.

Without embarrassment or preamble, the woman told the stranger that she had patiently allowed time for her husband to deal with a personality problem, but by the time she saw things for what they really were, it was too late for words. She had tried to help him see what needed to change, but it made him angry because he heard everything as a criticism. Between flare-ups, he was engaging to the world and sullen at home, but she could not speak to him. All she could do was escape, which is how she came to be there.

"My fathers," she said looking at the stranger, "have other views about this."

"Parents often do," the man agreed.

"Frozen by indecision," the elder father on her left said on the heels of the stranger's words, "she rationalized an untenable position into a conundrum about love and duty to give her suffering purpose. When she realised it might kill her, she left him and became unbearably sweet with new acquaintances from the relief of a new beginning."

"Father?" the woman placidly said, looking at the elder sitting on her right.

Sadly, the old man said to the traveler, "I think her inaction allowed the circumstance to become dangerous so she could justify leaving. She was young, and she abandoned her responsibilities with the knowledge this would ultimately help him and free her. In this way, she could feel sacrificially superior to anyone who might judge her." He looked at the other elder apologetically. "I have trouble reconciling her

[83]

claim of being patient, then leaving him from fear." He turned to face the stranger. "People who are patient and fearful are deceitful; they become actors who charge admission to their good humour, and when enough people recognize their game, they move the show to a new stage." His gaze lingered upon the stranger as he said to the gathering in general, "Our daughter's sweetness is a performance to be sure, but it is not deceitful for she has nothing to fear. For her, it is the most efficient way to conduct her affairs. Do you think you did the proper thing by leaving?" he said turning to face the stranger, again.

Although grateful for the hospitality, the traveler was disarmed by the candour of a communal conversation and disoriented by the glib responses that came to his mind. Wisely, he said the insights he had just been so graciously offered, were new to him so he needed to think about it.

"We know this is a difficult question," the elders said obligingly, in unison.

The gathering nodded in concurrence, but their collective gaze did not waver from the stranger: "Take all of the time you need," their expressions conveyed. "We'll wait until you're ready."

Ironically, by trying to incorporate both elder's views to justify his uncertainty, the stranger realised personal events had gone too far because he had avoided doing anything about them, and a fresh start became his best option. This is what he told the gathering.

"We all made that choice, one way or another," a young wife said, spreading her arms to encompass the abundance of fresh food, a glorious day, and the implied invitation for the traveler to make a new home.

Three twangs on the lute saved him from having to decide in that moment, which seemed to be the design of their conversation. However, this wasn't all good because the notes gave rise to a story about a silver-tongued stranger's arrival at a harvest celebration on the cusp of a change of seasons. This worried him, beneath the compliment of her attraction on display, for minstrels were the custodians of history, and his unremarkable journey might be heard in lands ahead of his arrival.

I set the pages down just as Bonnie returned to our table.

"Well?" she said.

The lack of names and obvious effort to entice the stranger made it easier to deal with the subtext of the scene, as per her request to look between the lines.

"Your theme seems to be that there are times when doing nothing is best and that offering help can be premature." I glanced down. "Reviewing the past is also important to understand what to do the next

[84]

time around because things might not be what they seemed to be at the time. For that matter, things might not be what they appear to be in the moment."

"I know it's choppy," she said, acknowledging that I had avoided commenting on the quality of her work.

"Why did these people plot to help the guy?"

"To have him realize he had arrived at a place he didn't know he was looking for." Her gaze lingered on me, before she said, "As for *these people?*" She dipped her head in anticipation.

"The woman is Aleena grown up?" I said.

"Correct."

"The elders would be the baker and ... another merchant?" I guessed.

"What about the traveler?" Bonnie said, taking the pages from beneath my hand.

I didn't have a clue.

"It's not *in* the chapter," Bonnie said to help me.

I shrugged, and she said no more about it as she reached into her bag to present me with another short scene beginning on page 340. I held my tongue about this annoying practice of randomness and dutifully read the extract...

The same characters had convened a council to discuss what to do about the unnamed traveler's practice of extracting praise and favours in exchange for his cooperation; he had not recognized that the elder was talking about him at their first meeting. The council's preamble dialogue pointed out that people who place this tax on relationships can never fulfill the demands of their self-image, and that this self-deception inevitably leads to a betrayal, so they were searching for ways to make the need to change his behaviour starkly apparent without damaging anyone. I followed their plan this far—you can't fix what you don't know is broken—before Bonnie lost me: the elder, Tartuu, said they should focus on the traveler's romance to come with the minstrel, and his companions discussion then revealed that the council was a cabal of psychics.

For pure disappointment, this machination surpassed resurrecting dead characters in dream sequences because, my specific objections aside, Bonnie's writing style generated an undercurrent of suspense by alluding to there being 'more' to everything her characters said. I had caught on to that much from Bonnie's roll playing.

I didn't get it. She was miles smarter than this.

When I looked up to comment, Bonnie pre-emptively said, "Teachers focus on the subtext of physical events, so when a stranger happened upon a group of people who were celebrating the change of seasons, they didn't have to discuss why he was there."

"I got that or would have. I'm thinking there's no depth to your plot if your guys know what's going to happen, even if the audience doesn't."

"By the time the audience gets to this scene they'll know the council can read the momentum of events, which is to say that some events may not have passed the point of change to become inevitable."

"Thereby making a thin gimmick arbitrary."

"Thereby creating drama, you'll see."

"Or not," I mumbled under my breath.

We paid our bill, and in silence headed toward the park for two city blocks before Bonnie said, "Every scene in my work has underlying circumstances, not unlike how you came to understand where you really were in the Middle East. I think you're frustrated with my manner of presentation because your imagination hasn't grasped the potential dangers of daily life here. You're still indoctrinated toward the more overt manifestations of conflict."

"Is understanding the dangers of daily life a step in learning a more advanced way to see things—or maybe understand the entire mission?"

"Absolutely." She grinned broadly. "You're on the same track as the students directly involved, because they had to appreciate the obstacles they would face; knowing where they really were was key to the success of the plan and their own safety."

"Okay, so what kind of dangers am I missing?"

"Let's see if we can find something that'll get your attention." She looked feverishly up and down Davie Street.

It took me a moment to realize she was making a joke.

Chuckling, I said, "When I was in the Navy, Campbell and I were standing an outside watch on the bridge wings in a dead calm when we passed a large log. A moment later, an officer cadet opened the hatch and shouted for the benefit of the captain standing inside the bridge, 'Did you see that log, Campbell?'

'Yes sir.' Campbell said, 'It was brown, long, and round.'

'Why didn't you report it?' the cadet said coldly.

'It didn't seem important.'

'Sir!' the officer cadet admonished him. Then he explained, 'There may have been a man holding onto it!'"

I told Bonnie that for the rest of our watch we scanned the horizon for shipping, the mid-distances for Russian periscopes, and the near distances for anything people could hang onto. Near the end of our watch, without comment to me, Campbell flung the hatch open and shouted, "Officer of the watch...sir! Port lookout reporting shit hawk bearing red one five, angle of elevation thirty degrees, range half a mile, closing fast!" Before the cadet could ask why Campbell had reported a seagull, he said, "There may be a plane behind it. Sir!"

Expelling a rush of appreciation through her nostrils, Bonnie said, "Are you making fun of me?"

"To the contrary, I am acknowledging that there could be danger anywhere."

"Umm."

We walked the rest of the way to the park in a comfortable silence before Bonnie suddenly became animated. Like a child making discoveries, she pointed to an ancient tree, a tide rip, then a cloud formation, and said things like, "It's elegant," and, "Watch the swirl," then, "Look at it change shape and still be a cloud."

I was envious. She didn't have to work at creating her commune characters.

Chapter Nine
Beauty and the Beast

Look, look!" she exclaimed as if my eyes required separate commands.
With exaggerated concern, I scanned the horizon for a tornado, then the sea for a tsunami before following her finger pointing toward a rotund man, dressed in a multi-coloured pullover shirt, playing with his retriever mixed breed wearing a matching bandana.

"The dog could have rabies?" I ventured a guess.

"This is important. Tell me what you see."

"I see a fashion-challenged guy playing with his dog."

"That's what our culture taught you to see. Try it my culture's way, and assess the nature of their interactions." Bonnie pulled me off the walkway to watch the duo work a cycle of heel, sit, down, and stay commands. At the completion of the routine, I had nothing 'advanced' to add to my initial observation.

"Would you agree she has been trained using appropriate methods?" Bonnie prompted me.

"No," I said definitively.

"Why do you say that?"

"She has a penis; otherwise I agree."

Bonnie managed her laughter into a distorted, "What tells you that his training has been appropriate?"

"Bozo's commands are calm, the dog obeys hand signals right away—maybe too fast because he anticipates them, which means it's all a familiar game." At that moment, the dog issued a plaintive cross between a reluctant howl and a whimper, which sounded like a blues horn refrain. "Otis is tired of basic training; he's asking for something to chase," I said.

"There's hope for you." Bonnie inhaled audibly through her nose, then slowly released the air through her mouth to settle her breathing. In a normal tone, she said, "Otis responds happily even when he doesn't get an immediate reward because his behaviour is governed by how his trainer conditioned him to respond beyond the command." She

[88]

mimicked the dog's antics at the foot of his owner, taking skipping half-steps around me before stopping at close quarters to say, "He has faith that his actions will benefit him," with a satisfied huff.

Taking her arm in mine, I said, "I don't think dogs are plagued by abstractions," as we started to walk.

"I didn't say he thought about it," Bonnie replied, squeezing my arm. "Which is the point; he doesn't know how he has been conditioned any more than we understand the roots of our behaviour."

"That may be true, but people can choose to act in different ways to identical circumstances. Dogs repeat a behaviour until they get a better offer." I thought about this for a moment, chuckled, and said, "Maybe that's not the best example."

"We're certainly capable of making other choices," Bonnie said, stopping to look back, "but our unrealised assumptions shrink those possibilities until we end up doing versions of the same thing in similar circumstances. Enslavement to our illusions about the way things are continues until we stop to assess the consequences of our beliefs." She nodded. "Set your version of the world aside, and look at them as if you're from another planet."

"Huh?"

"We're talking about illusions; just do it, and discover something."

After a moment of mental adjustment, I focused on a bipedal humanoid form moving his limbs in a repetitious way, then at Bonnie's direction I closed my eyes and opened them to focus on the four-legged creature moving his entire body in various ways.

"Switch rolls," she whispered. "Assume the smaller creature is the initiator, and you'll see that the big one is not as smart or nearly as agile. Otis stands on all fours, but all the man can do is lower his hand. The little one rests his body on the ground, but all the big one can do is raise his hand. Otis gives the human a break by patiently sitting in front of him. The human is happy for the rest, so he rewards the little fellow with a cookie."

These actions happened as she spoke, and for a brief moment, Bonnie's phrasing caused me to experience the incongruous perception that Otis was training an intellectually inferior creature to feed him. I laughed at the illusion, then again at the cliché that people are trained by their pets in just this way.

"You've got it!" Bonnie said bobbing in front of me like Otis at his master's feet. "Our predilections," she said, settling down, "are shaped by the commands of our culture, which we filter through how we view ourselves and the risks we're willing to take to maintain that view. Our

[89]

freedom to respond to identical circumstances in different ways is an illusion, just like the one you experienced." Grasping my hand, Bonnie took skipping steps trying to pull me along. "It takes discipline to break old patterns and to see what we're really capable of because we've designated our self-image to be the guardian of our assumptions."

I let go of her hand and began walking at a pace too fast for her to maintain her frolicking.

Stopping on the grass a few steps behind me, she triumphantly said, "And there it is!"

"There what is?" I said, turning to face her.

"You could have chosen to play with me, but your male upbringing dictated that you should be embarrassed. That's not manly either, so you became superior and distanced yourself from me."

"Not that I necessarily agree, but one point at a time: my action was one choice of many possible choices."

"True, but it was one you would make nine times out of ten. It's the tenth variation of the same thing that creates your misconception about free will, when the other ten times out of a hundred, guess what you'd do?" She closed the distance between us. Still catching her breath, she said, "Otis came into this world without ulterior motives. He has no abstractions to ponder or images to maintain so everything that's not a potential adversary in his world is a potential mate, food, a scent to be explored, or a circumstance of play. It doesn't occur to him to become nasty in new situations or when he has to work because his faith has been focused on inevitable success. He's happy!" she said, mimicking a dog chasing a bouncing ball.

Five paces ahead of me, Bonnie stopped as if she had hit an invisible fence. "Some dogs are trained through cruelty," she said, catching her breath, "which only appears to work because the animal's choices are basically limited to survival, pleasure or pain."

"I'm not advocating cruelty," I said, coming alongside her, "but you get the same result."

"You can't use inappropriate methods to create appropriate be-haviour with any creature. Obedience based on fear is submission, and that will always emerge in rebellion. Free will is like truth—like a falcon on prey—it will always present itself, and always unexpectedly."

"Doggie Uprising Ends Leash Laws!" I jested.

"The point I'm trying to have you entertain," she said wryly, "is that Otis sees the world in the way he was conformed to it, no different than normal people can become hooligans under the right conditions and

[90]

conditioning. Obeying his owner is not about hunger, power, or sanctuary; it's a pleasurable game he'll play with everyone because his actions faithfully generate circumstances in keeping with his focus of play, which constantly validates his conditioning and creates a positive cycle of play." Bonnie circled her finger as she spoke. "Kindly train a dog, and it may corner a trespasser and bark for attention or warn his pack, but his conditioning tells him that he's safe, so there's no need to protect anything. A cruelly trained animal will take a piece out of a stranger because the animal has learned that its safest place in the world is still hazardous. You've seen this kind of thing often enough."

"I have?"

Thinking I was being sarcastic, Bonnie gave me a sharp look only to realize I was legitimately clueless. Touching my hand in apology, she said, "You've worked with artists who believed their own press, politicians who indulged personal goals ahead of representing their constituents, and religious leaders absorbed by their status, haven't you?"

"All of the above, sure."

"The underlying threat is that none of them could act like that and maintain their status unless the public shared their assumptions."

"You're saying that everywhere," I waved my arm to cover all that we could see, "the tail is wagging the dog?"

"I'm saying our tales are wagging our dogmas and that good people derive beliefs from harmfully acceptable practices, which they evolve into personal convictions that camouflage the essence of their actions. Our society is now at the point where even clearly outrageous practices fly over our heads or confuse us if they manage to get our attention."

"An example of that would help me," I said, knowing it would be about me. Still…

"You've been tracking acceptable scientific, religious, and cultural beliefs to the grave for years, and I'll bet you lunch and a beer that you're still mystified when spectators celebrate a victory by destroying other people's property."

"You're not?"

"Trillion dollar contact sports, relentless and pointless violence on television, and arcade games based on brutality condition our children to think that wilful destruction is part of the entertainment package."

"Isn't it an outlet for pent up aggression, as well?"

"I'm not saying violence is categorically damaging. I'm saying the demands of social conformation put a lid on the free expression of our natural aggression, which is not damaging, but the force behind our

[91]

creativity, until there's a mass agreement to say screw it. That's when we emulate the celebrity players who are admired for taking cheap shots, cheating, and otherwise generating harm in acceptable ways."

"The courts don't hold game makers culpable when kids mimic them."

"Nor should they. That responsibility lies with the parents."

"My head might explode," I said, trying to organize my thoughts.

"Just say what's there," Bonnie prompted me. "You know I won't judge it."

Tentatively, because the ducks hadn't all landed yet, I said to myself, "We don't appreciate what our true circumstances are because we don't understand the underlying nature of events, and that understanding escapes us because we don't know what we're really like so we interpret events to suit our assumptions about our world, or ourselves?"

"Both...excellent!"

Not really. "Which has what to do with danger here and now?"

"Do you not find it even the least bit scary that two reasonably intelligent people can view the same scene, at the same time, in the same place, and see entirely different things?"

"I don't find it scary that we've got different opinions."

"Opinions are a lesson for another time," Bonnie said, apparently giving up on trying to make clear whatever I was supposed to be afraid of—a fit man living in Canada, in the daytime, in Stanley Park, with witnesses everywhere. I mean, really?

"I've said this before, but it requires repeating," I said to move on, "any Otis-like conformation analogy will be a lot for a movie to work through."

"We will simplify the idea, which we couldn't have done until you understood the connections between what we see, believe, and what we do. Great job. Thank you."

"You're welcome, but I was just piecing things together out loud." I pointed at my head. "A steel trap doesn't necessarily understand what it captures."

"Let's take the pieces of your reasoning out of the trap while they're fresh. Has a single experience ever changed something you believed?"

"I think that happens to everyone."

"So do I, but it's illogical for a single experience to form a cogent philosophy for life, which means there are events colouring people's world view that don't apply to much of it."

"Sounds about right."

"Let's cement that sound." She shouted, "Look around you!"

"At what!" I mimicked her exuberance.

"At the world!" she said, and her arm swept the misty meridian where sapphire sky dissolved into a crown of indigo ice atop spring mountains.

I did a 360 degree turn at the completion of which Bonnie examined my expression. Finding no ridicule etched in my lean grin, she focused on the distant landscape. Playing along, I followed her gaze into the darkened hollows of a descending forest, tracking pinpoints of light as they slashed through explosions of vital greenery where the sun punctured the canopy of clouds and conifer. I re-examined this vista for anything remotely relevant to her exuberant request, but like the outgoing tide grasping for rocks it had been polishing for millennia, I found no point of purchase.

"What do you see?" she finally said.

"Trees, water, and some shithawks feeding," I replied honestly.

Looking across the narrows and sighing with pretentious sorrow, she said, "You see nothing but endless days of competing for the survival of your self-image." She faced me, and looking puzzled said, "A man like you should be starving for a new adventure."

"Topography isn't an adventure to me," I said, wondering what I had done wrong.

She started walking. "Disillusionment and mistrust condensed create the cynicism that's blinding you to all of this, "she waved her arm as if to sweep the horizon free of my jaded view, "and caused you to see a clown where a free spirit was giving a dependent creature a good life."

Her bland assault kept my feet still as I momentarily struggled to make sense of what I had done—what I was supposed to see, and quickly conclude that she was again dealing with punctured expectations at my expense.

Bonnie was strides ahead before I realised that raising my voice to respond in any way would make me sound like I was pleading; and the sounds of water lapping at the foot of the sea wall marked off the next twenty yards as I tried to make up the distance without breaking into a trot of apparent reconciliation.

Bonnie must have thought I had decided to go home in this staggered fashion because, in a preoccupied manner, she contrived to wander in front of a jogging couple going in the opposite direction. Their near collision allowed me to make up the distance at a normal pace.

Finishing her apologies to them for having a wandering mind, in an adjusted cordial tone, Bonnie began talking to me candidly about her adolescence as if it were a stranger's life. She maintained this air of cool reserve until we reached her home, where she scheduled our next meeting as if it were a dental appointment.

Not until I was lying in bed that night did I put these events into perspective, ironically courtesy of her showing me how to assess the nature of events. Bonnie was trying to convince me that I should be afraid of the way things are in our world because, as she had stated, her characters had to be wary of where they were at all times; their fantasy world of energy efficiency made ours seem like there was danger lurking around every corner and bus stop. It followed that when I wasn't afraid of people simply having different opinions, I had created a run in the fabric of her intricate plot by responding as her audience would—the student thing aside. Her subsequent walk of disappointment, also her choice of topic, came from seeing the inevitability of having to restructure a key aspect of her story.

I felt genuinely sorry for her. I knew what that was like.

Chapter Ten
The Foretime

On the morning of our fourth consecutive day together, we met outside a fashionable bakery-cafe in West Vancouver, where a contagiously chipper Bonnie began telling me about her night of lucid dreaming. Two steps through the broad glass doors, Brandi greeted us with an orthodontist's smile and expansively declared that we could sit anywhere, before her youthful charm collapsed at the sound of a soft chime. I looked for a remote spot in case Bonnie felt like dancing.

Taking in the ambiance, two of the twenty-foot high walls were painted a light tan, accented by slashes of green neon under which stood snow-flake arrays of plastic tables surrounded by petals of tub chairs flaunting red slashes down the centre post to a Mexican tile floor. The impression of Christmas in Cabo San Lucas suggested that patrons should spend freely in the name of Christ. The other walls of full-length glass provided excellent lighting for customers to peruse the large print menus while wearing Ray Bans.

We headed toward a shaded spot in the back corner, ordered coffee, then to calm her I told Bonnie about an innocuous dream I had when I was between assignments, and still vividly recalled the setting for no reason I could explain. I was standing on a dirt roadway that bisected two rolling fields of calf high grass through which masses of trans-lucent people were slowly walking. I knew that the ones coming toward me from my left were returning from a physical life, and the ones walking away on my right were heading into one, not that I bothered to believe or question it, but it *was* a dream. Ten yards in front of me stood an elderly man dressed in a plain, off-white, and tan broad-stripped robe, holding a gnarled staff in his right hand. Quietly, he said, "Come with me," but there was no mistaking his authority.

We walked an indeterminate, but comfortable distance over the crest of a low rise, stopping on a tree-lined roadside where young men and women, none of them looking more than twenty-five years old, were sitting under a canopy of broad leaves. The group exuded an aura of tranquil pleasure, but there was an underlying power within their

[95]

casual countenance. Impish glances at me, then each another, made me want to check my fly as the elder introduced us.

That was it.

Nodding to herself, Bonnie reflectively said, "You got a pass between life and death so you could meet some very important people in your quest." She paused. "You were shown your probable future, as well."

"Not to be argumentative, but I have no recollection of anything about the future."

"If that's all you can recall, it was enough. When it's time, we'll revisit your choice—literally." She grinned then we got down to business.

Her latest offering of only four pages opened with a display of uncommon linguistic dexterity for a boy of Mihaleh's limited years telling his roommates what they could do with their suggestion that he wash himself and his clothing more frequently. When the usual merchants gathered to discuss the problem, a commotion by a monkey cage created a moment of grinning consent, and they assigned Mihaleh the responsibility of taking care of the animals.

He had no problem working for his keep—he expected worse when he first came to the commune—but he discovered that cleaning the cage properly didn't last long enough to pass inspection by the keeper. Upon hearing this legitimate complaint, the understanding man said Mihaleh was in charge, so he could change the animal's feeding time, camp out to observe their processing cycle, then schedule his duties accordingly. Mihaleh took his advice which worked well, other than the keeper noting that an unpleasant smell lingered. Mihaleh rightfully argued that monkeys always had an odour, to which the keeper replied they couldn't help it, as he locked Mihaleh inside the cage. Bonnie's scene ended on day three of Mihaleh's incarceration, when he finally grasped what it was like for others to live with him.

"To the point," I said, handing her the pages before she could snatch them from my grasp.

"Flat?" she said, with a tilt of her head.

"Not at all. It rides the edge of sparse nicely; if you described every little thing like you do with your dreams," I quipped, "It would probably dull the impact."

"What do you think about how they decided to treat the problem?"

"You've established that kind of decision making process, and your audience would get it anyway, but I'm not sure they'll agree with it. By the way, signs and omens weren't part of the decision making options you gave me when we met."

"I said there were five common processes. This one isn't considered common, but obvious omens are far from unusual. Again, do you agree with it?"

"It made the point when talking didn't work, sure."

"That's your standard—talk first, then do what has to be done?"

"If you have to, kind of."

"Meaning what?"

"Meaning the audience might think Mihaleh didn't commit an offence, just that he was offensive, and your guys literally put him in jail. That's a scare tactic, which pretty much screws up your view about not teaching by fear."

"Mihaleh's teacher's warned him what was to come, and he agreed to it. If they hadn't, the cage would have been a punishment, not a means of making their point."

"He didn't know he agreed to anything–or I missed it."

"We discussed this circumstance as an issue of avoiding taking responsibility." She took a breath and got back to her point. "I've also said that the only way anyone learns anything important is according to their own standards, so if any life lesson seems too harsh, you've banked too much credit in your wonderfulness account."

"The audience will probably see that he's just an angry kid."

"My teachers will make the point that you can't be angry unless you are afraid. It follows that Mihaleh rebelled as a way to keep himself safe because the safest place in his world is still hazardous. The same is true with adult tantrums, by the way." She briefly lowered her eyes then said, "We're going to show our audience that the human cage is constructed of our generous beliefs and that the true enemy is locked inside us. Bring some of your work over, and I'll show where you've built your cage."

"You think I've got one?"

"I know you do. Bring anything; the truth always finds a way to show itself. Ready to walk off some calories?"

"Sure."

Shortly afterwards, we were strolling along Marine Drive when, on no clue that I was aware of, Bonnie began painstakingly describing the mechanics of reincarnation that her merchants taught to the commune's children. Her conclusion, and the overt point of her speech, was that if we acted as if we came into physical life to engage specific developmental challenges, we wouldn't be so quick to avoid hardships we

[97]

knew we would face later in life or in another lifetime. There were some causes of turmoil, she said addressing my unspoken question, that could be deferred to a time when we were better equipped to handle them. However, this was a tricky business because poor timing is invariably a consideration when avoiding lessons that may have taken years to set up for ourselves. Ultimately, by not dealing with the smaller crisis that had inevitably evolved from not dealing with accumulating issues, we added momentum to a lesson that need not have become the devastating incident that it became.

She next reviewed the predictable stages of personal development, which to my lay experience seemed to parallel the clinical stages of grief and loss, although she used descriptors related to energy and core behaviours of self-image, i.e.: anger is fear dressed in an acceptable camouflage. She also spoke about how teachers dealt with these stages in swift, insensitive ways.

I asked her why confrontation was their approach of choice.

Bonnie said that what I, and most people, would view as confrontational was actually her teacher's empathy cutting short the pain of those who had the energy to make sudden and appropriate changes. She admitted her methods were not applicable to everyone, but it didn't change the unalterable fact that there was no kind way to deal with self-importance. That said, her story was not about everyone—not directly, she added cryptically.

"Why not?" I said.

"It requires evolutionary energy both to teach and to learn a process that can't be presented in a linear manner," she said hesitantly. She cleared her throat. "Stages of learning change with the student's distractions and the teacher taking advantage of the momentum of events in the world around them, like the commotion at the monkey cage." Seemingly finding more energy, she said teachers who had yet to identify themselves as such used a student candidate's personal history to lead them into excavating an embedded awareness of a sense of purpose in life. The teacher might also purposefully overlap lessons to aid in this revival, often to the point of overloading the student as they deem prudent or providential. Eventually, a new student begins to replace old beliefs with more efficient personal practices, no different from deciding to change how they serve a tennis ball, but to reach the stage of a complete transition takes years."

"Why so long?"

"While the student's lessons leave them with no secrets, their ego isn't deaf to the teacher telling them how to defeat the return of their

[98]

poor practices. The ego has lost only its mask, not the sense of purpose we program it with, so it will continue to fight to get its way, and it's remarkably clever at bargaining for what it wants when a belief has been wounded. In other words, by itself, discovering that you're being an ass in a given circumstance doesn't necessarily change anything."

"Back up a minute. How do teachers know how to approach issues the student doesn't even know exist?"

"The whole process involves an intricate teaching scheme called stalking. We can deal with that after we are finished this work, if you like, because it's not a large part of our screenplay. However," she said with renewed vigour, as an afterthought struck her, "there is a preparatory exercise about stalking, wherein a teacher helps a student to discover a buried belief. That would help me enormously. Are you up to that?"

"Do your students know this is the teacher's goal and agree to it?"

"Absolutely," she flashed a grin, "but they don't appreciate what it will mean to them until they have a shattering conversation with their teacher, or two—whatever it takes to pull the carpet from beneath that belief. By the way, I've written most of that conversation between Aleena and Tartuu, but I haven't set it up in earlier chapters. I know that sounds odd, but I'm finding that difficult to do without having the experience to draw from. Have you got any ideas about what they might constantly clash over so that they eventually come to an all or nothing scrap?"

"I don't have enough information to make an intelligent suggestion, but I would guess that anything not provable would do it." A question came to mind. "Why do teachers do these things, anyway?"

"Let me come back to that—so it makes sense that the confrontation would include both of them unloading all of their ammunition to make their points?"

"They would have to, and let the best man win. Or woman."

"Which means the student would have to consider bowing to the truth to... thanks; it works for me. You asked me why teachers do these things?" As I nodded, she blandly said, "They wouldn't be teachers if they didn't."

"I mean what business is it of theirs?"

"Are you objecting to them helping others develop?"

"Not at all, I'm asking why anyone would put out all of that effort for a stranger who fights them every step of the way?"

"The answer is rooted in the core assumptions of a teaching society, but I'll try to translate them for you." Bonnie pursed her lips, straightened her hair then, apparently dismissing multiple thoughts, finally said, "Teachers receive an omen that they should begin to teach someone, but it is more properly a command than a suggestion to them."

"Maybe you should explain why that is before you lose me on the omen part?"

"I'm not being glib when I say this again, they wouldn't be teachers if they didn't teach, and there is nothing more gratifying, frustrating, and personally advancing than formally learning How to Teach." She took a steadying breath. Using her finger as a wand moving in semi-circular motions to separate individuals in her explanation, she said, "All that a teacher's teacher put themselves through in order to teach— so that they could learn to embrace the absolute reverence *their* teachers held for all things—is ultimately designed to teach the ways of total responsibility. The newest teacher already knows that their hardships are the fires that forge knowledge out of experience, and the resolve it takes to apply this knowledge when eventually faced with unimaginable challenges. If you had a chance to take another step toward making your every act beyond reproach, so that even off-shoot events are positive, would you think it was a choice?"

"When you put I that way…." I grinned.

"Let's put it your way," Bonnie said as if I didn't grasp her explanation. "When something inside warned you that going around the next corner was a bad idea, did you turn back?"

"When I could. I get it. So what tells the student to learn?"

"That's an excellent question, which may have a less than fulfilling answer."

"I'm used to that."

Bonnie smirked and said, "A combination of influences are layered in an order arranged by the student's awareness in general, and Silent Knowledge in particular. Aspects of this knowledge nag at them while the teacher tries to awaken these memories and otherwise point out how the knocks of life guided their critical choices. This opens the student's mind to acknowledging that they received timing cues and directional clues in their important decision-making when it was required. For example," she grinned, "the deepest regions of your being knew that the mass of circumstances and political information you ingested about working in Lebanon meant nothing in critical moments, otherwise you would have to credit your intellect with God-like powers of deduction to have seen things no one else saw." Gurgling to keep the urge to laugh under control, she said, "A student's evolutionary energy compels them to investigate, but they have the energy to ignore even blatant clues, like you wrote off any event you couldn't explain," she smiled, "even though you don't believe your own explanations."

"I don't?"

"You wouldn't have arranged your conclusions to credit your intellect for your survival if 'shit happens' satisfied you," she said, motioning parenthesis in the air. "Think about it this way," she carried on quickly, "our default position is to reasonably act in ways that leave us feeling in control, which means it's inherently unreasonable to change the way we think." She pitched forward. "We pinch our reasoning to suit our sense of power and security then we focus on the slim point that we made any determination, regardless of its validity. We talked about this: the tenth choice causes us to believe we are free?"

"With you so far."

"You didn't have a first legitimate choice, let alone a tenth one, so you ignored what might otherwise have screwed up your sense of power and security." She leaned back. "The beauty of my teacher's system of retrieving students from their distorted views was they didn't have to threaten their views directly. Their technique was to have them make a conscious effort to withdraw their uninformed consent to mimic the ways of their world by embracing practices they didn't have to believe; they just had to act as if they were beneficial." She leaned back. "Ultimately, they would prove to be much more than that."

I understood that Bonnie's way around any credibility problem was to have teachers tell the audience, through instructions to students, that they should act as if they believed her premises for a few hours. It wasn't a bad idea...

"So what keeps students going?" I said.

"If and when they discover any self-deception or at least embrace the inner workings of deception, they become more willing to learn how they lead themselves astray."

"Is it safe to presume that discovering how a single belief changed their behaviour would be to discover a self-deception?"

"It is safe to presume that."

"Okay, so what are the mechanics of self-deception?" I said, looking for a path I might understand.

"Students are taught that their ego-accomplice is a belief filter." She re-seated herself for what I assumed would be if not a lengthy, then intricate explanation. "Picture a disco ball; our brain reflects our image from every angle, but it's hanging in the middle of the club so it's vulnerable. To protect itself, it takes inventory of everything it sees and stores that information in an inner sponge, while it filters the activity around it through the assumptions it thinks will serve or protect it while reflecting club life. The holes are pathways for rationalizations to pass through and mask contradictions."

"Hang on. Everything comes in, but we only absorb what suits us and reflect what we want others to see?" I said, trying to get it straight before asking how the hell she expected to incorporate that into a movie.

"The mirror is a two-way illusion: it accepts what it wants to see and reflects what it wants others to see. However, cutting remarks can break facets of our view, so we encase the ball in a layer of self-importance that transmits the impact of every assault to the sponge, which cushions the blow with personal assumptions. Still with me— even kind of?"

"Self-importance transmits shocks to beliefs that take the sting away. That's the anger phase of grief?"

Bonnie ignored my question.

"Actually, there are three layers." She slowed her speech as if that had anything to do with my ability to understand her example.

"A layer of self-importance defends against events that scratch the image. A layer of self-absorption interprets events that polish our image..."

"Denial?"

"I prefer to call it prejudiced evaluation, and there's a secret-filtering membrane of self-indulgence between them."

"Why is it secret?"

"The membrane isn't a secret mechanism; it filters events through our secrets—the secrets we don't know we have about ourselves—to distinguish between a polish and a scratch."

"Through the sponge holes?"

"Don't get caught up on the plumbing." She shifted in her seat again. "The point is that we process events through layers of pro-tection, deflection, and polish which collectively form and inform our self-image." She gazed into my puzzled expression.

"Another way to look at it," she persisted, "is that the sum of our assumptions is our personality, which we hone as an addiction to beliefs we can embrace, change, or discard as circumstances impress us. So-you-can-see," she said, running her words together, "we have all of the information we need to know what we are really like. It's just

[102]

that it takes a safe cracker to access our beliefs and a magician to untangle them."

"Your teachers play both parts—the burglar and the magician?"

"They do."

"Which means you have to know what they do?"

"I'm sensing you want to see if I can crack open one of your beliefs," she said casually.

I wasn't, but what the hell. "Sure, go ahead."

Bonnie nodded, took a moment to reflect, then she said, "In one of our conversations you said you hate war and a little later you mentioned that you had nothing against warriors. Correct?"

"You like war?"

"Don't play with me–not now," she said seriously. "There can be no war without warriors, so your declaration is either a lie you tell yourself, or you understand something deeper about yourself. This would be that you are outraged at the apparent helplessness of the entire circumstance because you personally know that war is beyond asinine and warriors' actions are the propellant for that great sentient void. This is not a condemnation of the participants, just their beliefs, and if this is your understanding, you need to express it in this way to avoid insulting soldiers directly; not that they'd be any happier about your view, but it would be accurate."

"Understood."

"There's more: what you might not realize from misrepresenting your own point of view is that you have entangled beliefs; one of these is that your distain for mankind's malice oozes on the participants and disguises your piety."

"Piety!" I exclaimed, spitting the "P". I felt no need to apologize.

"The distance your experiences separated you from those without them is vertical: you raise yourself above them because you know things they don't, and because your job was not to kill people, this belief applies to soldiers specifically. The nature of this attitude is piety. By the way, it was fed by your relative lack of fear of combat, but that's for another time."

"No you don't; I told you on day one that everyone was scared most of the time."

"So you did, but how you portrayed yourself conveyed something more."

"Which was?"

"When I suggested that it took courage just to get out of the hotel, you didn't say you were scared, you said everyone was scared, and

[103]

when I asked you about adjusting to fear you simply said, nope. You obfuscated that poignant point further by saying combat changes your thinking, that concepts like courage became stupidity before you realised it was all about doing what you had to do. In other words, you turned what most of us view as bravery into an intellectual endeavour to hide a belief that the entire experience generated in you. Only minutes later, you displayed your extensive knowledge to support your contention that heroes aren't what we think they are, that in fact, they're more like you. Between the lines, the elevation of your status gave away that one of your personality masks is piety, but this isn't a separate thought, either. You also use it to hide a secret that the entire experience generated."

I stared at Bonnie blankly.

"I told you we process events through layers of protection, deflection, and polish," she said hopefully.

Which is why it's called hope: I continued to stare.

"You know," Bonnie said casually as if changing the subject, "traumatic experiences can make us afraid of some aspect of the world we thought we understood, sometimes to the extent of feeling res-ponsible for the event because this assumption returns us some semblance of power—call it the tenth decision again. It's a normal part of our learning curve, but to repeatedly endure the kind of soul piercing events you did would have made your every decision seem extremely important. And when circumstances took some of those decisions out of your hands, you were left feeling extremely vulnerable. None of those events were your fault, by the way."

"No shit."

"No shit," she said evenly.

Wrong. I suddenly had more than enough of her shit.

Plotting my retreat from the arrangement she had coerced me into, I could only grunt.

"It follows that another belief you have entangled with piety," she said offhandedly, "is that you can't afford to be wrong. This means the idea of me being right about all of us being puppets to social con-formation threatens you more than if we were in real trouble, by your measure. No one is shooting at us," Bonnie continued, sweeping the café area with her arm. "There is you and me and the sweet smell of baking, but I bumped into the deepest secret you don't know you have."

Proving her point, something inside me snapped. "You might not know this," I said, with a tone of cold-rolled steel, "but I was at the

[104]

Sabra and Shatila massacre while it was still going on, and skeletons were tugging on my pants long before the Ethiopian famine became a fashionable cause. Acts of God would've been easy to spot," I grinned thinly, "but there was nothing supernatural at either place. If you dared to squint into that blissful beacon of light I'm sure you'll have healing crippled hearts in your book, you'll see that a soldier's high comes from drowning in his own blood. Raise your sight, and you'll see a boy, back-lit by the setting sun of life trying to tie a tourniquet on his pumping stump with his teeth. If he makes it, he might thank your God and swear to walk a peaceful path, but it won't be long before he'll be asking the ceiling, 'Why me?' and in the deafening silence lead a leper's life restricted by wheelchair access. And for the record," I said icily, "a loaf of bread doesn't feed the starving masses, that miracle would cause a riot."

"Ahhh," she said with satisfaction, "that's why the concept of miracles annoyed you so much. It lit the fuse on your view of faith, which set fire to your cynicism, which threatened the secret belief ..." She saw me reaching for my money. "No matter," she said easily, "that's how a single belief can taint so much that doesn't apply anymore."

As a single thought, I knew that the wind chimes in her head would forever filter out all unpleasant sounds: and the precarious balance between the joy of our intellectual rapport and my lust, versus the aggravation factors of both, swung mightily in favour of going to the Avalon. I would walk up behind Tom, hit him in the ear hard enough to make him think a phone was ringing for the next week, order beer on his tab all night, and he wouldn't say a bloody thing because he knew Bonnie was a nut job. I should have known something was wrong. Why else would he pass a beauty off to me?

"We don't apply anymore, either," I said, sorting cash from my pocket. "I doubt that anyone will spend the kind of time I have doing you a favour, let alone be trained to agree with you, but you're beyond clever, and I wish you the best of luck, but this will take up way too much time."

"How long did you say it takes to get a grant?"

"They're not given away, and it'll take forever if you have to explain the story instead of telling it, assuming there really is one." I put ten dollars on the table to cover my seven dollar tab; I wasn't sticking around for the change. I slid out of my seat, but as I stood, Bonnie grabbed my sleeve.

[105]

Looking up to make a show of squinting into the sun, a subservient pose, she offered me her other hand. "Fifty percent of everything across the board and we work every day that we can to get the scenes in the right order? I'm not that far away. Really," she pleaded playfully.

Looking at her breasts on the way up to her eyes, I formulated a plan that suited my mood, and I said, "Done." A few grand was about right for filling out another one of those God-damned forms.

"Let's celebrate at my house," Bonnie said standing.

"Wow—two things in a row we agree on," I jested weakly.

"Now you know that anything is possible," she said lightly.

Ten minutes later we turned into the short gravel driveway of a million dollar, beach front property on Argyle Street, and I briefly thought that anything could be possible.

Under the right conditions.

Maybe.

Chapter Eleven
The Message and the Messenger

Keeping my feelings in check about her alleged poor financial status, I asked Bonnie for a tour of the house as a circuitous way of getting a truer picture. I followed her first into the living/dining room where I noticed, on a back wall, a landscape painting of a winding country road, bordered by broad-leafed trees that ran between two open fields of grass. Neither of us said anything about it or my dream. Otherwise, during our trek through the double-suite, five-bedroom, three bathroom home, she made no reference to her expenses, so I was little wiser by the time we sat down to a ploughman's lunch.

"I had these all of the time in England. Filling and cheap," I said, taking in the details of the open design area, "which still wouldn't explain how you manage this place."

"My rent is probably less than Ed pays for his apartment," she said, crunching on a pickle. She leaned forward with unaccountable intensity. "I was about to close a deal on a townhouse in North Vancouver when I hurt my back." She quickly chewed, swallowed, and said, "Workman's comp wouldn't cover the mortgage, so I withdrew the offer. The next day, I met the man who was in charge of renting properties the county had expropriated to extend the park from the pier to the sea wall." She waved half a pickle from north to west across the room. "Getting this place convinced me that it was time to write my book, so I quit working full-time and sold a share of my novel to a good friend. Your injuries at Goodbye," she said, poking the green nub at me, "led you to writing, as well." She took a final bite and un-characteristically said around her food, "Tell me about why you moved to England; I cut you off—sorry."

"Four days ago," I replied, amused.

"I'm still interested," she said evenly.

Between nibbles of French stick bread and pâté, I meandered through my brief engagement to an Argentine beauty and a job transfer approved, to be with her and not travel, but I had to decline it when Graciela called things off. It was then that I realised everyday had

[107]

become the same for me and that I had nothing much to look forward to. On my next trip to England, when a friend mentioned the benefits of freelancing, I looked into moving there.

With Bonnie prompting me for insignificant details, as was her way, I told her about my living arrangements in Hampstead and later in Highgate while working out of the West End primarily for CBS and CBC News. I added that many local stories came from south of the Thames or the financial district, which led me to commenting on the wide range of accents that distinguished classes in a small geographical area. Bonnie aw-hawed as if I had said something significant, then she asked me to differentiate between local attitudes.

Essentially, I said the stiff upper-lip crowd claimed to speak proper English, and all things proper followed. As it is in most societies, people with "other" accents were generally assumed to be "less" in non-specific ways, but they were otherwise expected to follow social dictates. Working men and women learned this from the cradle, so that an underpaid street sweeper wouldn't hesitate to break your face for slighting the monarchy, while royalty tisk-tisked the savagery of the common man.

"Where did you fit in?" Bonnie said, apparently getting to her point of interest.

"I didn't. One way or another people reminded me that I was a visitor or a novelty."

"Didn't that bother you?"

"It was the most comfortable I've ever felt."

"Really?" she said, too surprised to really be surprised.

By this time in our fledgling relationship, I was less wary about her making fun of me and more suspicious about why she would punctuate aspects of our conversations, other than to imprint their memory. I mean, why else do it, and what's the big deal about feeling comfortable?

"I think it's normal to want to know where you stand wherever you are," I said cautiously, "which explains why people screw themselves into a single job or a huge mortgage." I took a bite of bread and rolling it to the side of my mouth said, "There were no social expectations of me," as I was demonstrating.

"I think you were comfortable because you had permission to be who you are, and the worst anyone could say was that you were from the colonies."

"There was an incident or two that helped enhance my stereotype," I said, her comment reminding me of an event. Swallowing, I said, "A

[108]

British comedy called Spitting Images used caricature puppets to mock celebrities. In Margaret Thatcher's scenes, two brass balls clanged every time she sat down." I sipped my wine. "Which is what I was thinking when we were introduced at Number Ten."

"And?" Bonnie said, grinning with anticipation.

"I didn't trust my face to agree with anything I was supposed to say about being honoured, so I just said, 'Hi. How are ya?'"

Inhaling a chuckle, Bonnie said, "What kind of area is Hampstead?"

"Middle to upper class."

"Wine?" she said, refilling my nearly full glass. "After your first war, you were never comfortable back in Canada, were you?"

My brain stumbled at the unexpected question, Bonnie interpreted my brief silence as agreement, then she asked me a series of rapid-fire questions most of which required single syllable replies dealing with my comfort. Initially, this was fun because we were speaking about myself and a time I cherished, neither topic of which was normally a cautious affair. However, when I was speaking about narrow attitudes, narrower streets, and a lack of parking to explain why you can't get a pizza delivered in London, she twice interrupted me to misquote simple points. Confused that she thought I might be lying about trivial stuff—I was all-too familiar with this interrogation technique for pin-pointing lies—I tapped the corner of my mouth to indicate she had crumbs on hers and said, "What's with the third degree this time?"

"The experiences we pay little attention to shape the ones we think are significant. Nothing comes from nothing." She dabbed at the corner of her mouth. "Ready to walk some of this off?"

"Sure."

Bonnie covered the leftovers with plastic wrap, and in a few minutes we were heading toward the mini-park at the north end of the sea wall that underlines the core of West Vancouver. During this three block stroll, a pervasive tranquility came over me, not the fatigue I had previously endured, which I ascribed to a letdown reaction from my recent anger, a full stomach, a new business arrangement, and a plan to handle it my way if hers didn't quickly pan out.

My mind ran free of concern as I gazed across the inlet to the former naval reserve that had become Stanley Park a hundred years earlier, and I casually envisioned a colourfully clad septuagenarian shifting a large chess piece on a patio board, twelve feet across, while a rucksack and sandals student frowned at a missed opportunity. This scene transitioned into seniors dressed in white, lawn bowling on this perfect day for an affair to begin at Lumberman's Arch: the woman would be

[109]

tanning during her lunch break, lose track of time, and in a hurry she would bump into the lawyer on roller blades. Eagerly at fault, both of them would apologize, information would be exchanged, and he would call to invite her to the Tea House...

....a silver/grey Mercedes drove by the front of the restaurant. I shivered.

Bashir Gemayel's house exploded. Lebanon's president was dead.

I jumped—or tried to.

"Gas?" Bonnie teased me.

"Sorry. Shit!" I said, embarrassed to discover that we were sitting on a park bench. Bonnie had her arm tightly wrapped around mine as support, not in a romantic way.

"Where were you?"

"Wandering," I said, feeling silly.

Gazing across the bay toward False Creek, she said with the sensitivity of personal experience, "Speaking about a nice time in your past can unlock the door to anything in your past. The average person stops short of walking through if it is unpleasant because no one has explained the benefits of taking that step. A student of their life will cross the threshold almost every time because they secretly know that to face the lingering unrealised is to render it harmless, or available for assessment."

"A thought caught me by surprise, is all."

"The abstract imparts guidance on its own terms."

"I don't have a clue what that means."

"It means the thought that jolted you was a consequence of your evolutionary energy bringing your core outlook to your attention." With a quick squeeze of my arm, she turned to face me. "Part of what makes people average is that they assume their thoughts happen on a single level, as an autonomous process they more or less control, in spite of how often they are surprised by insights. People with energy know there are inner resources available to them, if not yet at their conscious command, so most of them will explore those rare moments when the accomplice is not guarding the door."

"I didn't see anything important. Accomplice?""

"Your ego, and you certainly did. You're trying to dismiss it because it doesn't suit your assumptions."

"About what goes on in Stanley Park?"

"Whatever it was you first imagined was a set up for the finale; it tricked your ego away from guarding the door to a secret, which allowed the rest of you to experience that belief physically."

[110]

I still had no idea what she was talking about.

Bonnie looked into my eyes with precision, like an optometrist seeking signs of disease. Finding only innocuous incomprehension, she said, "You had another exquisite event, which if assessed, will inform you of the true nature of warfare and its influence on you." Bonnie stood and giving my arm a slight tug said enigmatically, "You are that message. Let events be the messenger."

"I mean no disrespect, and I'd like to think I'm not as much of an idiot as you sometimes want me to feel, but I don't have a clue what you're talking about." I stood, and we began a slow walk.

"We are talking about discovering the essence of warfare: If a child's territorial dispute in a sand box goes unresolved," Bonnie began her customary in-depth explanation, "the adult version may have property-line disputes. If they don't resolve those, other perceived intrusions on their personal space will draw them to foreign sands because what we think is what we do, is what we will create or be drawn to. The dispute is the messenger of what they are really like, which is insecure, petty, grasping, uncompromising, and afraid to give up anything they think represents their proper due, power or security. Dying on a foreign beach is the metaphor message about being this way."

How I was death on a foreign beach eluded me like partnered sex until I was sixteen.

"Are you saying we wouldn't go to war if our leaders had shared their sand boxes?" I knew this sounded trite, but I was serious and Bonnie took it that way.

"I'm saying they have never properly assessed their actions to realize there is a momentum and continuity to their experiences. If they had seen a pattern and understood the event-nature of their actions, they would have stopped being stupid a long time ago."

"And this means what to me?"

"Assess the experience you just had, and find out."

"I still need help with assessing things."

"What did you do at the end of your vision?"

"I jumped—tried to jump," I corrected myself.

"Why?"

"There was an explosion."

"Again, why did you jump?"

"I was surprised."

"What lies beneath that kind of surprise?"

"I haven't a clue."

[111]

"Of course you do. Take yourself out of the picture, insert some by-standers, and tell me what you see on their faces."

"They're afraid."

"Exactly."

"Hmmmm," I said with polite consideration. "So you're saying that fear is my core outlook?"

"I said much more than that." Bonnie suddenly switched topics to speak about her late teens and early twenties, surprisingly personal stuff, until we went our separate ways.

Chapter Twelve
Essential Acts

In her kitchen the next morning, I made tea while Bonnie read the chapter I had brought at her request, but tuned for this occasion; there were no omens, metaphors, or even vague references to cages as far as I was concerned. The scene was about a camera crew changing a flat tire on a deserted street that locals had recently renamed for a fallen son.

When she finished reading it, she said, "Your clinical setting and terse dialogue captures the potential of the crew's lethal circumstance well." She looked down at a page, then back at me to quote, "'Beads of anticipation trickled into thin eyes as the cotton curtain across the street swayed in the still air.' It needs a tweak, but it's good stuff."

"Thanks."

"Just one thing," Bonnie said, holding up a finger. "This situation came about because your driver was late for crew call, and he took a short cut across a shell-holed road to," she searched the page, "Hazmeih?" she said finding the line.

"Yup."

She slipped the pages back into order. "I think you could capitalize on the delay he caused by emphasizing that the sniper had only a short window of time to kill this Ely fellow, and you were running late for a series of little reasons that kept adding seconds to your estimated time of arrival in his sites."

"El-lee," I corrected her pronunciation, as I came to the table with our steaming cups, "is ambiance. The point of the scene is to establish that there were no real secrets between the press and any fighting faction so that anything can happen at any time. The delay was fortuitous and may even be ironic if it causes the sniper to die. I haven't decided."

"You have set up his impatience, but the drama rests there because you don't explain why the sniper doesn't wait for you guys to draw out his target for him." She slid the last page from beneath the thin sheaf and read aloud, "'There was too much danger in staying in one place.'"

She looked up. "The awkwardness of the sentence aside, you were lazy at a critical point."

Hearing my own words made her point; I had focused entirely on the crew's predicament and blew off the sniper's point of view, literally because he was waiting out of sight. Nodding, I said, "I'll setup those reasons while the driver loses time at the hotel."

"Good. That'll stretch your readers' interest because they'll know there's a purpose to you offering apparently unrelated details. Speaking of those," Bonnie said, turning the page, "LeBlanc's foul-mouthed prejudices don't go anywhere. I understand he represents battle-aged apprehension," she said before I could, "but racism steals tension from the scene which saps the readers' empathy for all of your characters."

Reaching across the table, I tapped the page number—eighty-one. "By this time, readers will know racism doesn't enter it; his comments are foreshadowing."

"His preference for working with black revofuckin'lutionaries, instead of Ragheads, are insights?" she cocked her head.

"Readers will know that with the exception of syphilis-ravaged Idi Amin types, modern African guerrilla leaders have degrees from the London School of Economics. They know that war is expensive, and bad press ultimately costs them money, which is why they try not to kill the press. At least, it used to be like that. Middle Eastern leaders may be cut from the same cloth, but having followers blow themselves up isn't something you can anticipate."

"Insulting millions of readers, while asking them to make abstract connections, guts the drama. Why not drop the obscenities and bigotry, and invest that space in suspense?"

"I could do that," I said, spooning sugar into my cup, "if I had a clue what you mean."

Bonnie set the pages on the table between us and poured milk into her cup. "Interpreting LeBlanc's imagery will get in the way of readers focusing on the potential of events, like juxtaposing your driver's delays with the sniper's chances of success slipping away, drawing their attention toward a greater intent at work. Anything could happen, anywhere, and at any time without angering readers, except snipers," she grinned. "You're fucking near there," she said as I sipped my tea. "Just don't dick around with readers' focus. This shit is complex enough."

Sputtering tea onto the table, I stared as her slow smile had me realize her remarks exemplified the problem she wanted me to see in my work.

[114]

"Twenty crews," I said, wiping the table with a paper napkin, "were on the ground for the better part of sixteen hours a day, and we all had flat tires—twice a week if we were covering combat." I leaned into her personal space. "The essence of danger was to be in the open and stationary, which means we were probably in a more precarious position when we were changing that tire than if we had been covering a firefight." I leaned back. "If your great unseen was helping us, it was to have us join them."

"This really happened to you?"

"Obviously, I made up the sniper."

"I wouldn't be so sure about that."

The twinkle in her eye trapped an obscenity in my throat, which I cleared indelicately to communicate that it wasn't a kind thought, as I said, "I appreciate the advice on creating drama. It's right there, and I missed it."

A quick sip of tea, then Bonnie said, "Another thing you seem to have missed is that LeBlanc's comments will sound gratuitous until you fill out the character so that people know him and where they're coming from."

"I've done that." To forestall endless inquires, I said, "I have him swear his way through history tracing tit-for-tat Jewish/Arab massacres back to tribes throwing rocks from opposite banks of the Jordan River; this establishes that kids on both sides know their versions of events like we know episodes of Bugs Bunny. In a chapter I called 'Twins', he also talks about the farce of good and evil and the capriciousness of war by looking through a telescope of time. He'll see Attila go into a revolving doorway and the Captain of the Anola Gay come out, Rommel and MacArthur trade uniforms in the club house after a round of golf, and Menachim Begin gets up in the morning to shave a reflection of Arafat. His comments are foreshadowing, and they apply anywhere, at anytime."

"Are there no good guys in your work?" she said anxiously.

"That's one of my twists. Everyone thinks they're the good guy."

"What examples of blurring good from bad does LeBlanc use?" Bonnie asked, looking concerned for no reason I could fathom.

"The main one is him telling a newbie that the Israeli Defence Forces were in charge of the refugees at Sabra and Shatila, and Elie was in charge of the Christian militia who massacred them. Ariel Sharon was Israel's defence minister at the time, and it's inconceivable that he didn't know what was happening for two days because fifty journalists called him for comments while it was going on."

[115]

"The Israelis did nothing?" Bonnie said.

"They kept us on the perimeter road until the shooting was over. The Red Cross gave us painters' masks soaked in cologne as we walked in." I sniffled. "Haven't worn any since."

Bonnie nodded as if she'd had enough of my reality, then she began talking about her later high school days. I reciprocated with a mixed sense of victory and relief, the tea eventually became wine, and we ended up talking about primarily pleasant personal events until it was time for me to go home.

Chapter Thirteen
Metaphor

I didn't bring any of my work to our next few meetings because Bonnie did not address where I had constructed my cage in my last offering. On the other hand, she brought fewer pages of her own work, which were so cryptic in their brevity that I understood little more than her apprentices were acting increasingly eccentric and subservient with their customers. I read the second of two instalments while sitting at her kitchen table after lunch:

A group of ten to thirteen year old youths from the commune came to the market at the end of a selling day to ask their nineteen and twenty year old apprentice friends/brothers and sisters for help resolving a dispute. They first explained their problem to Eirik, who bit his lower lip and shifted his weight from side to side. At the same time, the nearby butcher's apprentice grunted to the rhythm of scrubbing his cart, which sounded like punctuation to the children's sentences.

Believing he had considered every possibility, Eirik finally said, "Rohwan is much better at this kind of problem."

The youths turned to face the butcher's apprentice, who ignored them until the young flautist, Mahrli, asked him what he thought they should do.

"Do about what?" Rohwan said, huffing through a brisk series of scrubs.

Mahrli again laid bare the problem, but just as she finished, the apprentice's fingers slid into an awkward corner. Holding his injured hand aloft, Rohwan walked to the river's edge to clean the slight wound; all of the youths waited quietly until he came back to his cart and went about his business.

At this point, Brendah, the bee keeper's daughter, came out from behind her display to purposefully pace off the distance from her station to Mahrli. Thirteen paces. Turning around, she walked back six and half paces and sat in the middle of the ring of carts, staring at her feet. With a quick exchange of glances, the youths sat in a semi-circle around her. Village kids toting their mother's purchases home found this funny, a few of whom bothered to taunt the commune youths regardless of their well-known affliction.

[117]

Finally, Brendah intoned with mild surprise that the answer was right in front of her. She uncrossed her legs, unthreaded the leather calf bindings of her left sandal, and began a painfully repetitive description of how the youths should tie their sandals until the harvest festival, three months hence. The last of the village children lost interest when Brendah did the same thing with her right sandal, 'for the benefit of those who could not distinguish her right from theirs.'

This comment caused Rohwan to burst into laughter, while Mahrli thanked Brendah on behalf of the group, all of whom retied their footwear as they had been directed...

I looked up from the pages, and Bonnie asked me what I thought about the entire section.

"I think yesterday's section, where the apprentices coddle the public, was about money. They're saying, I will treat you well, and you will buy my stuff, but they're young, and they crossed the line between being pleasant and sucking up." I flipped through the current pages. "The kids respect the apprentices, but the apprentices were indifferent or abusive, so I'm guessing they knew they had tried too hard to please customers and they were making themselves feel better. Somewhere down the road, I assume your teachers will straighten that out?"

Bonnie sighed as if her elderly cat had taken its last wheeze, picked up her cup and walked out of the kitchen saying, "The youngsters think they're battling a complicated problem, but their apprentice friends know there's only one worthy battle to be fought—the struggle with self-image."

I followed her into the hallway, through the living room, then sliding open a panel of floor to ceiling glass, we stepped onto her narrow concrete balcony.

"Apprentices," she said, sitting in a cheap aluminum garden chair set around a matching table, "didn't contribute to problems by handing out gifts for the asking."

"Gifts?" I said, sitting facing her. "You've explained the laziness angle, but they ignored or made fun of them." I offered Bonnie her pages, so she could see that I was right.

Taking them from me, she explained, "Eirik's waffling represented societies' disinclination to commit to anything inconvenient. If you wait for those people to make a decision you'll wait a long time before they'll pass the buck. Rohwan had to have overheard the problem as it was first explained to Eirik, so he was teaching the kids not to presume upon others by making himself unavailable."

"In which case Brendah undermined them both."

[118]

"She *underlined* them both: Eirik did the last thing anyone expected of a teacher, and Rohwan, catching on to the ploy, inspired Brendah to seize the opportunity both of them had created."

"To sit in the middle of the street?"

"She would have stood on her head if that's what it took."

I scratched mine.

Taming a grin, Bonnie said, "During their lessons in Essential Acts, apprentices learn from their misplaced sense of compassion to teach at every opportunity because the moment might never come again. I think I mentioned that when I was explaining the teaching scheme my character had to endure."

"Did the townie kids collectively play the village idiot?" I guessed.

"In so far as they were mocking events they didn't understand, yes, but they also served the purpose of trying to distract those who should know better than to waste an opportunity because of embarrassment." Bonnie sipped her tea as I relived my embarrassment in the park with Otis.

"As young as they were," she said, "they knew enough to assess the nature of these events instead of reacting to them, and they recognized that Brendah had interrupted her life to help them."

"That's what the pacing was about?"

"It was more than drawing their attention to her leaving her work unbidden; retracing her steps meant she was going to cover old territory, and meeting them halfway meant she wasn't going to hand out a freebee. They were going to have to work for a solution."

"Because of laziness?"

"Her way of teaching made the additional point that the opportunity to learn may come at any time, in any place, and in unusual ways. If you are aware of that possibility, willingness takes you more than half way to solving a puzzlement because for a moment you have suspended your beliefs. The more you practice that, the easier it gets."

"Toying with them was a way to loosen their focus?"

"She didn't toy with them. She told them how to fix their problem."

"That it was critical to cross their straps right over left on one leg, left over right on the other, then reverse it the next day?"

"Exactly."

"They're simpletons to put up with that crap," I said, becoming exasperated at her drawn out approach.

"What conversations indicate that they're simple-minded?"

"All of their conversations are convoluted."

"So were ours until we began sharing assumptions."

[119]

"Different circumstance."

"Not really." Gathering the pages before a breeze took them away, Bonnie said, "Convoluted thinking is every student's default position and a condition through which they can't grasp much of anything important. Teachers know this, so they deal with every little point students bring up as they mention them, to clear away the debris in their thinking. If the student doesn't understand the answer, which is usual, at a minimum the teacher has laid track for a later discussion that will ultimately render the student's distractions unavailable when they get to the heart of the matter." She slid the pages under a potted plant. "This technique made almost every encounter they had difficult for the student to follow in the early days. Even then, as they began to grasp concepts, the teacher changed subjects the moment they finished with one, or they referred back to an interrupted topic as if it was connected to their last sentence."

"Where's the advantage in confusing them?"

"Actually, it's the opposite effect." Counting on her fingers, Bonnie said, "Ultimately, they're able to focus much longer than ever before, they've practiced losing their affront because they know there's no time for it, they're patient beyond their years, and their default position is of a keen observer of the world at large. Not much got past them after they lost their sense of self importance."

"Even if it looked like they all belong in an asylum?"

"They certainly lived in one before the merchants came along."

"You haven't mentioned anything about institutions."

"The world," she said. I could swear I heard, "duh" as well.

"The shoelace thing is psychotherapy?"

"In a manner of speaking; it's designed to help them break the rigidity of their thinking."

"I don't see how the way they tie their sandals would do that?"

"That's because you think too rigidly." She leaned toward me. "A core requirement of learning how to live properly was changing the routines of life, one point of which was to free their minds and appreciate things like the poetry of Brendah dealing with issues that living on the streets had stolen from them, on the same streets."

"Like what?"

"Their sense of play became less guarded, their trust in people was being restored, and their curiosity was poked with every teaching encounter."

"Your poetry may be too clever, and the apprentices will look suspicious, if not superior, by choosing such young friends."

[120]

"Your view of friendship is a balanced relationship of reliable exchanges?"

"Works for me. Why?"

"By that definition, two fools could form a life-long bond based on agreeing with each other's faults, and re-circulate endless sympathy as their lives never improve. Apprentices and teachers never agreed with flaws." She leaned her head against the house. "You have to understand what they are before you can have a true friendship with anyone."

Feeling that we were on the brink of a confrontation, I lifted a worn running shoe to table height and said, "Will the scene make sense if I tie my laces backwards?"

"It would help," Bonnie said, leaning forward to poke a finger through the slit in the side of my shoe where the glue had given way. "You're due for a new pair."

"That lets the water out." I lowered my foot.

"Treating yourself poorly leads to acting poorly, which gives others permission to treat you the same way. Treat yourself well, and you set a standard others must live up to if they want to share your company." Bonnie assessed my appearance, from head to toe. "Trimming your beard might make people think that growing it was an intentional act, and buying shoes will make you feel better about yourself. Maybe some shirts that aren't so tight would help as well," she said, glancing at my paunch.

"I began running a few weeks ago," I said.

"You must be very tired by now," she deadpanned.

"I'm getting there," I said crankily. "How does this encounter fit in your story?"

"My characters couldn't appreciate the abstract symmetry of their quest if they thought too rigidly, which meant there remained a chance that they might improvise in a predictable way."

"By which you mean like an average person?"

"I do. If they studiously practiced disrupting their routines, they will have become fluidly unpredictable, and yet deliberate within their new way of thinking."

"Meaning average thinkers couldn't anticipate their actions?"

"Meaning that even if they did, average thinkers would defend themselves in predictably inappropriate ways, leaving them equally vulnerable in a new circumstance."

"Clever...vulnerable to what?"

"Impeccable acts. We'll define those, as we go along."

[121]

Chapter Fourteen
The Guardian

I was looking through the picture window at a pedestrian drizzle that a soft-rock jock said would end by lunchtime, when the phone rang and Bonnie saved me from having to dress like a lobsterman to cross the bridge to her place. Forty minutes later, we were in our front booth at Nolan's having coffee and Danish pastries.

Taking new pages from an old envelope, she said her commune had designed helping others into their way of life, so their children took little for granted while participating in practical cycles of positive cause and effect. For example, the effectiveness of water proofing boats depended upon surface preparation, the quality of fine cloth, if required, and the proper blending of oils and saps. Not coincidentally, at some point in their early years, every child had gone fishing in a leaky boat and become exhausted while learning the rhythmic art of bailing water.

In this guided way, and at a pace suited to their individual abilities, children experienced the two-step recipe for creating a beneficial personal momentum. The first step was paying close attention to their economy of action; elders defined this as using the minimum amount of materials and labour to complete a task, while neither skimping nor over doing any aspect of that task. Achieving this balance required forethought, attention to detail, and precision in execution, while mistakes were welcome because teachers properly viewed these as lessons in fine-tuning. In later stages, they were a source of humour, or a sign of illness.

Understanding the condition of "complete" was the second step: a task was not finished until the user of community materials had reported their use, or replaced them, so there were no surprise shortages. Excess materials had to be properly stored and waste disposed of or prepared for other uses. In this way, no task imposed on another's space, time, or safety. Simply stated, which it often was with only the tilt of an elder's head, a person aspiring to live a proper life should leave no debris in the wake of their passing. This principle of living a "tight life" also applied to their relationships, which rendered pettiness, anger, and animosity short-lived experiences in the young.

Inherent within this process, children also learned to assume responsibility for their every action, and to regularly go a step beyond basic requirements because every mother, artisan, and craftsman had 'unexpectedly' needed an hour's help from them that somehow became three. Moreover, if a townie had to rebuild after a spring flood or winter fire, these surprisingly capable creatures appeared unbidden, their own daily supplies and tools in hand, because the seeds of thinking in cycles had taken root. For a commune kid, to help one person was to help everyone in unforeseeable ways, a seemingly fanciful idea that often revealed its potency through unexpected encounters with indirect beneficiaries of their labours during market hours.

Bonnie continued to explain that formal apprenticeships began for those who chose them around the age of twelve; they were a more mature twelve than television and computer games shape in our culture. By their late teens, apprentices had acquired remarkable powers of observation, including an understanding of the abstraction of momentum; they were adept at determining at what stage a given event was passing through, based in no small measure from guided assessments of their own experiences. This was humbling knowledge, and appropriately so because with it came the ability to influence events with little effort. As a result, regardless of outward appearances, they were cautious about how they spent their energy, the corollary of which being a deep appreciation for what one person can accomplish without the interference of personal concerns.

Years of working at these personal practices laid the groundwork for transitioning their many intellectual assumptions into a grand epiphany, which became a comprehensive assumption of how to live properly; they were in charge of every second of their lives, therefore deliberate, responsible choices were the only way to go. On this grand day of knowingly securing their freedom to succeed or fail on their own terms, at only their own expense, life became a bold, often hilarious adventure because pretending to be an average person leapt from a role-playing game into a practical art. In this way only did they sometimes fail to maintain their social facade in the public market, where every customer had become like a child, but because they intimately understood why this was so, there was no judgement in their joy.

[123]

Fondling the pages, Bonnie said that Cymhon, a teacher whose sight was taken in his youth, was in charge of everything related to the community sheep. Aided by his older brother Thomahs, their duties included teaching children the entire gamut from birthing, shepherding, and sheering, to designing and sowing clothing and tapestries. Of this seemingly dour duo, Thomahs taught his skills through riddle-statements intended to create uncertainty, while Cymhon's stark mannerisms effectively commanded the young to act without thinking. Only in this way, the younger brother said, could he tell which flock he was tending.

Bonnie finally handed me her pages...

The brothers took a group of youths on a quest to discover the kind of cultural transactions that drained people's energy like a holed vessel. Learning of a man overburdened with personal belongings from Thomahs, Cymhon extracted from the group a detailed description of his belongings and clothing, down to the length of his strides as he made short trips down the village's main street. Finally, he asked the youths what they thought was going on. Conditioned to look at the nature of an event, their careful consensus was that making more trips with less weight would allow the man to work longer and complete the job.

"Excellent, and what job is that?" said Cymhon.

Knowing better than to jump at the obvious, Donica said, "He wears the traditional garb of Hafnagurdar, so he is from the far north, and new to our area."

"What he carries is local," Evie said, pointing. "I helped make that blanket."

"He's probably working for a meal," Tobias said.

"That's good as far as it goes," the shepherd of wayward ideas agreed, disquietingly. "What about the things I can see?"

"But you can't see anything?" Carhmon, the youngest boy said, honestly.

"Is it not hot?"

The child didn't understand.

Donica cleared up his confusion. "The decision to move in the midday sun is poor," she said.

"Not if it has to be done right away," Karol, Carhmon's older sister said.

"Excellent! You've seen that the conditions of the moment are part of determining what is really happening. And?"

The girls' cheeks collectively puckered in a vain effort to squeeze time, the weight of the load, and the distance the man carried it into increasingly stranger speculations, to which Cymhon finally put an end

[124]

by squawking like a chicken: dip-twitching his head and bobbing cloudy eyes completed the effect. When the children's laughter subsided, he said they were wasting energy clucking at the wind when a direct and mutually beneficial act would clear up the mystery.

"Offer to help him," he said. "If he accepts, the stranger will almost certainly volunteer an explanation."

"What if he doesn't want help?" Karol said.

"Then carrying burdens alone is his path."

"Or atonement for an unforgivable deed?" Thomahs speculated.

"There is nothing unforgivable," the younger children said in unison, because they were still facing their own short-comings. They had yet to learn what the older ones were being taught: the act of forgiving was an energetic attachment to the negative and a judgement upon the 'offender'. Indifference to actions aimed at harming them personally, with compassion for those doing the aiming, was the elusive goal all of them would eventually learn.

Thomahs, "Ahem-ed," contemplatively. "You are correct, of course. This is the lesson I often get backwards. It may be a deed unforgiven."

"He may be punishing himself?" Gabriel asked.

"May," Chymon replied speculatively, as the young students took their first steps toward the road, "Either way, your offer will create an opportunity. Let it run its course."

"Unless he's stealing," Thomahs muttered.

"As always, so far so good," I said handing the pages to her. "Except I don't understand how you can achieve indifference with compassion. Aren't they mutually exclusive?"

"Indifference toward your own circumstance does not negate compassion for others trying to learn to be indifferent to theirs."

"Uh huh, so the point of this scene in the movie is what?"

"Observation and opportunities not wasted. In time, the children became formidable analysts of where they really were, with whom, and what choices they had to better their position depending on what they wanted to happen."

"So it's no different than how we learn to assess our circumstances, except it's guided by assessing the nature of the events?" I said.

"By understanding their lessons in Essential Acts, yes, "but they also learned much about what people were really like through the nature of the events people chose to engage."

"Got it."

As was her way, when Bonnie was satisfied with our discussions she began speaking about anything that caught her fancy, and we discussed her work no more on this day.

[125]

On day two of what was now a tropical depression, Bonnie gave me a passage written through the eyes of a young Roman wanderer...

Robust locks of curly brown hair made Teyo's five feet four inches appear taller, while a button nose affixed to angular features on a wiry frame made describing him a trial; he was virile and cute.

Raised in a culturally diverse orphanage, by twenty years of age, Teyo had command of three languages, five if you included flattery and larceny, both of which he judiciously employed when he offered to help fishermen unload their catch in exchange for a meal and a dry bed. The cook in the beachfront kitchen scanned a single face among the boat crews before feeding Teyo a hearty meal from the communal pot. During this time, the leader of the fleet, Rashaef, casually offered to teach the wanderer the vocation of harvesting the sea. Between mouthfuls, Teyo praised the offer generously, expending an effusive measure of seafaring bluster for one with no scars or calluses on his hands, before declining experiences best left in his past. He would, however, be waiting for their return to fulfill his end of the bargain.

Excited at overhearing this, Jehaneh, a pretty cook's assistant when one was needed, deferentially advised Rashaef that the arrival of a man of such talent was a good omen for the overnight session; they were a man short due to the imminent arrival of his first born. Surrounded by a brotherhood that literally had less food on their plates because of him, the traveler went to sea.

In Rashaef's eyes, Teyo's spirited excuses for nearly drowning three men with the reckless handling of a net constituted an omen of a different kind. And the young braggart's mournful proclamation with what was close to his dying breath, for he was one of the three, that an equilibrium problem meant he was not born to physical labour, cemented his destiny.

Early the next morning, Jehaneh effectively kidnapped him from a bed he had no time to warm, proclaiming that she would not allow Rashaef to make him pay damages so soon after his own struggle with death. A glance outside implied that he was moments away from this fate and Teyo followed her without question.

They crept behind homes, workshops, and gardens until they reached the farthest downwind point of the community, where they joined half a dozen women who were drying the catch. Rashaef would not look for him here, Jehaneh over-assured Teyo just as Rashaef's wife, Lei'a, came looking for her apprentice.

Seeing the connection between the two, Lei'a offered to smooth things over: "Few outside of the community can endure his idea of justice," she said. Teyo could ask anyone who passed through the market, some of whom came from as far as two days away for the commune's renowned products. Turning to leave, as an afterthought

[126]

Lei'a told Teyo that making himself useful would go a long way toward keeping him out of her husband's thoughts until she could come up with a solution.

Beginning with that first sleepless night, the women's chatter about their husbands, neighbours, and children's concerns imbued Teyo with knowledge of the community that had imprisoned him without tethers, and of the insinuated dangers that lurked in the nearby city.

There were also many work-related details told to helpers, and as the days became a week, then two, Teyo overheard everything there was to know about each species they cleaned and preserved while waiting to hear from Lei'a: between the lines of other's conversations, he understood that she was utterly dependable, and one simply waited on her.

During this time, Teyo revealed to Jehaneh the embarrassing secret of his poor sense of balance, which had caused the accident and now seemed to be getting worse in his stationary work. It seemed that mobility was important to his health, and he should leave before someone else was hurt. Jehaneh solemnly agreed, explaining that the skilled workers had noticed he struggled to fillet fish at a continuous depth, which left bones that could puncture a child's cheek or worse.

Not to worry, she soothed him, they had caught his errors.

The other women ascribed the miracle of his random swaying, without ever nicking himself with razor sharp blades, or raising so much as a blister from the smokers, to Jehaneh's nearness when a spell came upon Teyo, and she steadied him just in time

Four weeks passed before Rashaef asked Lei'a about Teyo's wondrously sluggish recuperation, so quoted Jehaneh before she speculated to Teyo that it looked like Rashaef still wanted restitution for his damaged reputation as a man of foresight and excellent judge of character. Teyo accurately interpreted this news to mean that his physical problems were not a solution to his predicament.

Solemnly, Jehaneh said he should make himself more conspicuously useful if Lei'a was to continue keeping Rashaef at bay and Teyo on shore until such a time as Rashaef would appear to be petty by demanding anything more of him. There was no other way out for, although he was a quiet working man, Rashaef was a leader, and children couldn't help but spread the word of the incident.

Teyo's affliction subsequently subsided as he began delivering the smokehouse products to Lei'a's godfather, Leith, thereby making his efforts more apparent to everyone in the market, and Rashaef.

A character among characters, Leith was annoyingly meticulous when he transferred the fish to display them alphabetically and according to their length and girth on his broad leaf-lined cart. This allowed buyers to choose between the heavier, more expensive cuts and cheaper species at a glance. In contradiction to this practice, he

[127]

was endearingly unconcerned about wearing bright, mismatched colours—a personal display problem of which he claimed to be fully aware. In confidence, he told Teyo that children had a difficult time taking their eyes off him.

Noting that Rashaef spoke deferentially to the old man, when their paths crossed more often than seemed normal for their respective daily tasks, Teyo applied himself to learning how to properly present Leith's products to the public. This was an art he knew the master monger demanded of his formal helpers, in part to honour all seafaring men's risk and labour.

Two more weeks passed before Teyo didn't make a single error in visual presentation, the naming of species and their characteristics, spawning times, feeding depths, and general habitat. The market day after this, Leith didn't review the work Teyo had taken the initiative to deliver on a ready-to-go display cart he had asked a carpenter to help him restore, and refine. Instead, Leith slyly said, "Would you like to learn the secrets of my craft? Not that they're real secrets." He chuckled, hushed his tone and said, "Not that it's my real work."

Teyo understood that gaining any merchant's trust would go a long way toward diffusing the situation with Rashaef, and he humbly accepted the offer he had been angling for.

Like a child, the merchant immediately showed him how to surreptitiously slide an extra half filet between the palm leaves for selected customers—always the poor who had learned the rewards of arriving clean, standing tall, and articulating their desires as equal partners in commerce with the old man. At the same time, he learned that, when possible, these people offered many half-cut bronze's to create the noise of coinage for the benefit of silver coin customers who were paying full value.

Teyo feigned awkwardness with his lessons in slight-of-hand, lest the old man deduce his past from his familiarity with a nefarious skill, which he gave away anyway when Leith "taught" him how to palm bronze half-cuts and exchange them for near equal value, or better value coins.

As time passed—Bonnie didn't say how much time—Teyo took over selling for the merchant when nature called and sometimes closed out the day's work when the patriarch forgot to return. Nature subsequently called Leith away more frequently, and during one of the monger's lengthier spells, Teyo came to the guilty realization that he didn't want the old man to come back, at least not that day. He loved the hustle of the market, especially shuffling fillets with one-hand while risking laying out the proper coinage when other eyes were watching, then exchanging them before the customer had closed her fist. He occasionally did this for well-to-do customers, as well, because that was Leith's directive. However, just who received these error-gifts was up to Teyo, with one caveat: the brisk and impolite were to be given the same treatment as the courteous.

After a short time, Teyo wasn't shy about filling in for his mentor's legendary banter, as well, because he too was born to talk; in combination with what the women had taught him about fish and the town's peoples' passions and concerns, his larger than life personality translated into sales nearly matching his mentors.

Nearly, he speculated in a moment of introspection, because he was a helper—a designation the village children guffawed over because the commune's helpers were almost always children under the age of twelve. He knew this circumstance undermined the peculiar relationship consumers assume when dealing with anyone other than the professional, whose polish and expertise they are more willing to reward. In their minds, the young man was knowledgeable and had proven to be trustworthy, if already mathematically challenged by the water in the commune, but he was not someone to spend their loyalty on because he had not formally dedicated himself to the business of serving them.

With this thought, Teyo realised he was no longer a stranger passing through, but a member of the commune. And although apprentices physically did no more than he, they were treated like fine sculptures in the making, whereas he was treated with genuine warmth and respect. Not that this was bad in any way, but it was different.Then there was the beautiful Jehaneh, a true apprentice to Lei'a, who Teyo understood was held in the highest esteem as an advisor on what the commune referred to as the proper thing to do. Rashaef was her counterpart, the energy and action behind what needed to be done.

It had taken him these months to appreciate the couple's importance to the commune because in face to face interactions they treated everyone no differently than anyone else, and they were in turn treated as equals. Behind their backs, however, an Aramaic appellative that Teyo translated into his native Spanish as dueño, Master, was often spoken in subdued tones, then quickly treated as an error in judgement. As a result of these common interactions, the town's people were unaware of their true status, which Teyo understood was how the commune wanted it and he respected. It also spoke volumes, yet to be deciphered by Teyo, about Leith's status.

On a day Teyo deemed appropriate, after returning to Leith's home with the day's tally, he reported his transactions and asked Leith if he could become his apprentice.

"I also want this, my young friend," the elder said, "but you must ask Rashaef. He is in charge of the sea and all that entails."

"Forgive me, sir, but how can one be in charge of that?"

"He embraces his responsibilities to it and to us from the moment he opens his eyes, to the length and depth of his every breath. I am a small part of his processes and designs, a component wearing into the end of its time."

"I don't understand. You have ten times the experience..."

"You may protest my station in life to Rashaef when you see him," the old man chortled, "but know that his knowledge was his father's knowledge and his father's before him—a man I had the good fortune to literally run into when he was establishing this place." The old man cackled, and said, "The roots of this community came on an overland quest, but they depended entirely on the sea until their crops were established. This happened quickly in this climate and with great diversity because their trenching techniques allowed them to grow almost anything, almost anywhere. They were a driven and industrious people who freely taught me a great deal, and when I had finally shown them that I could be trusted to complete my tasks properly, Rashaef's grandfather granted me the unimaginable gift of a purpose. In his language I became an apprentice apotropos, which to him meant guardian, but I prefer the translation of custodian."

"Pardon, Padrone. You became an apprentice custodian of what?"

"Of knowledge that would be needed when it was time." He paused for Teyo to react, which by this time, he had learned to better control.

Leith continued. "The grandfather told me all that he had learned from the true caretakers of this place, and I became the keeper of the living history of the sea in this time. I am a guardian of its secret vulnerabilities and so the custodian of its future. Is this what you chose to apprentice?"

Teyo's confusion was complete; it silenced him.

"Why do you tell stories to our customers?" the patriarch finally said.

"To sell fish," he said, hoping Leith was not having a spell.

"That somehow happens for me, as well," the old man shrugged, "but I can't say why. I am not a salesman."

"Not a salesman? You are the best I've ever seen!" Teyo blurted out. "The way you captivate the children to draw in their mothers is genius!"

Leith raised his hand. "Things are not what they appear to be. My sales are a consequence of quality, which allows me to teach children that we do not plunder our resources or challenge nature. Every merchants' story," he waved his arm in a small arc, as if they were in the room, "you would have noticed if you were not always looking over your shoulder, embodies the rules by which the world willingly provides for our needs. Our diverse skills and expertise are merely different ways to follow the rules of prosperity, and the way we prepare our products speaks to our respect for the gifts that they are because it's infinitely more difficult to destroy something you understand." Leith let the moment ferment, before he chuckled into a change of focus. "Rashaef lives in the ever-present because any moment may portend to unimaginable things for the rest of us. Possibly because I have known generations of his family, this includes not interfering with my ways, but this does not change what I am and will always be - his most grateful servant." Leith looked confused. "For some reason, he has not interfered with you."

"I have heard, sir, that you have been the senior monger longer than most people here have been alive. Would this not mean that Rashaef learned from you?"

"Upon his young father's death, I pledged to continue to teach all that his grandfather had taught to both of us. When I became the interim teacher of a young master by default, of necessity a gift of unimaginable consequence was bestowed upon me—a brief contact with the original teacher. Rashaef is of that lineage, as is Lei'a, so it was always in the design of their destiny to be taught directly by the original teacher when it was time. I brought Rashaef to this time, as an accidental apprentice to the most masterful of teachers through unforeseeable acts of free will. I am in fact and function no different from the women at the smoker, all of whom are teachers or apprentices in some aspect of how to live properly. So yes, I taught him when he was young, but only to make him ready to be taught the unimaginable. I am not of the kind of power that the wind and the sea deem to be ready to learn what a man cannot study with another man. But I think you might be."

"Are you servicing a debt to his father?" Teyo said, trying to understand the old man's position and reference to the original teacher, who he figured could not be less than a century plus twenty years. Even then...

"I am acting in allegiance with a gift." He shook off a thought and said instead, "It is my hope that someday you will be ready to meet the teacher and come to understand the importance of keeping his secret, and the history of his efforts alive until it is needed to awaken the complacent."

"I don't know his secret," Teyo said.

"That is why they are called secrets."

Leith breathed in deeply. "When it became clear to all of us that your malady may never heal, and you would surely starve if you returned to your world because of something we pushed you into, I asked Rashaef to permit you to apprentice with me. He said it wasn't time to decide the matter." The old master chucked. "Jehaneh may have thought she was keeping him away from you, but Rashaef was allowing time for your direction to choose you. Now that it has, it is the time to ask him, and I mean tonight, for time runs short."

"Why?" Teyo said.

"Time is always short when you're standing still," Leith said, looking at Teyo's feet.

Teyo immediately left to see Rashaef.

[131]

Leading the request by confessing to his original lie, Teyo asked to become an apprentice to Leith. Without comment, Rashaef took Teyo's hands in his and rubbing them with his thumbs said, "Prove that you can complete a task." He let go and pointing to an old fishing boat beside the drying room said, "Make that seaworthy."

"As you know, my skills are limited," Teyo said, examining the rotting relic of foreign design, the only monument to disrepair in the community. "I will need guidance."

"I will send someone."

Teyo set about the arduous and sometimes humiliating task of what he believed was making restitution. It would be arduous because he had to remove every scale, smooth every potential splinter point, and return all of the wood to the scent of forest and natural preservatives. The humiliating aspect was not anticipated: he waited an hour for help before trying to manoeuvre the craft away from the building wall, when a passing boy stopped to watch him. Sweating and breathless, Teyo said he would be grateful for his help.

Pointing at the ground, the boy said the poles upon which the hull rested could be pulled sideways one at a time but only to three times the distance of their diameter. Starting gently with the outer beam, the craft would gradually lie away from and abeam to the building. As Teyo pulled the remaining beams, the bow would orient to the subtle down slope that had been contoured for a rolling launch and which provided drainage while under repair. From here, he could skid the craft along the smooth surface of the beams to give him access to the port side of the craft. The deadweight of the hull would rest on the rounded keel and internal transverse beams, limiting the possibility of damaging the craft further, while Teyo removed the planks and restored their integrity and pliability with steam and oils.

This over-abundance of information prompted Teyo to ask the boy if Rashaef had sent him, to which the fourteen year old advised Teyo what tools and materials he would need and whom to see about acquiring them. Leaving a pouch of water, the boy said he would come back tomorrow to show him how to remove the old wood without damaging the internal structure.

Teyo spent the rest of the day gathering supplies.

The next day, the boy demonstrated how Teyo could work most efficiently before he again left water and went his own way, for this was how Rashaef's son defined the terms need and help.

A week and a day later, a carpenter's apprentice Teyo knew from building the display cart stopped by to show him how to determine if parts could be trusted. A new rudder, a double turning block, and the better part of a month later, a girl too young to be an apprentice came to teach him how to make a pitch solution that, along with an unusual fastening system, would seal any properly angled joint. Knowing about

[132]

the inevitable affects of wind and water on housing to be sceptical, Teyo questioned her claim. Elsbeth told him they were not building a house.

With no preparation other than picking up a double-walled skin sack on the way out of the village, she took him on a long walk to an oozing hole of sticky black syrup, where she had him choose a comfortable spot and curl his fingers to observe the surrounding landscape. With that done, but not questioned or explained, they gathered goo in the sack and walked most of the night to be back for his work in the morning. The girl did not reveal to him the preparation process that involved gummy tree saps to complete the sealant preparation. It was too early for that lesson.

In the days to follow, after swearing Teyo to secrecy, the metal smith taught him how to forge special spiral nails that pulled planks together tighter than straight nails merely joined them. This one innovation, he said, had led community carpenters to experimenting with designs that dramatically improved the efficiency of compression seals compared to those naturally created when wood expanded by absorbing moisture. They also discovered that squeezing a thin line of a refined tar between planks created seals that rendered plugging seams with cloth a cosmetic façade, done only to placate old sailor's ideas of seaworthiness. These techniques led to designs that made the commune's boats drier and sturdier than all known craft, which is why the community shipwrights always had orders on the skids.

The metal smith said the alchemist would have to explain the strange hue on the fasteners that would not rust, then changing the subject he said, "We should make a shackle for the mainsail foot, new sleeves for the rudder and winch, and add two stanchions aft; you're not the first person to throw himself overboard with his net. We'll also need a drain amidships—make it the size of the sleeves. Large."

"Drain? Is it not a hole into the ocean?" Teyo said certain he was not mistaken.

"It is required,' the Smith said.

These creations required metals, so into the hills Teyo returned with an apprentice shipwright to mine the ores required. During these journeys, four in all because the master of metals needed raw materials for other work, Teyo learned more about the architecture of the landscape—how surface characteristics portend to the existence of sub-surface elements, like the black ooze lesson he didn't know he had taken revealed the existence of that substance underfoot.

Smelting and fabricating came next, and when these fixtures were completed, Teyo again borrowed the carpenter's tools and his apprentice's expertise to make two turning blocks. Assisting with these installations, the apprentice demonstrated how one block affixed to a gunwale with a lateral rotation along the fore and aft line can lift the

[133]

mast and trim the sail by running a halyard through the topmast block, and by running a line run through a boom's eye, one man could also raise a heavy catch.

With the help of the same young girl making a modification to a sealing concoction, these mechanisms turned remarkably freely in any weather, which was how Teyo's days also began running together...

As often as she could, Jehaneh spent time with him around dusk, self-consciously commenting on the dropping temperature, moisture appearing on the foliage, and the changing speed and direction of nightfall breezes because it was her remark that, six months earlier, had put Teyo in this seemingly endless circumstance of reparation. Teyo could not convince her that he didn't mind, and spending time with her wasn't the only reason. He had adjusted to the routine of layering goals and entwining appropriate aspects of them because it was like being on the road of survival, except he was warm and dry and if he went hungry, it was by choice.

"I know you can do it," Jehaneh said, and she pointed at three stars to absently note their drift across the sky, just as she did every time she was about to leave him for the evening.

Time passed—Bonnie wasn't concerned with how much—until the day Rashaef inspected the hull, the hardware, and the innovative rigging that supported an ingeniously designed collapsible mast mechanism that made maintenance and replacement a one man job. Nodding his approval at each properly completed project, he said the craft needed only a small mainsail, for ease of handling because speed was not important, along with a finely woven net. Rashaef calculated the dimensions of the sail required based on a formula that took into account the former derelict's empty weight, waterline length and midship's dimensions, then he taught Teyo this technique for determining how much sail and load capacity vessels of various sizes could safely carry in a nasty sea.

The weaver subsequently taught him how to make the sail, but he said Teyo would have to see another man about making the thin, strong net cords, and learn how to knot them in a diamond pattern that appeared to stretch. Elsbeth next taught him how to embed eyelets in cloth, which needed protection against chaffing, and she sent him to a candle-maker who showed him how to wax eyelets and seams with a special concoction. This lesson included more than he cared to know about bees from Brendah, whose lessons went beyond teaching him about the industrious creatures to include a particularly irritating plant, which led to him learning about poultices and basic healing arts common to sailors, because sailors were also woodsmen.

During his recovery period, beginning two hours before first light, Teyo learned to tie knots from a sightless man who craved uncommon knowledge about common days. Was the sea running in the same

[134]

direction as the morning breeze? Had either shifted since he last spoke to Jehaneh or since he went to bed or after he got up? Had the morning dew evaporated? Were the clouds high or low, wispy and long, fluffy, or did they wear ragged crowns. "What about now?" he asked minutes later. Were his ears deceiving him, or did he hear the motion of water lapping on shore without feeling the air move? Had a vessel sailed by?

Teyo drew deeply upon his linguistic skills to turn things nature had surely intended to be nuance into fine points of information, such was the degree of detail the net-maker painstakingly demanded while his nibble fingers demonstrated a multitude of knots designed for myriad purposes. Some of these, he told Teyo, would never slip, some would lock one way but release with a tug from the opposite direction, and some could do both of these things depending on which end of a looped, wandering hitch was pulled.

During the many mornings it took Teyo to master the versatility of marine knots and splices, his teacher offhandedly explained various permutations and feelings that different weather signs Teyo had described generated in his senses. By the thirteenth day, Teyo could not help but check the state of morning dew, winds, and clouds then close his eyes to feel the day speaking to him before he decided which task he would do next. Telling this to Chymon pleased him greatly.

Overall, he thrived during a year and a half of unrelenting effort in which he felt genuine gratitude from the men whose boats he now knew enough to maintain, and for the friendly waves of camaraderie from the teachers and apprentices who had shared their knowledge with him, often as he was just walking by. Overall, meaning not entirely because, without it being voiced, he understood the community members must have deemed some of his tasks to be incomplete without a sea trial to test the physical quality of some elements and his workmanship; this brought into question his work ethic.

This one failing grew in his mind until he dared to edge a small craft into the bay after the fleet came safely home to rest. Upon his less erratic return, he had enough confidence to brave the deed as needed in sheltered waters, but he was not fool enough to believe he was a sailor. Nor were those who quietly watched over his awkward experiments while the townspeople saw only meticulous sea trails.

Balancing this uncomfortable requirement was that Teyo had great fun on market days when the increasingly frail, always jovial fishmonger taught him how to troll for a customer's self-interest by feeling the undercurrent of their words and adjusting the depth of his verbal hooks accordingly.

As always, there were the too-brief interludes with the woman who knew he could regain his freedom, a notion which by this time had become a disturbing thought to Teyo.

[135]

Bonnie next wrote that the intimate nature of his lessons broke down the walls Teyo had built around his past. In conjunction with his lifestyle of diligent study at the hands of masters of their crafts, who were never called such, it was inevitable that the old man who brought disparate elements of these lessons together became his life's confessor. When Teyo eventually told him about the ruse that had entrapped him, the old master simply said, "Everyone here knows you had never been to sea before that night." He laughed much longer than the moment required, but Teyo knew to be patient: the storyteller would explain his behaviour, or not, if and when the time was right.

Two years of training ended on the day that Teyo presented the sail and netting to Rashaef for inspection.

With only a cursory glance because Teyo's workmanship was consistently superb, Rashaef took him into a distant valley where he had Teyo recall every important event he could remember since his childhood, up to the time he offered to off-load the fish. Teyo did not struggle with these recollections because he and Leith had regularly compared misspent youths. Rashaef then simplified these events into themes, such as self-doubt, cruelty, betrayal, and fear then he had Teyo recall every event he had experienced in the commune under these same banners. With prompting followed by dissection and assessment, it took Teyo two uncomplaining days to recall his journey and to realize his old, well-travelled life coupled with his lengthy task, formed an obvious design—his destiny—after which realizations fell like torrential rain.

Teyo soon claimed as his own knowledge how the abstractions of behavioural momentum fed a synchronicity of events, without stepping on the toes of independence, to create the harmony this enormously loving and productive community enjoyed. He also knew beyond expression that the world had a natural order, that its secrets weren't secrets at all, but evidence ignored, and that everyone made a journey of imperfect choices to eventually discover themselves within a world of such beautifully diverse, yet harmonious complexity as to defy description and imagination. He envisioned each choice as a grounded boat that could be freed into its natural element by carefully moving the skids of fixed thinking. And suddenly his barriers were gone; he knew himself. He was free.

Elation caused him to mutter incoherently.

On this cue, Rashaef took Teyo's hands in his own and rubbing the calluses said, "You are ready to begin your apprenticeship."

"Begin?" Teyo babbled through a fresh rush of tearful joy.

"You could not understand the master's secret until you had none of your own. Rest before seeing him; his knowledge is weighty and he hasn't the strength to tell you twice."

Teyo rested less than a day before he went to see his friend, mentor, and official teacher of the secrets of the sea of life.

At the conclusion of their exhausting but joyful meeting, Leith extracted a promise from his formal apprentice; it was a pledge Leith had made to himself, he explained, but it was clearly impossible to be achieved on his own. Unsaid, was that he knew it would set Teyo free on his own journey. Sombrely, Teyo accepted the task before Leith lightened his burden by sharing his only secret.

"Like yours," he winked, "it's not really a secret." He chuckled weakly, and said, "When I was a young apprentice, a village fish-monger circulated a rumour intended to undermine my credibility. Without that, customers would suspect I was a scoundrel of indeterminate origins whom the elders were trying to rehabilitate. This perception was not far off the mark at the time, and it could certainly colour their view of my products and preparations, but the real damage lay beneath. Of course," he continued humbly, "when the curious tested my knowledge, I could dispel the rumour because my fore-runners had put me through the same meticulous preparations as you have now experienced." The old man lowered his voice. "Generations of children still repeat this rumour as a joke to be played on younger siblings, when it is a truth that has entrapped me for over eighty years. But to reveal it would undermine my stories, which are my purpose."

Leith then told Teyo the secret that had survived as such because the few that knew it had long since taken it to their graves: as two victims of identical design, the new apprentice and the ancient guardian were heard laughing until the pain of their joy was too great for them to stay together under one roof.

Privately and individually, in their hearts the village both celebrated and mourned the changing of the guard.

Short days later, every mother and child within walking distance formed an escort from the market, across the bridge, and all the way to the harbour, as their storyteller made his final journey. Their husbands and brothers, dignitaries dressed in finery, and beggars in laundered attire marked the route of his passage as a plain fisherman, a baker, a weaver, and a young apprentice carried the patriarch's body aboard an immaculately restored ancient craft from his native land.

Rashaef rigged a line between a turning block and stanchion, attached a perfectly knotted, fine mesh net, and the four of them lay the light body upon it. With elegant ease, Rashaef noiselessly winched their beloved friend off the deck, after which he delivered a short eulogy only the three heard: "As promised—no discomforting sway, old friend."

The baker stepped forward to place a crusty loaf in the ancient arms to honour the sustenance of friendship that had been his privilege to receive all of his life. The weaver next draped the body of the guardian

[137]

in a simple white cloth because, as his oldest friend had often said about this moment, "Custodians greet no one with pretence."

Three of them left the craft as Teyo unfurled a small sail. With the fleet following closely, he set a course for the ocean shelf that sustained the community, in the same vessel that had carried a runaway boy on the only sea sojourn he had ever made, nearly a century earlier. A falcon and a sparrow glided together overhead.

Keeping the promise the monger had made to himself so many years ago, to never again go to sea unless it was in his present state, Teyo could not contain a smile as he released the finely angled "bilge" stopper to send a servant of the sea home, steady and level, in the only vessel worthy of the journey.

It wasn't until Teyo had transferred to Rashaef's boat that he understood his teacher's final gift in two stages; by letting go of his greatest physical accomplishment, he could let go of his beloved mentor. And as the mast dipped below the surface, he understood the Custodian's secret—the key to masterful teaching that Leith had bequeathed him. Nothing could be about him. Anybody could learn how to build a boat, but few could teach without pity, and fewer could endure learning anything worth-while with it.

In time—Bonnie didn't say how much—the market mothers embraced Teyo's outrageous stories about the stars aligning one man's journey, while lighting every man's way, and a whispering wind as well as a telling sky giving directions to a living sea as the progeny of Leith's tutelage. The duo's only life skill confirmed for them that neither man had what it took to cope with the rigors of real town life... the well water, again.

"Whom may I serve?" Teyo sang out loudly.

"Serve us!" the children's choir chimed back.

"It's a great day!" Teyo played with them.

"No," Khol-The-Daring shouted, "serve us a story, apprentice Teyo!" as the newest monger would forever insist he be addressed because he had known a true teaching master—no matter what he called himself. Themselves.

As falsetto voices joined in the refrain, tears of awe and elation began to stream from Teyo's eyes for as clear as Jehaneh's first, "I love you," he heard from within his being the Original Guardian whisper, "We have been awaiting you; there is much more to tell."

And serve them the custodian did, as new mothers agreed their days were much better for Teyo's unfortunate malady keeping him ashore.

"What's next?" I said, handing the pages to Bonnie.

"No comment?"

[138]

"Again, I don't know where you're going with it, so I can't say how good it is until you pull it off." I grinned like a cherub. "But I enjoyed it."

"What points am I trying to make?"

In spite of receiving the most generous offering of pages to date, I was annoyed at having to interpret her work at all, let alone try to assess it through the uncommon perceptions she expected of me.

Petulantly, I said, "You've mixed elements of the Tortoise and the Hare, the Grasshopper and the Squirrel, a butcher, baker, and a candlestick maker...

"I wondered if you'd make that connection."

"Jack and the Beanstalk, the Good Samaritan, a clever reference to the Rhyme of the Ancient Mariner, and a not-so-subtle allusion to a fisher of men working with the Old Man and the Sea."

"I also have Simon Says and Doubting Thomas, but there's nothing about Jack and the Beanstalk," she said amused.

"Then there's one less plagiarism lawsuit to deal with."

"Ap-par-ently," Bonnie said, drawing out the word so there was nothing merely apparent about what was to come, "you were so busy judging the material that you missed the overview."

I expected her to pause for my response, but I guess that's why they're called expectations.

Bonnie carried on. "Along with the other scenes you've read, this section demonstrates how the teacher arrives when the student is ready, how teachers teach the unwilling, and how a student can assess his life and see that it is designed for a purpose."

"Like I'm supposed to have seen all of that."

"Don't be too hard on yourself," she said, putting the story away. "It took Teyo two years to understand it."

Chapter Fifteen
The Crafty Wraith

The next day, I crossed the Lions Gate Bridge through a mist of misery—the fine fog that forces bikers to wipe their faceplate every few seconds, to meet Bonnie at a café near her home. Neither of us had brought pages from our books so our conversation was affably mundane, talking about our early work experiences as the sky gradually lightened. When the first bright rays in four grey days poked through, we paid our bill and doubled up on the motorcycle to celebrate our parole in Stanley Park.

Walking within the casual quiet of our own thoughts, as had become our way to enter the park, Bonnie said, "Can you tell me why you're opposed to my metaphysical principles?"

Unable to deny her claim, I saw no point in delaying. "I don't think coincidences or suddenly knowing things are evidence of God at work or the devil at play. There's an explanation for everything."

"I agree, but you haven't told me what you have against it."

"I think the metaphysical world takes our focus away from things we could actually do to improve any of this." I waved a lazy hand at the world in general, almost smacking Bonnie in the face as she abruptly appeared in front of me like an ebony panther leaping from a cave on a moonless night.

Dauntingly impassable, her luminous eyes conveyed unassailable assurance in her advantage as I bumped into her, and she said, "What have you done for humanity lately?"

Stunned by the raw power of her challenge, I stepped back awkwardly and said, "What are you talking about?"

"Your objections to the premises in my book are based on their apparent impracticality to the ignorant, poor, and the down trodden. I'm asking what you are doing to help these circumstances."

Her challenge was petty, but the residual intensity of her inquisition intimidated me, so I was curt when I replied, "I support a foster child," as I stepped around her.

"I didn't know that," she said, turning to walk beside me. "Nothing else?"

"I'm one person."

"Some individuals have changed the world."

My gut told me to apologize, for what I was not sure, but the notion that a single person could cause significant social change on anything other than a nuclear scale was too supercilious to leave alone.

"After how many died paving the way?" I smirked.

"That would depend on what are you referring to," she said, setting a trap because there's rarely a perfect example of anything.

Cautiously, I said, "I'm saying it's not reasonable to harp on the way things are and expect the millions of people who made them that way to change, particularly when the people who try to change anything get a street named after them."

"You think the ratio is one in a million?"

"Now you're playing with me: I think there are lots of people who don't mind making futile gestures, but ninety-nine per cent of them tire of their defeats and settle for less. I think the one in a million has to be a fanatic," I said, saving her the trouble of asking, "who adopts the tactics of the enemy and justifies it with good intentions."

"Fanatics also investigate, inform, and explore the unknown for the good of the rest of us."

"The greater good being four wheel drive and zone air conditioning, sure."

Bonnie shook her head in puzzlement.

"Tom must have told you about Argentina."

"Nothing about cars."

"Maybe I didn't get that far," I said. It was hard to remember which version of what story I had told to whom.

"It's obviously time that you did." Bonnie leaned over, pushing me toward a bench tucked into a niche in the walkway. Off guard, I reached around her waist to keep my balance, she reciprocated, and the building tension of our conversation evaporated.

When we were seated, looking at the ships at anchor, she said, "You were scoffing at the greater good being about luxury," to get me started. "What was that about?"

"The day we were released into house arrest, we asked the press corps for footage to help with our defence. Jim Clancy, from CNN, agreed to give up his work on the spot, but all of the other head offices told their reporters not to get involved. Hilary Brown handed us her

[141]

tape anyway, saying the phones lines to ABC New York weren't always clear."

"What was on the tape?"

"The day after our arrest, the Argentines opened a training base to the press corps to show the world that they weren't a bad bunch—just peach-fuzz faces like everywhere else. The footage implied that access to the military was easy, so what we had done must have truly been criminal. For security reasons," I said wryly, "our footage couldn't be made public, when it was so innocuous compared to what they had authorized the day after our arrest, our attorney believed the judge would have been embarrassed into releasing us."

"Didn't the two tapes help you?"

"I didn't realize it at the time, but political circumstances demanded that we go through due process. I doubt that any amount of evidence would have changed the pace or the outcome for that matter."

"If the tapes didn't matter, what changed about your view of the greater good?"

"The official line was that any organization that helped us could be jeopardizing their access to future stories, which threatened the people's right to know. The truth is that we were expendable to the cause of advertising revenue. It's kind of ironic," I sniggered, "but a greater good cause freed me from that delusion."

Turning to face me for the first time since we sat down, Bonnie said, "The essence of the transactions between my merchants and their customers was to voluntarily sacrifice self-interest in the name of the greater good—the education of others." She paused.

"Uh-huh," I said, failing to see her point.

"You've never done that. You adopted a grand cause because it appealed to your sense of self-importance, which head offices then sacrificed to their own interests."

"How do you know I haven't sacrificed for anyone?"

"You would have found a way to tell me by now."

"Four minutes ago?"

"I had to ask you about that aspect of your wonderfulness," Bonnie said, looking across the water, "which tells me you became a foster parent to make yourself feel better. The part of you that knows why you needed to do that kept silent until it felt threatened."

"Diego's in school and he eats regularly."

"You didn't mention his name, food, or education, and that sounds like penance to me. Diego is lucky to be standing in the way of your self-pity," she tittered annoyingly.

[142]

"You're missing the essence of my act, which is what I stated without spin."

Patting my knee, Bonnie said, "I also told you that grammar *is* an event." Leaving Diego behind, Bonnie said, "You gave away that you were gutted by disappointment when the world didn't rush to your rescue. You thought, 'Good Guys Unjustly Detained,'" Bonnie announced the headline that never was, "would have created pressure for your release. When that didn't happen, you dressed yourself in apathy to disguise your outrage because nothing painful can happen when you're indifferent. Of course," she cocked her head, "nothing good can happen, either."

"I didn't know enough about your world to run and hide in there."

Bonnie looked away, inhaled deeply, and with a cheerless grin said, "It's the one place you can't hide because its underlying assumptions strip your descriptions of events to their core."

"You might as well have said that in Urdu."

"You know what I mean—you've been there with me—but you're too pissed to focus, so I'll spell it out. Anonymous strangers made a business decision that had such an encompassing negative impact on your ego that you can't imagine a wise person positively influencing large events. This is in spite..."

"You said changing the world, not large events."

"...in spite of history showing us that it is the individual who changes the course of history."

"What has that got to do with my view of metaphysics?"

"It has everything to do with one belief infecting another. Let me finish: the CBC put out every effort to help you, didn't they?"

"As far as I know."

"That seems not to matter to you."

"Hmmm."

"Good," Bonnie said, patting my knee, again. "So here is a remedy to your disappointment about Argentina: the media can't pretend to be a defender of the public's interest then throw even one of you away because the backbone of any cause is the individual. It follows that the whole can only be better off if its parts are better off. Like you, the networks didn't understand that the greater good has nothing to do with numbers. It's about principles of responsibility, about energy, which is how individuals change the world by tapping into an underlying momentum that's waiting for a push." She closed her eyes. "You have attached your crappy view of the greater good to all concepts of it, and metaphysics is squarely in your sights because you don't understand

[143]

it." She opened her eyes and looked at me sternly. "It's time to deal with your other illusions about the media, so you can begin to disentangle the beliefs you've unwittingly embraced based on a single incident."

"If you say so."

"I'm explaining this so you can grasp the validity of the teacher's approach to training and I can see how a student deals with it," she said, reminding me of our agreement.

"Uh huh. Right. Go ahead."

"Do reporters risk themselves to say, 'War isn't a good thing, but it's sometimes necessary, so we're going to focus on our brave boys doing their duty safeguarding our country?'"

"There's always an issue of focus, balance, and interpretation."

"Is it accurate to say that journalists cannot help but editorialize, while appearing impartial because the contextual fulcrum of their reports is fixed by their cultural bias?"

"Are you objecting to lessening people's ignorance because it's not a perfect delivery system?"

"You know better than most that informing people about distant wars is a camouflage cause for generating higher advertising revenues than a house fire can command. What is a soldier's job?"

"In what way?"

"This isn't a trick question; follow the bouncing ball," she said, illustrating the concept with an arcing finger in the air.

"Their job is to protect their nation from threats, real or perceived."

"That's their rationale—their cause. What's the event-nature of their actions?"

"They kill people."

"Now we're on the same page. What do journalists do?"

"They're the eyes and ears of the public. Guardians, actually."

"I agree. Did any of you carry weapons?"

"A few. Sometimes. It depended. Why?"

"I'm getting to that. On what did it depend?"

"Obviously, anyone who carried weapons did it for self-defence."

"That's obvious from within the assumptions you hold about the cause of the profession. In terms of essential acts, putting yourself in harm's way is what you have to do to chronicle the nature of harm," she shrugged. "What does arming yourself have to do with that?"

"Being in harm's way sometimes requires protection. Good people have died to get information to everyone."

"How does that change anything?"

[144]

"Jesus Christ…it shows exactly what a lack of information can do!"

"Momentum doesn't care about facts. Your colleagues followed erroneous beliefs into the fray, risking their primary responsibilities to family to potentially die for the public's right to know fundamentally useless information. In terms of what they thought they were doing, their deaths were pointless."

"I didn't mention colleagues."

"Jesus Christ, you're defending the risks you all took!" she shouted, making her point. Then in a conversational tone, "Someone you know was killed—maybe more than one."

"I doubt their families thought it was pointless."

"So do I," she lamented, looking across the glittering water. "It's a terrible way to learn that your husband's ego was more important to him than his wife and children." She cleared her throat. "Killing a stranger in his homeland, in apparent defence of *your* homeland is what soldiers do; their cause and spin is defence, but we've established the essence of their actions is murder, and the polish of patriotism, duty, and honour is their camouflage. Journalists' altruistic cause is the people's right to know, and I'm not saying we shouldn't have virtually unlimited access to information," she quickly added. "I'm saying that news organizations don't understand the effect their presence has on conflicts, although the conglomerate owners might well understand what they're really doing, but we'll come back to that."

"Still with you."

She nodded and said, "If a journalist uses a weapon, he becomes a soldier killing strangers in their homeland in defence of his own homeland's cause of the people's right to know. The journalists who carried weapons didn't think of themselves in this way because of their beliefs, but we both know that beliefs don't mean squat to the underlying nature of an event."

"In Vietnam…"

"Allow me one more point: nothing comes from nothing, energy can never be destroyed, and every action causes a reaction, so there is no true state of neutrality. This means concepts like necessity and fairness are pliable conveniences. Do you agree?"

"With that much, but I didn't carry…"

"It follows that as war correspondents have never ended a war, they can only be contributing to them. Their work is no different than a story focusing on the grief of a survivor after his family died in a fire; it can only enhance grief by generating it in the audience."

[145]

"If you had watched the news back when, you would know that many of the journalists who carried weapons are the same ones who brought the slaughter of Vietnam home to America, and the public protested enough for politicians to call off the war. That's information causing people to make better decisions."

"That's your camouflage cause speaking. In terms of essential events, viewing the carnage caused those who interpreted patriotism in this way to defend their national image. Voluntary enlistments would have gone up because of television coverage."

"You know that?" I sputtered.

"Let's walk." As we stood, she said, "It's an inevitable consequence of maintaining their particular brand of national image from the cradle to the grave, with too little time between the two."

"By the same reasoning, coverage of protesters and draft-dodgers would have contributed to the war by pissing off flag wavers whose influences would have pressured their kids into doing their duty."

"Nice try, and I mean that, but you've got it backwards. The *nature* of the protesters' actions was to peacefully demonstrate for peace in the face of tremendous political and social pressures. In this case, television coverage unified people of like mind, some of whom had chosen to contribute to the carnage and then came back to say no more, while others left everything they loved behind, breathing and intact. Television coverage would have promoted peace because that was the nature of the event."

"You know this from traveling the road of a housewife?" I snapped.

Bonnie held her gaze steady on the pathway for a moment, casually looked my way, then gazing across the water said, "Being a housewife taught me that short-changing experiences one hasn't had gives people's true nature away in interesting ways. One of the better ones my ex-husband taught me was that sarcasm is self-pity dressed in a tuxedo." She drank in a deep breath.

"So the point you've been skirting is that I contributed to warfare because I'm still alive?" I chuckled dismissively.

"And you're a victim." Bonnie pushed on before I could object. "The British rigorously contained their passion until an essentially harmless incident caused them to go to war with Argentina. Those who had committed to their culture's influences died in the name of a stiff upper lip, as did the Argentines die for whatever illusion they thought they had to maintain." She rubbed my arm. "You put yourself in harm's way because your media culture made the idea not just acceptable but

[146]

appealing, and you became a part of the conflict you went to observe. It could have been a lot worse than going to jail for nothing."

"Maybe not for nothing; we drew attention to the kind of government in power."

"Like your friends drew attention to the startling revelation that wars kill non-combatants?" she waived their lives aside. "I know this makes you angry, but if there were no truth to what I'm saying, you'd be laughing your ass off at the crazy broad who thinks she knows anything about journalism or warfare."

"Maybe I'm keeping that to myself."

"You're certainly keeping a great deal from yourself."

"Hard to know the difference," I muttered.

"Difficult to know the difference; concrete is hard."

"Shit—what's with the grammar lesson, now?"

"I'm trying to leave no gaps in our assumptions, which is especially important now that you're beginning to change them." She looked into my eyes and declared, "You're walking away from the slaughter of your illusions, but you don't know where to go." Bonnie stopped, flung her arms open wide and declared to the entire Lower Mainland, maybe as far as Bellingham, Washington, "I'm here! I'm right here!"

I knew it was asinine, but I said it anyway. "I can see you."

Bonnie's jubilant expression collapsed like Ali's opponents taking a head shot. Gathering her composure, she started to walk and said, "Try to suspend judgement as I put down another plank of logic for you to cross. Men have been conditioned to malice under other banners, so the true nature of their actions is no clearer to them than the networks' activities were to them or to you. That has been my point since we talked about another level of perception; we're not aware of the influences of our actions. Fighting for peace is a prime example of how we proudly sacrifice children to our illusions, which are fostered by those who benefit from them."

"History shows us that sacrifice is sometimes necessary. Your merchants did that." I raised my brow.

"They sacrificed nothing to a negative momentum, which is what you need to continue a war."

"Which ends in peace."

"That's the cruel illusion." She leaned my way. "Yes or no, expend energy toward the south and you create a momentum heading south?"

"All else being equal, sure."

[147]

"It follows that fighting can only feed fighting because the reason for fighting isn't being addressed. That momentum is stored in beliefs passed on to children, and on it goes."

"Okay, so where does it all start?"

Expelling a breath, she said, "For the most part, men form the governments who con the public in order to be elected, then they twist the power of their office that we grant to them into the belief that they are powerful themselves. Public concerns must pass through this delusion before they will serve the public and then only within the constraints of serving themselves another election victory. This process of selective representation demands explanations that officials route through an impersonal bureaucracy. Between those machinations and the blind alley of official secrets, inquisitors are worn down, account-ability becomes diffused, and important issues are reduced to a series of petty attacks on minor predators in the food chain and nothing changes. We accept this dog and pony show because we believe the bureaucracy is somehow separate from those who comprise it, as if it were an entity in its own right. After their convolutions have conned us into thinking we're not in charge, we're ripe to reclaim our sense of power through the exterior quests politicians have an interest in blaming as the source our problems, or claim will be future problems because we don't demand that our government perform responsibly if we don't demand it of ourselves."

"We enforce responsibility by holding elections."

"A process that comes without a minimum guarantee of perfor-mance, based on less than a sixty percent turnout split four party ways? I don't think so."

"Forcing a turnout would go against the principles we're turning out for."

"The results of the process are acceptable under the circumstances?"

"The circumstance of democracy, sure."

"If you're the victim of that greater good?"

I saw the traps of patriotism etc. looming, so I said, "The alternative being what your people would do—nothing?" I began saying this sarcastically but I lost steam to the realization that this would work.

"Absolutely! No government would last a second without the consent of the public. If we don't want a war, they can't make one, and we don't need to overthrow anything. We only have to withdraw our permission as a proactive choice." She took a breath of consideration. "We'd be taking back the power we granted them because they're abusing it."

[148]

"If you could save a million people by sacrificing yourself, would you do it?"

"Are you now arguing in favour of the numbers game, and that the networks were right to throw you away?"

"I'm trying to take a step away from my description of events to viewing the essence of them," I said seriously.

"If I sacrificed myself," Bonnie said, taking my arm in hers, "it would be as an informed decision uncluttered by losing face if I declined. I would not bow to the demands of the few who put the million at risk or the pleas of those who agreed to be put at risk."

"Agreed?"

"Through whatever combination of inaction and poor choices suited their beliefs, victims consent to the danger, no different than standing next to bullies or giving your uninformed consent to participate in the conflicts you thought you were observing." She squeezed my arm. "I know your writings are loaded with good people facing bad situations, and there are some particularly cruel acts between the two that you haven't resolved in your own mind. I also know that working in the shadow of war's wraith hardened your heart while restricting your vision to things that justify your jaded views." She squeezed again. "The essence of your written work is about moving out of your shadow secrets, which you have constructed to reflect the craftiness of cruelties' effects on all of you. Your Silent Knowledge of that goal won't let you slough it off because truth is relentless. Next time, bring some of your work, anything at all, and I'll try to show you how you are shinning a light into those shadows."

I didn't mention the personal cage issue, and we ended our formal meeting.

Back on my side of the bay, I put a dozen chicken legs on the bar-becue and opened my first contemplative beer because, the inherent strangeness of our relationship aside, something wasn't right. Every time we got together, Bonnie intimidated, ignored, insulted, or toyed with me, sometimes all four, and her explanation of research wasn't cutting it. She was too intense, too moody, and too flighty. Like two people, for that matter.

Mulling over our circumstance loosened a niggling thought, which like an embolism traveled to the heart of the matter: no writers I had ever known scribbled on top of anything other than first drafts. They made notes in margins or between the lines, and none of them folded their coveted inspirations other than those written on bar room napkins. From this, I realised Bonnie had to be knocking off pages as she

[149]

thought were required to interest me, and the only reason to do this was to create the appearance of her story being complete, not just unpolished or somehow misaligned. It explained why some scenes were watertight and others required preliminary explanations, which then explained her quick bail-outs through contrived flashes of temper to derail my inquiries.

The chicken bursting into flames triggered a deeper insight: Bonnie damned-well knew that her characters ability "to know" punched a huge hole in her story. To her credit, she had incorporated a surreptitious plea for the audience to suspend their disbelief, but she was smart enough to know this alone wouldn't cut it. She had to have reached the end of her options and was looking for a bigger kind of magic to fill the hole her gimmicks had dug, instead of scrapping unworkable premises.

I apologized to the tenants upstairs for the acrid smoke then I ate my blackened chicken with triumph. An unfinished story meant the path to starting the grant application was wide open. I didn't have to understand all of her premises. I could make up something that would fit them so far, as had to be her goal anyway, and update the outline if I learned anything interesting before I submitted the application.

I finished dinner wearing the cloak of confidence that Bonnie wore so snugly, and though the fit was on the smug side when I called to test the temperature of our relationship, her renewed warmth confirmed that she was afraid of losing the filter she needed to test new endings.

In the morning, ahead of plan, I called Rogers Communications to request a grant application before rough drafting a few scenes.

[150]

Chapter Sixteen
Changing History

Sitting on her couch the next afternoon, Bonnie gave me a scene in which a group of students were quietly chanting in a circle around a smaller group, who were meditating on objects in their hands. In the foreground, a young girl was dancing repetitive steps while a teacher quietly explained to everyone that by intentionally occupying her incessant here-and-now thoughts she was silencing her internal dialogue, after which she could experience a number of things.

One possibility was to have a pure recollection—full disclosure of a distant or suppressed memory. Another possibility was to enter a state of theme-like dreaming to access key memories of past lifetimes, or she could receive new knowledge directly. Any of these experiences helped to pave the way for more fantastic experiences. However, the teacher warned the group, information gained in any of these conditions belonged to that state of awareness, so the experience always required interpretation into physically related terms. It was not uncommon for an epiphany in one state of awareness to become a simple sense of understanding in another. It also took effort and practice to hold focus when making the transition and bring back what you had learned because to experience a mural of deep knowledge was useless until the student could explain what they saw. And language, as physically related symbolism, was often not enough to cope with aural and pictorial symbolism.

When asked for an example of a student having a problem with translation, the teacher said that seeing auras around trees proved to the observer that trees are conscious entities, not merely metabolically alive, the knowledge of which advises the observer to respect trees. The observer can easily bring back this knowledge, but they might not be able to explain a deep sense of sadness that comes with it. If the observer had explored their perceptions to the extent of aligning their own consciousness with the tree's, as an instant comprehension, they would have understood how to interpret colours of consciousness and be able to deduce the health and mood of not only trees but of other creatures because there is a continuity to representative colours. In this

[151]

and the subsequent aligning with other forms of consciousness, they may also realize that all things are connected, and in their own way, everything shares a sense of history in which contact with humans has always been detrimental; only mankind acts as if everything is a personal resource. Because of this, no consciousness welcomes mankind. It is an infinitely sad reality.

Bonnie's writings next described two personal experiences of students, one of which was little more than curious to the recipient, and the other profoundly moving.

That was it.

"Chunky," I said, handing the pages to Bonnie. "Where does it fit?"

"Practicing these arts made them considerably more aware of the world around them because in time they will need to be attuned to the ambiance of circumstances like you were when you had to be."

"I didn't stare at poppies in the Bekaa Valley."

"I didn't say you instigated the awareness. Something set aside your self-interest long enough to allow information to filter through."

"Is it necessary for the audience to understand the rituals, or can you show them as background?"

"Rituals are based on arts that have lost their meaning with time. These arts," she said, tapping the pages, "are formidable practices of personal power designed to evolve designated individuals. We'll make that clear to the audience."

"Designated, meaning teachers are nasty to weed out the ones who wouldn't make good magic?"

"Nasty?"

"The girl staring at a crystal has a tearful knowing about why her teacher is so difficult to get along with. I'm guessing that difficult in your world is related to putting kids in cages."

"The student saw through her personal mask to see beliefs she didn't realize she had. This knowledge changed her destiny from an average person's evolutionary path to a direct approach to self-evolvement. By this time," she tapped the page, "our audience will understand that she had crossed the bridge of reason, from old beliefs in preceding chapters, where her teacher was methodically tearing them down. With that preparation, she was able to make the leap from reason to accessing Silent Knowledge and claiming knowledge directly through pure understanding." She flashed a grin. "The student understood specifically how she had been fooled by a convincing world, and that knowledge put her in charge of her path. With training, the same thing might have happened to you after your experiences in Argentina."

[152]

"It did. I went freelance."

"In terms of essential acts," Bonnie said, getting up to stretch her legs, "you went from an unwitting sacrifice to a volunteer pawn, risking it all for the cause of compensation. Nothing changed, other than fast-tracking your path here."

"Thanks," wasn't the first thing I thought to say, but it was for the best. She didn't know better.

"I know that's a hard one to swallow, when you think you've learned key knowledge from a pivotal experience that has expanded to taint so much of your view. I earned my master's degree in uninformed consent at the expense of everyone in my family, but I don't blame myself or them for the things we didn't know. There'd be too much getting in the way of my journey now."

"You're a forgiving person," I said amicably.

"For some reason you're not."

"I don't see the point of taking a shot at the one person you say can help you," I said casually.

Bonnie's gaze seemed strained, then nodding to herself, she said, "You are correct. It's time to pull the big picture together, so you can see how our interactions fit into the grand scheme of my plot." She went to the rocking chair, tucked her feet beneath her butt and folded her hands in a Buddha-like pose. Breathing deeply, Bonnie rocked a few times before she bluntly said, "I psychically accessed the details of my society. I'm writing a true story."

"You said you researched Egypt at the University of British Columbia?" I said, too stunned to attack the principle absurdity.

"I said I researched what our scientists believe about ancient Egyptian culture." She stopped rocking. "My twentieth century characters will accurately represent our current beliefs about ancient Egyptian society, but mine existed thousands of years before the one we assume to be the first Egyptian dynasty. The teaching entities you have yet to read about, beyond their initial surreptitious contacts with the archaeologists, will tell them how mankind's social order attempted to evolve, failed, and what they intend to do about it."

"The second coming of Christ theme?" I said, shaking my head.

Bonnie nodded, and resumed rocking. "Osiris was a mystic of the most profound order, psychically linked to a teaching entity who was older than time. Various chapters will introduce the entity's guidelines for productive living, which resulted in a culture that outlasted all other organized societies in history because the population had been con-

[153]

ditioned to acting in accordance with the principles of peace and prosperity."

"What happened to them?" I said, looking around the room as if for clues to their mysterious disappearance.

"Bloodline heirs eventually killed the seers, or drove them into hiding because the seers knew who was supposed to become the next leader when the succession changed from being a family affair. This was the beginning of the end of their culture because only seers had the energy to teach the disciplines required to access and handle cosmic knowledge. Pretenders changed what little they knew into rigid rites and rituals for a public that was only generally aware of the abstract principles, and not knowing better, they paid homage to common thinkers as the source of universal knowledge. This was the killing blow because it fundamentally subverted the free expression of individuality, and as you know, repression is the stuff of rebellion."

"I get that much," I managed to say respectfully, "except the only consistency in family dictatorships I've ever heard about is the paranoid defence of their status. The bloodline heirs must have thought and our audience will think that the seers changed the rules because of personal agendas."

"We will explain that Spirit chooses its placement in physical life and that the first generations of leaders had to be safely born into the same family because it was ideal for launching cultural change. That said, it was flawed in the long term because their life experiences were vastly different from the average person's; they couldn't relate to their core assumptions, not unlike you and I when we first met?" she grinned slyly.

Or now. "Got it," I said, struggling to put myself in the position of a student first hearing this crap.

"To resolve that problem, prospective leaders were born into normal society and readied for training by having pure experiences in the ways of their world; they had no knowledge of their probable destiny to taint their approach to daily life. In this way, they embraced the convictions of their culture, and by undergoing extensive retraining, they understood what the average person was really like and how they became that way. In the first passages you read, the baker knew that an ordinary girl was destined to become a leader?" Bonnie raised her brow.

"Sure, but she didn't know."

"You've heard the expression, the teacher arrives when the student is ready?"

"Around the same time I was pondering the sound of one hand clapping," I quipped, hoping she would lighten up and 'remind' me that were role-playing.

"There's nothing to be afraid of," she scolded me. "Ready means able, not willing, because the prospect's assumptions are fixed in the mundane—in reason. This circumstance requires that the teacher arrive in disguise to probe the prospect's personality before coaxing them into an intricate teaching technique for direct evolutionary development."

"Why not explain what they intend to do, then draw from the people who were interested?"

"Volunteers don't have the energy to learn the ways of power, which is why Spirit chooses candidates by giving signs to a teacher." She shrugged. "It wasn't a completely blind ruse. If you recall, the baker told Aleena what his true interests were, and how he was going to teach her at their first meeting. And their second, and third, for that matter."

"Not unless you've added that to those scenes."

"He did it in between the lines." She leaned forward. "Their initial conversation was about introducing the idea of interpreting experiences in a different way, and how understanding the essence of these experiences propels personal evolution."

"Like we did—I remember. So?"

"So other conversations were about specific beliefs and their attendant behaviours that stand in the way of seeing things clearly." She waited for me to say something.

"Also like us, I get it—you were using me before I knew what you were trying to do," I said flatly.

"At another level of awareness, the student knows exactly what the offer is about so there is no need to risk frightening them off before events overtake their current views."

"You presumed I was a student."

"For now, let's just say that I knew you were. That said, there's a rule that says a teacher must tell the student what they're up to." Bonnie dipped her head to look over her nose, as if she was wearing glasses, "not how they're going to do it." She rocked again.

"Which you'll justify by claiming you're tricking me into something good, as opposed to deceiving me for your purpose of writing a screenplay?"

It took all of my energy not to walk out.

"Between lives," she said casually, taking my focus back to the fantasy world of her screenplay, "the teacher agrees to advise the student of their potential destiny when they meet in physical life and the road they will have to travel to achieve it. When they do meet, the teacher appears to be evasive when they're actually awakening the student to their agreement. Essentially, they're saying, 'I know you won't remember this in the traditional sense, but I also know that you know more than you think you know, and I'm speaking to that level of your awareness. Here's the scoop: the first part of your physical quest was to be fully indoctrinated to the beliefs and circumstances that create and recreate poor circumstances. You purposefully chose challenges to suit your personality flaws, which blossomed according to the time and place and to whom you were born, as well as the people you would meet because of these choices. All of the years we've spent apart and the people we have helped or hurt readied both of us for this meeting. Now, my first job is to show you that your interpretation of your experiences is nonsense, and I will do this in apparently separate ways. In the practical terms of breaking you free of society's conditioned reasoning and the rationalizing your personality flaws demand, I will teach you to view things in terms of core events. Simplistically, I will teach you logic. You will fight me as if you are fighting for your life because you are fighting for the life you know as I lead you kicking and screaming into seeing things as they really are. In that regard, I will introduce you to the abstraction of energy, specifically that physical reality is an illusion; it is one description of the manifestation of energy in one version of endless versions of reality.'" She slowed her rocking motion. "It is the teacher's hope that the student will piece the two together and claim as their own knowledge that the student is fighting a description—a description of their beliefs, nothing more and nothing personal. When the student gets their first real glimpse of how this is true, the teacher can more actively tear down old beliefs while leading the student to building logical bridges to the student's core events that shaped them. This is the only way they'll trust what they learn when their platform of reasoning turns into a gangplank. But," she said, head cocked with a realization, "you're familiar with the idea that the journey is one way; you know there's no going back, right?"

"When you see something as it really is? Sure."

She stopped rocking. "I'm confirming that you understand that an event like meeting Spirit would be striking a bell you can't unring. Something fundamental about your way of life would have to change."

"Consider it confirmed."

Bonnie continued rocking. "Tartuu modeled two points of view during his conversations with Aleena and connected them with a chain

[156]

of what were to her embarrassing self-interests. One view was her interpretation of the world in general, her experiences in it specifically, and where she thought these would take her. The other view was through his insights about her life, and where he knew the momentum of her beliefs would have to take her. At each meeting, he removed a step in her reasoning, polished it to reflect the truth, and replaced the span between their perspectives. Doing this put a constant strain on their relationship because as the days passed and the gaps between the beliefs she could rely on moved further apart, other views swayed from the loss of support because our beliefs are entangled. Unconsciously recognizing that she is losing her fight to maintain what have become isolated views, she will try to manipulate their relationship by bargaining for exceptions to his insights or threaten to leave. This will cue Tartuu to begin a final tug because she's ready to fall off her cherished opinions. This tug can take many forms, but the point is to cause her to willingly review all that she has been taught, so there will be times when he has to risk shocking her into making a leap of faith –and logic. If she's more ready than he knows, it's possible that she could leap directly from her reason to his logic. That would be a great day."

"And if she's less ready that he thinks?"

"She may quit."

"Couldn't Spirit ring the bell?"

"Is that what you would want to happen?"

"It would be stupid to go that far then pass on the opportunity."

"You passed on the opportunity to explore a terrific ending with your screenplay." She raised her hand to stifle my protest. "I'm saying it's possible for a smart person to pass on a grand opportunity, if at the time he's somehow not ready for it."

"Fair enough, but I don't see how a student could quit if Spirit chose them? How do you explain that mistake?"

"It's not about Spirit's judgement. It's about the student's free will."

"Wouldn't ringing the bell screw that up?"

"Not if the student agreed to it."

"If your people really existed, they must have left some evidence behind?" I said, stalemated on that point.

"It will be found in our lifetime." She shrugged a tiny effort. "It will still take time to convince people, though."

"But at some level we will understand it?" I tried not to scoff.

"Any assault on a core assumption becomes an insult to our certainty about everything, so leaders in politics, religion, and science will attack the authenticity of the finds and the integrity of those who

[157]

analyze them. The evidence will eventually rule because it's the nature of truth to stand squarely in one's way. Closing our eyes won't make it go away."

"What's the core assault about? Archaeologists find new stuff all of the time?"

Puzzled, then amused, she said, "They will discover writings that claim we're nearing the end of civilization as we know it, and teachers are coming back to help us change our ways. They'll also list what was to them future events that will have taken place and some that are still to come."

"This rescue—it's really about all of humanity–end of the world stuff?"

"Yes, but there will be people who won't want to change." She leaned back. "I'm not sure when to reveal the next step in the training, because..."

"Training of the rescuers—that's who your special people are? Why them?"

"They are universally old, they volunteered, they kept alive the core knowledge of how to live properly, how to teach, and the magical arts until they can all gather for the final phase." She leaned back. "I'm afraid if I give too much away, too soon, I could lose credibility."

"I wouldn't worry about that, now," I said flatly, looking at the clock on the credenza. "Shit, it's three-thirty. I've got to go."

I stood up and to her silent amusement walked away without making my usual promise of seeing her tomorrow.

"Bring some of your work the next time," she belatedly said. "We still haven't dealt with your cage."

I didn't reply as the door closed behind me.

Stunned by her audacity, I stopped at a pub before heading across the bridge, but by the time I ordered my third round, I was feeling foolish: Bonnie had invested all of her money, friendships, and as far as I could tell every waking moment her kids didn't need her to writing, and in that context her critically serious role-playing made some sense, some because why she needed to gauge a neophyte's reaction to a teacher's claim of talking to spirits about the end of the world should have been more than obvious. I went home wondering why she tested this, and trying to imagine how she would convince anyone that the universe was here and training people.

Chapter Seventeen
Losing Reason

I arrived at her house the next morning with two chapters for her to assess. The first one, an apology for my rude exit the day before, graphically demonstrated that my plot worked without the influence of the great unseen. I left the second chapter, a polished effort that demonstrated LeBlanc was not an idiot, stashed in my bike as a safeguard against her attacking the first one for being too impersonal.

Knocking twice, I let myself in, and as I climbed the mid-house staircase said a jaunty, "Good morning."

"Coffee's ready," Bonnie said, from the kitchen as if I had gone to the bathroom and not home for the night. "If the undercurrent of a culture's ideals is convoluted, it's inevitable that good people will integrate fear into their daily way of life and call it something else."

"The stress of daily living," I said, setting my envelope on the hallway table before walking into the kitchen.

Standing by the sink, Bonnie nodded toward the nook table for me to take a seat, as she said, "You can't live in between fact and fiction without confusing what you want with what you think is necessary or eventually taking what you think you're entitled to. For example," she said, to put us on the same page, "America's right to bear arms was about militias defending the country at a time when they didn't have a standing army. Two hundred years later, they've armed themselves to the teeth without embracing the underlying responsibilities that go with maintaining personal rights. Now they're defending themselves from themselves, which is the antithesis of living free." Bonnie came to the table with two mugs and added a third of a cup of milk to hers from a ceramic, jersey cow pitcher.

"Are we in an anti-American mode this morning?"

"Not at all," she said, surprised. "I've always been treated well there. I'm making observations about a country we're both familiar with because it's in a unique position to institute positive global change." She sipped her coffee. "Making them the goat also doesn't offend you like it would if I used Canada."

Cutting short a test sip with a chuckled slurp that trickled through my beard, I said, "You know I don't wave flags."

"You are a soldier at heart," she said, handing me a serviette. "You would rather kill our relationship than risk evicting your convictions by taking the time to evaluate mine, even in a written work. Push that behaviour to the extreme, and I'm an enemy of your state of mind. The fact is, you're dangerous to me," she said casually.

"That's a good hook," I said, understanding that she was getting even for my quick exit the day before. I dabbed at my lips, and said, "But you can't surprise me with crooked or crappy Canadian politicians. I've covered them from all sides."

"It's much more than a hook in my work," she replied. "Yesterday, you ran out of here when I offended your reason. What do you think would have happened if I had stood in your way?" she tilted her head questioningly.

"What you said was absurd on its face, so I gave myself the space to think about the context of what you said—research, which I obviously did because I'm here."

"What would you have done if I had stood my ground?" she persisted.

"Go over the balcony."

"And the next time?"

"You can't know what anyone would do from one moment to the next. People are too complex to be reduced to a disco ball or a tenth decision."

Bonnie blew across the top of her drink to create a casual air because her tea didn't need cooling, then with a dainty sip she set her cup on the table. "Thinking we're complex makes us feel safe and important, as if intricacy had some bearing on our pre-eminence or vulnerability. The most affronting fact I've claimed as my own know-ledge so far in my research," she said wryly, "is how much we are alike."

"Stop, you're making me blush."

"How much we are all alike," she clarified her statement.

"Uh huh, how so?"

"We accept a world in which businesses are bereft of social con-science, entertainment is based on violence, and where professions that require the intellectual prowess of professional wrestling are wor-shipped and rewarded accordingly. You can't evolve a society that way, let alone sustain a world."

"Your teachers knew there was no point in harping at morons about intricate personal development techniques when even your special people struggled with it. So what's your point?" Talk about piety.

"I didn't say we were all morons."

"Intellectual prowess of wrestling?"

"I didn't say wrestlers lack intellect, there's just little evidence of it in their sport, which directly correlates to the inhabitants of a global island with limited resources."

"Sounds like you're insulting everyone who you expect to understand principles like timeless momentum by tying their shoelaces backwards."

"And now I see that to forestall scorn from our audience I have to establish the veracity of celestial intelligence right away."

"Just hang on." It took me a few seconds to pull together what had happened since I walked up the stairs. "The point of this is to see how poorly Americans would receive news of how you view them by accusing me of being offended by Canadian flaws, that I am a soldier, a moron, or all of the above?"

"It's great that you're beginning to think in terms of assessments; it means you're confronting your sense of self-importance," she replied, "but none of the above is the answer. I was checking your point of view about living in between fact and fiction, and you confirmed that your general state of mind is fearful about that idea, which makes my point."

I slid my cup out of harm's way and pretended to read a tabloid newspaper. "Updating the gimmick of time travel to a New Age format, this film—what's it called?" I said.

"Probably Time—and Time Again."

"I think that's been done—doesn't matter." I pretended to read. "'Time and Time Again tip-toes the audience away from apparently innocent encounters in an ancient marketplace to trot us through time toward global cataclysms the film claims we are facing now. Secretly, in each of three incarnations the heroes painstaking recruit incorrigible youths to become part of a utopian culture that will take over when all the stupid people die by their own hand. To the screenwriters' credit, the script avoids directly aligning the audience with the dense and doomed by plaguing endearing wizards with foibles that encompass a broad range of mental and emotional problems. To disguise the discrepancy of unstable characters impressing criminally closed minds, unseen entities oversee the teaching process. However, by the rule of maintaining free will they must remain phantom characters capable of

[161]

generating omens and facilitating psychic suggestions only, which means the wizards have to consider the pros and cons of taking God's advice. Otherwise, being able to know things ahead of time, which still might be wrong because free will can change things, guts the ingenuity of a story that could have been a cult thriller cleverly constructed to create panic in the meek who shall inherit the debris." I looked up. "That's what they'll be thinking."

"You really have thought about my story!" Bonnie gushed.

"Enough to know you've trapped yourself."

"In what way?" she said without flinching.

"I just told you: you have extraordinary beings teaching exceptional people how to better their lives, and there's no guarantee that they'll get it, when the larger point of nurturing them through time is to train other teachers how to teach more unwilling people the same lessons. I know you intend to bridge that gap with meta-stuff or outright magic, but those fixes are never enough."

"Three things," she said, displaying three fingers. "You don't know how Spirit works, you are underestimating the impact of hearing predictions that invariably come true, and you have no need to be scornful."

"Three things," I replied. "Are you now saying your character's predictions will come true, that claiming they could be wrong some-how doesn't apply to them? And I am not scorning you, I answered your question."

"You're review was unusually succinct, which you become when you are pissed at me, regardless of your tone, and I said there were points of change beyond which an event will manifest. Do you think I would have the forerunners reveal maybes to the general population?"

"You also said scaring people into doing anything doesn't work."

"All we can do is offer people a clear view of the way things are, what they can do to better themselves, and tell them to not be afraid of making changes before they have no choice. You know what that's like, so you also know that it's your own fault."

"What about putting cage doors in cinemas?" I quipped.

Bonnie smirked. "Did you bring me something to read?" she said, taking the escape route I had offered.

My escalating emotions took a rest as I got up to retrieve the pages from the hallway. On the way, Bonnie said, "What did you mean when you said you've covered Canadian politicians from all sides?"

"When I was stuck in Argentina, my brother got the Minister of External Affairs private home number and, as I understand it," I said, coming back into the room, "acting familiar, like a colleague, he asked him about our situation. The Minister confided that he didn't have a clue what the caller was talking about, two days after we were arrested. Eventually, my brother's questions gave away that the minister wasn't speaking with someone he knew. After David finished telling me about their exchange, he added a heartfelt, 'Any Canadian in trouble overseas is fucked, so take it easy from now on.'" I handed her my chapter, and said, "Politics in Canada is still like the Kennedy era; lots of people know who is screwing who, figuratively and literally, but they'd lose access if they said anything because it's difficult to prove the insider trading, corporate thieves, contract kick-backs in forms other than money, and at least one kiddy-diddler."

Bonnie looked up sharply, admonishingly, and sadly.

"Sorry about the phrasing, I don't mean to lessen the brutality of the act. Anyway, I returned the effort when I was on a candidate follow-shoot—intimate access for days. I told my brother that our guy was very smooth, but beneath the oil slick he took hubris and raging at those close to him to a new level. I told Dave not the vote for him, that the bastard would plunder our pockets and that a year or so after he left office he would have an unaccountably comfortable life style." I shrugged. "Turns out I wasn't far off."

"Anything else?"

"I've talked to more than one ambassador who was not assigned to Canada, and to many of their aids over the years about Canadian politics...we're pretty much a joke yoked to American interests because they have us by the economic short and curlies."

"This annoys you?" she said, as if I of all people shouldn't be surprised.

"Not on its face; it's the way of the world."

"Then what?"

"I think they'll eventually squeeze us into a war, and my brother's kids could be killed for soft wood exports."

Bonnie contemplated my remark, as she looked at my pages, and said, "I think you may be right." She began reading.

I walked out to the balcony and watched the world go its way until she was finished reading. When I saw that she had begun to review some pages I came back inside.

"The narrative is so stark," she said as I slid the glass door closed behind me, "that I didn't realize how insightful some of your characters were on the first read through."

"Thanks, I think."

Uncoiling her legs, Bonnie sat up. "Clubbing readers with information at the same time you're assaulting them with action is a good way to distract them while you're setting up things to come. Except in here," she raised the pages to my eye level, "you focus on the predicament and not enough on the people."

"Readers have to know what being under fire is like."

"Isn't that one of the things you can't explain?"

"I had to take a shot at it to make my characters' thoughts credible."

"Hmm." Examining a point in space between us, she said, "You might be undermining your credibility by having obviously smart people repeatedly make Herculean efforts to get out of trouble of their own design." She focused on me, "Make the point that their beliefs led them into the trouble they're experiencing, and you've got endless dramatic possibilities because the reader will see how they contribute to their own fate."

A wise man would have heard the opening shots of a rebuttal to his film review, and said something to take the edge off.

"They didn't design anything, and there's endless potential in Leblanc's dialogue. Got any wine?" I said instead.

Bonnie got up and walking toward the kitchen, she said, "Have you got something to show me on LeBlanc?"

"In my bike pack."

"Meet you back at the couch," she said, disappearing around the corner, and I went to get the pages.

When I came back, Bonnie had filled a single glass of wine and set the bottle on the coffee table to occupy me while she read.

"It needs polish," I said, handing her the pages.

"Don't we all."

"Don't you ever let up?"

"I don't know." Her eyes fell to the top page. "I'm only thirty-eight."

She read the following:

You Taught Me Well   The Good Guys: Pt 2   Page 107

Rolling swells from a decaying hangover caused me to jostle a slightly built man in the baggage claims area, who in an unhurried motion pulled up his shirt to expose the handle of a pistol. Grinning crookedly at his extra-large companion, in Spanglish he told me that the shoot-to-kill curfew began in an hour and that the city was thirty minutes away, "Mas y meno." His buddy said something about the guerrillas owning the night and that I should be in a hurry but not to meet them. There is always tomorrow. He chuckled. My brain was on life support, but I knew something wasn't right about the too-polite exchange: I apologized profusely for the bump and thanked them profoundly for the advice. Corrupting stilted laughs with manly phlegm, the duo went their way.

I wouldn't have thought more about the incident, except I chanced to see them walk through immigration not just un-challenged but almost entirely unacknowledged, had it not been for a pudgy official awkwardly changing a salute into a head scratch.

Helping LeBlanc gather our eighteen corrugated aluminum equipment cases, I mentally juggled the tricky little bugger of language that had eluded me in high school French and Latin, possession, to see which variations of what I thought I had been told rang true. These included, "The curfew begins in an hour, more or less. The city is more or less thirty minutes away, the guerrillas more or less own the night. There is always tomorrow... more or less—" a version my mind attached to something my Uruguayan bartender in Toronto had said about Hispanic cultures. "Manana literally means tomorrow," she said, "but for practical purposes it means 'not today'. For gringo presna covering a revolution, they're probably implying tomorrow might never come."

"I'm not sure who I should be afraid of," I told LeBlanc as we stacked cases in front of an immigration desk. "I think I was just threatened by the good guys."

"Saaaw it," LeBlanc drawled, sucking on the last of his cigarette. "Could beeeee," he said, exhaling a plume, "the nuns bumped into your guys, as well," referring to four missionary nuns who had been killed on the road between the airport and San Salvador six days earlier.

"Funny."

"Not shitten ya." He lit another smoke from the butt and stuck the nub into a red, sand bucket ashtray. "A quick chat to find out where they're going, offer some friendly advice... Si-si!" he broke off our conversation to suddenly exclaim to an inspector, waving both hands toward the carton of cigarettes. "Take them all...da nada, da nada," he said, judiciously exploiting his entire Spanish vocabulary by doubling up on it.

This exchange prompted my official to squint at the fine print of the unopened toothpaste I had bought at the Syracuse airport. Looking grave, he ran a finger down the tube and said something about the environment. I shrugged my ignorance. Leblanc immed-iately reached into his personal wash kit, retrieved a twisted tube of Pepsodent, and offered it to his own man for inspection.

"Es correct," the customs man said, pushing LeBlanc's hand away.

My guy held my tube up to my eyes, and grimacing like we were downwind of a hog farm, ran a dirty fingernail underneath print so tiny that I needed the plastic magnifying glass on my army knife to read sodium monoflourophosphate.

While I was doing this, the official impatiently repeated, "Tienes receta," then in fractured English, "Papel medico?"

"Just give it to him," LeBlanc said, stretching a smile as if making room for extra teeth.

"He wants a prescription for Crest, for Christ's sake," I protested.

"J.R.," Robbie said, using my initials to end our discussion, "If he confiscates it, you're a fuckin' drug runner."

"Ahhhh!" I exclaimed, "I have another tube in the side pocket." For your wife, you thieving prick.

"Si-si!" Robbie exclaimed, in a second explosion of philanthropy as a third inspector, attracted by the commotion, confiscated his Yankee's jersey for containing a banned dye that apparently wouldn't bother his son.

The speed of the double rip-off cued Robbie to perils unseen, and he jerked me back a step that the surprise had me stumble into three before he steadied me. "Tick fucking tock," he hissed, and I shut the hell up as the pieces came together for me.

Tick: a guerrilla, terrorist, or freedom fighter by any name kills people. If his side loses, he's a murderer. If he wins, tock, he becomes the minister of defence. During the transitional blood bath, there is no practical difference between groups, and we were definitely in the transition time.

The three officials exchanged pleased glances over my public diminishing, and processing us became silently efficient and moronically transparent when they confiscated our chalecos – bullet proof vests: The senior man claimed the guerrillas would go for a head shot then take them from our corpses, so confiscating them made things safer for us. Protesting their rational ensured that their inspection of our equipment cases was meticulous, "In case there are other things the guerrillas can use, signor."

One official would tisk over an item, another would confirm the problem, their boss with the Yankee's jersey would raise an accusatory eye at one of us, and we would both nod our appreciation that we weren't being arrested for trying to smuggle toiletries into El Salvador.

Max's water purification pills and Tylenol went into a milk crate bin behind the inspection table shortly after his Cottonelle disap-

[166]

peared under the examining table. Brian was allowed to keep his contact lens solution, after he put some in his eyes, as well as a pre-squeezed tube of haemorrhoid ointment, the use of which they did not required him to demonstrate. Leblanc lost nothing he didn't plan on losing because the carton of smokes was a plant intended to influence how our equipment would be inspected. As it turned out, the Yankee's shirt went to the right guy: Every country requires an import/export carnet—copious forms listing serial numbers and the value of each piece of equipment. More often than not, officials pointed to a few expensive items and asked us to prove that they work. If they didn't ask, the inspection could be lengthy; five hours was our personal record. To avoid bettering this time, while junior agents finished sorting through our personal items for their family's benefit, LeBlanc took our paperwork to their boss and mimed the suggestion that he first look at the items listed on page two. Walking a few steps away, the official turned the cover page, pondered the list as if it were a Zen riddle, then still facing away he said, "Camera."

Robbie didn't have it out of the case before the official said, "You go." Resting the carnet on an empty examining table, he stamped and signed the temporary import sheet, while his underlings stopped their search and motioned for the rest of us to pass through.

"Fuckin' good guys," LeBlanc chortled as we pushed two heavily laden carts out of the terminal.

Loading our gear into a red Volkswagen van, out of earshot of our driver, Mad Max asked Rob what he had said to the supervisor to hasten our departure. LeBlanc came clean, and Max must have damaged something internally to create the kind of hiss that came with his refusal to authorize the bribe.

Rob shrugged, and looking appreciatively at the setting sun wistfully said, "Might not fuckin' matter."

We finished loading our gear within a strained silence, stacking cases so that when we were done only our driver, Carlos, and Rob could see out of the front window while we drove into the guerrilla's gathering darkness toward the good guy's curfew. Tick fucking tock.

On the way, dust, dimness, and suddenly braking for suspension cracking holes on the broken road had Rob swearing for reasons we could not see, and he did not explain. This unnerving practice turbocharged our imaginations, raising our collective angst so far above cruising altitude that I didn't dare mention how the authorities had put us directly in the line of fire, covered their ass, and I had pissed away precious minutes by protesting the loss of our vests.

[167]

The reality was that we made it or we didn't, and no official gave a shit which way it went; we had been "officially" warned of the dangers by a high-ranking officer as soon as we got off the plane. He had also told us how long it took to drive to the city and the hours of national curfew, after which the chances of actually meeting the Saviour and not driving to His city's namesake dramatically increased. There were many witnesses.

"I like it," Bonnie said, flipping pages back and forth. "Did you call him Mad Max because he was always angry, or did he put you at risk?" She stood and went to the china cabinet to get a glass for herself.

"He was an extremely bright guy who constantly failed to disguise his distaste for dealing with mere mortals... unionized mortals, anyway."

"Maybe he just didn't like you," she said, with a shrug that signalled a new topic. LeBlanc was your partner?" she said, sitting down again.

"For legal reasons, I will say he is a remarkable facsimile." I lifted the bottle and poured her a glass. Picking up the first pages she had read, Bonnie shifted closer to me, which was more intimidating than cozy under the circumstance.

"What was he like when he was not in situations of conflict?"

"He's a peculiar guy who learned to act as if he's critically inconvenienced most of the time so that people would leave him alone."

"With his secrets," she added to my sentence, as if to herself. "From our conversations, I know that he was more despairing over what he had seen than your serendipitous account of his profane and alcoholic behaviour makes apparent in your writing." She sorted through the material. "If you tone down the surrounding brutality, readers will be able to absorb evocative passages like this." She read a paragraph in which LeBlanc sagely pronounced a new born baby, "fuckin' beautiful," with a cracking voice, then he reverted to his cantankerous self to deal with a directive from Max.

"Explain why he was like that," Bonnie flipped her wrist with a magician's flare, "and voila! You've got the reader looking into the mirror."

I stared at her uncomprehendingly.

"LeBlanc looked into the abyss and it looked back," she said, somehow thinking this was helpful.

"He would have told the abyss to go fuck itself. Or maybe bought it a drink," I said.

[168]

"It's between the lines. It's, it's..." Bonnie stuttered with playful frustration, before inhaling deeply and saying, "He wasn't cheap, was he?"

"What's that got to do with anything?"

"It's not a trick question. You're not seeing the big picture of how his beliefs are the same as your readers taken to the next level, so we're going to another lookout point."

"He was generous to a fault."

"Did he lie, cheat, or steal?"

"He was blunt, he played to win, he congratulated anyone who beat him, and he claimed bribes as other expenses because we all had to. He also made people who didn't know him uncomfortable because his mind and his mouth weren't connected, but he's a good man at heart."

"He's a good man whose heart has been crushed; he became a reflection of his experiences, not a product of their assessment." Sliding the pages into order, Bonnie said, "The first scenes you showed me dishonour him by attempting to shock people at his expense, and the second section makes him look like an ass when his journey reveals the profound aspects of sharing energy with the deranged. You need to build the bridge between him at war and a younger version of him at home. What's that look about-what did I say?"

"Nothing. I had a dream that... nothing. The scenes are graphic because that's the way it was, and LeBlanc's attitude reflects the difficulty of a gifted man trying to cover events that defy representtation. That he's screwed up honours his drive and talent versus the difficulty of dealing with things people can't feel or smell."

"Did I tell you that you're succinct when you're angry? I did—never mind. Anyway, the impression your audience will get is that you're bashing him if you don't develop the character into a whole person." She raised her hand. "I know, you've told me what he thinks and why, but demonstrating his intellect doesn't tell me about the good man that lies beneath his jagged thoughts. Without that, you're pandering to a culture of pseudo-hero worshippers—doubly so if you don't develop scenes beyond a Roadrunner cartoon." She tapped the first section of pages. "You've got chase after chase for no reason other than to have your character's escape, then they go the hotel bar as if they had been delivering newspapers."

"Why would you run if not to escape, and what else would you do when you got away?" I said, perplexed.

Her gaze lingered to confirm my sincerity before she said, "Most of your readers haven't had these extreme experiences, so you should deal with the emotional quandary of your characters not just surviving on the heels of those who didn't but living well minutes later. Readers need to appreciate the deeper influence of those kind of events because as I said, they can make a connection to them." Glancing down, she read from the section I had left at the top of the stairs...a different war.

Less than twenty minutes later the night crews settled across from the rookies sitting with their backs to the street level windows.

"Fifty bucks, within half an hour?" Robbie said, tapping his ear to the bartender.

Releasing a soft fart between his lips at the sucker's bet, Hakim shook his head on the threshold of imperceptibility, as he poured three fingers of forgetfulness into Bryan's glass.

"LeeAnn?" LeBlanc said.

"Up yours," she said, without unfastening her mouth from the rim of her glass.

"A hundred and twenty bucks after twelve minutes," I said as Hakim moved toward Horst.

"Done," Robbie said.

Four minutes later, twilight detonated into a second crimson rain of sinew and calcium spikes piercing the gawking crowd. A moment later, our marble floor shuddered, and untainted hands reached for tables and countertops to steady themselves. Those in the know resisted this natural response, and instead covered their ears before ten, six by twelve foot sections of plate glass bowed in unison, plunging compressed air into every body cavity with a rolling whump that was surprisingly painful to the unwary.

Working his jaw to pop his ears, Horst looked at his watch. "Too late to feed the bird," he said to no one and everyone.

Bonnie looked at me questioningly.

"The second bomb kills the crowd and medics who were attending to the casualties of the first one. Birds are satellites."

She nodded, and continued reading.

Hakim wiped condensation from the base of Bartholomew Edwards' glass, as he sheepishly picked himself off the floor onto which he had plummeted as if he'd seen a thousand dollar bill floating by.

"When is cut off?" he said, reaching for his drink.

"Eight-thirtyish," LeeAnn said, painfully swishing a piece of lemon through her Perrier with a bandaged finger. "Depends on the kind of day and the condition of the driver."

[170]

Tilting his drink toward Edwards, LeBlanc toasted a supportive, "Tick tock, mate. Cheers."

"'Axe?" Nikki and Jolynn said together.

"Two mice ran up the clock," I translated his comment. "The clock struck the one who stopped to ask, what's that noise? The other one dropped to the floor and escaped without injury."

Bryan, who had forgotten more about the Middle East than any three of us put together would ever know, nudged my elbow. "I can't remember why hitting the deck was a good idea."

"Me neither," I said.

Turning to Edwards, he said, "Cheers, we needed that," meaning we all should have been picking up thousand dollar bills.

Edwards nodded with uncertainty as the first wisp of a pungent odour arrived at bar level. Bryan lowered his eyes to read a beer label printed in four of the five languages he could negotiate in a pinch. Soon after, everyone's eyes inspected the architecture of their fingernails lest they influence the decision the multi-million dollar anchorman had to make in the brief stretch of time before another round of sirens echoed through the downtown core.

"I'll be fucked," Edwards said, shifting from one foot to the other, "I shit myself."

"In which case, it won't be anytime soon," LeeAnn said blandly.

"Jockeys or briefs?" Hakim said, seriously concerned about his bar stool.

Turning toward the elevators, Edwards said, "Put that strange fellow's tab on room nine-twenty. His translator's, as well," he said, nodding toward me as I slid the $120 bet across the bar to Robbie.

"Stairs," Nikki said, not raising her voice.

With a chop-step, Bart angled toward the stairwell and said, "Hakim, everyone who's ever done this gets doubles."

Horst glanced toward LeeAnn, who shrugged at Jolynn, who ordered gin ahead of everyone else who had eaten a salad washed in hotel tap water, or who otherwise weren't strangers to an unexpected shit. It was just the way it was.

Bonnie placed the pages on her lap, and a shallow smile faded into contemplation as she closed her eyes, and there she sat. *Tick. Tick. Tick.*

"That scene helps to demonstrate how combat kicks the hell out of normal values. Like I said, context is everything."

"By glamorizing their risk-taking before this scene," she said, "you missed the point that some of them just sat there."

"What point; they were used to it?"

"Exactly."

"Exactly what?"

"There was a time when life and death issues weren't a usual part of their day, a time before the possibility of being shredded by plate glass had them take precautions, a time when they thought about what they had seen, like you did after El Salvador, and events changed them into who they were in this scene. Right or wrong?"

"I'm not saying they didn't."

"Why didn't you investigate why they just sat there?"

"I just told you, they were used to it."

"So used to it that living well immediately afterwards was normal?"

"What else would you do?"

"These news crews are metaphors—they're messages to readers who are lounging in the midst of their unacknowledged dangers, until they reach the point your characters have reached and suddenly find themselves asking what the hell they are doing there, and why they didn't take action?" She began searching through the pages. "You allude to this quandary a number of times." She found her spot and said, "Here, LeBlanc asks himself how killing farmers makes the world a safer place." She looked at me. "This internal dialogue suggests that his personal cause is blowing apart before his eyes."

"I'll have him say it to a buddy," I said, missing the point.

"The question isn't rhetorical." Bonnie shifted on the sofa to give us breathing room. "You implied he's on the verge of realizing that recording depravity for a noble cause doesn't create a revolt against the disgrace of the human condition. His pictures are revolting on their face and perverse in that an audience finds them riveting. More to the point, in that moment he glimpsed his crossroads and now he secretly knows that his bang-bang days are numbered."

"You lost me between depravity and nobility."

"It's in bee-tween," she stretched the word. "He has created a pre-dicament of entangled beliefs: he saw this kind of thing in his first war, knows he will see it in his next one, and secretly fears that his artistry is raising the standard of acceptable atrocity to an audience that's doing nothing about it. That would be the killing blow."

"To what?"

"His humanity. He can barely function as it is." She shuddered as she shook my pages and forcefully said, "This work airs *your* assumptions and internal dramas. Different characters represent the different options you've taken in similar circumstances, but you inevitably come back to where you started because the 'tenth' choice," she paraphrased in the air, "made you think something will be different, but it's the tenth time you've made the same tenth choice."

Rubbing the top page, she looked at me compassionately. "You're style represents what you think and how you came to think it, both of which portend to an inevitable end that's staring you in the face if you can't resolve what happened to you."

"Which is?"

"Becoming LeBlanc."

Staring, I said, "Your eyes look normal."

"Mocking me doesn't change anything. Your characters represent different aspects of your personality, which you test from event to event to try to resolve personal quandaries, but you corner yourself by emphasizing peripheral issues, like you did with your screenplay, because the core issues either offended or made no sense to you."

"What personal quandaries? It was what it was."

She cocked her head in a come-off-it manner.

"Really," I said, not feigning my confusion.

Still suspicious, she said, "The first time we met, you said the necessity to act is the basis upon which I should evaluate your character, albeit under the guise of evaluating your character's character." She grinned slyly. "In other words, necessity is a qualifier of bravery for you, but your characters created necessity simply from being there. You couldn't distinguish courage from idiocy or hero from villain because you volunteered to be part of the problem and that, my friend, is your cage. You became a part of the insanity in order to survive *in* the insanity." She pitched forward. "But you are right on one point: courage and heroes aren't what we think they are in warfare because you can't turn a fundamentally flawed event into a virtue." She relaxed her shoulders. "That's like a medic shooting someone then getting a medal for saving his life under fire." Bonnie leaned back and placed her palms on the table. "This is no different than giving medals for murder under the banner of a duty, awarded by the very people who created the drama while sipping their daiquiris, oblivious to the sirens outside. Or by design."

Uncomfortable because through my beliefs and confusion she was still making sense, I chuckled at the imagery while she took an overdue breath.

"You also haven't fixed an ending in your mind," she next said, "because you're secretly searching for meaning in experiences that everyone freely admits are insane, yet they still go to them, which can only mean one thing." Dipping her head as if from the weight of

[173]

sudden wisdom manifesting, she said, "Within the midst of this madness, LeBlanc had a peek at himself, and he questioned what he was doing there. This tells me that you glimpsed a slice of what you are really like, but your ego slammed that door before the secret could slip through the crack in the mirror of self-reflection."

I heard her words clearly, but I understood she was comparing our works under the guise of our characters' beliefs, and that her fervour was antagonism, regardless of her tone, to goad me into changing my story. It was a covert way of causing me to validate whatever she had in mind for hers. It ticked me off. A lot.

"My work isn't about special people sowing the groundwork for peace of mind," I said carefully. "It's a glassy stare at the casual cruelty of seeding minefields in fertile land. Mutilation and involuntary crapping may be less appealing social transactions to you than discussing their philosophical implications, but we aren't all on the same step of the evolutionary ladder. I can't write about things I don't know, and neither can you." I steeled myself for the counter assault.

"Christ," she said exasperated, "am I speaking Mandarin? Do I have to throw you down the stairs to get your attention?"

"Only if the lesson is about gravity."

Breathing a sigh of defeat, Bonnie picked up my pages and placed them lightly in my hands, as if they were ancient parchment. "Let's move on. Assess events you saw for their underlying nature, and question the odds of these things happening to one person. If you do this throughout your entire book, you should begin to appreciate how your experiences are unique by virtue of what their totality represents. From there, some of your shadow beliefs will fall, and the extra light will shine on a purpose." She leaned into my personal space. "Your first thirty-five years are an extraordinary tale that you're turning into a common war story because you can't make a single leap of faith."

"What leap is it this time?"

"You haven't examined any of your exquisite moments even though you believe nothing happens by chance; the leap is being willing to accept whatever conclusion you arrive at."

Bonnie suddenly stood and shouted, "I'm right here!" launching her cat into sanctuary under the couch.

"I can still see you," I muttered, my irritation dissolving into consternation over a crazy lady standing as if she was nailed to a cross.

Bonnie dropped her arms, and said, "Would you like a Tarot reading?" as if this was a chore. Realizing her delivery wasn't exactly a gripping invitation, she lightened up and added, "Just for the fun of it.

[174]

It also might loosen you up so we can have more interesting discussions like this. This one was great, wasn't it?"

"Yup."

Not until that night, in bed, did I fit a critical piece of my daily puzzle together: Bonnie trashed the context of living in conflict that she believed was my general focus, ergo the world's focus, because she faced her days within the cozy context of metaphysics. This meant that something bad must have happened, something particularly cruel for her to have run so far away in her mind that she needed me to filter her views through the levels of damage she had guided me to use, to regain her sense of safety. I was her disco ball. No Matter, the grant proposal was well underway.

***

Zzz: Drifting from a conversation on an El Al flight, my thoughts melted into a camera crew eating lunch at a Kibbutz patio, which became the deck outside of the Horse and Hound. Across the street, a family was having a picnic in Hyde Park, a loin-clothed jogger stopped to feed a Chinese chow scraps, and the animal turned into a statue of a lion. A small crowd admired it while a weeping man herded sheep into Starbucks. The aroma of coffee wafting from the kitchen lulled me into the present.

Chapter Eighteen
Remodelling Beliefs

A nnoyingly, this colourful dream left me feeling enthusiastic about the Tarot card reading, a feeling I fought by abbreviating our ritual exchange of small talk when I saw Bonnie the next morning. This change in our routine felt transparent even to me, but Bonnie said nothing about it as she led the way to the dining room table.

Sitting across from each other, she said, "I'm going to deal nine cards face down in a cross formation, then a key issue card to the side." She handed me the deck and mimed shuffling. "I'll turn them in order, explain the metaphorical significance, and as we go on I'll integrate the focus of each card into the next to refine the big picture until the tenth one brings everything together."

"Dabble?" I said

"I didn't say I was sloppy. Cut them into three stacks."

I did as she asked, and Bonnie laid out the cards. Without emotion, she plucked meaning from the first four in clipped tones, spot-welding sentences together with what for her were unusual "ums," and "ahs" she seemed unaware of uttering.

The first card signified impending wealth, the next death, which she said could mean the death of a person, a relationship, or a belief. The third card was about personal development, which turned the death card's meaning to the end of a debilitating idea, and wealth toward knowledge gained from opening my mind. Go figure.

During this first run of cards, the pitch of her voice dropped as she repackaged information from previous cards, until we came to the ninth card. Haltingly, she said it was about journeys, but not the getting on and off planes kind. She closed her eyes. Speaking in a distant manner, her words became more formal than her everyday vocabulary while still flowing with the easy rhythm of forethought. A cynic might call it "well-rehearsed."

Occasionally speaking in the plural such as, "We see that you will travel extensively on a sojourn that has rippled through time," she served up information that went well beyond the parameters set by

[176]

previous cards. I managed to wrangle my smirk into a stingy smile over her contrivances aimed at enhancing my interest, until she said I had lived some lives as a soldier. For reasons unknown to me, beyond being unable to separate the student's role from reality, I took offense.

"This occupation performed different roles at different times," she said into my derisive grin. "In one period, they were deterrent peace-keepers watching over their borders, and those of neighbours who acted in concert with the principles of peaceful coexistence. They neither instigated nor intervened in other's hostilities because doing that postponed a lasting resolution to problems the warring society had not dealt with sensibly. At this time, soldiers practiced tact over tactics, and mental patients over medical patience, although they were well-trained in the deadly arts beyond anything your world knows. Foreign societies honoured their total commitment to their tasks by leaving them alone."

Apparently seeking a better response than "uh-huh," Bonnie said that, at this time, I had intimate knowledge of thirteen couples who were learning evolutionary lessons about conflict, both personal and external. These couples shared a telepathic symbiosis that made the sum of their parts a remarkably powerful force. Essentially, the women preferred to align neighbours, and people of influence with the side of reason, by verbally launching events that drained the mental and emotional coffers of antagonists. On the practical side, whisper tactics, for example, were so inexpensively effective that large segments of populations withdrew the tacit permission their governments presumed from citizens, through verbal protest and subtler acts of civil disobedience. Undermined, maybe even embarrassed but not stupid, they had a good look at the ingeniousness of their quarry, and they thought twice about forcing the hand of the people who originated diplomacy.

The men implemented the bolder aspects of the women's machinations, using surprise and opportunity to coordinate sudden cuts in lines of communications and suspension of trade to demonstrate the scope of the siege that was possible, without resorting to battering rams. A key to the success of using coercion to avoid expensive conflicts was that they never threatened to swing the economic stick, for example, they just did it as a shot across the bow. If only because no adversary knew for certain where these people's alliances may lay in wait, they saw that it was both logically and financially in everyone's best interests to prefer peace.

Bonnie's tone clearly favoured the patient approach, without dismissing the use of force she described as a "necessary potential of other's making." She finally said that I had experienced the former mode of conflict resolution in one life, the butchering kind of soldiering in others, and my most recent occupation had completed my investigation of the illusions that cause all manner of conflicts. I was now assembling the beliefs all of these experiences had required and then generated.

I felt betrayed: Bonnie was putting spin on our moments of candour and casual conversations to lend credibility to her card interpretations. Surprising me, following this recognition there was a wave of disappointtment that shaded my anger as she mechanically said, "Do not be distressed. You are not subjugated to a fate based on the past, as you know it. You have endless choices, all of them influenced by the totality of experiences yet not assessed."

"What card tells you that?"

The glaze over her eyes vanished with a twist of her head and in her usual voice, she equivocated, "It's a composite view from an unusually in-depth session." Turning the tenth card, she said I was neck deep in a quest that would take a couple of lifetimes to complete.

Certain that I was neck deep in something, I made an excuse to leave, and I headed to the Dover pub for lunch.

I didn't call Bonnie until noon, two days later, because it took me that long to see past her abuse of confidences and clever reconstruction of known information, to recall that she had warned me about teachers shocking students to move things along. It only then became clear that this was an excellent deception to mirror her fiction and see what I did with it. I was again impressed by her all-out commitment, as wacky as it was, and as strange as it was becoming. Still...

Bonnie answered on the fourth ring with a breathless hello, allotted me half an hour to get to Nolan's, then hung up as if her tub was over-flowing. Thirty one minutes later, we were chatting about everyday things, as opposed to the paranormal. When I was as close to at ease as I ever was with her nowadays, I opened my manila envelope and asked her to comment on the flat tire rewrite I had done.

Bonnie took the chapter from me appreciatively, her hand lingering on mine as she said. "I understand what you're feeling, but scepticism is something only you can resolve."

"Fair enough," I said as a thinking student would, waving at Bréta for coffee as Bonnie began reading.

The changes I had made included our inability to find a special tool that released the jack from its moorings, so we forced it from a French-engineered locking mechanism that would have sent Houdini into

[178]

retirement. Also following the driver's manual instructions, it took us fifteen minutes to remove the spare tire, then we couldn't get the jack to function under load. We solved that problem with C clamps from our lighting kit, then the spare went flat by the time we had repacked the tools. Previously included, but now polished, was that we caught an elderly man peeking from behind a curtained window across the street, and we asked him where we could get help. He said there was a garage a few blocks away, but it was an uncertain day; it might not be open. It wasn't, and we ended up buying a spare tire from a passing motorist for the price of a used car because he was the only other person on the road, and he knew it.

In the meantime, I wrote about the sniper's opposing thoughts of being caught and tortured and of imagining his friend's faces when he described the moment the precise, red hole in Ely's chest exploded out of his back in a pulpy spray.

Finished reading this section, Bonnie lowered the pages and said, "You've done a good job blending in the delays."

"But?" I said, holding a small aluminum container of milk for her.

"I still don't know what your sniper is seeing." She blew across the top of her drink, then pitching forward said, "If you put him on a hill overlooking you guys, you could describe everyone from the sniper's point of view to make the physical distance intimate. I mean," she snapped out words with a gulped breath, "he could tell us if they're tall, have a scar or nose hairs—that kind of thing."

"And have Ely meet us there," I said as the image came to mind, "but he's never quite in sight, so the flat tire gives the sniper many borderline opportunities that he ultimately doesn't take. I like it. Except...hmm."

"You can also give the sniper an internal dialogue that has him speculate that he was not destined to get his shot on that day; the pace of fixing the tire was like an omen saying, 'Not here and not now,' so he left without taking it out on you guys."

Not willing to go down the road of omens or Allah's will, I said, "I have pictures of the real people for reference."

"You don't strike me as the type to save...." she paused, "anything."

The implication of her statement flew over my head, as I said, "Lynda organized dig-me press passes and photographs into albums of bar stories that ended in a story about an ex-wife that turned out to be her." I shrugged, "I kept it up."

"Let's go," Bonnie said, sliding sideways to stand free of the table. "I want to see the faces of the people who defied the odds with you."

[179]

"We were a motley crew."

"You could have been the Grateful Dead," she said, leaving a ten dollar bill on the table for two medium cups of Peruvian coffee, winter blend, whatever that meant.

Chapter Nineteen
False Creek

Vertical blinds behind Ed's cobalt blue couch slashed bars of light across pictures of colleagues and cellmates as I turned the page from the Central and South American section to the Middle East. "These cameramen," I said, tapping the edges of a group photograph, "don't work conflicts anymore. The work didn't suit Horst, and Terry is dead."

"It sounds like it didn't suit either of them," Bonnie said quietly.

"Terry didn't die in combat. He got sick after working in Laos, but the Brits couldn't find out why. They suspected AIDS in the end," I said, turning the page.

Bonnie stopped my hand. "There's more to it."

"He was gay," I ventured the plausible explanation.

"That's not important," she said, concentrating on the picture.

"It's all l know... other than it was a strange call."

"In what way?" She gently pushed my hand backwards.

"I hadn't heard from Doug for more than a year when he phoned from England to say that Terry had died. I figured it was an apology call of sorts because—it doesn't matter," I said, turning the page back to Amritsar, "Terry was barely a passing acquaintance. This is the Golden Temple. It's like the Sikh's Vatican."

"There's more," Bonnie said, turning back the page. "The official version of his death is what others wanted the world to think happened," she said tentatively. In a disinterested tone, she then accurately described the leaden motion of joint grinding fatigue and pounding thirst of jungle travel. Pausing, she concluded with the stunted wonder of unexpected thoughts rolling off her tongue. "He surprised a group of very private people. The deadly aspect was that he saw a gathering of criminals and government officials, and your friend was employed by a security agency. The officials knew him because they were plugged into the intelligence community. They poisoned him."

"Don't know if I can squeeze that in, but I'll keep it in mind."

"You've acted like a spy," Bonnie said, in her normal tone.

[181]

"Straddling laws was part of the game. I suppose I could tie that to spying, but it doesn't fit the rest of my story."

"What do you mean by straddling?" She took a pillow from the backrest and then the scrapbook from my lap. Shifting to the end of the couch, Bonnie put the cushion behind her neck and reclined to look at the photograph and me, from between bent knees. I figured she had settled in to see if I was any more open-minded because I had summarily dismissed her psychic suggestion from force of habit.

I made myself comfortable at the other end of the couch, placing our feet strategically heel to heel to keep us from sliding down. "That must've hurt," I said, pointing to a large circular scar on her right foot, as I slid mine into position.

"Surprisingly little. Straddling?" she said, avoiding an explanation.

"Right. In Chile, we gave undercover police the slip before a dissident took us to the salt mine where the government executed *los desperacidos*—the missing. In Pakistan, there were aspects of President Zia Al-Haq's campaigning that he didn't want the world to know about, so we ditched our minder. In Teheran—"

"Hold on. What do you mean by gave them the slip and ditched a minder? These are trained people."

"There was one car following us in Santiago, the traffic was bad, and the driver didn't expect us to take off. In Pakistan, Ski and I worked a chance remark into an opportunity to lose our guy, and we were jailed for a few hours in Iran for looking suspicious, like we were taping forbidden sites."

"What was the chance remark?"

"On an internal flight, we bet on how long it would take from full power to wheels off, like we always did. The closer we came to our numbers, the more we glanced at each other, the more our cocoa-coloured minder turned a whiter shade of pale. When we finally began our climb out, he leaned close to Wizichinski and asked him if he had ever covered a plane crash. Ski said, 'Just small ones.' Our guy looked panicky-curious, so I told him that metal fatigue from micro-vibrations and years of flying in hot, humid climates caused all of the turboprop crashes I knew about. Ski added that the kiss-your-ass- goodbye clue to the passengers would have been the plane's downward attitude increasing while the air speed slowed. It would feel like flying through mud, which made no sense until you looked out of the window and factored in the extra drag caused from a wing twisting on Fokker turbo-props like ours."

[182]

Visualizing how a normal, full flaps decent would affect our man, Bonnie nodded for me to continue.

"We did our thing in Lehore and got back on the same plane while our guy took a bus back to Islamabad. That gave us a full day to go where the army had polled some towns with fifty calibre certainty of Zia winning."

"Tom said something about you guys insulting the President when you did the interview?" Bonnie said without humour.

"The office, not the man: his press secretary was floating our appointment until election day to make sure we couldn't be in Karachi where they expected protesting. When Gavin and I showed up with a backup camera, the chief of security clenched his teeth in a frozen smile and asked us when the President could expect our producer and cameraman to arrive. Gavin offhandedly said, "Oh, they can't make it," as if half a crew didn't reflect poorly on the importance of having access to the President."

Bonnie smiled at the image.

"I shot the interview with Zia while Ski and Smitty shot some tame stuff in Karachi."

Cocking her head, she said, "The office might have thought little of shooting you." Her expression lingered before she said, "Did you cross battle lines?"

"And vice versa, sure."

"When it was in your plans," she honed her question, "were you considered to be consorting with the enemy?" Her confident manner warned me that Tom had told her about that time in Central America.

"That's a rare ban," I temporized.

"The question remains."

"The few countries that care about that kind of thing confiscate passports when you arrive, so you're stuck in-country if you're caught breaking rules. Hypothetically, you could get around that by bringing a giveaway passport."

"You're talking about crews with dual citizenship?"

"A lot of them considered themselves citizens of the world, so they had other passports."

"Hypothetically, wouldn't that would be against the law?"

"They considered themselves part of an advanced association of kindred spirits who were doing the right thing for the right reason. Sometimes, that looks like something it's not," I said, tongue in cheek.

"Which is the credo that landed you in an Argentine jail."

[183]

"No—well, kind of. We were screwed by the lens seeing things we didn't."

"All of it if you don't mind," Bonnie said, turning back to the first page of the South America section.

I explained that federal interrogators asked us if a portion of a panoramic shot could be still-framed and electronically enhanced, and we said that it could, subject to technical limitations. Doubling the size of a car half the distance to the horizon, for example, would make it indistinguishable from a house. Tripling the size would make traffic look like golf balls in a blizzard. Why, they next asked us, had we twice held steady on extremely wide shots that showed almost no activity?

Ski explained that he had followed a light aircraft's landing and roll-out until it went behind a row of hangars, frame right, then he held steady for a few seconds before swish-panning to hold on the space where the plane would roll into frame left. This was Film School 101 stuff: cutting screen time while sustaining continuity.

They said we held steady on a fuel dump, centre frame, on the first pause and a fighter bunker in the second pause.

Bad luck, we said, but the British would hardly consider finding fuel or jet fighters at the closest airport to the Malvinas Islands strategic information.

This didn't matter, they said, because we had broken the law.

"Had you?" Bonnie asked me.

"Technically."

"Is there another way?" Bonnie said, curling her toes to poke the bottoms of my feet. "You've got to admit that journalists are well placed to engage in spying activities."

"Not as much as you think."

"Obviously, more than you'd like to believe. Your footage was viewed by the embassies of all concerned, correct?"

"That's hardly covert."

"Secrecy is not a prerequisite to espionage, it's a method. What was the nature of Terry's assignments? Where did he go?"

Sean, a cameraman I often worked with was Terry's close friend, so I knew more about him than a passing acquaintance normally would. A fact I didn't appreciate until my list for Bonnie grew to include Afghanistan, many trips to the north and south of Ireland, plus all of the countries in conflict I had been in—a baker's dozen if you included repeats and internal strife.

"Did he do volunteer assignments?"

[184]

"He made me look shy."

"Well?" she said expectantly.

"I said I'd look into it."

"You said you'd keep it in mind. Listen," she sat up, "I'm not trying to push the spying angle for your book. I'm trying to have you see that your friend didn't understand the world he was playing in." She looked cross-eyed at me, a thought found a home, then she said, "I think you need a demonstration of that, otherwise we're going to get bogged down. Let's figure something out over lunch on Granville Island."

"Sure—my tab—I've got some money coming," I said, getting off the couch. "A demonstration of where I really am, like you did with Otis?"

"If you recall our first meeting," she said heading toward the door, "I said intellect had little to do with grasping my premises because you needed an experience to embrace them."

"I recall you saying that in a number of circumstances."

"Good. Otis was the theory part. The experience we are heading for will show you how your version of reality is reasoned from your personality, and you'll see how your so-called facts are actually interpretations of events that apply only in your mind."

I opened the door for Bonnie and said, "I'll probably figure out what you just said by the time we get there."

Moving past me, she said, "It's important to show our audience how dangerous it would be for my rescue party to try to reason a circumstance to suit a belief. They can never lose sight of the nature of events—so we're going to show you how that works."

"Got it," I said.

"Let's take the Aquabus," she said, as I locked the door. "The tip is mine, by the way."

"Done."

Bonnie clicked her tongue like an Arab grandmother discovering too late that her granddaughter had decorated the kitchen floor with flour and water.

We walked a kilometre to the foot of Hornby Street in casual conversation, then boarded a twenty foot, generously rounded craft of Boston Whaler design, with broad gunnels and unobstructed panoramic views through large Plexiglas windows, helmed amidships from a raised pilot's cabin.

According to our captain, a young woman honing her spiel in preparation for the lucrative Asian tourist invasion, Spanish traders were taking otter pelts from the Pacific rim to the China market when, in 1792, Captain George Vancouver arrived to negotiate for territory and to map the shoreline. The island of Vancouver, not Isla de Ferdinand, speaks to his success. She next told us that shallow waters extended much farther into the strait than seemed reasonable for a mountainous region. As a result, it was rare that a summer's day went by without a sailboat skipper spending quality time with his family stuck in the soft mud of the Spanish Banks until the flood tide released his ego. She speculated that as brilliant a sailor as the Captain must have been, it was likely that he also did six hours of penance before ghosting toward land on the evening's onshore breeze.

Tracking parallel to the bluffs of the future English Properties, and the site of the University of British Columbia, he would have crossed the area where John Barrymore would twice anchor his schooner to watch Pacific International Yachting Association races during prohibition, before dropping anchor at the mouth of what appeared to be a river draining a continent—the protected cove we were crossing.

A century ago, the city stabilized the tidal flats of False Creek so that, mining, logging, and various other industries could settle there. The area became officially known as Industrial Island, but for social and historical reasons the name Granville stuck as industry left or was burned out, to gradually be replaced by more visitor friendly, commercial endeavours. Almost two hundred years since Captain George first saw the twin sand bars of the flats, Granville Island hosts a marina, a private community of floating homes and an eclectic array of markets, shops, bars, artist's shops, two theatres, and the Emily Carr University of Art and Design.

At this well-timed point in her monologue, our captain pitched the ferry service itself, declaring that the two tonne vessels of twenty to twenty-four feet traveled eight routes around the peninsula that is otherwise accessed by the Burrard, Granville, and Cambie street bridges from the south. The service is a huge tourist draw while it facilitates the movement of island workers from key parts of the city without concern for parking. Checking her watch, about three minutes for the crossing, she expertly brought the craft alongside the island's ramp at the Arts Club Theatre and wished us all a great day.

Walking behind a young couple who were holding hands, back to front, as they rose from the bench seating to disembark, Bonnie nodded at a stranger who was waiting dockside and whispered, "He's in for a surprise today."

"Tell him that on the way by to make sure," I quipped.

"Behaviour designs destiny, so we are all self-fulfilling prophets."

[186]

Into her elfin expression I said, "I was making a joke."

"Oh—sorry," she said taking my arm. "You meant he would have been surprised by my comment. I get it, now, but I meant he had already arranged his surprise."

"You knew what I meant," I said as we exited the ferry amidships and stepped onto the heavy planking.

Bonnie tightened her grasp as we walked side by side up the broad dock. Reaching the paved landing, she said, "Months ago, I was amazed to discover how much difficulty people create for themselves by not saying what they mean or truly meaning what they say. Case in point, you just took a shot at clairvoyance because you think it's crap, whereas I interpreted your comment to suit my focus. Then I remembered where I was—with you."

"There was no confusion until you contrived an assumption no one else would have thought of... but you're entitled to your opinion," I said, reasonably.

"I used to think I was entitled, but what a mistake that was!" Bonnie giggled at a private thought until we stopped to read a menu posted on varnished pine boards bordered by a hunter green frame. Surrounded by some kind of a creeping plant, the design proclaimed a tofu and wheat-germ establishment.

"Public speaking," she said perusing the menu, "taught me that the less hyperbole I subjected others to, the clearer my ideas were in my own mind, as well." She faced me. "In time, I realised that I viewed reality through how I twisted its fabric, and I made a point to avoid superlatives for a week. I sounded... there's that look again."

"It's nothing." I tugged on her sleeve. "Look—vegetarian lasagne for six-ninety-five!" I said, mocking her dietary preference.

"They have burgers," she said, tonelessly mocking mine as we moved toward the door. "On the first day of avoiding hyperbole, I sounded like an answering machine, and from that perspective I could already see how the way I said things influenced my perceptions of the moment." Bonnie opened the door and walked through ahead of me. "This is when I decided to use plain language, beginning with clients who expected hype from me."

"You used to lie?"

Rocking her head from side to side in a more-or-less manner, she said, "I didn't need to be so thrilled about quoting before-and-after sales figures of ads, and I always posed the ominous "what if" question to have them see how the train may be leaving their business behind if their competitors were onboard."

[187]

"Got it, so what happened?"

"Without the hype or implied promises, clients began to see me as more of a marketing advisor than a telemarketer. That change had me appreciate that I was negotiating peace of mind through good business sense, and that realization led to a moment of clarity." We walked into a cantilevered section over the water. "To my horror, I saw how common gestures had led me to think of some people as inconsequential. Is this good for you?"

"Sure—great spot," I said, and we sat in a shaded corner. "To your horror, sounds like hyperbole." I grinned.

Bonnie flip-fluttered a linen cloth before drawing it across her lap in a fluid motion. I snapped mine open and dragged it over one leg as she said, "I'm not overstating the moment I realised that saying have a nice day was a hollow gesture but far from meaningless because it brought to my attention how other apparently innocent circumstances could lead to something unimaginable."

"How can they be hollow and meaningful?" I said, sliding two menus from a wire stand and offering one to Bonnie.

"Thanks. I saw how practicing social graces as part of my job generated a momentum that ran contrary to my beliefs. Automatically saying things like, 'Thanks for your time,' sloughs people off. Essentially, it's laying the ground-work for neglect, and without curbing that momentum my business relationships would eventually fade away. I would also become disillusioned by the unfairness of my polite life and redouble my efforts to talk a good image, which would only add energy to the poor circumstance. Finally, I would talk myself into despair, which is what we all joke about when empty promises have made the recognition of the proper course of action nearly impossible." Looking intense, as if she were entrusting me with launch codes, she said, "Everywhere you go you hear people convincing themselves that they're doing something about the issues they prattle on about, even in jest." Bonnie glanced at the wine list on the back of the menu and returned it to the holder as a hyper-personable waiter introduced himself and asked if we would like a drink to start.

In a single-breath parody of Daryl, Bonnie ordered a carafe of house red, the veggie mush, and two glasses of ice water. I ordered a fish burger sans seaweed; she hadn't lied to me, they did have burgers.

Smiling deferentially, Daryl bowed and moved away with a "very good," parody of an English butler.

"The underlying nature of rote social graces is insincerity," Bonnie said, sliding her cutlery to one side, "because we are invested in other's

[188]

welfare only to the extent that it affects ours. Essentially, we're negotiating safety or affirming a peaceful transaction, which is a positive thing, but we don't realize our words are a pervasive force of self-conditioning that can bring unexpected consequences. We've both seen smart people do stupid things."

"I guess."

"You make my point. Your poor grammar and habit of communicating in incomplete sentences, while leaving gaps you automatically fill with assumptions, has finally caused you to guess about your own experiences."

"Come on—you know that's just a phrase."

"Why did you use it in a straight forward circumstance? Really, think about it before you say something else inane." She grinned.

"I suppose I wasn't sure where you were going."

"What does that have to do with anything?"

"You obviously understood me," I backtracked.

"But your ego-accomplice is not allowing you to understand me." She leaned in. "Your turn-of-phrase was based on the assumption that I might be leading you to agree with something you could regret. It follows," she said as Daryl returned with our wine, "that gaps in your thoughts represented by gaps in your sentences allow you to misrepresent yourself and conceal the fact that your underlying concern is about upholding your image." Bonnie leaned further forward, forcing Daryl to lean away from an attempt to pour for us. "That's why you didn't commit to a simple truth. It follows that if you don't have another's best interests at heart in comfortable circumstances you will, at a minimum, abandon them when the pressure is on. If they are the source of that pressure," she leaned back to shrug, "you could be dangerous to them."

I thanked a patient Daryl, holding up a dismissive hand so that he would set the bottle down, but he reached over to pour two half glasses before leaving us with the apologetic bow of an inadvertent intruder.

"Intentionally setting out to confuse me punctures your point. I think I've got a better handle on what's dangerous than most people, and I would never hurt you," I said, reaching for my glass.

"I see that you haven't taken the time to assess our conversation about me standing in your way, yet."

"Nope," I said taking a drink.

"Mmmm," Bonnie said, sipping her wine. "Is it cruel to be entertained at the expense of another's fear or pain?"

[189]

"That's probably the dictionary definition," I said, irrationally feeling like I was throwing a boomerang blindfolded.

"Isn't that what you did with your minder in Pakistan?"

"He was playing in the big leagues, and he struck out." I shrugged.

"It didn't cross your mind that the Chief of Security might shoot him, if only to appease Zia because you insulted him?"

My mouth opened, but no sound came out.

"*That's* why I used the word horror," Bonnie said, swirling her wine under her nose.

"He knew he was working for a despot," I said, finding my voice.

"What your minder knew has nothing to do with the essence of your act."

"What Zia did isn't my responsibility."

"I didn't say it was." Incongruously, Bonnie flung her arms wide to encompass the entire vista as she exclaimed, "Isn't this terrific!"

"Ya—great spot," I mumbled, as the idea that I might have set up a man to be killed slithered through my conscience.

"No—really, it's beautiful, isn't it?"

"I said it was," I snapped as Daryl returned with our meals.

To his credit, being the elephant in the room did not affect his show of grinding pepper from an unusual altitude, which is why Bonnie and I initially failed to notice that he hadn't brought the parmesan, or ice water, before he left us.

"Good thing personality is worth something," I said, looking over my shoulder to get his attention.

"Don't be too quick to judge. You don't know what might be distracting him."

"Maybe the distraction will take his mind off the tip."

"He owns the social graces, and he's well spoken. He's probably a U.B.C. student, and it's near exam time."

"How are his exams my fault?"

"Fault?" Bonnie said as if I had belched. Setting her fork down, she folded her hands in front of her as a sign that she was lining me up in her sites. "Do you think he's punishing us?"

"No, but tipping is based on the level of service he gives customers."

"My cheese has nothing to do with your lunch, or do you think I'm not capable of handling the situation?" She unclasped her hands to sip ice water.

"Hardly, but..." I had nowhere to go, so I shrugged and smirked, letting the words dangle as if she had missed an obvious point.

"You did what you did in Pakistan. Now, you won't do that kind of thing again, and you'll be more careful about doing this again, as well."

"Doing what?"

"Sexism aside, you tried to regain your good standing with me at Daryl's expense, when you haven't lost it."

"Give him whatever you want," I said.

"I will, and your passive-aggression won't change that." Bonnie picked up her napkin and patted the corners of her mouth. "Some friendly advice: you're an all-or-nothing kind of guy at heart, but the world has forced you to pretend to be cautious, so your initial threats sound like sulking. Most of the people who recognize this mode make the mistake of thinking you're negotiating for your way because that's what sulking is about. However, they don't know where you've been or what you've seen, so it doesn't dawn on them that you're actually giving them their last chance."

"Huh?"

"You challenged me at Daryl's expense: if I give him a small tip, you'll think I capitulated to your way of thinking about fault and punishment. If I give him a large tip, you'll think it was an in-your-face kind of thing and still think you're correct."

I topped up our glasses. "Give him fifteen percent and be done with it. No harm, no foul," I said reasonably.

"I think ten percent will make the point. Wait!" she shouted as if there were Hemlock in the glass I was bringing to my lips. "He'll just think I'm cheap; better make it five percent to emphasize that he screwed up. No," she vacillated. "He didn't spill anything—that's a five percent offense. Seven should sting him about right. Maybe nine—no eight sounds…"

"Jesus Christ, it's just cheeeeeese." I hissed.

"Exactly," Bonnie exhaled the word with relief. "It's just cheese," she said, repeating the gesture that had first brought our surroundings to my attention.

Briefly noting how clear things could sometimes be when I was with her, I grasped what had just happened between us: still thinking about Pakistan and unhappy about Daryl overhearing Bonnie speak unflatteringly about me, I had lost sight of our reality: we were two friends and business partners having a quiet lunch in a terrific setting, the underlying point of which was to give me an experience about how people do not appreciate their true circumstance. Damn.

I chuckled self-consciously.

[191]

"Good," Bonnie said, tinking my glass with hers. "Now that you've seen the absurdity of making a stand for your ego, you can be on guard for it." She sipped her drink.

"I won't do that again," I assured her.

"You certainly will," she said lowering her glass. "Nothing has changed beyond you understanding how it happens. It could take years of practice to stop that reaction entirely." She grinned. "That's why they're called disciplines. By the way, I'm going away for a week."

"What? Why didn't you tell me?"

"Would it have changed anything?" she said innocently.

"I—it would have been good to know," I muttered.

"It would have interfered with what turned out to be a GREAT DAY!" she exclaimed the last two words, startling Daryl as he came to our table with a bowl of parmesan cheese and the ice water.

Apologizing to Bonnie, he explained that he had grated it fresh. She thanked him as he spooned coarse filings over her pasta.

A part of me felt vindicated because Daryl should have told Bonnie what he was doing, but mostly I felt used; Bonnie had designed the lesson to smooth over the moment when I was bound to realize there was more to her going away than she was saying, and that something more was Josh.

I got the impression from her double glance and grin at me between bites that she knew what I was thinking, so I held my tongue for the rest of the meal, taking care to speak politely and limit my comments to remarks that were on point. Conversely, Bonnie didn't push me, other than leaving a twenty percent tip, which I said nothing about.

With no dialogue underway, the ambiance was on the cool side when we were walking back to the ferry, and Bonnie made an ironic comment by shivering and noting there were waves at the dock. Not risking a misunderstanding, I agreed that the wind had come up, and we were not dressed for it. Soon afterwards, I graciously thanked her for paying my fare.

On the return crossing, a Simon Fraser University student told us that Vancouver had loosely formed around fishing, forestry, and a gold rush, but it didn't become a real city until the Canadian Pacific Railway built a terminal at the foot of Howe Street. Putt-putting under the Burrard Street bridge at four knots, he lamented that otters had nested here until twenty years ago, his tone implying we had lost the creatures to a hundred years of unchecked progress, him trolling tourists through their domain notwithstanding.

[192]

As we came alongside the Hornby Street landing, I commented on this oversight in his monologue as a springboard to asking Bonnie how she practiced appreciating her true circumstance, as well.

"I found it easier to think of it in terms of practicing clarity, then applying that to where I am. Do you want to try it while I'm away?" she said.

"Sure. That's why I asked."

"Every morning before you get up, imagine packing your entire life's inventory for a journey into physical reality. When you enter this world, act as if all events are new, and pause to examine what you are about to say before setting your words free to take on a life in other people's minds, because that's the nature of the world you've chosen until you get home." Making our uphill way home with stilted breath, she said, "It won't be long before you appreciate how easily we mislead ourselves and become distracted from what we're supposed to be doing."

"By inventory, do you mean taking stock of my circumstances?"

"All of our so-called facts about physical reality are part of our inventory. In narrow terms, if you think you've got a huge problem, the weight of your waking inventory can crush your will to achieve anything before you get out of bed. If you collect things, you drag your decisions through the underlying reasons that made you a collector. Typically, it's insecurity or hubris. In broad terms, your inventory is a repository of all knowledge and assumptions about physical reality from which you engage the journey of self-discovery. We'll come back to that."

"We'll have to."

She chucked. "You should engage every day with a sense of wonder to avoid tainting it with judgements, thereby freeing yourself to ask why you say the things you do. Part of what Tartuu is teaching Aleena," she said, tapping the back of my wrist with her hand, "is to not waste energy maintaining images. When she begins living the way Tartuu will suggest in specific terms, her energy saving will allow unexpected insights to add to her positive outlook, like the one you had in the restaurant."

"You're saying energy set my self-interest aside, and what I understood was waiting behind it?"

"Insights are conclusions drawn from untainted inquiries. As your world becomes clearer, your days become less daunting, your outlook becomes more positive, you expend less energy, and the easier it becomes to draw correct conclusions. Most people use all of their daily

[193]

energy converting events into acceptable ideas. You already know you do this, and that you react like a black belt on speed, so your first discipline should be to do nothing as a proactive consideration in virtually every circumstance you can. It's that, or you should find and fight to the death for a worthy cause because living in between is a living hell for you."

I understood exactly what she meant, and I used the remainder of our walk to silently review and remember how events unfolded at the restaurant because I had the illogical sense that once we were apart they would become like 1969, foggy.

Bonnie occasionally tittered for no apparent reason.

When we arrived at her car outside of Ed's apartment block, she gave me a quick hug and said, "If you practice clarity by stopping to assess what you're about to say, as if you've never said anything, one hugely humbling insight you'll arrive at will be how much you've been missing. See you on Sunday." She got in her car and drove away.

Chapter Twenty
The Language of Chaos

During the week that Bonnie was away, I reworked sample scenes for the grant application, jogged in the afternoon, and in the evenings made a game of assessing what I was about to say to Ed. Not all of the time, mind you, but enough that by Wednesday my halting manner caused him to call me to the Avalon to ease my apparent stress over my screenplay deadline. I didn't tell him that I had finished it because he would want to read it, and that wasn't ever going to happen with anyone I knew: trying to incorporate the ringing chord of mystery with my altered design of suspense that culminated in Tom's practical solution had gutted both. The measured ingredients of my psychological soufflé had become instant pudding.

Ironically, as the postal agent weighed it for shipping, I had realised that Bonnie had been bang on at our first meeting: My deadline hadn't been too close to make subtle changes, if only I had faith in the process leading me to where it wanted to go; I saw that destination too late to do anything about it. As it was, choosing the expedient way pretty much defined the quality of the story—written in a hurry for money.

During that liquid therapy session, I explained my flat tire scene to Tom and said that I intended to bring the sniper forward to make him an immediate threat to Ely, but I wasn't sure how to explain why he didn't shoot anyone when Ely was never quite in his sites.

Tom shrugged and said, "Didn't the guy who sold you his tire help the infidel?"

I had one of those Zen moments wherein things become clear around corners: the farce of good and evil would show when the stranger didn't make it around the next corner, and there was poetic justice attached to his blatant profiteering. The scene would also further establish that there were no safe places to work, thereby silencing Bonnie's appeal for me to include ethereal influences in my life, and book: these would have undermined my portrayal of the capriciousness

[195]

of warfare when the sniper, highly conflicted by moral indecision, regrettably fired the round that tore through Ely and into R.J.

Boom-boom taking a shower in a large glass box drew my attention away, and as the warm mists revealed other women apparently in need of public cleansing, I mentally relocated the sniper in chapters where the paths of Ely and Robbie literally crossed. Between dancers, I idly tuned into my friends' banter and unexpectedly experienced them as characters in my book; I knew their dialogue as if I had written it. The tigress creeping beneath fluorescent netting, to stalk three-piece prey out of mourning their losses at the exchange, interrupted their conversation. But when she was finished, I listened intently to my friends to make sure I really could anticipate their words. I was both exhilarated and embarrassed to hear their personal fables unfolding between the lines.

As the final dancer contorted to a punk racket that ended in the kick-bass beat of the damned thumping through a cloud of dry ice, I heard their conversation as a series of punch lines from a comedienne's routine specifically about them. I was only a small step away from becoming cocky over this perceptual accomplishment, when Bonnie's comments stormed into my thoughts; first that I was no different from them, then that most of what I'd been missing by filtering my conversations through my self-image was about me. This smack to my ego became my motive to listen to other "characters" in the club, to try to specifically see how they gave themselves away, before Bonnie came home and I embarrassed myself more than I already had. With this decision made, the relative ease with which I was making distinctions between my friends' words and their undertones, dissipated into a struggle for my attention between rock songs and rollicking breasts.

For the next three days, I gave the practices of clarity a reasonable effort, but I never achieved the depth I had experienced when I was with Bonnie. Even so, by Saturday I had personally absorbed a piece of knowledge that I had previously embraced only intellectually; people don't stray far from validating themselves in their casual conversations. I also discovered that my urge to be heard was remarkably strong, which I tried to curb by imagining silence as a supernatural event only special people could achieve. Still...

On Sunday, Meaghan and Rachel showed up at Bonnie's door less than a minute after I arrived, their overly bright greetings testifying to a rift between them and Bonnie, which Bonnie confirmed for me by exuberantly dragging them in for tea.

[196]

With our own reunion on hold, I tried to stay in the background while the women repaired their association, but the sassy brunette had other ideas. Rachel first offered me the warm, wry remarks of a social teaser, to which I uncharacteristically responded with restraint. She then became more of a sultry temptress, and as I pretended these comments flew over my head, she became a brazen street hustler confirming her attraction to me, while overtly fishing for reciprocity.

Bonnie's amused glances had kept me focused until, in an effortless moment, I recognized Rachel's preoccupation with the harlot's role was about having suffered at the hands of unmentioned men, and she wanted it acknowledged: our eyes met often, but hers did not linger with promise or sparkle with challenge. Her gaze loitered in memories, even as her words tried to set fire to my crotch.

I later learned that Meaghan had been Rachel's pragmatic counter-part and prissy alter ego since their grade school days. An intellectual C-130 transport plane, she moved bulk cargo slowly and reliably toward the horizon of reason, but lacking the guile of a fighter, she chastised Rachel's flirtations with expressions of shock that melted into a waxen pout I didn't place until it was time for them to leave: when Rachel repeated that their children were waiting, Meghan shook her head and said she was thinking about a leaky faucet. The abandoned look of a single parent, whose ample frame relegated her to the category of "also ran" before the age of thirty, washed her countenance transparently bland, and I saw the deeper meaning of her pout. She felt that she had disappeared.

I knew there was a lot more to both of them, as my thoughts became common, but I had no doubt that my sliver impressions were accurate.

When they both were gone and the room remarkably quiet, Bonnie said it had been great to see them, but she needed to recharge her psyche. Without further comment, she headed out of the door toward the sea wall.

Comfortable within a rejuvenating silence, we established an easy pace on the rocky beach before Bonnie asked me what I thought of her friends. I went straight to the important point and told her that I had experienced a moment of clarity about how her friends portrayed them-selves, and what lay beneath their words was so clear that I felt like I had invaded their privacy.

Bonnie looked pleased with me, like the first time a puppy sits on command, but I didn't mind. It felt good to get something right.

[197]

In the next few minutes, we condensed aspects of their reunion into essential points without the loss of ambiance because essences implied more than words would have limited us to. I was unusually calm while my brain was fully engaged in its first ultra-efficient dialogue when Bonnie asked me to describe the moment in which I had decided to practice clarity of thought as a serious endeavour. I began to tell her about my evening at the Avalon, but I stumbled so badly that my delivery became comical. Imagining that I sounded as if I was mocking her advice to pause and edit my words, I chuckled and said, "I need a moment to switch topics."

"Self-delusion isn't a simple thing to stop," she said with a broad grin.

I stared silently.

"You're struggling because you're trying to hide something, otherwise we would still easily be sharing assumptions."

"I didn't do badly with your friends, though."

"You know I'm impressed with your effort. Why did you just pull for a compliment?"

"I didn't—hmmm."

"It's a lot easier to see other people than ourselves, isn't it?"

"Sure is."

"Sure as in certain, confident, or indisputable, or sure as in non-committal, deniable, and I heard your question, and I'll get back to you?"

"You may assume the former from now on."

"I will. While we're at it, saying things like, 'Don't think so,' as opposed to 'I don't think so,' distances you from the subject, and by failing to assume responsibility for your words, you give yourself permission to avoid taking responsibility for your actions. As I told you before I went away, words are events that program our actions, so prudence requires that we handle them like explosives until discipline makes everything we say a deliberate choice. Are we still on the same page?"

"Yep," I joked.

"Yep and ya convey the assumption of an agreement, but they lack the commitment of personal attribution, just like na and nope resonate with indifference or inconsequence while implying impoverishment or illiteracy."

"Poverty and illiteracy would be assumptions of the average person, not you."

"The point is, you wouldn't have to do battle with our culture's assumptions if you didn't play into them by suggesting you are uneducated or possess a meagre intellectual capacity. More often than not, the barn door will be closed before your actions speak to your true capabilities, and you can't know who else is listening. To represent yourself properly is to become aware of how you create a continuity of confusion in yourself and others then shatter those practices. Are you up for that now that you've experienced clarity as a reward?"

"Sure. Sorry—I mean, let's give it a whirl."

"Meaning you're not serious about it?"

I cleared my throat. "I'd like to break the continuity of how I create confusion and all that comes with that."

"Excellent. Why did you add, and all that comes with that?"

"It's clearer to me that all of these lessons are connected, and my first success tells me that we've just begun."

"You are a beautiful man," she said as if... as if I was a beautiful man.

I left it at that—gift-horses and all.

Bonnie's delicate facial contortions thereafter noted my inappropriate use of language, or opinionated phrasing on what became a full day of endless offences to clarity of thought. I was particularly surprised at how often I used words like ass, crap, and shit, a rampant habit Bonnie put an end to by offering to help me explore the origins of my anal fixation. She also quashed anthropomorphic references, explaining that aligning any aspect of Mother Nature to fearful or disdainful activities could only contribute to the neglect of our environment.

In part, she said, "Wind is not wrathful, seas are not in turmoil, storms are not angry, and fires do not rage. These are beautiful, natural processes acting in concert to rejuvenate our world in ways we cannot appreciate because we are mostly unaware or indifferent to the intricate fragility of our existence."

"What about as literary devices?"

Chirp-chuckling she said, "I have three points to make. The tone of your utterance indicated that you were asking me a question, but it was too vague for me to determine what you were specifically asking. It's also possible that you do not know what you were asking in specific terms and that you were relying on me to supply the context of your inquiry as part of my response. Taking these things into account, I will say that it is generally wiser to communicate in the style of 'See Spot Run,' when you can't afford a misunderstanding. Otherwise, using

[199]

literary devices for a specific affect requires that you address a literate audience, not a literal audience like impressionable children whom you might inadvertently make afraid of the wind. Personally, I prefer simplicity because things usually only have to be said once. It's also a discipline that undermines pretence." She breathed deeply. "If I have not answered your question, please narrow the field of your inquiry so that I might respond directly."

"I appreciate the demonstration of what can happen when the same assumptions are not shared in even a simple sentence," I said formally.

"Good, now let me presume to add to your appreciation: all things human expand at the speed of their presumed convenience. This is why it's critical to avoid even the smallest of open-ended self-entrapments, like saying sure, or uh-huh. From there, it's a small step to concocting lies."

"Without your training and vocabulary," I said, feeling accused, "I might not articulate my ideas the way you do, but that doesn't mean people can't understand me, or that I'm not telling the truth."

"This is an excellent point on its face," Bonnie said indifferently. "However, my training and vocabulary have little to do with why I'm more articulate than those who may have less of either. My comm-unication skills are unhindered by having to wrestle my self-image for an appropriately reflective adjective, and I am otherwise unconcerned whether others approve of me. If and when I modify my mode, I do it to communicate ideas outside of my internal concerns, not because I've lost control of them." She beamed like a child having recited her first poem.

"All I'm saying is that a little spice adds flavour, and a well-placed emotional reference can add depth to make communication more personal to others. I'm not denying the value of your exercise, but it's also become clear over the last hour that decorations are sometimes required to affect precision."

"That's too bad," she lamented. "It should have become clear that your thoughts meander, and because they're not always appropriate, you have to conceal them. We'll come back to that." She waived her comment aside. "Your versions of depth and flavouring are based on emotional attachments to ideas that skew the point to suit your moods. Case in point," she glanced my way for the first time in a while. "I first told you that maintaining secrets is difficult because the truth is constantly prodding them. A moment ago, I prodded you until you leaked a belief by arguing that my background gives me an advantage."

"What's my belief?"

[200]

"You argued the fairness issue, which means you still assume we are in a competition, and you haven't embraced energy efficiency as a way to determine the correct action over the capriciousness of beliefs."

"I didn't argue."

"Did too!" she exclaimed.

My testiness wobbled into a grunt.

Putting her arm around my waist, Bonnie said, "Grunting is an egotistical contrivance that generally flows from ignorance toward condescension. It is intentionally subject to misinterpretations such as yes, no, maybe, I'm thinking about it, or I disagree. A grunt can also be tuned to imply a threat, while avoiding responsibility for any of these connotations."

"Okay, okay, I get it!" I said raising my hands in surrender.

"Okay does not necessarily designate an agreement, level of quality, or acknowledgment of understanding precisely because it can be any of these things. In addition, doubling the term may commonly emphasize the assumption of agreement, but it can also be interpreted as condescension, remorse, defeat, or leave me the hell alone, any of which may be a deception because there is no personal attribution."

"The context of a conversation clarifies its meaning," I said, automatically leading with my ego.

"Okay, okay," Bonnie said tonelessly, which put my point to rest.

After this illuminating exchange, Bonnie simply went silent if I erred, leaving me to discover my offence to clarity. During these lulls, passers-by provided me with evidence of how pervasive our use of verbal colouring really is, therefore how frighteningly extensive the continuity of confusion is in our culture. All cultures, I assumed.

One enjoyable example of this came in the form of a twenty-something girl complaining to her friend, "Whatever happened to the customer is always right?"

"Retail is a gyp," her girlfriend commiserated.

Bonnie grasped the opportunity to help me understand the process of assessment.

"Gypsy's aside," she said clinically, "customer service is about correcting company or customer errors and misunderstandings according to the policies of manufacturers and retailers. There is no moral imperative, spoken or implied, and little that is personal about transactions between strangers, other than what their perceptions of personality can create out of an act of commerce. The continuity of the girls' thinking dictates that other aspects of their lives will be plagued by affront and confusion because they don't realize they have made

[201]

their happiness subject to availability, credit approval, processing fees, and that reality may not be exactly as illustrated. Their emotional investments come with thirty-day manufacturing defect protection before their satisfaction becomes a warranty issue. True joy for them," Bonnie quipped, "has to be hand washed, never bleached, and if the girls read a promise into a sale's philosophy instead of reading the label, they will end up calling one-eight hundred Tough Go. Does this make sense?"

"You're in the groove we were in before," I said.

"If you make a conscious effort to avoid seemingly unimportant self-deceptions," she continued, "it becomes increasingly difficult to generate the momentum required to make a complete ass of yourself. Moreover, as a matter of intellectual continuity, you'll more easily see how other people operate, and as a matter of emotional stability, you'll face your days head on because you've set no traps for yourself. Does this make sense?"

"It does. In the last four days I've experienced flashes of the under-side of many conversations."

"Then it's time to move on." Which she did without taking a breath. "We deal with events based on how we feel about them before we stop and think which means other people can manipulate our emotions to their advantage."

"We talked about that."

"This time we're going beyond advertising gullibility and into how people try to manipulate others, often without either of them realizing it. For example, you nearly popped an artery when I raised the tip to twenty percent because you thought my kindness overshadowed your offer to pay for the meal. Proof of your indignation came when I said there were waves in the creek, and you noted how chilly it had become. Your comment was not about the climate."

"I'm not denying that I thought you tricked me in more than one way," I said, "but the wind made it colder, and neither of us was dressed for it."

"Tricked, not betrayed?" she said.

"There's a difference?"

"I tricked you into seeing something clearly, which your affront translated as a betrayal, even though you were better off."

"Do you agree that the wind made it colder?"

"I agree that it did, but let's take a moment to assess your version of that moment for authenticity."

"The moment is all yours."

[202]

"Thank you." Bonnie bracketed a phantom scene with her hands. Slowly panning from left to right, she said, "Exterior, day, tracking shot of a man who stood winter watches in the North Atlantic and who has sailed thousands of ocean miles in all kinds of weather. A man who has been wounded atop a foreign mountain, jailed in three or four countries, and deported from God-knows where for playing games with terrorist heads of state. Widen the shot, and we see that he's walking with an unaccomplished, single mother of teenagers who makes a casual remark about six inch waves in a sheltered harbour, and he comments on his frailties?" Bonnie nudged me. "You also turned an interesting shade of red when I handed the ferryman two fares. Overall, your behaviour last week made my theoretical point personally relevant today, especially now that you've seen yourself in your friends." She took my arm in hers. "Which is what you were trying to hide from me."

"What do you think I saw that was so bad I would want to hide it from you?"

"I'm not sure I can separate that from all I can see," she smiled coyly, "or that you're ready to hear it."

"I said I would never hurt you," I quipped.

"Never is a long time, but a student who finally puts their faith in the teacher deserves a reward."

"Thanks," I said, somehow thinking I was going to hear good things.

"You saw that you are a shadow created by social dictates; shadows have no substance, no depth, so you are also transparent, predictable, and superficial. Last week, I saw that you are possessive of things you do not own, like my time and affections, and you expect things that are not your due, such as knowing my plans. Our silence on the boat unnerved you enough to seek reassurance by asking me about something you couldn't care less about, but was important to me, so you are manipulative. That said, I saw your ploy as an opportunity to motivate you into playing my game, which you did, the first success of which you used to learn more so you could hide what you're like from me, which is deceitful. Today, I see that you've learned you can't hide what you don't know is hidden, and this realization should now propel you to correct what you discovered about yourself at the Avalon for your own evolution."

I managed to remain quiet for that often regrettable half-second that can change a relationship, before I said, "That works for me."

She squeezed my arm. "Obviously it's already working; you've been succinct for over an hour without being angry and without making a single reference to rectums or bodily functions. Possibly more importantly, now that you know it's possible to be tricked for your own good, you can cut me some slack, and our research will go more quickly."

"Done."

Bonnie and I thereafter monitored and commented on passers-by conversations to help me assess events and cement my appreciation of how accurate and efficient communications could be when our assumptions matched, due in no small measure to the unusual depth thinking in terms if essential events offers. Conversely, I far better appreciated how much others misinterpreted their true circumstance, when they filtered events through concern over their image. By the time we reached her home, I was exhilarated from hearing so much in-between-the-lines of other people's lives and so drained from editing my ~~crap~~-racism, sexism, and other grievous categories of ignorance that I said goodbye to her from within in a dull and floating awareness. Bonnie noted this about my demeanour, said it would pass without harm, and that I was due for another infusion of energy—whatever that meant.

Emphasizing the utter mediocrity of my mood, traffic on the way home seemed bizarrely slow, even though my gauges said this wasn't true. Also strange was that I didn't find it funny when a middle-aged Caucasian male shouted at an erratic driving Oriental man that they should all walk to math class. Not at the time, anyway.

Entering Ed's apartment, a colossal fatigue overcame me and I collapsed on the couch feeling like I was under the weight of a ~~trillion~~ …I felt so heavy that I literally couldn't move, yet I remained unconcerned. Eyes closed, I listened to an internal buzzing through which I swear I could feel my heart beating. Wishing this sensation would stop didn't seem wise, so I focused on the rhythm until the buzz faded into chirping birds; fifty minutes had passed. I got up feeling invigorated, not unlike the last time I had dabbled with cocaine while covering a lazy firefight that became a three-day debacle.

I called Ed to see if he was available for a beer. He wasn't, so I went for an effortless jog that took me a full kilometre beyond my usual range before I turned around, still feeling like I could sprint home. Knowing the penalty I would pay in the morning, I didn't do this, and by bedtime my youthful level of vigour had settled back into its battered thirty-five year old container.

Chapter Twenty-one
Practical Magic

In spite of making steady progress, by the sixth day of Bonnie interjecting her practices of clarity at every opportunity, she grimaced at my unusual number of errors at such a torrid pace that I began to feel as though my personality was fragmenting along character fault lines. My mind finally shut down over a simple menu choice at a Greek restaurant on 4th Street.

Grinning foolishly when Andrea asked me what I would like, all I was missing for an involuntary incarceration in a soft-walled room was the drool as Bonnie explained, "He's exhausted from eliminating reason. We'll share the number three combo, a carafe of house red, and ice water please."

"Excellent," Andrea said.

"Now that you know intellectual prowess is your worst enemy," Bonnie said, facing me, "you should approach our meetings as if you need them to survive. That's what a student would do at your stage because they would understand they're straddling the old and the new as if they were options."

"Before I ask you why they're not options, how do I know that about intellectual prowess?"

"You're a sputtering example of what hiding inappropriate thoughts and trying to uphold inconsistent views does to people. Look at you— you're exhausted. It's a terrific day!" she raised her voice.

"Why is the slow death of my brain a cause for celebration?"

"You've got it backwards again, but until this day you couldn't help it: you've finally disrupted the automatic routing of events through your ego, but you haven't claimed enough knowledge about yourself to make a permanent shift onto the clarity trail. For the moment, and I mean in this moment, the Olympian levels of intellectual gymnastics you have always incorporated to make sense of your world have run their course and left you pending."

"Meaning?"

"Are you concerned about anything?"

[205]

"Nothing—still waters run deep." I tapped my temple.

"Peh-ending," she said, hard on the "P" as if she had mispronounced the word the first time. "Let it fill your mind."

I did this without effort because nature abhors a vacuum.

"I'm pending," I said, aware that I was opening myself to whatever might happen but not like a predator on the instinctual prowl. I was poised to interact without feeling guarded. It was a curiously free state of placid awareness, apparently run by the low voltage tingling sensation running through my body.

"You are potential," Bonnie said a cut above a whisper.

Without the interference of an internal dialogue upholding my daily assumptions, her words tendered the sense that every second was a moment-choice within which I was free to agree with or change the momentum of my decision-path because nothing was pushing me onward or stacked against me. I was in between my decisions; they still existed, but were suspended, and I was indifferently aware that my future pended.

"That's a perfect description," I think I said aloud, awed by realizing the power I had over my life, as another encompassing fatigue beset me. As swiftly as this recognition had come upon me, it was gone, and I was embarrassed because I felt like I just forgotten my mother's name.

Bonnie leaned forward and addressed my unspoken feelings.

"Since we began these lessons, you've literally had dozens of opportunities to tell me where to go, but you chose to put your ego in a temporary trance and address your underlying state of mind. After only a couple of weeks, you've discovered the lucidity available to you by not constantly spending your energy on reconstructing the world you think you know. This was no small feat."

"Thanks for the perspective," I said, struggling for a deeper breath, "but where did it go—the clarity?"

"It belongs to another perspective. As you continue to practice, you'll have access to the memories you think got away. Imagine what years of practicing clarity would do for people who used it to address the nature of human behaviour? No one could hide their underlying motives from them, including the secrets they are keeping from themselves," she answered her own question. "Couple that with their intimate knowledge of the magical arts, and our audience will have no doubt how powerful the teachers really are."

My attempt to respond turned into a Lamaze breathing exercise. Looking tearfully pleased, Bonnie said I had ended my journey of

[206]

living exclusively in the cognition of the average man and realigning assumptions takes its toll on the body. It's also normal to feel like a lead bar when you're new at polishing your link with a massive energy that's becoming free to flow your way.

I wanted to ask her to define almost every term she used. Instead, I accepted her reply as given because she had to have been down this road to have described it so precisely, and Bonnie was nothing if not thorough. She would explain everything when it was time.

We ate our meals in relative silence. When we were finished and had placed money on the table, for no apparent reason Bonnie said, "How do you understand the concept of spiritual Intent?"

"Spirit sees things for what they are, so they don't get side-tracked. They also know how to work with momentum, so their intentions equal done deals."

"Take it one step further; if they have no personality as we know it, then who and what they are would be indistinguishable from what they do, correct?"

"I can see that in the abstract."

"In which case using the term Intent in place of Spirit would be accurate. Correct?"

"It would."

"Good." She set her cup down, inhaled deeply and formally said, "Physical experience is an artifice for spiritual development, so it makes perfect sense to use our life-force's intentions as a personal guidance system when we're in a physical form. The trick is strengthening our link within the territory of an ego that wants what it wants when it wants it, thinking it is protecting us from threats that we make up. You had to experience the clarity that a simple practice can bring," looking out of the window she continued, "to know that it's more than possible, but stupid beyond words to deliberately remain a shadow character in your ongoing autobiography." She looked my way. "With exercise and caution, you will eventually be able to open the door to other exceptional perceptions at will."

"What kind of exceptional perceptions?"

"The kind you'll find disagreeable until they prove themselves," she chuckled.

"Such as?" I said, believing the alternative was to be perceived as being stupid beyond words.

"We can start with simple things," she shrugged. "I shop without keeping track of prices and always choose the fastest checkout line by feel, to keep Intent consciously active in my everyday affairs."

[207]

The pervasive fatigue I felt lifted as suddenly as it had come on, as I said, "You must be important for your spirit friends to guide you to a checkout line."

"They're not concerned with those details. I practice to keep the link clean. Come on," Bonnie said, getting out of her seat, "It's time to see it in action, so you won't argue about having it in the screenplay." She paused. "We're going to park beside a blue Volvo, fifth row from Zellers main entrance."

"Those are long rows, there's bound to be a Volvo, and I think blue and grey are their bestsellers. Maybe their only colours," I said as I thought about it.

"Dented front fender on the driver's side," she said, leaving me behind.

"This I've got to see," I said, getting to my feet.

Bonnie stopped in mid-motion and said, "You practiced clarity until it proved itself as a magical art, correct?"

"You could categorize some of my understandings that way," I said, baffled.

"What's different now?"

"The difference is that you're claiming to be able to get something out of nothing which might work in a screenplay, but...." I shrugged, looking around at reality. "What does it have to do with a student?"

"It's part of reaching a new understanding—a new cognition."

"Are you saying I can practice being psychic?" I chided her.

"Of course, but let's not get ahead of ourselves."

On the way to the store, Bonnie drew on past relationships to speak humorously about the ways people retouched the truth to suit their images. I reciprocated with tales about politicians on what became a comfortable exchange relative to how internally volatile our meetings could become for me. After a short while, we drove into the parking lot, and after a few turns, Bonnie drove to the car she had envisioned, which was where she said it would be; there was a small dent at the height of a shopping cart basket on the driver's side.

"Well?" she said.

"Do you need groceries?"

"With teenagers? I always—" she caught on. "Ah—you want more."

"Wow—you really are psychic."

Bonnie smacked me on the arm playfully then she wheeled her car closer to the grocery store, where we picked up milk, fruit, vegetables, tinned soups, and cereal. When we went to the front to pay, there was no angle from which we could see how full the carts were at the four open checkout counters, only that they each had queues of two or three people.

"Pick a reference line you think I can't beat through the paying process, and I'll join one that will beat it," she said.

"What if they're the same?" I said.

"They won't be," she chuckled. "I'm focused on the positive."

I made my choice and Bonnie joined the line she preferred, which was in third place behind two men while I stationed myself to watch everyone leaving.

A bagger-boy shifted stations, an older woman fumbled with her purse, and a yuppie swiped a credit card then changed her mind about which card to use, but a price check ultimately decided the matter. Bonnie ended up paying before our reference shopper was finished, and with taxes she was a penny short. The cashier waived it off.

Handing me a grocery bag, she said, "Don't get hung up on the details. Developing your awareness is about more important things, like recognizing a delay could avoid a car crash, or missing a turn might bring you to where you need to be."

What I heard her saying was, "Don't look too close, or you'll figure it out," but it was too late. Taking the parcel from her, I said, "I know the trick: the time you spent choosing a line was about finding something in another cart that wasn't marked properly."

"Pardon me?"

"A sceptical student would also say the Volvo belongs to staff in the mall, so it's always there, and that you can do math in your head before they'd believe angels shop at the Superstore."

"How did I price the tomatoes without weighing them?"

"I haven't figured everything out."

"Let's take these things home, then we'll go for a drive, and I'll explain my trick."

I thought so. "Okay."

Twenty minutes later we were cruising Marine drive on a gorgeous day, quietly heading for a Cypress Mountain Lookout that rendered a spectacular view of the city, Stanley Park, the Lions Gate Bridge, and the harbour.

When we arrived, Bonnie shut off the car, took the keys out of the ignition, and dropped them into her carryall. Turning to me, she said, "Original Intent is not a trick. It is our Source Soul and a library of timeless knowledge that some people can tune into for help in any number of ways." She shifted her weight, making herself comfortable for a long stay. "Following the designs of Intent is to learn how to

[209]

gather the energy we need to ignore a taunting world, so we can tackle worthy challenges. Today's demonstration was about you and I sharing another teacher/student experience, which will help you cross the bridge between your version of the world and into the one you encountered at the restaurant." She relaxed her pose. "Later in my work, you'll read that a conscious partnership between Intent and a teacher is so powerful that events which can fell strong people can be dealt with as simple challenges or pushed aside as a matter of impeccable intentions commanding the right of way."

"How is this relevant to your... our work?"

"The success of my archaeologist's quest depends on them embracing Osiris's ideas as if their life depended on them because it does. Aligning your personal power with Intent can be dangerous. I need you to...."

"You need me to demonstrate how someone tries to align themselves with it, I get it. Are you saying Spirit is dangerous?"

"No, but some lessons are based on aligning a student's momentum with a flow of events, and I've told you that momentum doesn't think. The student's free will could cause them to metaphorically stand in front of the bus. I didn't mention this before today because it never crossed my mind that after all we've invested in our project, you would accuse me of lying to you."

"You drove up here to tell me to take your premises seriously?"

"Don't be offended. It's a long walk back."

"You're threatening me with exercise?" I said, incredulously.

"That's your ego misinterpreting our circumstance. I'm saying that complaining about what we have to do won't change what we have to do, other than annoying you enough to get out and start walking back." She shrugged like I did with her. "You already know I'll drive on by."

Grasping at straws, I said, "Is this is the confrontation scene?"

"You have nothing to confront other than your affront, and that's not a challenge worthy of my time."

I paused, thought about the distance back to my motorcycle, and in spite of it being entirely downhill, I said, "Or mine," capitulating to a truth.

"Excellent." She fished for her keys, which tinked against another metal. Bonnie upended her carryall in her lap, and a penny dropped out.

"I knew it had to be me," she said. "Intent doesn't make mistakes, not even a penny."

I said nothing.

After this chat, Bonnie and I often shopped together so that she could demonstrate what she claimed was a growing ability to tap into the stream of Intent, while I continued to look for ways she could stage the show. I wasn't truly baffled by her charade until the day she took all of her money out of her purse, turned away, and asked me to pocket enough to cover our lunch. If the bill came out to the penny, I was to agree to replace my efforts to find other explanations for her trickery with seriously trying to tap into my spirit's stream of intent; she said her Original Intent had ratted me out.

I agreed to the challenge and put some of her money in my left front pocket.

Having a glass of wine each put us over budget, but I said nothing until Bonnie ordered a second glass only for me. I declined, saying that we might be short on funds. I knew I had between seven and ten dollars—a five dollar bill and a bunch of change I had grabbed from the top of my dresser on the way out that morning. She said worrying muddied the waters.

With tax, our bill came to $22.65. A fifteen percent tip brought this to $26.05. Emptying both of my pockets, I had $26.05.

"It was a good try," I said, stacking coins on the table."

"What are you talking about, we're perfect?" she said incredulously.

"*We* are bang on—you weren't."

"I told you to take enough for lunch. How could I know how much you had?"

"You implied your money would cover both of us."

"You inferred my money would cover both of us." Laughing, she said, "Are you saying I cheated by intuiting exactly how much money you had with you?"

"I think you told me not to worry because you have more money in your purse," I said, scrambling.

"What does that have to do with anything?"

I hesitated, came up with nothing, and gave in. "Okay, so how do you practice this cosmic wire-tapping thing?"

With an errant grin occasionally leaking out of her poise, Bonnie explained the basics of how to stop my internal dialogue without her help. She said these practices ultimately led to another framework of reality called the Second Attention, but I was probably years away from achieving entry on my own, as a deliberate experience, if I kept up the practices. That said, just trying to access Intent as a guidance system automatically loosened my death-grip on the First Attention, which is entirely fixed on the inventory of physical reality. There was a

[211]

lot more to know about how our perceptions assemble the world we experience, she said, but focusing between the lines of conversations went a long way toward preparing me for extraordinary perceptions.

Bonnie then explained that "intending to know" made her plot edgy because the apparent meaning of the resulting information played on the assumptions of the First Attention of her audience. As the scenes we had discussed amply demonstrated, what her teachers saw, said, and did, rarely agreed with what we thought they represented, but things still worked out. In this way, a simple pause could be dramatic and possibly create an access point for the audience to touch their Silent Knowledge about the screen circumstance. Bonnie reached into her carryall and took a scene from her screenplay. I knew she was working on it, but I was unreasonably annoyed that she had completed something entirely new without consulting me. But I could hardly object.

"I'm still working on the set description, but imagine that the chamber is translucent and that we can see spatial infinity outside. Our solar system will be recognizable off to one side of the Saa-ra character. She pronounced the character's name 'saw-raw'

"Got it."

I read the following:

SCENE TWO
INTERIOR: CRYSTALLINE CHAMBER WIDE SHOT
Saa-ra, Kha-lib, Jerome, and Phillip are seen as astral bodies with a particular hue differentiating them from the rest of the twenty-six astral body characters. They chat in the foreground of this group, thirteen men and thirteen women who are grouped socially: a few men talking to each other, a few women doing the same, three people in non-specific gender order, a group of six, etc. Off to one side, PHILLIP is talking to MAN ONE while SAA-RA stands beside him.

PHILLIP
You have shown them much and taught your-self well, but the journey is not complete. We see that it will be brought to a close in this way.

FX: SECTION OF WALL IN FRONT OF MILKY WAY
SAA-RA opens a scene of infinity with a wave of her arm and points to a whirl of rolling events, as if from news casts that span centuries of warfare, flood and

[212]

famine, etc. Time is represented by ripples between events.

SAA-RA (pointing)

Probable, (pause), also probable.

With a slower view of news events dating from the 1950's, she says,

There—inevitable.

MAN ONE nods, seeing what is to be, his expression conveys that it could be no other way without regret.

SAA-RA

To have chosen this time and place to seal your destiny is to embrace a hard and lonely path, for you once again meet with those who believe themselves to be powerful and so important as to not treat others with the love we teach. It will again be them who make you what you are to become, and in the doing you will have need to trust and then lose all trust, love, then lose your capacity to love; it will be a struggle to find reasons to live until you understand your purpose of mastering these lessons of illusions. Such teachings are not for the meek, as only the demand for the completion of tasks will bring true under-standing. It will also cost the image of all who will learn and all who will teach.

MAN ONE

I will have to learn who I am and bring that character to his end in this one time?

SAA-RA

In this last time, and you will, but be warned: the task is not to blame yourself for being the message of imminent destruction, as some will perceive, but the messenger of our love. For such as you have agreed to carry that burden, then such is your destiny and lesson, though you will not remember this until we touch you with this knowledge.

MAN ONE

How will I come to know my purpose?

[213]

PHILLIP and SAA-RA exchange a glance that
speaks to an amused secret.

PHILLIP

We have sent a messenger in time; your
journey will take you to her, and to you she
will say that we have sent many of ourselves,
and that you are one, if you so choose. Your
Silent Knowledge of us and this place will
determine your decision as she offers you
knowledge to know who we are once again.
But beware, messengers do not linger, and
our teachers teach only those who will learn,
so know that you may not choose that destiny
turn. And if memories of this place fade with
the damage endured, and you find no relief
from terrible knowledge secured, and tears do
not cleanse the memory of your quest, and if
your silent reply has the messenger leave you
to rest, know that you are never alone. You
can always find me in this place, for I am
your source, and I walk with my children
until they understand the nature of all dis-
course. That is who I am, that is my word,
and they are the same for my actors in the
theatre of the absurd.

SAA-RA points through the crystalline walls toward the Milky Way.

SAA-RA

As we leave at the same time here (she smiles
at the word Time), we enter into the depth of
linear time at different points in physical life.

She circles her finger three times, and the atmosphere appears
to ripple around the motions in slightly different hues with
each circle.

SAA-RA (cont'd)

Your different years of birth (she motions with her
arm to encompass the twenty-six) correspond to
the experiences you have chosen in order to meet
us at specific points in destiny. This one is the
present (her finger ripples a brownish hue), this
one is the time of the beginning, and...

[214]

KHA-LI ENTERS THE CHAMBER
As seen over the shoulder of MAN ONE.
SAA-RA (cont'd)
It is time for introductions.

That was all Bonnie had written.

I straightened the pages and for no apparent reason set them down gently. Bonnie tried to hide any physical indication of anticipation, which only enhanced it, as I thought about her work and said, "I liked it. A little tightening here and there and you're good to go. Except maybe the poetry thing is—it's not consistent." There was something gnawingly familiar about it, but I couldn't recall what book or movie I was thinking of.

Bonnie watched and waited, as if I was supposed to say something more.

"I gather the first scene would introduce Kha-li?" I said, breaking her focus.

"Correct. Are you ready to deal with the premise of Knowing as if your life depended on it?"

"I'm all ears."

"That'll have to do, for now."

Chapter Twenty-two
The Nature of Knowing

Officiously, Bonnie said, "My teachers say that everything is conscious, and all consciousness vibrates at a frequency specific to its
genus and individual nature." She moved her finger across our table in
a waveform pattern. "Everything is also electromagnetic, so like-
minded people attract and contribute to the momentum of similarly
natured events. The more evolved the consciousness, or nature of the
act, the faster it vibrates. Unconditional love is the most rapid event:
malice is the slowest."

I nodded to confirm that I had not fallen behind.

"You are magnetic, so the thoughts you generate are also independent magnetic forces. We talked about this at our first meeting." She
leaned forward. "At some point in your life, you were unable to recall
information that was familiar, then later in the day, or the next, it
popped into your mind. The effort to find this information is akin to
sending a messenger that rides the momentum of will to attract a
response that matches the frequency and sequencing of the question.
When we turn our attention to other matters, we put ourselves in stand-
by mode to receive the answer. If we don't turn away, and have
practiced gathering energy, we can access information at will, eventually even our Silent Knowledge.

"Our beliefs work the same way," she said, when I nodded in
apparent appreciation of however important that point must be to her.
"They lead us to people and experiences of a similar nature so that our
actions seek and seed events long after we have turned our attention to
other matters. It is this turning away that has us miss how much in
control of our lives we really are. The bottom line is that we assemble a
daily reality that unerringly offers us a view of ourselves through the
nature of our relationships to other people and the kind of world in
which we participate."

"Otis and a guard dog," I acknowledged her lesson.

Bonnie nodded in the affirmative. "Knowledge vibrates at a speed
that reflects its nature, and we can access it to the degree that we focus
our will, and the extent to which our personal speed matches the speed

of the information. This information can be outside of our direct experience, but its components must be familiar for us to process a conclusion. If we gather pieces of past events, a sudden knowing can feel like a coalescing of information you hadn't thought about in that way, as long as the messenger is free from erroneous assumptions."

"Is that a loop-hole in intending to know something, like free will screwing up a psychic reading?"

"No. Let's take the example of sending a messenger to resolve the paradox of what happens when the irresistible force meets the immovable object. All objects are the product of will propelled by the irresistible force of catalytic momentum into a physical manifestation. It follows that the apparently immovable object is less powerful by the degree of will required to maintain that form. In other words, your question presumes a paradox when there is no such thing in nature; they are a creation of man in which at least one component of a theoretical state is erroneous." She tapped the table. "Identical forces of will also presupposes duplicate experiences with interchangeable interpretations forming identical intentions. Granting that absurdity, both aspects of the paradox would still lose energy in an encounter until an outside force eventually determined the outcome. You must have covered battles like that."

"So you're saying there's no such thing as a stalemate in nature?"

"A flexible balance is inherent to the ebb and flow of all energy."

"The body dies. Where's the balance in that?"

"Death is an assumption based on the limitations of physical perception. Remember where we began…everything is conscious?" she said rhetorically. "The body changes form to become part of the earth, the earth becomes part of the plants, plants are eaten by animals, and we eat the plants and animals. Everything cycles and recycles—everything is connected." Bonnie opened her palms to indicate an irrefutable conclusion, then setting her hands on the table to suggest simplicity, she said, "It follows that if any single thing could die, everything would eventually die. In reality, when a physical form makes an apparent change, the spiritual essence has been released to take on whatever forms its speed allows, while the body takes on whatever forms it can in the absence of the spirit rider."

"We become ghosts?"

"That's one form of energy the speed of our consciousness allows."

"What about a rock?"

"What about a toasted bacon and tomato sandwich?"

"Sorry. Are you saying rocks are conscious?"

[217]

"Certainly, but most of us can't perceive their vitality."

"Meaning some people can?"

"Very fast people—seers can focus their perception to see the energy fields in everything physical. They know that the earth is alive because they can see it like a surgeon watching a heart beating in their hand." She clasped her hands studiously in front of her. "Close your eyes and imagine that all things are events when viewed from a different underlying order of reality."

"For example," I said, closing my eyes.

"A pane of glass is solid within our perception of time," Bonnie explained, "but if we weathered reality from the perspective of a thousand years passing for every second, we would experience glass as a liquid gently flowing in the direction of gravity. The pane wouldn't be an object so much as a circumstance connected to an array of exterior settings, like viewing a bend in the river isn't just about water moving by a single point. The flow has created conditional events downstream, like deltas, based on upstream events, like erosion creating canyons, when our point of observation is the flatland between the two."

"I know that old glass is thicker at the bottom than at the top."

She nodded. "Our point of observation reveals the cumulative effect of the river's experience in that specific time and place only, and under those specific conditions, no different from you and I observing an instant of each other's lives right now. Neither of us is entirely apparent to the other, nor are we complete in and of ourselves. We are riding different tributaries toward the same destination of evolutionary fulfill-ment at our own pace."

I nodded, unnecessarily stirring my drink. Bonnie looked out of the window.

"What about..." I started to say.

"I wonder how they stay open?" she mused.

I waited for her to continue.

Bonnie appeared to be as dazed to hear herself say that a company across Davie Street was a front for a smuggling operation as I was stunned by it. A brief pause, then she haltingly said the contraband was people, a two-way operation, illegal immigrants in, babies out.

"How did you piece that together?" I said, stretching my unplanned mockery to hopefully mimic wonder because her demonstration was so juvenile, and unnecessary; just write the scene and be done with it.

"Days ago," she said seriously, "I noticed that the staff cared for customers lackadaisically. We're in a high rent area, so I asked myself

[218]

how they make a profit selling inexpensive items to so few customers. The messenger came back today. Look at the sense of secrecy about them."

"How do you look at a sense?"

"Do it and you'll discover the answer."

I watched for about ten seconds before turning my head to comment; Bonnie pointed her finger back across the street. The next twenty seconds were no different from the first ten other than it being twice as boring, until my mind isolated individuals from the context of commerce. I thought I saw a furtive quality about one of the staff and his customer's posture. Both of them were slightly hunched, implying they were speaking under their breath. I also saw a clerk cover his mouth when he spoke to a customer, who did a quick head-bob snigger.

Bonnie cleared her throat, and I came out of my reverie.

"Well?" she said expectantly.

"The sense I get is that they know people well enough to tell dirty jokes."

Bonnie levelled a granite gaze at me. I wasn't kidding, so I stared back.

"Ahhh," she exhaled as if she had received another delivery. "The information is difficult for you to accept because while it agrees with your views about mankind's malevolence, it subverts your certainty of its whereabouts, which threatens your sense of security. By the way, that's entirely based on your prejudices."

"My prejudices might be more earned than learned, than most peoples."

Bonnie took me to task on the sidebar point: "Yes or no, per capita gays, aboriginals, and Asians of all nationalities are more prevalent in Vancouver than anywhere else in Canada?"

"Probably."

"How many friends do you have in these groups? No—how many friends have you ever had in any of these groups?"

"I grew up in a middle class *wasp* area long before it was fashionable for gays to come out, in an era when political intrigue was about who was screwing who on the school board. When I moved to Little Israel in north Toronto, I hung out with Jews, when I lived in Little Italy, I hung out with falling and fallen Mics. When I began traveling, everyone in Canada dropped away except Ed, and he was born in Germany."

"You haven't mentioned any women from any time or background."

"There haven't been any who could keep up."

[219]

"One of your secret needs is to feel superior—it's tangled with having to be right—so you can't have any women friends who aren't sexual conquests. When you think you've bested them, you throw them away as unworthy opponents, which is another of your prejudices."

"Does it make sense that anyone who has seen destruction on the scale that I've seen it because of prejudices, would fall into the same trap?"

"You comprehend why you should embrace noble ideas, but your interpretation of world events has impressed you with a different set of facts. These are that white, heterosexual, secular, apolitical males are more trustworthy or somehow less scary than any other people." She touched my arm. "Your experiences have sabotaged your most treasured beliefs, and thinking you know better is camouflaging that fact from you like it did from me."

Unsure of whether to laugh or utter an obscenity, I did something I had never done in my life. I harrumphed. *Funny how it sounds just like the word*, I thought as it filled that critical half-second before Bonnie noted the event with a fleeting smile.

"The affront you're struggling to contain is not directed at my ability to intend to know because that's a part of the way things are between us now. Instead, I'm trespassing on the monopoly on danger you assume is yours from having paid so dearly to develop what you consider a philosophy."

"You don't think it is, after all that I have explained?"

"Your views are the remains of repetitive assaults on your self-image, the importance of which you have elevated by virtue of their survival. You assume other people couldn't possibly have acquired similar understandings from different circumstances because you have been honing your defences ever since you... ever since. How you came to your understandings is certainly personal, but what you came to understand is not exclusive information. Like it or not, I understand the depth of mankind's malevolence better than you because I didn't have the freedom to avoid it or leave when the adrenaline rush passed." She inched back. "Neither do the hundreds of millions of women whose lives didn't unfold like an action-adventure. They experience cruelty in other ways." Her tone was cool, her eyes accusing, and I thought I saw damage lurking beneath her stare.

Aware that I was staring back as if in defiance, I lowered my eyes and swallowed bile to digest a sudden between-the-lines understanding: Bonnie's world view was an insurmountable obstacle to us having any real fun, in any kind of relationship, and as a sense loss trickled

[220]

through my bowels, I thought it could be time to cash out. I wasn't far from finishing the application.

"By leper's lives," Bonnie said, looking out the window as if my answer would walk by, "did you mean begging?"

I had no trouble recalling that outburst of weeks earlier, nor in assessing this moment: she knew she had gone too far, and the time shift and topic change was damage control.

Too late.

"That's one ending," I said amicably because I could afford to be. "Losers become social outcasts, or they move inside to keep their secrets company."

"That sounds too deep to have come from observing your stories."

"I knew a couple of Americans in Toronto. One dodged Vietnam, one didn't, and both of them sometimes wondered or maybe wished they had made the other choice. The split in public opinion between branding them killer and coward made them both casualties of conscience."

"Well put. Is that what they moved inside—guilt?"

"Or resentment, maybe both."

"They said that to you?"

"Not in so many words; they knew I had a clue about what it was like, so the odd comment was enough."

"Being the coward *and* the killer?"

"No—that the overall context of everyday life was changed for both of them, and those changes are more or less the same in everyone who experienced what they did. We were on the same page, without having to compare anything."

"You still don't think I understand what the silence is about, do you?"

"Feel free. As you said, it's not exclusive information."

Bonnie did not flinch or hesitate.

"I think it's common for combatants to avoid discussing their experiences with anyone who hasn't been down that road because there's a huge gulf between public assumptions about warfare and a fighter's intimate knowledge of it. I think that chasm is created whenever religious or political motives disguised as moral certainties are pitted against events so abhorrent that participants can't forgive themselves for shattering any number of beliefs, and that the restraint of this expression caused them to seek relief in a bottle or a needle. I also think what an anonymous enemy couldn't do with bullets, their countrymen did with personal judgements."

[221]

"Impressive—I mean it."

"So when did you develop empathy for the so-called coward?"

"I didn't think he was a coward."

"Identifying with a casualty of conscience, then?"

"I suppose—if I thought I had done something wrong. Can't you just like someone?"

"No; I explained the principles of magnetic energy." She dropped the subject and said, "My place tomorrow at nine, and bring some of your work." Bonnie reached for the bill.

Covering the slip of paper with my hand, I said, "What's the rush?"

"You gave me a way into the confrontation scene, and I want to get it on paper while it's fresh. Thanks." She stood up, blew a kiss in my general direction and muttering "casualty of conscious" left me sitting there.

"Anytime," I said meaning it because there was little of it left. It was just a question of opportunity.

Chapter Twenty-three
Cataloguing Discord

Zzz: Drifting in the periphery of consciousness, I was on a catamaran in the Mediterranean when instances of colleagues "knowing things" rolled through my mind unbidden. No situation was more definitive than a feeling to stop or turn, but after three examples easily came to mind, I accepted that we all had experienced definitive psychic feelings at some time in our lives, just not with any control over them. The claim of control connected to another ruse, her apparent ability to sometimes know what I was thinking, which became clear as a consequence of her manoeuvring conversations toward landing points I could not anticipate, when she had previously checked these out under the guise of the many "what ifs" she had stored for future reference.

Checked out. Store: I could eliminate two-thirds of the checkout lines by the age and gender of the customers and clerks. Young and male were faster because they didn't fill their carts, chat about the weather they had just walked through, or suddenly search their wallet for a payment method as if groceries were usually free. Men were the house odds for speed. Bonnie would certainly have a refined list of clues; she was like that. Some magic.

She was good, I thought as my imagination squeezed the catamaran between the Palma welcoming lights and the outer breakwater... good enough to palm a tomato, and by squeezing it for ripeness accurately guess it's weigh from its circumference.

Almost awake, I tried but couldn't figure out how she did the lunch money trick, but it had to be a modification on the shopping scam. Scam: The penny in her carryall was laughable.

At four-thirty in the morning, it was too early to get up and too late to go back to sleep, so I let thoughts about her story make their own connections. In the half-hour before I got up, I came to see her work as a New Age morality play based on religious propaganda. Mystical intrigues aimed at personal development represented the bible's teachings, while diabolical theories that fostered blind obedience under the guise of faith represented the devil. The Christ figure would come from

[223]

the cult—no personal rights, unlimited investigative authority—had to be a cult. The man with no name would attempt to teach people how they were enslaved, but not enough of them would listen to make a difference. He would seed lessons, then come back to conclude them.

I got out of bed, made coffee, and began honing my sample scenes for the grant, to reflect my new understandings. At nine o'clock, I packed a chapter of my own book in my tank-top bag and headed across the bridge to her house.

Seated in her kitchen, Bonnie hadn't finished reading my work before setting the pages aside to offer me an insight that was more implausible than the smuggling scenario because I was supposedly a participant.

The true event and scene she was reading opened in Beirut on December 23, 1983, with a crew arriving at a hospital amid a steady stream of car bomb casualties. Our pictures of outrage and gore were so good that we lingered at the emergency entrance until soldiers threatened us for imposing on their grief.

We went inside to tape the triage tango.

Following the natural progression of events, we went to the morgue; seeing that it was full, we went in search of the makeshift morgue to impress our audience with the extent of the carnage. At one point, I walked past a storage room and did a double take when I realised the sacks on the floor weren't laundry. It was here that Bonnie said she had seen me in her mind's eye, catch a glimpse of someone inside the room guaranteeing the occupants were dead.

"Interesting, but it's a trap—nowhere to go with it."

"It's a trap of a different kind," she said. "An integral aspect of our sense of security is our perception of morality because it can exclude all kinds of nasty things we think people wouldn't dare do to us. You shut the incident out of your mind because what you saw uprooted the last of your generous assumptions about people, in spite of your penchant to think the worst of humanity. You couldn't afford to embrace that moment of utter helplessness, so you banished the memory to suit your less brutal core."

"Thank you."

"You know you are a kind person, you just don't think you can afford to be," Bonnie said evenly. "You should try to recall every detail about that night to rid yourself of its affects." Crisp lines at the corners of her mouth suggested that I try this right away.

"What affects?"

[224]

"That will become clear when you examine that event," she said patiently.

"Now?"

"That would be nice."

"Give me a second." I re-seated myself before trying to conjure a memory I knew wasn't mine, but why make waves now?

After a short while, I recalled being repulsed by the first mutilated body but no others, including the guy who was brought in on separate stretchers.

"Aloud would be helpful," Bonnie said.

With the dispassion I had felt at the hospital entrance, I described the strain on the drivers' faces, the tense efficiency of too few doctors trying to cope with the slaughter, and my cold indifference when a soldier fired warning shots to make us bugger off: a warning shot in Lebanon was generally anything that missed a vital organ.

We were so close that the concussion of his rounds popped the left lens out of Steve's glasses, but the carnage made the rest of his world disappear; he didn't notice it fall.

I next recalled conversations with crews up to and including my approach to the storage room, where I again experienced the pungent stench of disinfectant, feces, and sweet flowers. Saying nothing about my olfactory illusion, I told Bonnie that I had called Sean back to the door then I fiddled with recording levels that needed no adjustments while he took an establishing shot, before moving inside the small room. I stepped aside to allow the NBC crew room to pass, handing Steve his lens as he squeezed by. Ann, his wife and soundperson, stopped outside beside me. I said they paid cameramen to live with that shit. She went in anyway, heedless that bodies make no sounds that can be broadcast.

I told Bonnie that I honestly didn't recall a man with a knife bend-ing over anyone.

"Send a messenger," she said perfunctorily.

Squeezing my eyes shut, I pursed my lips to focus on the moment before I looked into the room. In a short while, I heard Bonnie tittering as I repeated a mantra in my mind, "Come back with a replay." Imagin-ing a bullet-shaped request racing into deep space.

"Done," I said, opening my eyes to see Bonnie silently convulsing in her seat.

"What?"

Gulping air, she said, "You looked like you were having a bowel movement."

[225]

"The messenger had a long trip ahead." I nodded at my pages and said, "There's more," as I got up to get us another cup of coffee.

"Give it another try tonight," she said.

"A bowel movement is a regular part of my routine," I replied.

Bonnie didn't find anything else metaphysical in that scene, nor did she say anything more egregious than pointing out awkwardly constructed passages. I reread these, understood the flaws, then setting my work aside took her to lunch to prod for a reward of information. It couldn't hurt to try.

To my pleasant surprise, Bonnie was very accommodating and filled in parts of her novel's overview nicely: Her twentieth-century bad guys were part of a secretly connected group of the most influential people on the planet, two thousand individuals who had their fingers on the political pulse of the globe, which collectively formed an iron grip on the planet's economic carotids. They bought, sold, traded, and manipulated events in an underground dance of commerce that could finesse a country's financial stability, change educational and agricultural practices, instigate and control the spread of disease through planned outbreaks, and discovering cures timed to the rising need of cartel-priced medicines. Their bottom line, annually in the trillions, depended on the promulgation of greed, fear and fanaticism couched in God's word and patriotism to keep nations, regions, and races divisive. If one of their hand-picked dictators, or duly elected presidents developed a conscience or otherwise began to think they really were in control, a takeover of some kind followed. Conversely, they allowed the obvious good guys of the world to run all of the equal opportunity, level-the-playing-field social activities they desired because they understood that supporting any bias ultimately promoted the isms for which it was designed to compensate. For the same reasons, they quietly supported Band-Aid acts of social conscience, such as needle exchanges, soup kitchens, and homeless shelters, because superficial fixes were ideal for helping the world's scavengers, sociopaths, and other forms of specialized groups to endlessly impinge on the public's security. Bonnie called this odious bunch, whose depravity and despotism knew no boundaries, the Players.

While the Players practiced their dark trades, she said her protagonists were studying the disciplines of handling energy. In time, their skills and growing numbers would influence the Players' focus on negative applications of power to enhance the impact of the irresistible forces' return they had made inevitable. As I understood her, the focus of these emissaries of change was not directed at felling felons, like

[226]

cops chasing robbers; it was about stalking the footings of corrupt empires and sticking in thorns to cause them to squeal. Under the relentless sting of these small but well-designed punctures, trusted members and associates would think about a *coup d'état* to deal with these annoyances because that was what Players did. This kind of thinking would inevitably create a tiny crack in their global operations, which would never seal; like water dripping through a pinhole in a dam wearing through exponentially into a catastrophic breach, so great was their greed and concomitant suspicion that the erosion of their empires would become unstoppable.

This was great background stuff for the narrative section of my application, and I thought that trying to remember my morgue scene was a small price to pay for what I might get in return later.

It did cross my mind that I could have lied about trying to do this, but there's often an aspect of an experience that either isn't known or can't be faked for those who are in the know. People who claimed to have worked the bang-bang showed me this, and Bonnie certainly knew her stuff well enough to explore my reactions to exploring deep memories. Anyway, it made no sense to fake something I could take two minutes to try, no matter how stupid it was. And only Bonnie would ever know.

Before going to sleep that night, I tried to recall the crucial moment from a meditative state, but I fell asleep amid a mishmash of events. I tried again in the calm of pre-dawn until the draw of the bathroom became too great. To cover my bases, because Bonnie wasn't above probing my failures for authenticity—it might even be what she was after—I tried again after three cups of coffee, but all I managed to do was exhume memories that were better left alone.

With my promise kept, I worked on the grant application, and then a section of my book. Three hours later, I printed six pages of rewritten "rutted" pages, showered, then I met Bonnie at Nolan's where we ordered blueberry muffins and herbal tea before I handed her my edit. Pre-empting the inevitable question, I told her nothing had changed about the hospital scene.

"It'll come," she said, taking my work in her hand.

Bonnie took the entire morning to dissect the minutiae of my changes, asking me dicky little things about my characters' feelings from one moment to the next and to explore comments like "making the world disappear." She said she was not confused about what I had written, but she wanted me to be fully aware of the internal nuance of my own experiences.

[227]

I wasn't sure what that meant.

"The wind and water references stimulate an emotional sense of your personal presence, as opposed to you physically occupying space," she explained, "then you abandon the natural world to make calculated references like caches and ROMS."

"There's only so much the wind can do."

"What happens after this?" she said, flicking the corner of a page.

"A reporter is killed in a chapter called The Road to Kfar Matta."

"Aaah," she said, tilting her head back. "His death scared you away from intimacy."

"I doubt that I ever met him, but I knew his cameraman, Bryan. Anything else?" I nodded at the pages.

We next had a general discussion about foreshadowing under the banner of omens, then she tied these to other every day events in a clear and clever way. She said omens aren't necessarily manifestations of a designed mOMENtum, because to a trained observer all be-haviours portend to a predictable culmination. At the conclusion of this conversation, Bonnie seemed unusually pleased with my input, and our day ended positively.

Trying to recall the morgue scene before going to bed that night, I could not stay focused in the corridor. Instead, I repeatedly wandered through unfriendly memories, until finally falling into a troubled sleep. Shortly after five o'clock, one of these memories hounded me awake, and I got up to write.

For reasons I can't explain beyond willingly going where my mind takes me, because it so often paid off, I managed only a few minutes of reworking ROMS into personal terms before I scrolled to the days immediately after Clark Todd had been killed. To my unexpected satisfaction, there was an abundance of emotional bloodletting in this section because network poo-pahs had published a version of his demise, their glaring focus on highlighting their own heroic efforts to retrieve the body from a hot zone.

Lacking the fundamental ingredient of selflessness required of heroism, this article elevated the danger to their wonderful selves at the direct expense of the crew's integrity, by declaring they had abandoned a wounded colleague. They also took a pot-shot at the international aid agencies who would not enter the contested area from which the highly experienced crew had taken many hours to escape, sometimes under fire and on foot, in a literal life and death effort to get their friend medical attention. This otherwise comprehensive personal tribute somehow failed to mention how many medics had been killed, or wounded, in the preceding months in that area, or that their own network had refused to pay compensation to Clark's widow and children.

As I understood it, this decision had crossed the authors' desks, as well.

I didn't change a word before scrolling back to the ROM references where my thoughts now flowed like molasses: this is a good thing for nuance, so I had an unusually productive three plus hours of work on my own book.

After a hot shower cleansed the remaining vitriol from my system, I drove across the bridge feeling lighter.

Bonnie read my morning's work over tea and toast in her kitchen, concentrating as if it were an English translation of Albanian assembly instructions for a Korean made ceiling fan. Wearing a faint smile of satisfaction, when her lips weren't moving, she then read it again. Finally setting the pages down, she said, "You have engineered a series of subterranean references that flow with the electricity of uncertainty and disaster, until your cameraman's musings sucker-punched my assumptions. For a moment, I looked at life as you guys saw it, and it scared the hell out of me. Excellent job," she said pushing the pages my way. "No, not excellent, outstanding."

"Thank you, but it's not much different from my other stuff."

"It's a personal payoff: you discovered what stood in the way of writing the entire scene like this the first time around." She tapped the pages. "The first part is a delicate balance between too thin and enticing, which would have lost its edge without the full-blow hammering thoughts of your characters."

"I didn't think about doing that, but I guess I did."

Bonnie frowned and said, "We really can't have you guessing anymore." To my chagrin, she began listing all of the meta-principles we had ever talked about, as if I understood few of them and was guessing at the rest. These premises included how parents nurture an infant's beliefs into inevitable acts, that the nature of all actions cycle back to their originator, and that a continuity of similar acts builds momentum. Impeccable actions also come back as positive influences, while polishing the link to Intent, which as a simultaneous force and purpose makes any goal a *fait accompli*. It follows that the key to living a productive life lies in learning what we are really like, for only in this way can we do the right thing, for the right reason, while gaining energy and awaiting the inevitable return of these events to help smooth our path as we challenge larger issues. Eventually, we will earn

[229]

the energy that a mortal manifestation of the earthbound spirit requires to make a permanent connection to their / our Original Intent.

It was old stuff, but by reconnecting these ideas, the designs of Intent came into focus in terms of practicing personal disciplines; it was like taking a course in Destiny Cartography, the other side being to wander a relatively uncharted path designed by uninformed consent. This understanding was comprehensive to the degree that it was momentarily incomprehensible to me why anyone wouldn't want to take charge of their lives in this way. However, as the criticalness of this idea began to lose its edge, I thought that examining the stuff in life that sucked wasn't something people just decided to do on a Sunday afternoon; that without Bonnie's two-tiers of understanding pretty much beaten into you, all you'd end up doing was corroborating your original actions.

"Are we close to sharing a monumental assumption?" Bonnie interrupted my thoughts.

I touched my thumb and forefinger together as my insights slipped into something comprehensively interesting. That said, it somehow suspended my use of the word 'guess'.

[230]

Chapter Twenty-four
The Lifeline

Finished our meeting, I went home to write, run, shower, then have a couple of brews with Ed at the Dover, before going to bed around eleven and trying to recall the morgue incident again.

Initially, I drew a literal blank when I looked inside the room this time, then the bundled sheets suddenly popped into view. I assumed my mind was finally creating the fiction Bonnie had suggested so there was no point in carrying on. I fell asleep amid swirling memories of general unpleasantness.

In the morning, I awakened feeling sombre, a mood that stayed with me while I worked on another chapter of my book until it was time to leave, a mood that was still with me when I arrived at Bonnie's. In little time and with no obvious inspection of me, she suggested that we hold our morning session outside, "So you have something positive to look at while you bask in melancholy."

I saw no point in commenting one way or the other.

Ten minutes later, we were sitting on a park bench at the north end of the sea wall where Bonnie began reading my latest offering.

A few minutes into it, she asked me why I had phrased my deportation as being "invited to leave Iran," and how that had affected my professional reputation.

"I borrowed the style from British newscasters who say things like, 'An alleged I.R.A. killer is aiding police with their inquires,'"I explained, "and if the event changed anything in my career, it was for the better; countries that deport journalists have a history of killing or jailing their best minds." Seriously, I added, "Most of us hated those places, so it wasn't as if we fought very hard to stay."

"A country is not a thing one can hate," she said placidly. "It is a gathering point for like-minded individuals and you can't hate millions of people you haven't met. What you're saying is that you feared what could happen because their way of life is radically different from the one you think you understand."

"We've been over that with Otis," I said.

"And you've still written about it in the old way of thinking," she said, holding a page toward me and tapping the top line of a paragraph with her index finger. Leaning forward, I read where two characters were having a vulgar disagreement about what to do in a circumstance that might get a wrist slap back home but their hands cut off where they were now. Leaning back, a montage of similar circumstances, recycled from my uneasy dreaming, flooded my mind. I don't know what this looked like to Bonnie, but she seized the moment like a fifty-dollar bill in a laundry hamper.

Placing her arm on the bench backrest, she said, "What are you thinking?"

"I just got the culture of fear thing you talked about."

"Here, or as it applied to when you were working abroad?"

"Away. Why?"

"For the past few days, you've become increasingly morose in spite of me responding favourably to your work and your own clear efforts to understand mine. Maybe some of that knowledge is leaking through to our here and now?"

"I couldn't say. Events suddenly fit into what you said about me not understanding where we were. I didn't think about it applying here. Not yet, anyway."

"I've got you," she said softly, putting her arm over my shoulder. "You're safe now."

Her words made no sense to me, but inexplicably, I felt like crying; it had been so long since I had last done that, the best I could do was breath strangely.

"What's your body telling you?"

It wanted to get up and walk away, but my legs felt like lead as a wave of lethargy overtook me. I have no idea how long I sat there playing mental ping pong between feeling like an ass and wanting to know why I felt like my father had just died, but it probably wasn't more than half a minute before I became a spectator in this internal struggle. Bonnie was saying something about body memory being stripped of emotion when this equidistant point of view evolved into a specific mural of memories, categorized by their destructive content, and presented as if on a roller for my inspection. Then they were gone, leaving no impression on me beyond marvelling at their sudden appearance and cohesion.

I heard Bonnie say, "Flatten the experience in words, and let everything else get on with whatever memories do when you're not trying to make them serve you."

[232]

"What if..."

"Shhhh. Discussing the moment ruins it."

I took a deeper breath, paused to still my thoughts, and then I spontaneously said, "Humanitarian acts could have been rendered by the victors, but all of them declined the opportunity to begin the healing process."

"That's how you felt about what went on, but your sadness is a manifestation of what lies beneath. Peel back that layer. It's safe. I've still got you."

I felt a surge like there was a jail break pending on my tongue, and I whispered, "Don't pick on every word."

"Don't cloud the moment with any concern and never about me."

I slipped into an easy, emotionless flow.

"Working on the morgue incident brought back memories of the winners punishing losers until they became tired of getting even for their losses, but their contempt was a constant reminder to the losing side that they were frauds and cowards. That's the secret they took into their next war because there was no honour in having fought the good fight if you're not willing to die for the cause you killed for. Parents teach hate to their kids before they're toilet trained, which means the next war is fought for their parents' stupidity, guilt, and shame. They are killing their own kids to justify their own beliefs."

"Almost there," Bonnie said quietly, gazing at the water.

"I think that's it," I said, feeling the depth of my ease becoming shallower. "My late night walks in the hospital corridor always ended in snippets of this kind of crap. I guess that's why I've been a bit off," I said, looking across the bay toward Point Grey.

"You're very close: surfacing those memories has frightened you anew," Bonnie said as a matter-of-fact, "and what you call a bit off is a sense of defeat wrapped in the shawl of relief because you don't have to keep the secret from yourself anymore. Let those ghosts get on with whatever they do when you're not using them as a blanket of suffering. Set yourself free."

"Pardon me?"

"The secret is on your tongue. Let it out...don't think, just say it."

My mood, or lack thereof, had me accept her words as a command. Speaking mechanically because I didn't know where I was going with it, I told Bonnie that amid the chilling rains of an early Asian spring, crews came under the constant assault of half-naked children begging for food or clothing while their hollow-eyed mothers offered themselves to us in exchange for either. On occasion, a fourteen year old

[233]

punk carrying an assault rifle would appear and, imitating his favourite screen revolutionary, shout that we would all die if we dared to help his enemies. We walked away because there is no single group, in any country, more dangerous than adolescents with guns. A block farther on, we came across ragged groups of elderly survivors huddling around smoky refuse fires they had built inside the open garages of bombed out buildings. Their eyes asked us for help.

"*Shocran*," thank you, they said with dignity when we gave them something. "*Insha Allah*," God's will, others said without animosity when the kid came around the corner to check on us.

"That's it," I said.

"It certainly is. The punk confronted your self-image, and that's why you feel defeated. It's also why you could feel equal empathy for the Vietnam vet and the draft dodger, but we'll come back to that."

"It wasn't my job to help. Agency reps took care of the refugees."

Holding up a defensive hand, Bonnie said, "You hated the position the kid put you in, and because the agency people dared to do something you couldn't do, you felt ashamed. In part, this explains why you risked your life in meaningless ways after you came home."

"Pardon me?"

"For short but critical times, you challenge fate in the only way you understand the concept of control, which is by riding motorcycles on slick mountain roads, sailing small boats on large oceans, and crawling through pubs to celebrate your survival. You've been down in the dumps for days because your efforts to retrieve a pivotal memory put you in touch with core events that changed you." Bonnie casually looked across the narrows toward Granville Island while the truth settled in my stomach like a lump of cold lead.

"In this moment, you are acutely aware that your life can depend on the whims of a child strolling around a corner with a weapon, or a corporation polishing their Ethics in Journalism Award at your funeral. Your safe place in the world was taken from you, which in part is why you're so angry."

"I'm not arguing against the impact of those events, but they were rare, years ago, and thousands of miles from here."

"That's the bargaining phase of the numbers game speaking." She looked away. "I knew you were deeply disappointed in yourself from the moment you said, 'Not even us,' when you were telling me about witnesses not coming forward in El Salvador. It's clear now that an act of mercy gutted the soldier of fortune image you concocted after the global adventurer phase died in Argentina." Bonnie patted the back of

[234]

my hand. "Don't lose sleep over it. Few people understand when to intercede on behalf of others without interfering with a journey that's not theirs. Many are as careless with their lives as you are."

A sudden rage arose in me, and I dared not speak until I figured out what to do with her body: in Asia, the Red Cross and Green Crescent retrieved wounded from all sides, and many of them were shot for their trouble. In Africa, Doctors Without Borders were twisted into emotional knots by the cruellest of ironies. Unable to save people for a lack of staff meant that losing someone they were treating inside the tents doubled the tally. Understandably, "heroic measures" became the standard of care for the nurses who carried this nightmarish burden into the dying throngs to choose another child patient, not by the degree of their damage or pain, or the pleas of an emaciated mother, but by weight. If they were too light for their age, they wouldn't make it anyway. Next.

Enter a mother's love.

Local helpers caught on to the significance of the staff asking for birth dates while weighing the children, and in the strictest confidence told relatives how to tip the scales of justice's ultimate simplification. It took little time before every mother was swearing their six-year-old was three if only to have the child die warm and dry. The meaning of "rounds" for those magnificent people was forever changed, and here sat a placid bitch telemarketer shitting on them.

Suppressing violent urges I did not know I had, I settled at being aghast over her view of what I was like.

"Motorcycles and oceans are how I have fun," I hissed, redirecting the force of my fury into sibilance.

"You can't have fun as long as you act from fear," she said evenly. "You don't know how to have fun."

My anger fizzled in the face of this asinine statement. Taking a couple of steadying breaths, I said, "You're seriously saying that I look for danger to convince myself that I'm in charge of my life because dangerous events have convinced me that I'm not?"

"I'm saying you became a media mercenary, a fanatic willing to die for the cause of compensation. This is the act of a man with no sense of self-worth, a defeated man whose cheques are written in other people's troubles to pay for bar stories to convince himself that he's in charge of his life."

"Huh?"

"You really have to stop saying that. It reflects poorly on your college."

[235]

It also consumed the half-second of hesitation that may have saved her life.

"You've got it backwards, this time. Risks are what make living worthwhile," I said.

"When they have a purpose. What was yours?"

"To have fun, to recover, to recover from having fun—who cares?"

"Meaning your existence is pointless." Bonnie cocked her head.

"Meaning I'm recovering from trying to make a point of my existence!" I snapped.

"That's the wisest thing you've ever said to me. Speaking of which," she leaned back, "a wiser part of you is constantly showing his hand by prompting you to reorder your thoughts about your life. It's what drove you away from big money to tackle the frugal challenges of self-discovery."

I stared open-mouthed.

"Your thoughts led you to viewing the cause and effect of your feelings about yourself, but you couldn't make the connection because they contradicted years of hiding the truth. Your inner awareness knew that I could explain things to you when you were ready, but only you could make yourself ready, which is what walking the corridors was about. Good job." She grinned like the proverbial cat.

Her tension-breaking effort was too little and too late, not to mention too spooky for me. I stood to leave; her fucking inner awareness could explain that.

"You always come back," she said as I turned to walk away, "because I answer the questions you have been surreptitiously asking yourself for years. Your Silent Knowledge also tells you that I'm correct. I can see the look a moment before your ego registers my words as a threat."

I pivoted to face her. "I come back because I am seriously attracted to you," I blurted out. "Why else would I do this—for a fucking fairy tale?"

"You have no control over what I think of you," she said, patting the bench beside her, "and you come back every day to argue about fiction? I think not." She patted the bench again.

Feeling used and drained, I sat down; if I was going to feel like an ass either way, I might as well be comfortable.

"Two things you need to take away from this conversation: in a matter of a day or two, you went through denial, anger, depression, bargaining, and finally acceptance of your own experiences, which means you have grieved the loss of some core illusions. You need to

[236]

fill those voids with an assessment of events to stop the crappy ramifications from coming back, and you need to do that soon. This is a grand opportunity to picture those disturbing memories as pieces of a puzzle that form a quest. At the least, you'll discover the lifeline that will allow you to tackle challenges that go beyond writing a book or a screenplay."

"If the lifeline is faith," I said, "you can't eat that."

"Let's put the issue of faith to rest: it is not logical to believe in yourself beyond the point of hubris when even you admit that you shouldn't have survived God-only-knows how many incidents that would have killed a normal person. All I'm asking is that you grant me a little piece of that trust and have faith in the search for a life purpose that will lead you to the certain knowledge that you have one." Bonnie stood up. "Brunch is on me," she said, turning to walk toward the commercial core of West Vancouver.

"Apparently the egg is on me," I quipped.

Doubly so when Bonnie ignored the comment.

Chapter Twenty-five
The Road to Damour

The next morning, I worked on my book until eight-thirty before I showered while steeling myself for a push to the pay-off scene I suspected she had not written, but had in mind pending my reaction to hearing it; Bonnie had been dead right when she said I couldn't live in between pivotal events, and I had written a decent grant proposal that was missing only a suitable ending...one that incorporated and stream-lined her premises into an aha moment, preferably.

Drying off, I realized the fifty-fifty split for work she had originally claimed only needed tweaking wasn't exactly a lie, but it wasn't the whole truth, and it was time for that or the fifty-fifty would become something else. Her choices would be to give up her plot or try to distract me. My position would be that there is no reason not to start the application process, which I would miraculously finish in a day or two, after I understood how to bring together her disparate teaching elements. If she was not forthcoming, I would disengage from daily meetings while polishing the mediocre pay off scene I had drafted. If she gave up the information before I was finished, because she had too much invested to let me walk, then great. If not, I would submit the proposal myself.

Arguing to learn her dramatic closer meant I couldn't lose focus, I reminded myself as I got dressed, because she could twist a phrase so smoothly that by the time I realised she had skewered my objection I had to wonder whether I was narcoleptic.

I couldn't telegraph my intentions, I thought as I motored into the park minutes later. With Bonnie, even one word out of place would be like trying to hide a cow in a closet, bell and all.

I had to wait for her lead, I chanted as I ramped down to Marine Drive.

If she somehow changed the conversation, and I didn't get what I was after, I had to remind myself that the shoe was still on the other foot: she wouldn't complain when I handed her some of the cheque, maybe not fifty per cent, because she could add all of the complicated shit she wanted. That's why they called it a development grant.

[238]

I spooled up my courage by running a reddish light at closed-casket speeds, steeled for a battle of wills I knew I couldn't lose. Still...

We had been walking the West Vancouver sea wall for half an hour when a jogger passed between us from behind and Bonnie said the runner was in financial trouble.

I saw my open door.

Two steps later, I said, "I don't doubt that things come to you because there were times when crews felt things and changed their plans. But I think our audience will have a problem with your character's unverifiable Knowings if you don't somehow distinguish them from their imagination, their shopping habits aside," I joked.

"By which you mean you're having a problem with the concept even though you're experiencing insights nearly every day?"

"I'm not dismissing the psychic experience; hell, I've taken real risks to avoid the potential of something that felt wrong, but there are only so many of those you can rely on before it becomes a cheap device. If you had insights every day, you might anticipate them, your anticipation would insinuate itself on normal circumstances, and you would need a way to distinguish between a Knowing and a speculation. There'd have to be some kind of mechanism of control, and the audience will want to know what it is. Even then...."

"Tell me about a risk you took."

I hesitated, realised it lent credibility to my objection then I said, "There's a lot of background, again."

"We've got all day," she said, spreading her arms as if encircling time.

More like ten minutes, I thought.

"Most factions," I said, a few paces later, "could capture any village south of Beirut as a Monday morning exercise in prestige, but they couldn't hold them without controlling the outlying areas because that required resources no faction could spare. They would spend Tuesday and Wednesday sniping at anyone coming within half a mile of them, then on Thursday, abandon the place. On Friday, another faction would attack the empty village, claim a decisive victory, and stay only long enough for us to get footage of their presence. With me so far?"

"Different groups insinuated power and political control through tactically meaningless territorial victories," Bonnie summed up the situation.

"Exactly. We called most of the roads in these areas Sniper Alley, but there was one that everybody called The Alley." I drew a map in the air. "Damour was on the coast highway a few klicks south of Beirut at a pincher point between the Chouf Mountains and the Mediterranean Sea. Israeli Defence Forces levelled it, but wannabe militias still went there to shoot civilians going to and from work in the city. In early eighty-four, there was a half mile stretch of roadside strewn with bullet-riddled cars that our drivers called Death Row."

"Why shoot civilians? Why was the rubble important?"

"The town overlooked the airport. Controlling access to a country is a big deal. Temporary, but big."

"Go on," Bonnie said, with a spring in her step.

"We were assigned a scouting route that a BBC cameraman called, 'an absorbing excursion into hell' because he had been pinned down by a sniper, inadvertently saved by Phalangists, then on the way back a P.P.L.F. gang told them to take another road, and they hit a mine. Anyway, there was a refugee story at the Awali River Bridge—that's about an hour south toward Sidon—the day after a skirmish for Damour's sniping rights. I was primed to turn back if I didn't like the feel of anything because the winners hadn't had time to calm down, and there was another way through the mountains."

"Why not take that in the first place?"

"It was an hour longer and the story might have gone away."

"The hour wasn't worth your life?"

"Nothing was wrong."

"Carry on."

"We were past the airport grounds in no-man's land when Kamal slowed the car to pick up a belt of heavy calibre ammunition lying in the middle of the road. I told him to keep going, and he spoke Arabic for Sammi to translate, "What's the problem, friend?"

I pointed out that we were on a flat, straight stretch of shell-holed highway littered with car-wreck range markers.

"Pointed out," Bonnie snickered.

"I also drew his attention to the coincidence of the ammo lying between the safety of a runway access road behind us and a dirt road that ran into the foothills in front of us, the significance being that a sniper had maximum time to shoot the enemy soldiers he expected to stop and die of stupidity. Sammi knew it as well. He sat upright, waiting for the thunk."

"What did Kamal say?"

"He said we weren't fighters, and the sniper wasn't likely to shoot."

"True?"

"Yes, but the press had no reason to carry arms or ammunition because that undermined our thin shield of neutrality, making it difficult to convince fighters to let us go about our business. Kamal said, 'Friend, you do not understand my country. I am going to offer this ammunition as a thank you for our safe passage,' and he opened the door to pick up the ammunition on a slow drive-by, so I leaned over the back seat and grabbed the wheel to turn us away. Kamal threw a tantrum at Sammi in Arabic, ordering him to put me in my place. Sammi knew I was right, but Kamal wasn't used to driving techs through front line areas, and without a producer or reporter along, he thought he was in charge."

"A local driver was not accustomed to frontlines?"

"He owned all of the cars CBS leased. When he did drive, it was four-man crews to do stand-ups in safe places. Safer places," I corrected myself.

"Didn't he have some say?"

"All drivers had the right to refuse to go anywhere if they felt their safety was on the line, but that cut two ways. Kamal either didn't appreciate the circumstance or he didn't care that he was taking the bait someone had risked his ass to put there, and shooting people for spite and sport was common a day after a battle. In our circumstance, 'not likely' to shoot us was a long way from wouldn't shoot. Another problem was that Kamal wouldn't say a word about the ammunition if we were stopped because he wanted to sell it. He didn't know I was on my third trip in country, and I understood that 'the deal' was equal parts honour and commerce in his world, so he quietly expected us to risk dying for one of his."

"After his tirade?" Bonnie prompted me.

"I asked Sammi to ask Kamal if he knew who was crouched in the debris, and in excellent English Kamal said it didn't matter. I told Sammi to tell him that I was sure Kamal could recognize the military uniforms of Lebanon, Syria, Israel, America, the United Nations blue caps, and probably the principle Shiite and Sunni militias by their badges. But I doubted that driving between Embassy Row and The First National Bank had familiarized him with factions who wouldn't be around long enough to design an emblem. If one of these groups was in Damour and they asked us who we thought they were when we picked up the ammunition, Kamal would screw CBS by supplying them with ammunition or screw us by guessing wrong because that was admitting supplying their enemies. I then agreed that it didn't

[241]

matter who was in Damour as long as we weren't passing through with ammunition."

"What did he do?"

"You know Eskimos have something like thirty words for snow?"

"Inuit."

"Them, too. The same thing applies to an Arab tongue click. Kamal's words meant I was ignorant and uncultured, which in western terms was to call me the scum spawn of an American soldier and an Israeli hooker."

"Sounds more like fuck off, to me."

"True, but that lacks a sense of historical significance."

"Like most things North American. What happened next?"

"He reversed the car, picked up the belt, then stared at me."

Not unlike how I stared at Bonnie now, who processed the circumstance and said, "You were stationary, in the open, blocking the sniper's view of his trap. Everyone was playing chicken?"

"You're very good."

"Yes I am. Who blinked?"

"Kamal did, when I spoke to him in his own language."

"You don't speak Arabic."

"Money. I said if he didn't put the ammunition back, I was getting out of the car and walking back to the hotel. It made him think about losing his contract and maybe becoming a full-time gunrunner—lots of frontline driving," I smirked.

"I didn't know you were that important in the CBS hierarchy," Bonnie grinned.

"Dead or alive, everyone would know what Kamal had done, and Lucy would have a little chat with him, maybe even renegotiate their deal."

"If I've got this straight, you were willing to risk the sniper because you weren't his preferred target?"

"That works," I said, thinking more along the lines that Kamal and Sammi would cause the sniper some indecision while they became bigger in his scope. But it didn't matter. "Kamal reset the trap, then booted it into Damour with his eyes slitting my throat every time he checked the rear view mirror."

"After you drove through town without seeing anyone?" Bonnie guessed accurately.

"A fact Kamal reminded me of until it was time to head back, and I still felt the longer road was a better bet, but he insisted on taking the coast road because the mountain route was terminal to travel at night. It wasn't even dusk when we began to argue at the side of the crossroads, but the moment the sun dropped behind the highest hill it was over." I shrugged. "He must've felt something wasn't right as well, because we booted it over broken road at around sixty then punched through a hundred when we dropped to sea level on Death Row...miles per hour, not klicks," I said.

Bonnie nodded.

"Anyway, Kamal crouched behind the wheel when the first shot came, Sammi sat upright in the passenger side of the rear seat, and I crowded over next to him to leave a clear path through the trunk to the driver's side."

"What other Knowings have you had?" Bonnie said, apparently not appreciating my sense of fair play.

To further substantiate my view that anticipating Knowings would demand that one have a definitive way of distinguishing them from speculation or wishful thinking, I said, "I had one after my father had a heart attack. He had been in the hospital for six weeks when my mother said he would be coming home the next Saturday. I knew he wouldn't."

"What did you do in the moment of receiving that Knowing?"

"I made the mistake of saying that he'd die with the certainty that I felt. I think Mom wondered whether I wanted him dead."

"He died?"

"Yes."

"When else did you experience Knowings?"

"None," I said, shaking my head after a brief search.

"There are more, but you chose to forget them because you couldn't explain their source or defend their validity without risking ridicule. Maybe subconsciously you even believed you were the cause of some events, so you banished their memory, but their affects are still with you." She winked. "It would explain why you didn't acknowledge having the experience when we first met."

"I don't think..." a stark picture popping into my mind shut my mouth.

"Don't tell me nothing just high-jacked your thoughts," Bonnie chortled.

"It has nothing to do with knowing things."

Slowing our pace with a gentle hand on my forearm, she said, "Fair enough, so what do you think just happened?"

"I can't say."

"Actually, you can. The experiences you have when you're with me are a consequence of gathering energy through your own efforts and of me lending you some of mine. There's nothing to argue about. It's just the way it is, so you might as well go with it. We can talk about the process later and where it fits in our work, but these events are not random. Now is the time to explore it."

I told her the flash was about the famine in Ethiopia: a World Vision plane had flown us to the foot of some mountains where other employees drove us up to a feeding station, seven thousand feet above sea level. Cresting the final rise, my eyes were taken hostage by a foliage-free moonscape filled with starving people portentously shrouded in the steely haze of campfire smoke and ground fog. Dumbfounded, I got out of our warm vehicle, a cacophony of pneumonic coughs besieged my ears, and with embarrassing volume I exclaimed, "This cannot be."

"Which," I told Bonnie, "had nothing to do with a Knowing."

She nudged me to the side of the path. An acute gaze, designed to compel unconditional surrender, caused me to step back against a chain link fence.

"Your feelings were whispered directions to keep you safely on the path of your destiny. You didn't understand this because the point of having those experiences was to avoid proving them accurate. Each of those incidents was a sign of our friend's presence in your life, even to the point of them speaking directly to and through you in Africa."

I didn't bite. "The point we're discussing is that too many Knowings undermine them."

"If you had learned to trust your feelings like I did," she said, taking a step back as I moved around her, "you would have no doubt about Knowings even if they arrived by the truck load. You would also have heard our friends by now. Let's go to the Greek House. It's only another ten minutes."

"You hear voices? I mean you, not your teacher character," I said, bewildered because there was no net for this claim and trying to shock me with a hallucination was just plain stupid.

"Yes," she said evenly.

Perched between fact and fiction in my novel, dangling between hope and delusion over bedding Bonnie and getting paid for it, licking a wall socket couldn't have made me more wide-eyed. "Uh-huh," was the least offensive thing I could think to say as my saliva migrated to my palms.

"You don't believe me." It was a statement.

[244]

"Would it be rational?"

"One who denies their experiences because they don't suit their opinions is hardly in a position to determine another's sanity."

A creeping pleasure filtered through my wonder. This wasn't a shock tactic, it was the resolution to her plot! The cosmos had decided to do things directly because mortals interpreting their instructions wasn't working. Of course, this undermined the reasoning behind the lessons —all of the personal disciplines, the need for three time periods, the magic, everything was diluted. But how she intended to overcome this flaw in the Universe's plan would have to remain a mystery because I was done with her: she should have levelled with me from the start, and we would certainly have come up with something better than completely undermining her admittedly clever set up.

All that was left was deciding how we would part company. I could push the voices issue into a confrontation, and our ending would come quickly with acrimony, or I could continue being a student for the day. We'd go to lunch on innuendo and sip double entendres until we went back to her house where I wouldn't say, 'See you tomorrow,' and Bonnie wouldn't reply, 'Nolan's at nine.' I would leave without the look-back wave that seals little deals, and that would be that.

Either way, it seemed fair to offer her a dignified way out.

"When I was in trouble as a kid," I said, pushing my glasses up the slippery slope of my nose, "I rehearsed the excuses I was going to use on my parents and imagined confrontations that included the stuff they usually came up with. When I was older, I wrote down things like best-man speeches and memorized them in context by bantering with a phantom audience. It also helped me see what I should or shouldn't say. Does that sound familiar?"

"Did you ever get proper advice?"

"I'm talking about imagining people's reactions." Jesus Christ, take the bait!

"So am I. Did you ever lose an argument, for instance?"

"To myself?"

"This isn't complicated. I'm asking how deep your imaginings went."

"Not so deep that I crossed a point of intensity where I tricked myself into believing independent voices were telling me what to do."

"You've just described how your inner voice has been talking to you for years." She waved her own comment aside. "My inner voice asked to speak through me to some of my friends, but my lifelong ties weren't of immediate interest to them. An entity named Kha-lib said he wanted

[245]

to speak to just Josh and you. I channelled him out loud to Josh two days ago. Come on," she said, pulling me along. I didn't realize we had stopped.

I mumbled something about a quack without a duck being a decoy.

"I've always embraced intuition as a normal part of my awareness, so it wasn't as big a leap as you might think to become familiar with its source over the years. That said, in spite of a clever progression of events to make me ready, I wasn't exactly calm about it."

"Mmm," was all that came through my mouthful of cotton.

"How many demonstrations do you think you'll need to accept that I have a personal relationship with our spirit friends and that I know things I couldn't know because they tell me about them?"

I bent over to remove a phantom pebble from my shoe. Clearing my throat, I said, "Even a student would demand proof." I stood up and began walking without looking back.

"Come over around noon tomorrow, and speak with Kha-lib," Bonnie said, tugging on my sleeve to catch up to me.

"More words won't change anything."

"Words are what had you come this far. How likely was that a month ago?"

"Tell me how the voices fit into your payoff scene and you've got a deal."

We turned a lazy circle around a garden display at the far end of the sea wall and headed back toward her home. Ten paces later, Bonnie said, "We already have a deal; maybe Kha-lib will tell you tomorrow."

Putting my honour at issue was not as compelling a reason to stay alongside her as the distance to my motorcycle represented an infinitely awkward silence. "So we do," I said. "Can you at least tell me about the experience?"

A short pause later, Bonnie said the voice directed her to sit in her wooden rocker where a general fatigue soon engulfed her. Feeling as though a large weight was pressing down on her shoulders, she moved her head from side to side to relieve a kink in her neck before she began rocking mechanically. A minute later, with elbows pivoting on the armrests, her arms were pumping in the rhythmic manner of a slow motion runner. Finally, she felt an irresistible pressure to speak, and she was as surprised as Josh to hear a male voice introduce himself in a business-like manner.

Bonnie lowered her voice in imitation: "We are teachers. In time, you will find the experience of channelling us effortless, for it is a natural act of acquiescence to those who have the energy to handle the

[246]

physiological and psychological process. For now, your earth-time consciousness considers us intruders, so we are distracting your ego by giving it something to do."

"Considerate," I said.

"They told me this right away," Bonnie said, evenly, "because the physical manifestations of their presence were exaggerated." She chuckled. "The word intruder tweaked me, so Kha-lib said there had never been a single case of spiritual possession in the history of mankind. I could stop channelling him by simply deciding to stop. Otherwise, they would add these physical distractions until I let go of my bodily armour—that's tense muscles." She grinned sheepishly. "I didn't want to fight any movements, but struggling to stay calm while Kha-lib countered my struggling over anything made me so stiff that by the time we were done Josh had to pry open my fists."

"Who are we and they—how many intruders were there?"

"Kha-lib said the plural reference was a term of reverence that recognized everyone who helped him to become all that he is."

"Which is what?"

"He said he's an inseparable aspect of a family of energy-consciousness who are ever-developing in their own ways. We could call him Kha-lib because we needed to make such distinctions, then he didn't refer to himself after that."

"Why did he say he was talking through you?"

"Part of their purpose for making contact is to explain the context of our existence, to have us understand how we are much more than we believe we are, and that what we do has far more impact than we realize."

"What did he want to tell Josh?"

"He was speaking to both of us, but he told Josh about my internal struggles before getting to the point, which was explaining the evolutionary process we all go through." Bonnie took deeper breaths as she slowed her pace to a geriatric stroll, after which she integrated concepts like our secret accomplice and uninformed consent into a rolling carpet of beliefs that generated a cyclical momentum within a multiplicity of realities. She next interwove mankind's core follies with the disciplines of spiritual development that countered them, which ultimately made hearing Spirit a logical closing stage in our physically oriented development—call it the post grad degree.

Early in this dissertation, I knew the grant version would say that everything we do matters because everything comes back to us, and in this way, the truth always shows itself. I would combine these into a sensational catastrophic event. The survivors would be the ones who were trained; at least those scenes wouldn't go to waste.

I neither needed nor wanted to hear anything more, because I now knew that Bonnie believed everything she had ever told me, except why she needed help if the Universe was chatting her up made no sense. Always a huge hole to fill.

With this thought staining every word, her monologue took twenty-five excruciating minutes to complete during which my amazement fluctuated between vacant stupefaction and wondrous shock over her ability to concoct such an intricate load of shit. By the time we crossed the mini-park to her narrow roadway, I was dumbfounded by the dichotomy of such a brilliant mind so convincingly supporting its own madness.

As we turned up the short driveway to her house, Bonnie said I had been learning how the Universe would help mankind change our ways from the moment I asked her what her book was about. My Source Soul had plans for me in this regard.

"Hmm," was all I could say as I straddled my bike.

Resting a hand on my shoulder, Bonnie leaned close and said, "Don't be angry. I said your beliefs were skewed on day one. Your reactions to hearing how this is true told me that nothing less than an experience in my world would decapitate the opinions you hold about yours, which you also agreed to have the first day we met. Now you are ready to meet them, so suspend your disbelief for one more day and don't throw it all away. That rhymes." She grinned. "I'll see you tomorrow."

I nodded mechanically, kicked down into first gear, and pulled away at a reasonable speed for my narrow vision on the slim road.

I was across the bridge before anger over my colossal waste of time collapsed into a bout of giddiness when I dared to wonder if the revenge of watching Bonnie try to maintain her poise was worth the trip. The transparency of her ruse would be my immediate pound of flesh, the grant money my back pay.

It was nearly two o'clock when I turned onto Davie Street, so I stopped for lunch.

Sharp thoughts snuffled from my nostrils until I was sedate enough to arrive at the ironic conclusion that *I* had too much invested to quit one day before possibly hearing how her story ended. Or the punch line, in which case I would have to find a way to make her death look like an accident.

[248]

Chapter Twenty-six
Kha-lib

I arrived at Bonnie's just before noon, where without preamble she led me into a living area flooded by the light of a southern exposure and softened by sheers covering the wall of glass facing English Bay. An onshore breeze waved the diaphanous material above her lethargic cat's head, keeping the room cool.

"It'll take a minute," she said, sitting in the oversized oak rocker beside the fireplace.

"I'll be here," I said as she closed her eyes.

Fifteen seconds or so and she began rocking in her chair, followed by twisting her head from side to side. A series of stilted breaths preceded pumping her arms, which was closely followed by deeper breaths that seemed to synchronize all of her motions. Embarrassed for her, I turned my attention to her cat, but Ginger wasn't any more at ease with me watching her than I was with watching Bonnie's theatrics; she left the room to lie on the balcony.

Not a bad idea.

When Bonnie finally stopped moving, she opened her eyes to explore our surroundings as if she were unfamiliar with them. When her gaze fell on me, it was with such calm assurance, not the stare of mental vacancy I must've been expecting, that I felt undressed.

"We have been awaiting you," she said, in a sonorous, distinctly male voice, not at all like her imitation of it. "All times are now, for the end has met the beginning. This does not mean the end of the world as you think of it. Rather, humankind has reached the end of a cycle of evolution wherein your cultural experiments have gone as far as they can go within their current focus. You are now repeating the essential events of your history."

I felt mortified for the rational Bonnie I sometimes knew and intimidated by the tranquil idiot sitting across from me. Inspecting my toes took care of both feelings.

"Do not bow to us or to anyone. We are not your masters but your servants," she/he said.

[249]

I looked up to protest her error, but words would not come: her facial features had become square—manly, and continued to change in subtle ways as she spoke with a simple elegance I found compelling even from within the turmoil of my sceptical fascination.

In part and paraphrase, as it will always be when I "quote" Bonnie, or the cosmos by any name, the Kha-lib persona said the aberrant ways of our world will come to an end by way of cataclysmic ways that have nothing to do with the wrath of God. Before encountering humanity, spirit/energy/consciousness, hereafter called the Universe, had never encountered malice. This concept was the antithesis of all that they knew about life, as foreign to them as Aramaic is to an amoeba.

At this time in our evolution, he said the momentum of mankind's destructive path is turning back on itself, accumulating energy at incompatible frequencies like sound waves exciting the natural resonance of a wine glass beyond its structural tolerance. This circumstance was magnified by a cascading collapse of energies that exponentially propel events into physical manifestation sooner than would otherwise be their natural flow, resulting in life as we know it becoming increasingly more dramatic.

I envisioned a spinning figure skater pulling in her arms to gather experiences, both wobbly and true, as she increased her rate of rotation. I understood it, but the vision and its nature were both unusual.

Kha-lib continued: "Mankind develops within evolutionary cycles which manifest according to the nature and degree of the momentum generated by acts of free will. It follows that the closing of your loop of development is not fixed in terms of fully preordained events; the momentum-consequence of some of your key choices has yet to pass the point of change beyond which circumstances become inevitable. Overall, we see that mankind will experience the end-time as a transition in your way of living over the next eighty-five years. This does not mean change will be subtle, for your kind demand an inordinate number of similar experiences before you are convinced of the necessity of change. The purpose of making ourselves known at this time is to reveal the fundamental practices of your daily lives that are literally killing you. This knowledge will be spread by our emissaries, for it is destined to become the foundation upon which future generations will evolve productively." He paused to allow me to digest his words.

"Do not be misled by the timeline," he continued. "Now is a more crucial time in history than has ever been, for within the opportunity to learn from the effects of an entire evolutionary cycle you have

[250]

developed the ability to annihilate entire universes. It is critical to learn of this peril, for how you each behave will determine in which reality your next physical journey will take place. If you continue to choose greed, prejudice, war, and deprivation, you will return amid these circumstances until you have understood them.

"This transformation," Kha-lib said, after again allowing a moment for me to grasp the significance of his words, "must take place on your own volition. Otherwise, we would be robbing you of your hard-earned lessons and we would have to return."

He stared. I stared back; apparently Ginger had walked out with my tongue.

"A general insanity pervades mankind," the persona said. "This circumstance requires that proof of your destiny, our existence and intentions, be offered within a strategic process that will undermine the myths you have entrenched in doctrines of morality and terrorism your nations disguise as God-given rights, servitude, and piety to justify your ways."

Finding my voice, I said, "It sounds like you'll prove you're good at arguing a point. I'll concede that right now," I told Kha-lib. "They're just more words."

"To an extent," he replied, "we will establish our credentials through physical representatives demonstrating the inherent magic of your existence while they speak of time's immutable projections that will subsequently take place in front of your eyes. These events will draw your attention to the reappearance of the masters of The Arts of Life among you."

"The Second Coming thing?"

"It will the fifth and last teaching intersession in your ways."

"Uh huh. Why not pop in, state your beef, and get on with it?"

"If we were to arrive unannounced no one would know us, whereas immediate demonstrations of our abilities would scare you into sub-mission, thereby tainting everything we have come to teach."

"Which is what?"

"We will assist the first waves of representatives to reveal their underlying beliefs to themselves, from which they will understand how specific aspects of their behaviour generate distinct events. We will teach them responsibility, and they will leave the world of average men and women to gain conscious control of their destiny. Their personal development will set the stage for those whom your masses will recognize as your prophets returned. Some of these emissaries will

[251]

emerge from among the families of the forerunners. Others, cast off by mankind, will be adopted by the Original Family of Man."

What had begun as an undercurrent of hubris in her manner finally clawed at my throat, and a stark foreboding stripped away the bullshit she had fed me since day one: I envisioned Bonnie standing amid the six-point lighting of a techno-cathedral picking the pockets of sinners by way of electronic salvation. The chyron crawl at the bottom of the screen read, Dial 1-900-Saviour. *Three minute minimum, heinous crimes may take longer. Must be nineteen or older to be forgiven. Long distance charges apply... and all of the carnage I had seen generated by religions coalesced into a rush of rage that rendered me immobile. Breathing became a discipline. The systolic thump in my chest began to hurt.

Unconcerned with my paralytic apoplexy, Kha-lib said I was a direct emanation of an entity I could refer to as Phillip, under whose direction I could advance my own development. "These lessons are difficult because mankind is difficult," he said, ludicrously challenging me into an alliance.

Kha-lib bid me farewell with a crisp, "We will speak again," the absurdity of which cyclonically whirled through my mind until Bonnie's eyes fluttered her back into our own space and time.

Beaming as if I had won a lottery, she said, "Well?"

"Well what?" I said, with the innocence of dealing with a collections agent.

We searched each other's eyes until it became a contest.

With no punch line in sight, I stood up and said, "I have a job today."

Bonnie did not challenge my conspicuous lie, possibly because the effort not to laugh twisted her face into a post-stroke grimace that sapped every ounce of energy she needed to control her bladder.

1-900-Fuckyou looped through my mind as I left her house for the last time.

Standing by my motorcycle, I forced myself through a meticulous safety check routine because I had a habit of sharing traffic lanes when I was vexed, and the bridge didn't have a ditch of forgiveness. Well it did, but I didn't have a parachute attached to a dingy.

I was still incredulous over the extent of her hoax as I leaned into the on-ramp, a feeling that dissipated with the rub of the curb and Newton's Third Law kept me heading toward my fate. Refocused, I made my way to Davie Street like a probationary driver on weed, then I inched toward home through Saturday shopping traffic. Feeling supremely stupid for going back to see her actually served to calm me while two-foot advances grinding away my clutch connected me to a sense of loss. I hadn't moved two blocks before I was debating with myself again, because it wasn't as if I made up my experiences with clarity or intrusive thoughts.

My tentative thinking was that I could still embrace Bonnie's performance as part of her research, which wasn't far-fetched within her meticulous preparations, or I could accept that there was something seriously wrong with her wiring. Maybe both. A fourth option came to mind as I pulled over at the Dover Pub; she was researching how a well-traveled, reasonably intelligent man when subjected to endless conditioning by untouchable tits and ass can be turned into an idiot.

I went inside to soak up courage enough to decide which one of us was an asshole, and which one was crazy, not that one necessarily excluded the other.

Everything Australian was in vogue for some reason, except Men At Work in concert, so a number of Fosters fat cans later, I over-enunciated "fuck it" into the smoky air and scraping my chair on the plank floor stood up to dig out my cash. Two tables over, a stranger grunted in agreement while his muddled buddy had turned to look for the bar's resident drunk, Delores.

"Women troubles?" Miriam said, sidling up from wherever servers lurk to scare the shit out of contemplating customers.

"Investment problem," I said, offering her an uncounted wad of cash.

First taking the correct amount of bills, she pried open my fingers to snatch away my keys and said, "I saw you leave yesterday. I wouldn't want to lose a good tipper. Any tipper," she corrected herself, looking at the sparsely inhabited room of indigent regulars. "Who was she?" she asked, as I moved to step around her.

"Who are *they*," I corrected her, offering her a five dollar bill.

"Have it, already," she said, refusing the extra money and I walked outside as free as a man can be in the world I knew.

Chapter Twenty-seven
The Question of Sanity

To leave the memory of Bonnie behind, I also left the grant application alone and instead concentrated on filling out the civilian ambiance in chapters of my book that preceded events in Lebanon. Background colour aside, my thinking was that readers who were familiar with my characters' environment and upbringing would better understand why they made some of the otherwise incomprehensible choices they made, when the war came to their doorstep.

The drafts of family scenarios took a tedious nine days to complete because writing about social conformation inexorably led to thoughts of Bonnie and her premises, which I dismissed as best I could until they finally struck an inner chord: I wondered if her eccentricities were a manifestation of an unusually agile mind, kind of like LeBlanc's but intelligible?

The thought of translating his world into ours triggered one of those aha moments for me, and I focused on tracking Bonnie's fanciful views back into their source possibilities: She had been with a good man whose spirit had been crushed, seen his generosity as a ruse, and tried to heal him. Maybe they were emotionally starved as a means of discipline—there were two kids in her book and she had a brother. It made sense that her older characters, all kind parental stereotypes, were an ideal that somehow compensated her or gave hope for the future. No matter, snickering with sad satisfaction, I marveled at how her survivor's instinct had segregated and insulated memories into layers, and that using trickery to unwrap abstractions was mental masturbation for an ingenious flake in a world of cerebral eunuchs while her need to dominate to feel safe was satisfied. I concluded that I was an excellent disco ball, just not what she wanted reflected, so she had to fight for her version of the world at the direct expense of mine.

With a celebratory beer over my genius, considering all that Bonnie had done to drive me so nuts that I would even contemplate believing her story, I realized I needed to get away. Taking a motorcycle trip with Ed to Sooke on Vancouver Island, a weekend piss-up in a Victoria hotel before taking a Sunday afternoon ferry back to the mainland should rid me of her influences. I would check ferry sailing times in the morning.

***

Zzzz - Sailing close-hauled toward granite cliffs.
Jimi plays chartreuse chords into a pear-scented breeze.
Gusts in C. Gales of grey rolling seas. Can't see.
Narwhal slides to the surface, I hang on.
The beast glides under, we dive deep.
Surfacing with a gasp, I drift on a kapok preserver.
Scarlet orchids rise from John's orchard.
Keith beats on a row of pumpkins.
Janice sings lime-toned sandpaper.
The Narwhal hums rose pulses that push me toward shore.
The distance between artists creates a cacophony of echoes.
They reach me in sync.

A car horn outside my window called the entire street to attention, as I hazily understood there were five soloists working in concert to show me that I was where I should be, before the fanfare of an inharmonious world returned me to my futon.

I pushed the ON button of my radio at five fifty-nine to check the weather. The news was the regular crap—pretty much a tape loop of the last decade, except for the last item. There was a police alert for residents of Horseshoe Bay and surrounding environs to be on the lookout for a prisoner who had escaped from a nearby island penal facility. The weather would be sunny with afternoon cloudy periods…

I called Bonnie at seven o'clock.

"Sorry I haven't called. Things have been going well…"

"That's terrific—half an hour on your side," Bonnie cut me off, the hardened plastic bang emphasizing how much on my side she wanted to be.

I sauntered to Nolan's, turning onto Davie Street just as Bonnie walked across it from her parked car, and we met at the door sporting the decorative grins of a first date. Entering the cafe arm in arm, Bréta cocked her head in a pleasantly surprised "Glad you aren't dead," grin, and we ordered mocha lattés, taking our seats at the recently vacated window booth.

Shifting empty cups to the side, Bonnie cast the first line. "Unusual experiences can change the course of one's life," she said.

[255]

"Through the isolation they create, if nothing else," I replied, easily.

"That may be true in some circumstances but not this time. I heard from other entities while you were away," she said, eagerly. "Now there's Saa-ra, Kha-li, Caroline, Jerome, and Phillip."

"You've been busy."

Grasping my hands like an excited school girl, she squeezed and said, "They told me f-a-s-c-i-n-a-t-i-n-g stuff about how the nature of physical reality impacts perception and how the teaching scheme incorporates specific perceptions to enhance our development." Letting go, she took a calming breath. "But you must have lots to tell me about your book."

"You first," I said, flexing my fingers.

"Sorry," Bonnie said, without remorse, but with the foresight to place her palms on the table to minimize my sense of peril.

"Physical reality is a realm within which each decision we make unerringly reflects our beliefs in that moment. Broaden that idea, and you can see how the point at which we chose to engage or abandon any event reflects our understanding of the relationship that always exists between our freedom of choice and our responsibilities to that event." She tapped the table with her forefinger. "These choices determine when and where we will continue our development."

"Kha-lib said something about that."

"They've all added something to what he first told us." With a finger occasionally tapping a lacquered pledge of love between Geri and Theo to underscore her favoured words, Bonnie said, "There will be three core versions of Earth at the conclusion of our current cycle of evolution. One will be inhabited by those who assumed their responsibilities as far as they understood them. In every way this will be the best place to continue learning. Another version will be inhabited by those whose behaviour demands that they experience the effects of their actions directly. Teachers will be there to help. The other version," she settled back in her seat, "is this one. We're literally choosing our destination right now."

I grasped Bonnie's hands as Bréta arrived with two oversized cups and a Danish pastry cut into quarter sections. Picking up the used cups, she said, "A new company delivers these fresh every morning. Tell me what you think," explaining the welcome-back freebee. "Where have you guys been?"

"Traveling the Universe," Bonnie replied expansively.

[256]

"In economy—she's jet-lagged," I said, to explain why I was restraining her. "You might as well bring us another one of those when you come back this way. Thanks."

Snickering without offence, Bréta said, "I haven't had a straight answer from either of you yet." She turned to greet a regular customer.

"Nice girl. Interesting future." Bonnie sipped her drink while I tried the pastry. Setting her cup aside, she said, "The Universe's teaching style is about showing us how the decisions we make and the challenges we create set our course. In simple terms, we save ourselves from ourselves, and it's easier than you might think."

"Except?"

"There's no catch. Every mother who rubs away a child's pain, every shoelace tied by a busy father, every moment of need shared with a friend, every promise made or broken determines which passport we get." She pitched forward. "Don't you see? We don't have to be brilliant, a physical prodigy, or possess one iota of talent. All we have to be is kind," she said, with a wave of her arm, and her hand struck a glancing blow to the rim of her cup.

"Some people are missing that gene," I said, pulling a serviette from the brushed aluminum holder.

"Some people need more help to see beyond themselves than others do." Bonnie took the paper from me and wiped up the minor spill.

"Does where you live matter? I mean, is a life in ancient Cairo better than one in Palo Alto? Are there places that guarantee certain points of view?"

"Every place and time provides their own challenges."

We subsequently discussed examples that ultimately made the point that we all manufacture our evolution with every decision regardless of where we are. Marvelling over the simplicity of what felt like suddenly crucial knowledge, I was embarrassed over having chosen living in the moment as a philosophy that separated me from the bar-prowlers. I knew that Bonnie really understood it and me…maybe not so much.

Wryly, Bonnie said, "The same thing happens to me in the moment that I understand something beyond the intellectual grasp of reason."

"Pardon me?"

"I'm talking about what just happened to you: A comprehensive understanding suspends the equivocations we rely on to face our days. You didn't know how to act in the moment of comprehension that just passed because you were entirely free to embrace the fact that you are responsible for the events you encounter. That idea took my breath away, as well." She leaned forward as if to pass on a secret. "If you

[257]

think about it, you haven't known how to act since Kha-lib disrupted the continuity of your existence."

"I've been doing what I usually do."

"Because that's all you know how to do, but I know your days weren't the same and that you are unsure of how to respond to me now because you're still not ready to give up your reason."

"My reason for what?"

"To give up reason as a mode of assessment."

"What else is there?"

"Logic renders reason archaic."

"Are coincidences logical?"

"Coincidence is how the average person recognizes the presence of Intent, and the Universe is nothing if not logical. That's what happened to bring you back?"

"Yes."

Apparently not interested in what specifically had caused me to call her, we subsequently drank and ate within a comfortable exchange of information about our time apart. When we were finished and had split the tab, I tucked in my shirt and tightened my laces then we headed for the park five blocks away without speaking, but it wasn't an awkward stroll. Bonnie window shopped while I pondered the idea of disrupting the continuity of existence as something to put into the application as a plague. I hadn't completely abandoned my solo plan; it was on hold.

With four blocks behind us, Bonnie casually said, "I struggled to accept the validity of my first encounter with the Universe, as well. Not so much at the time because a nine-year-old accepts most things as they are. It wasn't until years later that I wrestled with the question of my sanity."

We stopped walking to lock level gazes for that fickle stretch of time that implied she knew she had addressed my thoughts and that I had wrestled with the same question—her sanity. Turning to cross the width of the sidewalk to a bus stop bench, Bonnie sat down with her back to me. I sat beside her, waiting to hear why she thought she wasn't nuts.

Looking past me at who knew what, she said, "I was standing beside my father on a Chicago street when I became mesmerized by the lights circling the marquee, Cat on a Hot Tin Roof. Without warning, I was propelled into a realm surrounded by countless points of light brilliantly pulsating with a life of their own, then a cushioned, rocking motion enveloped me in a sea of blackness, but it was light. I felt warm, but there was no heat or cold to compare sensations."

[258]

"A place of contradictions?"

"A place that had none," she said, casually looping an arm through mine. "I was struck with an incredible calm and an illuminating clarity of mind so profound that fear became an out-dated emotion. I felt as if I was cradled in the hand of something immense, yet benevolent and protective, when a deep voice began to speak to me."

Taking in the street scenes with a slow turn of her head, she said, "He told me his name was Kha-li, and that it was of ancient Egyptian origin meaning 'All That Is'. He said he was the messenger of the Universal Source and a direct emanation of the creator then he spoke of his time on Earth and of his purpose and mine. He said he was my greatest ally, and throughout time I had been his; he had served my purposes while I had been his messenger preparing the way."

"And?" I said, nudging her along.

"He spoke about the rise and fall of innumerable cultures, of the future, and of the purposes of humanity in the twenty-first century. He also spoke about the dimension from which my life-force, Saa-ra, emanated and of the great scholars and luminaries of history, among who was his son. He also said that the end of the world cycle was not a physical condition because life would and must go on. What the creator has given is a beautiful gift conceived within a flourishing and indomitable passion born of immeasurable love and sent forth in the grace of freedom to live, to love, to experience, to gather wisdom, to apply knowledge, and the courage to address the challenges of aware-ness while assuming total responsibility for your acts." She looked at me. "Twenty-eight years later, I had my second formal contact, apart from thousands of fabulous dreams."

"When was that?"

"Seven months ago. I know how difficult this is for you to accept; I sat on my balcony staring at the ocean for three days trying to grasp the enormity of it all myself." She took a deep breath, stood up, and pulled on my arm. "Let's walk."

"He spoke to you then?"

"Like wearing earphones," she said, stepping away.

Bonnie's idea of "walking" was ten feet to a clothing shop window, where she continued unfolding her personal plot. "They asked me to search my past for signs of their presence. I wasn't sure what I should be looking for, so they started me off. When I caught on to the abstract style and context of their contacts, I discovered many instances that pointed to my destiny when I thought they weren't around, just as your experiences brought you to this point in your life. Our lives are remarkably similar. That's a good buy," she said about a fifty dollar sweater.

"I'm glad you think ours is a match made in heaven, but claiming to have friends there will lead to a rubber room. People aren't accepting of that kind of thing."

"Channelling is more common than you realize," she said, strolling to the window of a man's clothing store.

"So is rationalizing advantages out of a loss. I mean," I said hastily, "you can't be the same person after meeting Kha-li, and people don't let you change, they leave you alone. The other side of that coin," I said, pausing to feign sensitivity, "is that you might be pushing people away to hide the inevitable losses meeting him created."

"The people who think I'm nuts have fulfilled their purpose in my life, and parting company is the natural order of growth. What do you think of that belt?" she pointed toward a brown belt with a brushed brass buckle of a steer's head with curved horns.

"I might wear it to a hootenanny. What you call the natural order is what a student might see as abandoning old friends for better ones."

"It's the truth unencumbered by how I feel—felt because missing them isn't a loss anymore." She looked my way. "The Universe explained the underlying nature of my experiences as they apply to a specific plan for this lifetime. Along with experiencing their world directly, I had to abandon my penchant to rationalize any event to suit my feelings, beliefs, or desires, like my old friends still do." She took a full breath. "The bottom line is that the unspoken agreements that bound us are gone. What about this one?" She pointed to a narrow black band with a nondescript, brass buckle. "The ache I still some-times feel is from appreciation for what they did for me. Now, all I can do is go the way of my destiny and leave my friends with a gift."

"Bewildered is a gift?" I quipped.

"That's the wrapping of knowledge. What about this one?" She pointed to a medium width reversible, brown/black belt, with a silver buckle on one side of the clasp and gold on the other.

"That's good," I said. Her son didn't dress flashy and he would have a choice to suit his pants.

Looking at other options, Bonnie said, "I catered to people's silent demands to maintain harmony by telling myself that compromise was fairness, and when it didn't seem fair to me, I was being an altruist. Eventually, I saw victimization at the end of that road, and I broke my unspoken agreements to shoulder the burden of other's responsibilities because it wasn't doing either of us any good. Now, friends are dis-

[260]

covering they have to face themselves or find someone else to carry their baggage. In the first case, they'll unwrap the gift to discover the source of their hurt feelings, and they'll be better off right away. In the latter, they'll present their new friends with the opportunity to learn if and when to assume responsibility for their circumstances. Either way, they grow."

"How—," I hesitated to sound less offensive, "how would they learn this on their own if they didn't from Kha-li's ally?"

Bonnie examined my reflection for sarcasm. Finding none intended, she said, "Whiners use up friends because the fine art of sucking the life out of people is never an equitable exchange. Someone always feels they're giving more than they get, and they eventually move on to share their misery elsewhere. In time, they wear those people out, or they're thrown away so often that they have to consider they might be creating their own isolation."

"Aren't you're doing that—isolating yourself, I mean?"

"My experiences with the Universe removed me from the world of common thought in a single act, but it's their lessons that'll cement the specifics and make that change a permanent gift of separation from the madness." Reflectively she said, "Every day that I work on changing my ways is another day I can honestly say I like who I'm becoming. It's slow, but I'm low maintenance now. Come on." She went inside the shop, picked up the belt, and had me put it on. The salesman commented that Bonnie had good taste, and she bought it.

As soon as we were outside the door, I said, "I'm saying you might not think there's much to change about yourself because you're pretty much alone now. You have no points of reference."

"And I'm saying I don't feed off other people, so I don't need the touchstone of their approval. As you assume responsibility for your life there will certainly be ostracism."

"What if you need help and your friends are all gone?"

"Following my heart has always led me to what I really need, not what I think I want." Before I could ask, she explained, "I used to think accidents or being without money was unfortunate, but now I can see how those circumstances motivated me into making choices that benefited me in the long run." Restraining a smile, she said, "Like you, I've always been fine in spite of myself. I told you how I got my house?"

"Falling down stairs, sure."

"I cracked my tailbone. Even a little movement hurt, so I limited where I went and shopped at places I wouldn't have normally gone. A man at a checkout line asked me what I had done, which led me to telling him I lost my townhouse deal. He was the rental agent for the county."

"You told me. I think the Universe plays too rough."

"We choose our accidents as certainly as we choose our pleasures."

"Why would I want an accident?"

"To put an end to a particular phase of living and the momentum of poor choices. You see, it doesn't matter if we are aware of our purpose because learning how to live properly is everyone's purpose. Mind you, on occasion the Universe directs an apprentice to enhance an experience if both parties agree."

Nearing the park entrance, Bonnie chose to bypass it, and she instead headed toward the sandy beach strewn with large, sun-baked logs.

"If they didn't push you down the stairs," I said, "what's the big deal about meeting the agent? It's still a coincidence, granted, but there's no mystery about a stranger talking to you."

"At other levels of awareness, I chose the event to prevent me from deviating from what needed to be done. Our friends probably softened the blow."

"Deviating from what?"

"A mortgage might have stopped me from connecting with you and Josh."

"You don't know?"

"You didn't know that turning back was right when you did it in Lebanon."

"Our physical friends connected us, which was a lucky thing because there were a lot of people over a lot of time and miles that could have changed either of our plans."

"I'm sure they did many times. The fluidity of a universal intercession can seem so reasonable that we don't think to track contributing events, or as in your case, they were acceptably inexplicable."

"A student would think it's more logical that you are contriving personal intercessions with the heavens because you don't consider yourself a common person. You know—greatest ally?"

"My experiences don't make me a better person than you or anyone else. I am better off than most because I embrace the minimal chances that life offers us to improve every day. It's that simple and that profound, and being an ally is their claim. I'm not comfortable with it, at least not until I know what it means."

"Minimal? I thought every moment is a new decision?"

[262]

"How many of them do you embrace?"

"One more than I did an hour ago."

"Excellent, and now we'll see if you can pay attention to individual events and act as if there's a point to everything."

"Why wouldn't I?"

"Because a lifetime of dismissing everything that didn't serve your myths has crushed your point of view into the breadth of a hair compared to what's possible." Bonnie sat down on a huge log and patted the space beside her. "Teachers say it's extremely difficult to get the hang of stopping propensities because it's so difficult discovering what they are on your own. Few people will ever challenge them directly; even students need a huge push to change the way they think. That said, as you embrace each moment, you're rewarded with far richer experiences than the parameters of weights and measures other people impose on themselves, which then feeds the momentum to continue your efforts. Case in point, this morning you recognized a coincidence that clearly had a huge impact on you, and now you're bargaining by looking for loopholes to put the event into a perspective you can accept without changing how you think."

"You gleaned that from me asking about coincidences," I accused her.

"Of course," she laughed. "I don't need to intuit the obvious."

I sat down beside her. "What kind of push are you talking about?"

"Pushes to stay on track: these lessons inherently subvert a student's faith in themselves, so they have to act as if they believe in them more than they believe in their own judgement. It's difficult to replace one with another, so teachers constantly remind them to not react, to remember to act as if you have an agreement with the Universe, then that the Universe always keeps their bargains, so there's no point in putting things off." Watching joggers in the park many meters away, Bonnie said, "One of the reasons you can't accept that the Universe has an interest in you is that you expect crashing cymbals and thunderous drums to announce and prove their existence, when they have already saved your life half a dozen times, given you Knowings, opened career doors, and orchestrated many coincidences that culminated in the one that you couldn't ignore today." She gulped air as if it were on sale.

"Why don't they just show themselves?"

"Because you still think in religious terms; you would run."

"Not that I agree, but I'd eventually have to face what happened."

"Not necessarily. Your world of fixed dimensions still has you denying the validity of mystical experiences and generally ranting against the outrageous because to acknowledge a sentient unseen would be to admit you aren't in control. Which of course you aren't but only because of the way you think. That leaves religion as the only context to deal with the inexplicable, and you haven't seen anything other than a master slave relationship in any of those."

"A show of some kind would make anybody accept them."

"What would you do if a burning bush spoke to you?"

"I'd look for the speaker in the ground."

"When you didn't find it?"

"I'd have another beer."

"And forever after shout, 'Do it again!' refusing to accept anything less as a confirmation. If you got those, you would obey the Universe when the point of them revealing their existence is to fast track a student's path to voluntary self-development." Bonnie raised her hand to stop my protest. "The difference is that you have to experience their information or recognize how you've already experienced it because that's what turns events into knowledge. They don't waste anything."

"How is following an order different from taking advice?"

"Bowing to anyone taints the experience when the point of the teaching scheme is to learn how to discern the proper path in any circumstance. Ultimately, their lessons align you with the unstoppable forces of Catalytic Momentum, so they can't risk having your last word be 'Oops.' If their lessons were about memorizing core solutions to standardized problems, you would not appreciate the full ramifications of those solutions, whereas taking suggestions adds personal interpretation. Together, these lead you to discovering much more about a circumstance including the belief that blocked your view. It's a win-win situation."

"Crashing cymbals would make me take them seriously from day one."

Feigning fatigue, Bonnie sighed. "They don't make anyone do anything. Mind you," she softened her tone, "depending on the agreement they have with a potential student, the Universe might make their presence known in an undeniable way. As I said, the ramifications of that are further reaching than you can begin to imagine, so you're better off uncovering their benevolent presence in your life before anything else happens."

"Else?'"

Like a surgeon removing a splinter from my cornea—absorbed by something connected to me as if I weren't there, Bonnie said, "I've spent the morning telling you what I learned about the nature of reality to help you realize how and where the Universe may have helped you, even though you know they have. Come on." She stood up and brushed the back of her jeans. "Your words may deny the source of the help you received, but your actions say you've accepted an inexplicable source of guidance as not only functional in your life but necessary to your survival. You fight that knowledge because you fear it, and your only recourse is to challenge it through me by thinking I'm a victim of groundless faith."

It took me a moment to catch up mentally. Still sitting, I said, "What about me tells you that?"

"Why else would you have acted on your awareness of impending danger when there was none apparent to others? By your own admission, you're not a strategic thinker."

"I trusted my senses in those situations."

"If that's true, why is learning the source of your extraordinary sense experiences an issue now?"

"Maybe flying out of my body would change that."

"Be careful what you ask for. It can change more than your opinions."

"Uh huh." I stood up and we started walking. "Queasy feelings in tricky situations are normal for most people, and there's nothing mysterious about the average soldier being a piss-poor shot. It also makes more sense that an experienced non-combatant would survive than it does to make magic out of falling down stairs."

"A student of life would want to know why an otherwise intelligent teacher would make a claim she apparently can't support."

"That crossed my mind."

"The teacher would speak about unusual events in their own lives to awaken memories of similar experiences their student has had but forgotten because the student had no reference point from which to assess the source or value of the experience. It wouldn't resolve anything right away, but it would be the proper time to lay the foundation for a student's epiphany."

"Why wouldn't it resolve anything?"

"The student would think the teacher is trying to secure their self-image in the student's eyes because that's what students are doing when they tell their intimate tales and reveal vulnerabilities. They are competing instead of comparing, so the underlying point is obscured."

"Competing for what?"

"For power and control, if only over their views. Getting me into the sack has been your prize since you first saw me, for your own reasons,

[265]

more so now because it represents a conquest over threatening ideas. Ironically, all of the progress you've made would be lost if you won that competition."

"After all of the time I've spent trying to pry a story line from you?"

"Your prying has always been aimed at undermining my views."

"I don't have to agree with a premise to write about it, and arguing is a method of investigation."

"Novice students secretly believe their teacher's metaphysical affairs are more important than the student's physical experiences, when in fact they extend the significance of their lives by revealing the unimaginable potential in all of us. In your case, you have bet your future that people will be interested in reading about a version of the world you think you know better than most of them. It follows that if you slay my dragon, your kingdom is safer. And *that*," she said, emphatically, "will be the end of us."

"If I win an argument, we're through?" I stared in disbelief at the threat.

"I'm saying you can't continue to compete *and* learn enough to help us both do our work." Bonnie faced me. "It's important to listen to every syllable of what I have to tell you right now. If you have the slightest doubt about anything, ask me about it until there are no issues in your mind. Can you do that in this new moment?"

"Go ahead," I said, bewildered at her suddenly cold demeanour.

"Do you agree that each fragment of knowledge we gain can change the way we live?"

"Sure."

She waited passively.

"Yes, I can see that," I said definitively.

"The knowledge I can access, and the lessons that will make it your knowledge will eventually render your current way of life untenable. If we are to continue to work together, you must agree to being taught how to live properly, so you'll know what to do when your old version of the world falls apart."

"If I trespassed somewhere on our walk, I apologize."

"What are you talking about?"

"The ultimatum," I said, turning back toward Denman Street.

"I'm taking responsibility for my actions. It only looks like an ultimatum."

"I think you're getting even for my time away, because a change can't be inevitable if I have free will."

[266]

"Phillip always fulfills his bargains, so he will continue to teach even when you think you can't go on. Fair warning, this time will come because the lessons push every student to the limits of their ability. Kha-lib wishes to speak with us. Let's go home."

Twenty minutes later, Bonnie sat in her rocker, and I took my place on the couch. Following an abbreviated download routine, her Kha-lib persona greeted me with the disinterest of speaking to a house plant. Apparently, this was his teaching mode because it was without pleasantries, emotion, or emphasis of any kind that he launched into the following lesson:

Essentially, Kha-lib said mankind evolves through trial and error because maintaining endless images stands in the way of seeing the underlying order of a circumstance. Teaching me an ancient philosophy he called, 'The Way To Live', will put an end to my circuitous learning pattern and heal my wounds within a triage of safe arenas. These influences will be the Universe's, Bonnie's direct and directed care, and through teachers in my dreams.

While speaking of dreams, Kha-lib said I thought of continuity and momentum as a series of like-natured events when they are much more. Mankind creates their continuity of existence by continuously assembling our perception of reality through a focal point seers rightfully called the assemblage point, which feeds the cocoon-like energy essence of our being. He would teach me about this at another time. For now, it was enough to know that we literally create our impressions of time, distance, form and texture, and validate them through the same means that assemble the perception. In this way, there are no seams in our impression of physical continuity, which is our fundamental source of conditioning. Unfortunately, we have given our egos far too much influence, and we underestimate the value of things we cannot measure. He said we do not give our dreams their due because we do not understand their source or underlying order of their continuity. Without dreams, we could not sustain a physically oriented presence, so important are they to our mental, physical, and emotional health, as guided by our Source Souls when we are "home" i.e.: sleeping. In other words, the reality of our existence is the reverse of how we perceive it. We are not the dreamer, but the dreamed. The Universe uses our perceptions of physicality to create scenarios in which it is known what choices we will make, choices that invariably reveal a core belief that may avoid causing the kind of damage we are capable of. May, because free will prevails.

A typical lesson dream might begin with things going surprising well before they methodically fall apart. Every fix we try leaks, our tools are never where we left them, and finally, the stairs to the basement tool room disappear. The underlying message may be that we didn't complete each step of the job properly or otherwise fulfill our responsibilities to a task, and we end up repeating the task until we get it right. But a dream is just a dream to most people, and their influences only temporary.

To deal with our assumption of reversed realities, the Universe will train teachers how to impart the same kind of lessons but in a physical context. They do this by reading the nature of a student's behaviour in a spontaneous situation then they wait for or recreate the scene so the student will repeat the behaviour without thinking or excuse. What they are really like beneath their customary calm in an ordinary social circumstance rears its head, and the student sees themselves. In conjunction with other poignant dreaming scenarios, the student cannot escape themselves.

I told Kha-lib that entrapment taints everything.

"Apprentices learn that every circumstance has the potential of eliciting a secret from their intricate disguise because one cannot be trapped by behaviours they do not have, and dreaming lessons are agreed upon by the Source Soul and their earthbound presence. There is no subterfuge other than what the physical portion of the Source spirit conjures from his or her inability to grasp the true nature of the event. In this way, they learn that all behaviours flow from a few categories of influence, and within a moment of clarity, the myriad examples of what they are really like coalesce to force the unconditional surrender of their self-image. In esoteric circles, this event is called a Conditional Death. In laymen's terms, it is the moment when the beliefs upon which one shaped their personality no longer apply, and they know without reservation what they are really like."

"Uh-huh. What's left when the beliefs that shape personality are shot down?"

"You are ready to deliberately face challenges to the extent of knowingly putting yourself in circumstances that will demand your best."

"If our personality is a concoction of aberrant beliefs and they no longer apply, what's left to challenge?"

"A lifetime of conditioning inexorably draws you back to your old ways unless you actively pursue new standards to make them your core conditioning. In this way, the influences of your old personality become reference points for learning the thirteen principles of The Way To Live. This is everyone's inevitable challenge."

"How does the conditional thing compare to what happened to my way of thinking in Argentina?"

"Narrowly speaking, you understood that the media's purpose was a ploy, as was the world's basic goodness a deceit because the media reflects the world. Knowing that you had been duped meant you were no longer a pawn, but as a meaningless cog in a corrupt world, you felt free to adopt the tactics of the enemy."

"I was paid for taking risks other people wouldn't take."

"This is another subterfuge. Without a purpose, your life did not matter, and that frame of mind freed you to punish corporations by way of large invoices written in the blood of those upon whom you both preyed. Acting with fervour as you always do," he said as my stomach lurched, "has made a large shift in your perceptions inevitable sooner than might otherwise be. If you focus on learning about yourself, these shifts will bring you to your Conditional Death. If you focus on despair, they will bring you to the brink of your death because you will have nothing to champion and none to punish for your circumstance."

"If it's just the brink…"I quipped.

"You have never found death amusing," Kha-lib said placidly.

"Then why are you talking to me?" I snapped.

"Because you volunteered. If there are no more questions, we will leave you to consider your choices in this moment."

"Ummm,"

Bonnie was her normal self in about thirty seconds. Keeping a straight face, I asked her what the Universe's lessons were like.

"I lived in two worlds from the moment I met Kha-li. In the world of average people, I lived in relative ignorance of what was going on, in relative safety compared with what could have happened, and by modest means relative to the wealth around me. My other life was full of magical events where knowledge became the means through which I achieved my goals, and safety wasn't an issue because my lessons, feelings, and knowing things put an end to most of the risks I might have taken."

"Most?"

"Going out of my body proved that we transition, not die, but I haven't fully incorporated this knowledge into how I live every moment."

"In what way?"

[269]

She got out of the rocker and came over to the couch to sit beside me. "My certain knowledge of life's continuance brought with it the awareness that I'm here for only a short time. I'm not saying this as a parental concern or philosophical advice, I mean that we're here for a really, really short time." She snapped her fingers, and I half-expected her to disappear. Smiling at my reaction, she said, "I'm aware of how easy it is to waste an opportunity, which is why I try to make my every action as deliberate a choice as I'm capable of making, as opposed to a person who misreads warnings as challenges. I still catch myself doing silly things because reprogramming the way the world insists I think requires constant attention. I get help with that." She looked up.

"What about that conditional thing changing what you're like?"

"What about Martian weather?"

"Sorry. Have you had a conditional death?"

"No. I'm still cutting the elastics when I recognize the tug of a poor belief. You help me with that more than you know."

"Thanks," I said missing the slight.

Swallowing hard, she said, "Well—what's your decision?"

"What the hell, let's get on with it."

"Done!" Bonnie said, so firmly that her ancient cat jumped up off her belly. Looking over her shoulder, Ginger trotted out of the room.

Had we been in Tripoli, I would have noticed the crowd thinning and headed for Jordan—best salads in the world in Amman. As it was, I chuckled over Bonnie's imitation of me as she went over to the fireplace mantel.

Picking up a paperback by Jane Roberts, she said, "This will help to clear up the first hundred questions you'll have. And this," she said picking up the bag with the belt inside, "will keep you from having to hike up your pants. Your jogging is working well."

"I thought it was for Karl," I mumbled unappreciatively.

"We are not in a financial competition and the value of this gift does not constitute a condition of reciprocity," she said coolly.

Her eyes brightened. "If that's too much to take for a lesson example, think of it as a teaching aid. You can hitch your thumbs through the loops as a reminder to pay attention, like a real student would, to every syllable of what I'm saying." She cocked her head to one side. "Come to think of it, I need the exercise. Do you want to run together; we can do lessons at the same time?"

"Sure."

"Your commitment is underwhelming."

[270]

Chapter Twenty-eight
Momentum

Jogging together didn't happen for many weeks, which didn't break my heart because I enjoyed the solitary aspect of running and the freeness of a wandering mind. Bonnie was sure to be slower, unable to do my distance, and would probably talk the whole bloody way. What stopped us wasn't a lack of resolve but a lack of time because, after my formal agreement to be taught, she began channelling descriptively illusive entities virtually every moment we were together. And when I went home at night, I read Jane Roberts' *Seth Material* to better grasp what Bonnie had told me during the day. I did not bother to question the authenticity / multiple personality issue.

Typically, our days began around nine, always with the Kha-lib persona setting up timeframes and cultural backgrounds for the physical lifetimes of other personas who would then tell tales of personal growth that I could relate to the larger quest: I recognized that Bonnie was acting out the prologue reminiscences of characters in the first material she had allowed me to read.

As an example of this approach, Phillip told a story about sibling rivalry driving him to accomplishments he might not otherwise have attempted, then Caroline spoke about a youthful jealousy that drove her to become a prima donna. Kha-lib then explained that focus was the difference between the two experiences: smouldering resentment had propelled Phillip to greater achievements but his fuel had been acrimony, so the journey was without joy and the conquest bittersweet when his sibling was happy for him. Examining the experience, Phillip thereafter pursued challenges for appropriate reasons.

Propelled by whispers and ridicule, Caroline evolved an inventive package of patronizing behaviours, which eventually elevated her so far above everyone that she was utterly alone. When her pedestal of pretence crumbled, because there was no support for her lofty views, the impact of her fall caused her to realize the climb back to changing and accepting who she was had to be honest. During that trek, she discovered that she could be loved for who she became because of the fall.

[271]

Kha-lib added to these stories, saying there was a time when he had played fair, but rarely came in ahead of the cheaters. Those experiences nourished in him cynicism to the point that mediocrity became his standard, and numbing days dutifully followed his lack of vision. With no pleasant memories to comfort him, and nothing to look forward to, he eventually realised that the journey is the thing, the arrival but a temporary place to reflect upon the quality of the voyage. In sharing these human experiences, he said the collective consciousness—the family of entities—came to understand that hate is a manifestation of the desire to be loved, the opposite of which is indifference. From here, they thought they may have unravelled the mystery of mankind's universally unique behaviour of malice, as a confluence of ignorance and fear becoming a tide of self-destruction when we allowed the influences of our ego-accomplice too much latitude.

At this point, I asked Kha-lib why he said "may have unravelled the mystery," to which he replied, "Our experience with an endlessly resourceful species has caused us to not underestimate the potential of your irrationality."

This segmented teaching style filled eight to ten hours of our day, the information from which Kha-lib built upon the next day. All of it was potential grant proposal material, so I stopped working on it for the time being, awaiting a coalescing of material that would apply to a screenplay climax.

On Saturday, when Rachel and Meaghan again stopped by, Bonnie told them she was a channel of universal knowledge and they were welcome to listen. I enjoyed this because they did not know, nor would they have appreciated how they were participating in the development of scenes in our screenplay. They came inside because there was no other polite option.

Shortly afterwards, Kha-lib introduced them to their Source Soul personas, who talked about their personal evolution. After they were brought up to date, Rachel's Higher Self asked them both to come back the following week; out of channelling mode, Bonnie volunteered my expertise if the ladies wanted to know more about what the Universe had told us so far. From their initial shock to feeling trapped, then enthralled, and now uncertain, both of them were noncommittal.

The first Sunday of lessons, and how most Sunday sessions would be, ran about four hours after which Bonnie made lunch, usually a smorgasbord. My usual contribution was a little shopping if needed and dicing or peeling while Saa-ra channelled ancient recipes.

[272]

My weekday lessons then continued in a layered fashion until the next Saturday when, to my surprise, both women arrived just a few minutes behind Josh, which wasn't startling because I assumed Bonnie was subjecting him to the same ideas she doled out to me.

On this day, Kha-lib stayed in the background while Saa-ra initiated a discussion about religion influencing social evolution, saying that most of our laws and ethics are based on ancient teachings that have been misrepresented over time; the culprit for Christians was the Ten Commandments. She said these started out as simplified disciplines derived from the core principles of how to live properly, and that they were first presented in a manner suited to a particular culture in a specific time, when the apostles had designed their lives to be meta-phors of the male and female principles on The Way to Live. Saa-ra said she would tell us a more complete story about the time of Jesus* as our progression warranted such clarifications before saying that, as these principles of personal growth spread to other lands, various sects incorporated them into their belief systems. An eye for an eye, for example, was meant to convey the existence of the immutable law of catalytic momentum that brings us face to face with the nature of our own deeds. When this idea spread to the self-important leaders of other cultures, "immutable law" became a demand, and the myth of an angry, vengeful God was underway. His anger could be mitigated, of course, and rewards brokered by His earthly representatives.

In our time, Saa-ra said writings will be discovered that reveal there are twelve disciplines which culminate in the thirteenth principle of living a *whole* life. It was not a *Holy* existence mired in worship to the unexplained desires of a petulant unseen. How our cultures skewed these teachings is an historical testament to the ingenuity of self-interest that has forced the Universe's emissaries to return to the physical plane on four other occasions* to set things straight. Even then, the momentum of our ways out ran the truth, which is why previous envoys left writings that will make it clear how and why mankind has reached the wretched state we are currently in. She said she would say more about these previous interventions at appropriate times.

On the next Monday of my solo lessons, Kha-lib focused on man-kind's ingenious ability to manipulate awareness: Our First Attention holds our root assumptions, which the ego embraces to keep us safe while we're on the physical plane. Root assumptions are things like gravity, time, distance, and the standard values of weights and measures that literally root our attention in the physical realm. The

[273]

more energy we gather, the more versatile becomes our ability to manipulate our awareness into the Second Attention where assumptions hold little more sway than as reference points to make sense out of Second Attention experiences. This is where we begin to explore the world, and ourselves, as conscious energy constructs. The Third Attention is the ultimate human accomplishment, for one's life-force is outside of the physical construction looking in, literally straddling realms, and there is nothing to stop one from staying out other than the recognition of an incomplete physical journey. He said the Second and Third Attentions can be experienced at the behest of Spirit, the memories of which have to be translated into First Attention terms.

In midweek, Bonnie gave me a copy of *The Power of Silence*, by Carlos Castaneda, "to help you understand the rules and processes involved in the journey to knowledge from a first hand perspective," she said, sitting back in her rocker. She immediately followed this with, "Who are we?" the signal that another persona had come for a visit.

Reading this work at night, I discovered that Castaneda's teacher, don Juan Matus, was twice the crackpot that Bonnie had become with me, which initially made understanding the book difficult. Ironically, this second source of confusion during my acute learning curve breathed new life into my old suspicions that Bonnie may be a recruiter, as opposed to ingeniously nuts. I dealt with this concern on a warm, May evening, during a stroll along the West Vancouver sea wall.

"Why did Carlos bother going back after their first meeting?" I asked Bonnie, on no cue other than we had finished speaking about another matter.

Accepting the topical change as if she had been thinking about it, Bonnie said, "His self-importance rendered it unimaginable that a Yaqui Indian elder could be smarter than him." She started to laugh, fought it off, and then said, "You were unable to fathom how I could know anything about conflicts that you didn't know, but you've developed more tolerance for my ideas because they are showing up in your writing by now." Her statement was not a question.

"I did borrow some background ideas while I was away," I admitted.

"I'm not accusing you of anything," she chuckled. "What I say to you is a gift. Do with it what you will."

"Thanks. Did Carlos suspect there was some kind of deception going on?"

"Like you do? Of course."

"Why didn't that screw up Juan's credibility?"

[274]

"Juan knew how to polish an ulterior motive, which allowed him to lead Carlos into participating in the sorcerer's culture until validating experiences made it impossible for him to stay away. Carlos always struggled to rationalize Juan's ways into a sociological structure he could accept," Bonnie said, with a shrug, "but he didn't realize he had already made the leap into the unknown." She leaned into her explanation. "Your friend Sammi knew that committing to a decision meant leaving his feet, after which all you can do is engage your destiny with dignity." She paused and explained, "Initially, you tried to manipulate your fate by hunching low, then you understood your commitment to your decisions at Goodbye. The part of your awareness that's designed to protect your physical journey still thinks I'm crazy, but there's a deeper part of you that knows you've already left your feet. Otherwise, you wouldn't be bargaining to maintain your reason *and* leave it behind to embrace log as your core cognition. You'd be at the pub conveniently forgetting the special moments you can't properly explain, especially since we met."

"I'm researching your premises like you asked me to, and my experiences with you are a large part of why I came back. I didn't dismiss them."

"You've softened your approach, but you're still serving an ulterior motive."

"If you say so."

"I just did."

Before I left for the day, she gave me a book written by Lynn V. Andrews about her unexpected journey of becoming a Medicine Woman, and another book each by Jane Roberts and Carlos Castaneda.

---

*Soon after this lesson, Saa-ra explained the nature of the first four intercessions, with a special focus on the time of Christ. This information is presented in Volume Two, Stalking The Bridge of Reason, and Volume Three, Stalking The Designs of Intent. Both works are due for release in 2012. Check www.axelson.ca for updates and pre-orders.

Chapter Twenty-nine
The Gathering

B y the end of the first month of Bonnie's elaborate chats with her Universal friends, a typical day consisted of getting up at five-thirty, writing until eight-thirty, then showering before meeting Bonnie at nine. In the early evening I jogged, then kicked back for some TV, or I might try editing my morning's work. I say try because I was interrupted by calls from Meg and Rachel asking me about thoughts seeded by Bonnie on Saturday. As a result, I added an official night session of writing to my schedule—in lieu of having no better offers.

After a supper with Ed at a pub, on one of these scheduled nights I sat down to write, and as happened often enough to allow it, my creative flow went into scenes that ignored established parameters. Unusually, this time I found myself mentally trotting to keep up with what became an historical hallucination narrated by an unidentified party in my dying character's thoughts. Two paragraphs in, I knew it wouldn't fit in my work but I continued recording this internal dictation as an investment in something I could somehow use later on.

After an hour, my mind emptied as if a tap had been shut off and I settled back to read what I thought was a rambling parable about a band of wanderers seeking shelter in a town for the winter. To my surprise, the story was clearer on paper than it had been in my mind because I had to scramble to describe the scenes as they continuously unfolded, the essence of which follows:

A caretaker group of one of five gemstones that comprised the tribe's only physical wealth, wanted to sell the stone because their new landlord demanded much labour for low pay. This crystal was one of four that when polished in times of need reflected the true circumstance from which the proper course of action could be determined, then the vision would fade as a lesson learned, and the stone's hue became lighter. I did not know how many levels there were in the stones, only that the last vision revealed a core principle of living.

When all four caretaker groups reached this stage, a wizard—I wanted to say seer, but my fingers fought the change—arranged the gems to the cardinal compass points. Focusing the rays of a rising sun, the cornerstones of life illuminated a fifth crystal which projected the design of destiny to the students from its every facet. As the new day fully dawned, all of the stones returned to their rich, black lustre, and another journey of learning was ready to begin under the guidance of the leader designated by the centre stone's projection.

I did not define a time of need or have a clue what the design of destiny might be as I read the tale with increasing immodesty: in one pass, I had orchestrated an intricate metaphor about looking into the darkness for points of light, and in a moment of illumination, everything became clear... but I digress.

The wizard objected to the sale, telling the group that he needed all of the crystals to guide them to a place he had been enticing them to seek by calling it Freedom. However, years of living hand to mouth had the splinter group wanting more, and tired of being judged because they were poor and presumed to be ignorant, they made the deal knowing how the layered visions would affect their landlord. As did the wizard, who warned the wealthy buyer that the stone's reflections required deciphering by someone with no interest in the outcome, otherwise misinterpretations of its prophetic properties were inevitable.

Absently manipulating the gem in his palm, the landlord took pity on the tribal patriarch who was transparently seeking an easier existence, and he offered the vanquished leader a menial job serving in his expansive household. The seer, wizard accepted because the keeper of the stones was duty-bound to pass on his knowledge; the landlord carelessly dismissed him to view a vision of affluence in the stone of gratitude.

As the weeks became months of polishing through layers of illumination that increasingly reflected his laziness and greed, the landlord promoted a tenant-wanderer who proved to be equally adept at managing the landlord's personal affairs as he had cleaning and repairing his things. The seasons cycled, and as more business matters fell to the discretion of this employee, other tenant-wanderers were brought into the fold. These people also proved to be more efficient workers and administrators than the local labour pool because they knew what having nothing was like.

During this time, a powerful confidant learned about the stone, and seeing how its reflections came true, he quietly set out to purchase an indolent future of his own. A second caretaker group, seeing that their peers had become very comfortable, offered their gem for the price of the first group's current wages and circumstances. The businessman did not hesitate, his new employees soon proved themselves, the man's

[277]

fortunes began to rise, and there was a bidding war for the third stone, the losers of which formed a partnership to afford the fourth crystal.

The seasons again cycled as the old guard spent their days peering into layers of desire, while their servants became masters of new systems of commerce by which the landlords blithely and blindly profited.

Eventually, realizing their predicament when, one by one, the stones began to reflect only lush, idle landscapes, the landlords came to the wizard for advice, which was something he had become renowned for in the town square by simply waiting to be asked what he was doing there. They said they would pay any price after they were in control again because their wealth had become ensnared by complicated investment structures that amounted to liens held by each other against each other's interests. No wanted to be the first to blink. They were also more than prisoners of their mistrust because some of the former wanders sometimes declined to see their "bosses," until a more convenient time.

The wizard said he could help them become powerful beyond their wildest dreams; however, it could not be done quickly, or in this place. In the meantime, their empires were in capable, if misguided hands.

In the spring of the fourth year of the wanderer's tacit rule, the landlords and those among the original tribe who had refused to barter their future, left with the keeper of knowledge to find a place he had often talked about during his servitude.

In time, this incarnation of seekers of knowledge reached the cores of every crystal, and at the dawn of the summer solstice, all except one among them saw a clear reflection of themselves framed by the lush valley in which they stood. The one, who had remained true to the wizard's teachings during "the winters", as they would forever be known to the descendants of the clan, saw the old town. Gathering the stones that had already begun to glow with an eerie darkness, the new wizard began the odyssey of leading his lost friend's home.

The internal narration of my character's vision ended when he opened his eyes for the last time, and he told his friend not to mourn him, things weren't what they seemed, then he died.

I told Bonnie about my free flow experience the next morning, joking that her work had infected mine to the point where I didn't understand it; I handed her the pages to see what she could make of the scene. Still on the first page, Bonnie chirped a stilted cry, then stifling a series of sniffles left the room. I made toast for me and tea for both of us. Ten minutes later, wearing new mascara, Bonnie came into the kitchen and said the Universe had given me a message.

"Ed and I rearranged our perceptions a little bit last night but not so much that we were communicating with the cosmos," I grinned.

"You should make a gesture in return," she said, with a reproving glare not to be trifled with. "Visualize meeting our friends, so you can thank them, and another scene will come to you like this one did." She set the pages on the coffee table. "Be bold. If a door opens, walk through it." She stood and went to the credenza to retrieve more pages of her screenplay. Handing them to me, she said, "Read it tonight just before you go to bed. First draft," she reminded me.

I didn't question why she wanted this, Bonnie changed the subject, and we got on with another day of persona hopping.

In bed that night, I read the following:

TIME AND TIME AGAIN
SCENE THREE: SPATIAL INFINITY
MEDIUM WIDE SHOT: REVERSE POV.

As Kha-li walks away from a translucent rose gateway, it rapidly recedes to disappear between quadrants B (upper right screen) and D (lower right screen). As this happens, the stone pathway he is creating extends from what was five-fold the distance of his every step to finally reach a glowing energy construction of a pyramid that enlarges to encompass screen left. The top third of it is a golden aura. As camera DOLLY's in, we see that the front of the pyramid has two golden doors with distinct carvings of infinity and the trinity symbols. The doors open outwards on their own as Kha-li approaches and enters a chamber. He moves through the pulsating crystalline structure toward a hallway. The floor is of a golden radiant cast, still translucent. The walls and ceiling are as if hewn from a single crystal. Spatial infinity can still be seen faintly outside.

FADE IN BG SOUND:

Voices of twenty-six people mingling are heard, the predominant voice by a small amount is Saa-ra concluding her talk with MAN ONE

FX (cont'd)

Kha-li continues his walk toward the voices as choral music rises in the background. It reaches a consistent volume of a repetitive pattern that western ears would consider New Age at its core. However, it clearly contains instrumental qualities of a First Nation's percussion, Asian vocal pitch with African syncopation.

WIDE SHOT: Entire chamber

DOLLY: Camera moves around the perimeter of the chamber to behind KHA-LI as he enters the chamber. We see SAA-RA over his shoulder saying her last line to MAN ONE as he begins to walk through the gathering. As the twenty-six entities notice KHA-LI'S arrival, their conversations politely stop, they group into couples and make their way to front of the raised dais. Four entities move through them to stand on the dais, their clothing transforming to formal, long flowing robes of iridescent colours further disting-uishing them from the twenty-six. The order of the four now standing in a line are from CAMERA LEFT - PHILLIP whose colours are mauve and purple, JEROME in yellow, PETER in red, then SAA-RA in sea-green with blue trim. There is a space of a single person's distance between her as KHA-LI steps up, nods to the four, then he turns and speaks to the twenty-six who await expectantly.

KHA-LI

We prepare for the return; you will not be alone. I send with you the emanations of my own heart, (his arm sweeps toward the four) the portions of my personality which together complete my identity. They are the keepers of time and the gate-way of knowledge. They will act as catalysts that you may understand your past and return to you the wisdom that is yours. We shall return the world to the position from where it began as it was intended to be. And when the way is paved, I will send you my son, for I must finish what I began millennia ago.

MUSIC: A distant singing voice is added. There will be four a cappella voices added over the music and a rising in volume choir with each addition as KHA-LI makes the following introductions.

KHA-LI (cont'd)
The angel of the west—number one.

[280]

(Phillip bows his head—voice one Aahhhh aa—ahhh-ah is
   added)
>   The initiation of action. He will be known as
>   PHILLIP.
(PHILLIP raises his head)
>   KHA-LI (cont'd)
>   The angel of the north —number two
(JEROME bows his head—voice two is heard Ohh ha ohh-oh)
>   The angel of union. He shall be named
>   Jerome.
(JEROME raises his head)
>   KHA-LI (cont'd)
>   The angel of the south, number three.
(PETER nods—voice three is heard Ayya-yaa, aay-yaa)
>   To complete the union of Earth, Heaven and
>   Spirit shall be named PETER. (pause)
>   KHA-LI (cont'd)
>   The angel of the east, number four—who is
>   the last cornerstone of the pyramid and the
>   messenger. She shall be named SAA-RA,
(SAA-RA nods—voice four Ahhh-ohhayyyohh)
>   Number five will be myself, Kha-li. I will be
>   known by another name. I will not be as I
>   was, for when I was once the beginning, I am
>   now the end as a rebirth.
>   (Pause to look at everyone)
>   You all will make the way ready.
MUSIC: The four voices blend in with a full choir.

KHA-LI walks toward the exit, his astral body FADES as
BG voices of the twenty-six saying good-bye and farewell
to each other blend with the choir. Soon after KHA-LI
disappears, in pairs the entities draw in their astral bodies
to pinpoints of light and streak away through the crystalline walls into spatial infinity toward the rose petal gateway. The rose becomes more solid looking as the crystal
walls shimmer with less density.
ZOOM IN:
Pinpoints of light gather at the gateway, which reform as
astral bodies. As the first astral body floats toward the
centre of the gate, the tempo increases and expectation

[281]

builds. KHA-LI greets this first entity with an exchange of warmth and love in their glances but no words. Kha-li looks into the rose, the music builds, crashes into a crescendo, the aperture instantly opens—Earth is revealed one third screen size rotating past the continent of Asia. The entity flashes from his astral body into a streak of light which laser-like streaks toward Earth. This streak is joined by two outrider streaks of light which have separated from the first: the main light enters at Bombay India, passing through a ripple in time which the outriders go through, creating smaller ripples of their own to signify slightly different times of birth. Other entities station themselves at the aperture to watch. It is a spectacle of majesty and reverence as the aperture opens again and again, allowing one streak, which become three to enter Earth at Buenos Aires, London. Moscow, and Washington—each with ripples that are never identically placed.

SAA-RA joins KHA-LI at his side.
                    KHA-LI
          Come, a place has been made for you.
                    SAA-RA
               I will see you there.
Her smile of departure is of infinite love, she moves to the gateway. The camera moves to highlight her entrance. The music swells, the gateway opens, and SAA-RA's light streaks into Stockholm Sweden, with a ripple of the present (brownish). KHA-LI pauses the opening of the gateway slightly longer than for other entities, then he turns to face the next entity, bidding him farewell with a simple mention of his name.
                    KHA-LI
                 Percodemus.
The entity streaks into Rio De Janerio.
                    KHA-LI
                  Pamela.
The entity streaks into Holland.
WIDE SHOT:
     From a wider perspective the remaining entities streak to Earth, the ripple of time signatures are all shades of the

present (brownish to yellowish hues.) The rose petals snap shut.

FULL SCREEN CLOSE UP

The central petals of the rose snap open crisply and precisely, revealing the slowly rotating earth, 7/8 screen, surrounded by a rim of space in C3. KHA-LI and his outriders streak toward Egypt. We see the ripple wake of the main streak time signature as a bluish hue, and the outriders turn green and brown respectively. EARTH rotates slowly toward North America and the circumference of the frame (spatial infinity) turns to the hue of the present.

MUSIC: CROSS and FADE CHOIR with BG SOUND
RISING:

Summer sounds of birds chirping, soft wind blowing through tree leaves, clothes line screech, being pulled in two feet at a time, light traffic sounds, distant aircraft.

ZOOM IN:

As the United States comes into view, the shot centres on the Great Lakes and syncs with the earth's rotation. DOLLY IN as if from a spy satellite to the final focus on a suburban back yard near the city of Chicago.

HIGH ANGLE WIDE SHOT:

A little girl singing a children's song enters the yard and sees gardening tools. A pitch fork is leaning against the garage. The astral bodies of KHA-LI (screen left) and SAA-RA (screen right) emerge into a hover slightly above the little girl. SAA-RA smiles down with an expression that portrays influence on the girl. The girl interrupts her singing as if she forgot the words. Looking puzzled, she begins to play with the pitch fork. SAA-RA's expression implies that she is influencing her again. Wide eyed, the girl plunges the pitchfork into her foot.

SAA-RA

It is alright little one. It has begun.

The girl only then notices what she has done, pulls the pitch fork free, and drops it. Staring at her foot, she leaves the yard confused but not in pain, weeping quietly.

I liked Bonnie's work and appreciated the premise of simultaneous time better than when we had talked about it. The only reservation I had was the same one I had with her last offering; the choral music and grand entrances into Time were familiar in a peculiar way, but I'd be damned if I could figure out where I knew them from. This was troublesome because if it was familiar to me, educated people in the audience would certainly pick up on its true source.

Setting the pages aside, as Bonnie had requested, I then envisioned walking up an endless flight of stairs. The echo of my footfalls was a conscious addition, a soundman's flare, but the staircase became circular on its own. I walked, and walked, and walked. Zzzz

This is what I told Bonnie in the morning.

"Work at it," she told me.

"I did—I walked until I fell asleep," I said.

"I'm not accusing you of quitting. I'm saying meaningful gestures are timed to other's needs, not our convenience."

"What could the Universe need from students?"

"A sustained effort."

She did not ask me what I thought about her work at any time during another day of channelling multiple personas. Strangely, it was as if the mention of it was breaking some kind of rule, so I left it alone. She also seemed preoccupied but not as a distraction, because I knew it was about me. I didn't understand; I felt fine, and I was playing our game with the serious attention she wanted of me.

I walked the staircase for three more nights, but little changed other than I had a last recollection of looking at stairs disappearing into an opaque background. On the fourth or fifth attempt I had a nightmare.

Thoroughly terrified, I was running through an inky void of viscous air, struggling to get away from a wraith-like form that was steadily closing in on me. When it finally reached out to take my life, I turned, planted my feet, and defiantly shouted, "Fuck off! You can't hurt me!" The sooty hue passed through me, dissipating harmlessly in the darkness within seconds.

I am no stranger to nightmares, but it had been over a year since I had last awakened with a pulse in my beard, so the event was as disappointing as it had been frightening. This feeling lingered into the lessons of the day, in that I didn't meet Bonnie's gaze where I would normally confirm my understanding of something, but she let it go because I was otherwise participating. Over lunch, however, when I failed to carry my share of the conversation, she said, "Whenever you're ready is fine."

We had been down the road of denial and knee-jerk delays so often by this time that neither was a consideration. I confessed to what had happened, adding that I was anxious because nightmares tended to hunt me in packs.

Bonnie contemplated my story for the time it took to tilt her head in empathy, sit up, then formally say, "Now that you have faced your death head on, there is no point in skulking around the periphery of your fears when you can freely access and assess your beliefs for their influences. Who are we?" she said, and I felt a twinge in my gut.

Kha-lib subsequently told me a personal story about inner cowardice evolving outward defiance that stoked the fires of what others saw as valiant until it became true. He said I should give this some thought before I went to sleep that night because I had literally created a turning point in my life.

I was not thrilled about going to sleep that night, so I did as Bonnie had asked of me. In a short time, Kha-lib's personal example combined with my lessons on human behaviour, and an understanding blossomed: my evolution was based on falling, getting back up, and facing the next day. There was no other way.

Feeling better about failure in general terms, and holding onto the lingering sense that I was where I was supposed to be, I slipped into a deep sleep. For that matter, for the next two weeks I luxuriated in coma-like slumbers devoid of dreams I could recall: I got ready for bed, lay down, sniffed and scratched, and that was that.

I didn't tell Bonnie about this change in my sleeping habits, but as a by-the-way kind of thing, I did tell Ed's ex-girlfriend Gerri: after months without contact, we chanced to meet and went for lunch on a restaurant patio.

A waiter cleaned up the deposit a soaring seagull made on our table just after we sat down, while I told her about meeting Bonnie and working on her screenplay. This led us to discussing metaphysics, during which Gerri asked me to arrange a reading for her. I called Bonnie that evening, and she said she would be happy to do it, paused, and then added that Saa-ra had just pointed out how Bonnie was between cheques and low on groceries. Gerri's timely request was an omen to begin charging for her services.

"She offered to pay," I said uneasily, "but I thought it was a no-no to use the gift for personal gain?"

"Saa-ra said she'll explain later. I need to trust in the design of my destiny." A short pause. "Everything they've ever done with me has been about making me a better person or keeping me safe, so I'm embracing the cue and putting an ad in the weekend paper, as well."

Gerri became Bonnie's first official client, paying forty dollars regardless of the length of the session, which turned out to be three hours. This was a great deal in a crowded marketplace of less knowledgeable cosmos speakers, but taking money to research her book bothered me. Nevertheless, I said nothing to Bonnie about this as Gerri spread the word of her positive experience to her flight attendant friends. This resulted in Bonnie booking regular sessions with them, which took up a lot of my usual time with her but it didn't matter; I caught a freelance gig with an independent production house, then another with CTV News the next day. After Bonnie worked her regular job, I was called for a last minute shoot after which another show called to book me for Friday. When it rains it pours.

Only a week after officially hanging out her shingle, by word of mouth and a simple advertisement, Bonnie had booked sessions for up to two weeks in advance to accommodate her client's schedules, while I continued to get gigs at an alarming rate, as if I had a real job. In the next two weeks, we may have mentioned our screenplay only three or four times, until the day I showed up unexpectedly, and Bonnie answered my knock with tears tracking mascara down her cheeks. Before I could ask, she said Saa-ra had just concluded a lesson.

"This phase is over?" I said, climbing the stairs behind her.

"We need to discuss some changes," she said, sniffling as we came to the landing and turned into the kitchen. "Tea's ready," she nodded toward a pot wrapped in a blue cozy. Two mugs sat on the counter beside it.

"Has researching what society wants to know changed how your bad guys can trick them?" I said, guessing this was what the readings had been about.

"Mostly confirmed it: They all ask about love, money, and health," Bonnie said, "but they're more desperate to hear good news than they are interested in learning how to generate it. This is why Saa-ra told me to be careful because we don't want followers."

"I thought the point of your movie is to help people to live better?"

"Glorifying the source of that knowledge is how religions get their start."

"Tough enough raising two kids without heading up one of those," I said. "So is that something you needed to confirm–how easily you can gather followers?" I sipped my tea.

"I hadn't thought about that until Saa-ra made the point with me." Bonnie slid her cup to one side. "Our guides have always emphasized that choice is the only road to evolution, and they will never take our choices away. Good advice," she said sardonically, "is difficult enough to follow from free will, which is why so many people think they need more guidance than they really do. If I played into their laziness, I'd be taking away their lessons, which is what I've apparently been doing." Smirking self-consciously, she said, "Saa-ra told me I've fallen victim to my teaching role because I believe I have to do all that I can for as long as I can to spread the gift of their knowledge. She had asked me a number of times if I wanted a day to rest." Bonnie chirped her lips to quell a rush of emotion, I presumed because it had been a long time since she last had a day to herself. "She said I've become a follower, not a partner, because I don't distinguish between serving the needs of honest ignorance and being a slave to people's doubts and fear. She said her knowledge came without obligation, and I should stop pandering to everyone, including her. She also said she had lessons for me that would take up more of my time." She shuffled the mug between her hands. "This means I will need your help for a while."

"In what way?"

"You have a decent grasp on how behaviour designs our world..."

"Stop, you're making me blush."

"And your grasp of abstractions like probable events is excellent."

"My heart's all a-twitter."

"With practice," she said, flicking a finger at my forearm, "you'll be able to apply these ideas to other people's problems accurately."

"What kind of practice are you talking about?" I said warily.

"Most of my clients call after their sessions to try to better understand the principles of building their future, and I won't have the time to deal with them. If you would agree to bring them up to speed so they can make informed decisions, we wouldn't be pandering. They'd be better off, and our screenplay will be better because you'll know firsthand what readings can do for people. What do you think?"

"You'd be risking my charisma starting a religion."

"Your impatience guarantees followers wouldn't last," she grinned.

Bonnie subsequently schmoozed me into familiarizing clients with concepts from readings that sometimes took her five hours, and they still didn't get it. With that concern out of the way, Bonnie said she was going to make whatever arrangements she could make to better her financial position, then quit her full time job to become a full-time psychic reader and teacher. This decision included advertising Saturday morning gatherings as classes in The Way To Live. Admission would be free, but she would pass the hat while I became the inbound customer service representative, after the fact.

Reluctantly, I was again impressed by how far she was willing to go to research her work, but after calculating the minimum number of readings she would need to live, it again crossed my mind that she might have lost hers.

Chapter Thirty
Layering Lessons

Bonnie rerouted a call from a client later that same day, and I was pleasantly surprised to discover that I could flatten concepts and integrate aspects of diverse premises to satisfy most of her questions. I say most because my answers invariably gave rise to new questions, and I had to explain that I was Bonnie's writing partner, not a psychic. After a second call forced the same issue, I phoned Bonnie to tell her to pass on this information to her clients. The next evening, I learned that she had done both in practice and neither by design.

She had told Rochelle Fletcher-Smythe that I was researching the practical applications of mystical disciplines for a screenplay, and in this capacity, I was knowledgeable about cause and effect beyond what was commonly apparent to most people. She had also said I was attuned to the abstract, that I could align earthly and ethereal clues to see around corners and that I had been doing this since long before I met Bonnie. So said Mrs. Fletcher-Smythe.

As a result of Bonnie's non-disclaimer, call-me-Rochelle-darling wanted new answers to replace the ones she didn't like, which eventually forced me to be curt when I referred her back to Bonnie for that kind of information. With a wonderfully executed quiver in her voice, Rochelle-darling said Bonnie had warned her that I was eager to display my intellectual prowess, but I was reluctant to acknowledge my metaphysical gifts, then Rochelle pleaded for help; important people were coming over, and she couldn't wait for Bonnie to come home to answer a few simple questions. She would pay full fare for my reading. Money was no object.

I couldn't accept the money, but I had made a promise, so I asked Rochelle what she had specifically been told that puzzled her. Instantly tearless, she gave me a detailed version of one aspect of her reading, adding a blow by blow account of her feelings, should I somehow fail to realize she had been verbally assaulted. The bottom line was that she didn't understand how the time she got out of bed mattered in the grand scheme of things.

I understood that Bonnie's reading had focused on the downward spiral of arrogance, and that "Rocky" to her close friends was asking for an off-the-shelf fix, preferably something her butler could do. I also thought that Bonnie's persona of choice, Saa-ra, (Sara to Rocky) might have been too subtle in laying out the process of revealing the core of any problem to ourselves, subtly being the stuff of threats to a frightened person.

Peeved that Bonnie was probably having dinner with Josh, I aligned the bug of Rocky's laziness with the windscreen of behavioural momen tum to tell her that she needed to get her shit together at dawn and stick to a productive plan until sundown. Rocky could rest but not loaf. She had to put away the things she touched in a state ready for reuse and otherwise not litter or tisk at either her hired help or the general in-efficiency of the world that existed beneath hers for the sole purpose of supporting it. When the day was done, she could read and relax but have no social contacts that were not responsibilities and otherwise break the routines of her daily life until she realised it was a fairy tale.

What specifically could she do that was productive? She could clean, paint, garden, walk her dogs, or take an hour to repair her nails by herself, anything that resulted in an improvement from her own efforts. After a while, she might understand that there was no physical debris around her because of what she had done. From here, she could see how cleaning up the litter of her social encounters would drama-tically lessen the oppression she felt by way of social obligations implied. In time, she would be astounded to discover that she truly owned her time because she had nothing pending that she didn't want there. She would be in control of far more than her bank accounts, and she could get on with a life devoid of the petty encumbrances over which she had called Bonnie in a panic. I added flatly that the chances were good that this work wouldn't kill her, as she seemed to think it might, or she wouldn't have called me. I also reiterated something Bonnie had told her: Rocky should make a practice of looking back when she left any room at the metaphorical inn of life. If she could tell that she had been there, she had not appreciated the creativity of the designers, the effort of the builders, or the comfort that daily workers had provided her. She had left a responsibility behind.

Rochelle argued that she paid people to make her bed and otherwise keep her house in order.

Losing patience, I told her that Bonnie's exercise wasn't about doing the maid's job, it was about doing the right thing, for the right reason, for herself, and that this always benefited other people in both direct

and indirect ways. The bottom line was that Mrs. Fletcher-Smythe—
two Anglo-Saxon references to skilled labourers—should make her
passage between worthwhile causes inconspicuous, and otherwise
tread lightly so as not to disturb the neighbours. By taking care of the
two square feet she occupied when she was vertical, the angels would
have less to review with her when she was horizontal.

Rocky hung up on me.

You're welcome, darling.

Maybe five minutes later, Bonnie phoned to wryly ask me if I had
told Rochelle to put her affairs in order right away.

Snickering, I said, "It was you who told her there's no time like the
present because no force in the universe can guarantee any of us will
see the next dawn." I chuckled.

"She didn't get it, so you had to get her attention?"

"And I couldn't risk being charming."

"I wouldn't worry about that," Bonnie said.

A short silence. "You think I blew it?"

"No. I knew when she didn't name her house staff that she would
shop around until she heard something she liked."

"So why did you give her my number?"

"It wasn't about you. Good job, see you in the morning."

This time of changing individual roles brought with it a change in
our relationship, in that Bonnie became annoyingly insistent that I
assess my life for evidence of Universal Intent—for a life purpose. My
efforts to help others see a point to their behaviour, in terms of a
continuity and direction of momentum, should have opened the door to
wondering about my own path. She added that, although I failed to
mention this to her, she knew I had read between the lines of her
client's queries and that I knew more than I had told them.

Annoyed that she had again tricked me, that she was correct aside, I
argued that if Kha-lib would bother to hint at what it was, I might give
it a shot.

"Take it up with him," she said.

I joked about the irony of getting advice on how to live from the
dead, and the more I thought about this the funnier it became until a
cool voice said, "If there be death, then you are more dead than we."

My gut contracted, smothering my snickering before I realised
Bonnie had slipped up; the egoless Universe had misinterpreted my
comment as a slight.

[291]

Taking her to task as any decent student would, I said, "My humour is geared to a mortal audience, so it's understandable that you would misconstrue my comment."

"We have lived in your reality many times, and we understand mankind's idea of humour well. There is a time and place for it."

"Humour is a spontaneous part of my being, so are you objecting to free will?" I tried to say this lightly.

"To you," Kha-lib said tonelessly, "our presence represents the oppression of free will because your religions have caused you to equate faith with desperation and worship to victimization. You know that we do not seek recognition, nor have we ever commanded anything of anyone. Yet, you scorn us under the banner of a freedom you abuse, thereby making yourself your own victim."

I had no idea what he was talking about.

"You rob yourself of opportunities through self-deprecation disguised as recreation," he continued, "when your remarks are judgements that demean all who have helped you. In larger gatherings, the cynicism you flaunt as wizened scepticism taints everything you legitimately wish to convey, and your peers dismiss you as an angry man attempting to gain solace by having them agree with your fears and disgust. We suggest you stop this, for when you recognize what you have stolen from them, it is your own development of personal power that will be interrupted."

"Stop being funny?"

"You cannot cease what you have not begun. We speak of self-pity."

Shifting my weight to manufacture concern, I said, "What do you mean by personal power?"

Bonnie rocked in her chair once.

Kha-lib said personal power is based on a ruthless examination of our motives and responsibilities to consciously excavate our secrets. Discovering these secrets leads to selfless acts that have no barriers of self-pity to undermine their completion. In time, we choose only impeccable challenges.

"What makes an act impeccable to people who can't see energy?"

"If you choose the scenario, you will better understand our reply."

"Okay, if I'm standing with my back to a cliff while a robber takes my wallet, is it fair to antagonize him into rushing me?"

"His momentum will determine his fate."

"Even though I intentionally pissed him off?"

"The precariousness of his position arose from a circumstance he initiated."

[292]

"What if I grabbed him, and he dragged me over?"

"You would both fall."

"I mean—right —so, it's okay to tease him to death because he's a short-tempered thief?"

"He volunteered for the journey." Kha-lib flatly stated, "You did not kill him."

His phrasing inexplicably gripped at my chest.

"With training, pure logic will determine your actions," he continued, "not the conditioning of your past, or the influence of emotions that are better focused on pushing your will toward a proper assessment of circumstances."

"How does logic apply when I'm speaking to invisible beings?"

"Is our conversation illogical?"

"Not on its face, but I haven't surrendered any responsibilities to you, either."

"Has she shown a lack of courage or anything less than devotion to her children?"

"I didn't say she had, but following imaginary rules of invisible beings looks more like fright than discipline."

"In the deepest depths of love's anguish and despair, when every sinew is focused on placing one foot ahead of the other, who were able to travel the barren lands?"

A lightening image of the famine stole breath from my chest: women with children were almost always the last to die. Men gave up much earlier.

Finding my voice through thoughts of Kha-lib's comments about self-pity, I said, "If she's not afraid, it looks like she's giving up her role as a parent, and that's worship."

"Is it more logical that our goal is to free her from the clutches of an aberrant world, or that a family of timeless consciousness would be validating their wonderfulness by manipulating immeasurably less capable beings?" Before I could respond, he said, "What would we do with your adulation?"

"Entertainment."

"There is no species in any place or time that views the callous disregard of their potential impact upon other's as entertainment."

"I'll have to take your word on that."

"Then we have an agreement to build upon: to deal with your query, she knows there is a time in the teaching scheme when the student is dependent upon the teacher's impeccability. This is the transition time between faith and conviction. You are mistaking her discipline for submission."

"Faith is leading her to making objective conclusions?" I snickered.

"Every breath begins with an act of faith; you are objecting to the nature of reality."

"Huh?"

"You take a breath believing you will live to speak your next sentence, just as you blink without fear of losing your sight. You know your physical abilities inexorably diminish, yet you act as if time stands still until you feel like accommodating a circumstance. She acts as if a probable destiny can be made concrete as a consequence of impeccable choices, thereby learning to assume our lessons will lead to her mastering the disciplines of freedom she can pass to her children."

"How long does it take to go from faith to conviction?"

"If you stopped viewing our lessons as personal judgements to assume our apparent ambiguity is not fabricated to make you look foolish, you would conserve the energy you currently expend contriving diversions and race headlong into your destiny."

Taking an organizational breath, I said, "Scepticism seems prudent when anyone asks for trust up front. It's a form of investigation, not a diversion. That I'm talking to ghosts who say they can choose to be seen, but don't, notwithstanding."

"How we manifest is integral to a teaching scheme that requires you find your own answers, for only in this way will you never doubt them." Bonnie shifted her weight forward. "Your scepticism is a consequence of your surreptitious study of politics. When you grasp how this fits your life's quest, your view of us and our methods will change."

I admit that Bonnie had me on the ropes, again, until she made this preposterous claim, and I laughed in the face of the proverbial bold lie—the one we tell when the little ones stop working.

Bonnie waited, her indifference shortening my glee until I was able to say, "I know nothing about and couldn't care less about politics. Hell, I've never voted!"

"To the contrary," Kha-lib said, placidly puncturing my self-assurance, "That you have regularly voiced your intricate knowledge aside, you were constantly immersed in political intrigue often at great risk. The depth of your education is not apparent to you because you observed politics from the point of view of their failures. This personally acquired knowledge is no less valid than the formally educated among you; it is the other side of the coin, devoid of the

[294]

distortions demanded of academic publications, but infected by your own reactions, which she is dealing with."

"Leaving me with an un-degree?" I smirked.

"Leaving you unable to acknowledge your accomplishments. Optimism for you is a sedentary place in which time pointlessly passes without insult or injury. This moribund state of mind is also a grand achievement of passivity for a core predator, such as you are; a clear mind paves the way for the mastery of your lessons in illusions."

"Mankind's illusions are double sided; to believe one, is to be run down by the other."

"Did she not say your journey has two tales during your first hours together?"

"Funny."

"It is your joke. You have been excavating the secret of your destiny by calling it Twins."

"That means nothing to me."

"It is yours to discover, but we will assist."

[295]

Chapter Thirty-one
Alpha and Omega

K ha-lib began his explanation about 'Twins' by saying that any idea may be expressed in endless ways; a grain of sand is to us a miniscule aspect of terrain, but in other perceptual circumstances, it's an entire world. Interpretation of "things" depends on the speed and nature of the observer and the experiences that allow a consciousness to make connections between apparently disparate events in their version of reality. For example, to us, music is created by pulsing air molecules at mathematical values that conform to malleable rules of orchestration. Where a conductor may focus on the relationships between the different instruments' notes, bars, and phrasing to create a mural of sound, the musician may feel that her notes are telling a private story. Together, they can create a sweeping emotional journey, like the William Tell Overture, or they may organize our discontent through discordant, metallic riffs while choreographers interpret these into physical motions.

Simplistically, artists are the architects of experiences and experiments that enrich their own lives, after which audiences respond as an internal collaboration based on the degree to which they are exposed to the medium. However, there are always a few who extend that collaboration, forcing audiences to stretch the fundamentals of the form. These are the unreasonable ones who tread the line between an inmate representing their personal asylum and the trailblazer making lives richer by unlocking the doors to perceptions that others may walk through. To extend the metaphor, these people have gone from the audience to the orchestra, to become a solo artist then a conductor of experiences aimed at having new effects on their audience.

"Conductor, meaning teacher?" I said.

"Our conductors use their knowledge to stalk students out of their assumptions and into their freedom, no different from how we orchestrated the lesson we imparted on this day. You knew about this process when you chose your personality for this quest."

"I chose who I am?"

"We will discuss the construction of personality in your next phase."

"The same applies to Bonnie?"

"Her preferences are derived from Saa-ra's entire identity, in the same way that you are a portion of Phillip. She chose to be the kind of person who, literally propelled by her genetic makeup, would succumb to the cultural cruelty and domestic brutality of even your so-called enlightened societies."

Bonnie was born in Sweden, and she had lived in the United States and Canada.

"In this way, she knows these circumstances extend to all societies."

"Why did she choose a hard road?"

"She chose the path necessary to experience the ways in which your world mistreats females. This forced her to adapt her mindset toward survival in her cultural milieu, and eventually become an archetype victim to the pressures and practices of society. Her life represents Alpha, the beginning."

"The beginning of victimization is at home, or her lessons lead to a new beginning?"

"Both are true," Kha-lib said.

I didn't bite. "What about Phillip and me?"

"You came from a loving home in order to later recognize the brutality of so-called disciplinarians. In time, you catalogued crimes, edited cruelties and tragedies, and met the pompous, greedy, and neglectful people whose collective acts led you to witnessing where their momentums collide. In this way, you fell victim to the require-ments of surviving in cultures of conflict. Your life represents the end, for living by the rules of men will destroy you."

"Uh huh."

"Collectively," Kha-lib said, "your experiences form the bookends within which the core influences of your culture can be found. How-ever, this is the first time you have challenged these lessons in your present personality structure."

"You're sure you're speaking to the right guy?" I said, feeling like Bill Cosby doing his Noah routine. "I've never been accused of being saintly, and what about brains and education?"

"How many Down's syndrome children did you meet in the battlefield?"

"None. They're disabled," I said, confused.

Kha-lib held his gaze until I realised their liability was peace.

"In your world, education and intelligence are applauded as reflect-ions of refined prejudices when they have no bearing on your global

[297]

plight beyond your captains of industry, intellectual elite, and nobility convincing entire populations to serve them."

"I know you're not saying everyone should have Down's syndrome, but my thinking stops there."

"Many of your so-called deficient individuals have chosen to explore emotions directly. This takes enormous courage in a world made hazardous by your clever people and a distinguished intellect to assess these experiences when they return home. Their paths are not for the meek because they are pure journeys of heart and grand gifts of challenge for those who have the audacity to be their guardians. As for saintly matters, your remark reveals how religions have influenced you deeply, which is a matter you have yet to assess."

"I don't know where to begin."

"We will lead you: in part, you presume human imperfections preclude one from attempting meaningful challenges without God's permission or help. This is nonsense. Sufficient to say that none of your biblical figures came into the world knowing everything, but they all learned that The Way to Live is a springboard to the unimaginable—a clear view of how to shape destiny—and they left your world knowing they were co-creators of it, as you all are."

"Uh-huh, so?"

"Koram," Kha-lib said coolly.

Shocked at hearing a word I had not uttered since leaving Eritrea— not even one tiny lie—I blurted, "Where the hell were you?"

"We are referring to one who did not fall victim."

His laconic words enticed the memory of a medical outpost run by an order of Catholic Sister nurses to fill my thoughts: a three year old girl lay on an examining table breathing in a shallow rattle that, amplified by a Sennheiser 415 shotgun microphone, echoed around the Spartan shelter. One Sister said she had heard pneumonic gurgling fall shallow into the stillness so often, as she gave the girl an injection, that she knew the girl had only minutes to live. The penicillin wasn't remotely close to even a heroic measure; it was something to do when there was nothing that could be done.

Unusually for the Canadian Broadcasting Corporation, our producer decided we should record her death, and we rolled tape for a few minutes before stopping to wait for signs of change. A short time later, Birhan Woldu began to pant. We rolled tape again. In a whisper, one Sister said, "She's recovering."

"We've never seen anyone come back from this stage," the other nurse said. "It's truly a miracle."

I thought it was the final goodbye because some people experience a period of well-being just before the end, and the Sisters were pre-disposed to seeing the bright side. Minutes passed while colour returned to Birhan's death mask.

On a follow-up shoot weeks later, we found her playing in front of the station with her father and some young friends.

"One out of how many?" I said, a second later.

"How many miracles would change your beliefs?"

"One won't do it," I sputtered an impotent mix of menace and exasperation.

"Seek out other unlikely incidents, and you will twin your dismay with the miraculous. Only then can you assess events properly and come to see the path you have been walking."

Taming obscenities into a terse, "It's not time for that." I got up to leave.

"Lunch tomorrow—barbecued salmon?" Bonnie said in her own voice, "Come around twelve, and bring the wine. You can tell me what just happened thennnnnn," she said, in a rising tone as I went down the stairs.

Chapter Thirty-Two
Assumptions of Physical Reality

That evening, I could not help but consider Kha-lib's words because the impact of working the famine was highly resistant to forgetfulness, especially after even clipped scenes of suffering had been resurrected. I resolved that he may have a point about me being influenced by religion, but still I wanted to shout, "What about the rest of them?" which took me back to Bonnie's view on fairness; my anger bled energy into a bleak sense of wonder about the ways of her Universe. "Cruel bastards," slipped from my lips before I slept fitfully.

The next day, I arrived at Bonnie's house on time, with a bottle each of red and white wine. Tapping on the side door twice, I let myself in. She called a quick "Hello," from the kitchen, and as if joining sentences with elastics, she said, "Remember when Kha-lib told us that everything is always changing, but subjectivity influences how we adapt?"

"Can we get a glass of wine first?" I said, topping the stairs.

Apparently not: "We both know that physical experience is an artifice for spiritual development, the natural grace of which is that mankind's endeavours are ultimately self-developing, correct?"

"Yep," I said, walking into the room. "But I have a question. What did Kha-lib mean by calling my core predatory?"

She grinned, and said, "He was speaking about the base approaches to self-development; there are only two kinds, stalkers and dreamers. You are a stalker by nature—a predator's approach to gaining knowledge, while I am a dreamer by nature. We'll come back to this at another time, but sufficient to say that one is not better than the other. Fair?"

"Go ahead."

"With lifetimes of gathering energy, the earth-bound spirit can be aligned with spiritual Intent, and when that integration takes place, you have become all that you can be in the human form. So if my characters become a unified force and the momentum they align themselves with is unstoppable, what do you think they could do with their power?"

"Not a trick question?"

"No."

"Anything they wanted to do."

"Exactly. Hold that thought. I've said that intellectually we know personality is no more fixed than our tangible selves, but we refuse to change unless we agree that we need changing, in which case we would have begun changing unless an outside force had influenced us." Bonnie looked up from sprinkling croutons into a bowl of salad, and I nodded. "So it makes perfect sense that the broader the view of reality we have, the better we can see ourselves in the grand scheme, and the greater the changes we can make. Is the white chilled?" she said, nodding at the bottles in my hand.

"Just cool," I said, setting both bottles down to rummage through her utensil drawer.

She nodded and said, "Kha-lib also said energy takes forms that reflect its speed, and this form is only apparent to forms that vibrate in the same range."

"Uh-huh—where'd you hide the corkscrew?"

"Check the dish rack."

"You wash your cork screw?"

"You don't?"

"With twist caps?"

"In that case, I'm honoured that you bought corked wine." She picked up the salad bowl and napkin-wrapped utensils. "Yours," she said, nodding at the plates and marinating fish as she headed downstairs.

"In effect," I said, taking the glasses, an extra plate from the dish rack, and the fish to follow her out to the back patio, "you're saying that a ghost sees other ghosts as real, and we're illusions to them?"

"Yes, but hold that thought." We negotiated our way through her son's bicycle, basketball, and assorted sports paraphernalia on the narrow side path to the front of the house and set our dishes down on a weathered picnic table that a previous tenant had liberated from the Provincial Park Service.

"As we engage new experiences," she said, arranging place settings, "we transcend the apparent limitations of our physically related insights." Bonnie stopped and looked at me as I lit the barbecue. "So you see, freedom really is a state of mind!" The fiery whoosh acted as an exclamation point.

[301]

"Got it. Experience liberates us from incarcerating ideas."

"Experience is the catalyst to attaining knowledge." Bonnie looked at me questioningly, as if I wasn't taking her seriously. "Try to think like an apprentice." She looked down to find her next words. "Fear focuses our attention on experiences we don't want, when it's our focus that inexorably draws us to or creates those experiences. It follows that focusing on not being desperate is the reverse of striving for joy because the focus is on desperation."

"Don't focus on the negative as something to avoid, focus on the positive as something to achieve. Got it."

"Good. Now we know that our physical orientations will be the catalyst for change before we come into a physical life, so we choose historical timeframes and social circumstances that will provide us with a stage to act out specific scenes. By the close of the show, assessing the consequences of our choices will cause us to realize that we created the events we experienced based on how we perceived ourselves in the earlier scenes."

"You've said all of that." I took a sip.

"As an intellectual idea but now I *know* what it means." She took a quick sip of wine then she leaned into her words. "The scope of our freedom to choose a destiny is so great that even the shape of our nose represents part of the image we project into a reality where overcoming appearances is the core of personal evolution. Hair colour is part of our self-stalking process!"

"A little less stalking each year for me," I said, taking a dark slab from the marinade.

"Let the grill get hotter. Cajun blackened is what we're after."

"My specialty."

"Eventually, we realize that everything happens from the inside out. Physical form," she motored on as I put the fish back in the bowl, "causes us to assume that our senses define reality, and we trick ourselves into believing we can buy or build abstractions like happiness."

"It helps."

"What helps?"

"We get satisfaction out of building a new deck—things like that."

"Meaning money helps?"

"You have to buy the wood," I shrugged.

"Take your example to the end point: a lot of money can free us from having to do the work ourselves, but free time doesn't bring us any closer to understanding what caused us to focus on collecting money or what our personal expenses were on the way."

"Such as neglecting other things?"

"Exactly. Another thing Kha-lib said is that our creative abilities can't be granted or taken away because they are not rights or privileges. They are a consequence of being; our speed determines our abilities."

"So when we say that someone is slow, we're being precise?"

"Clever but correct only on the surface. Remember the Down's Syndrome talk?"

"Vividly. The brother of a friend in boot camp had Downs. Hot enough?"

"Give it another minute. Speaking of speed, events instantly manifest as we conceive them in our cardinal reality, which would severely disorient us if we hadn't experienced the drastically slower manifesttation of our ideas here."

"Kha-lib mentioned that." I forked the fish onto the grill.

"Is something bothering you?"

"Just hungry. We experience slower events, you said?"

Bonnie's gaze penetrated my interior as she said, "Kha-lib also said our cyclical development is tied to Catalytic Momentum, which functions by the rule of like attracting like. This means there's no greater attraction to an event than those we seed for ourselves. It's the ultimate justice because there's no judgement involved except our own."

"It's a great idea, but doesn't the slowness of an idea manifesting in physical reality disguise the cause and effect from people who don't have teachers to explain things?"

"Most people don't need to see evolution as a function of energy, continuity, and momentum. They need only try to do the right thing, and they'll learn to ascribe a particular motive to a specific action."

"By themselves?"

"Of course not. Our choice of parents, friends, and enemies boxes in our lesson plan."

I poked at the grill. "Why not face all of our ignorance at once then let the good times roll?"

"You know better than most people that we couldn't survive that. Look at how much destruction it takes just to get our attention. Even then…"

"Point taken, but what about people like Rashaef or Lei'a?"

"What about dandelions?"

[303]

"Sorry. I mean, there's not much happening where they live, and they're still calculated about everything, so how much crap could be coming their way?"

Bonnie sipped her wine slowly, then impassively said, "You don't appreciate what it means to be alone, making deliberate decisions that can affect the entire course of people's lives."

"They're together."

"They weren't always. They both had to understand that the journey, by which I mean all journeys, to becoming impeccable are solo treks and they must be willing to carry on alone. Finding each other is for them a union of power to fulfill greater goals because their love makes no demands. A consequence of this is that they're comforting and comforted, amused, and bemused by endless reminders of where they came from. Saying they're 'together,'" Bonnie mimed parenthesis, "Is like ... like..." she stumbled.

I caught on. "I'm not dumping on single-parenting. I'm sure it's tough."

"I'm not talking about me," Bonnie said, surprised. "I'm talking about a consequence of achieving true freedom. People like Rashaef and Lei'a could shoulder mind-boggling responsibilities because they understood their true circumstance."

"Didn't Kha-lib say self-stalking is an unalterable condition for everyone?"

"It is, in a physical reality, which is one choice of many but once you've started you have to finish it. The rule is a function of responsibility transcending time," she explained.

"Okay, so how could any of your teachers make people turn right if they had pre-programmed life for left turns?"

Bonnie held my wrist and with excitement said, "If you came into a life designed to interact with a known flow of events, including meeting people who showed you how some left turns took you down dark alleys, what has to happen?"

"Whatever the design dictates."

"Exactly."

I looked at her blankly. "And?"

"Thousands of emissaries are coming, and all of them will understand their rolls. Don't you see—nothing can stop them!"

"I see that it will work great in a film where dying doesn't matter.

"You do know that you're coming back to finish whatever you do this time around?" Bonnie said, perplexed by me not playing my role to the end.

[304]

"Right, sorry," I said.

"I think the emerging apprentice in you recognized the inevitable loss of your old way of life, and you're objecting to an inevitability that doesn't appear to be a choice. Don't worry about it. Martyrdom wasn't in your cards, and I'm not going to set myself on fire."

"Let's pretend for a second that you did do that. What do teachers say goes on between lives?" I said, moving things fully back into her work premises.

"We return to our spiritual state and re-join our higher selves, who are us in our entire identity. From there, we learn that a circumstance we ignored was the opportunity we had meticulously seeded then avoided because we were in a crappy mood, that we had yet to recognize as part of our challenge. We'll see how some of the events we instigated in fun were not funny, how some things we didn't really mean took the same toll on our victims, and we'll learn that we saved a life with a kind word or an appropriately harsh one."

"How often do we recycle ourselves?"

"Saa-ra said a thousand life-reviews and refresher courses weren't unusual."

"Okay, so how do you explain the Universe talking to a person who is on life number one?" I said, addressing the next grand hole in her evolutionary premise.

"They said you are on life number one in your *present personality structure*, which is true for almost everyone." Bonnie cleared her throat. "Lifetime after lifetime, we acquire the energy to engage experiences that were formerly beyond our capabilities, and when we're ready to accept certain truths, we reveal our secret selves to ourselves by engaging irrefutable lessons like you went through before meeting me. We just haven't dissected them yet. When you do assess these properly, you'll understand how cognizant self-stalking resolves contradictions in our personality, trains us to think positively, and guarantees that we encounter less negative experiences because we know better. Phillip's personalities have collectively traveled the full course of physically related evolutionary events, and your personality is designed to tackle the final steps."

"Then we're done—like the fish?" I nodded toward the grill.

"Ready to move on," Bonnie said, handing me a plate. "When we've understood the principles behind creating events responsibly, we're on our way to mastering our personality. This is to become a master of our destiny, not a master over anything else."

[305]

I put the salmon on the dish, shut off the gas, and served us leaving one piece on the third plate.

"You'll like this part," Bonnie said as I quickly steel-brushed the grill and she served salad. "Saa-ra told me that the body is alive within its own measures of consciousness, but it's the energy of Spirit that gives it the means to continue. In other words, our experiences are based on a grand partnership in which the body has no more of a human experience than a barnacle has captaining a ship. That's not to say the body's experience is less profound to it than our experiences are to us. They're just different."

"Why should I like that?" I said, poking my spinach.

"It puts you in charge." Bonnie grinned, snatched a quick sip and said, "She also said some of us choose short experiences and are still-born, while others choose a short experience outside of the womb, then die of things like sudden infant death syndrome. The rest of us chose our time of death as well."

"Every death is a suicide?"

"Yes."

"There goes the Catholic audience. Speaking of which," I said as the thought came to mind, "when do we actually begin a physical life?"

"We insert our consciousness into the developing foetus at a time of our choosing, and we can leave it almost as easily before conformation to physical sensations convinces us we can't. In between these times, Saa-ra said children regularly speak to their source selves because they still have their connection."

"Neat." I took a bite, as did Bonnie.

"It's the vibratory speed of all things that distinguishes them from other things," she then said. "It follows that when the speed of our perception is in the same range as the speed of other forms of con-sciousness, we grant them the status of being real."

"We covered that," I said, around a piece of some kind of purplish vegetable.

"I'm making another point." Bonnie stabbed a cherry tomato. Leaving it resting on her plate, she said, "The pilot of a low flying jet would see a constant white line on a highway, whereas the pilot of a propeller craft would perceive the broken lines."

"At the right speed, height, and angle."

"This isn't about physics," Bonnie said, tapping one finger at the corner of her mouth to bring to my attention that there was something on mine. "If our visual acuity weren't automatically attracted to the brightest light, we would focus on the broken black lines. With me?"

[306]

I blotted off a drop of salad dressing with a paper napkin. "I am if you're going to say that the white lines represent our personality, and the black lines represent the beliefs we don't know we have and that to see both would be to survey the entire road."

"Excellent."

"So is lunch. Thanks."

"Anytime." Bonnie jabbed her fork in the direction of the remaining piece of fish, indicating that it was mine.

"I'm good, thanks."

"Yes you are," she said, spearing the fish so that it broke in half. Leaving it on the third plate, between small bites, sipping wine, and daintily wiping her lips, she continued explaining her realization.

"Less than impeccable actions always create casualties, the majority of which we don't perceive because they lie between the white lies, or they're too far down the road for a short-sighted species. However, we can still help ourselves by acting as if we are always heading for a lesson that we can learn before we fly into it because pivotal events rarely come without a shower of clues."

"Such as?"

"Witnessing an accident may be telling us we're one decision away from having one, and it's time to assess our own circumstances. It may be that we're going too fast on wet pavement." She shrugged. "If I ran a light, it may be that the impatience of self-importance is an issue, and I'm about to be T-boned with my attitude." Bonnie raised her brow for me to acknowledge my understanding. I waved my fork for her to continue.

"Being aware of our own actions to this degree, leads us to the power reference point for self-development–there are no accidents— every event is of equal value."

"Then five bucks a pound for this was a steal," I quipped.

"You're impossible," she said, shaking her head.

"Not true," I replied, shaking mine. "I'm just not easy."

"Not true," she said.

Bonnie next set up life-lesson examples for specific behavioural challenges, which included how a higher self could help to create a probable destiny: an old soul deliberately chooses to be born as an early twentieth century female, amid circumstances it knows will curve destiny toward the practice of medicine, and create personal challenges for friends who have agreed to reincarnate in his/ her play for their own reasons. The entity knows it will use personal struggle as a springboard to positive acts, therefore choosing an impoverished childhood will

[307]

provide her with impetus to better her circumstances and those who are in her sphere of influence. Whereas most cultures will consider females "less" by the men who run them in that time, her environment will demand that she live within an ongoing self-examination to keep a clear picture of her self-worth. A lifetime of quashing self-doubt based on irrelevant circumstances of race and gender will cause her to look beyond all apparent limitations, and her medical methodology will intuitively peek into the underlying order of health. After a well-earned revelation, she will publish the factual bridges she discovers between attributes of self-image and their concomitant ailments. One of these could be documenting how liver disorders are common to individuals who are unable to cleanse circumstances that tarnish their secret self-image. She first clued into this by aligning the arrogance of the Old Boys Club with the pettiness of prejudiced ignorance she experienced for most of her life. Exemplified by the derision with which they dismiss her new ideas, she will also realize pretentiousness is common to those who secretly know what they are really like and drink to deal with it.

A different entity might approach these lessons from the point of view of a wealthy, white, male doctor in a predominately black country. While in a detox centre, he would realize that the ways of his world caused him to assume his status didn't require him to contribute to the quality of life of those who weren't like him. Upon his release, he might fight the inequities of his social system by setting up clinics.

"In these examples," Bonnie said, "the woman's role is not necessarily more difficult than the man's. It's the choice of environment that guarantees a lesson will be faced, but not how well the individual will do."

"Like I said, a crap shoot."

"With loaded dice; ultimately you can't lose."

"Uh-huh—so how does poverty figure into personal development?"

"Learning to discern the difference between need and want is integral to discovering ourselves. This means that at some stage we include a form of poverty in our lessons, but it doesn't have to be torturous deprivation. You and I are broke, but we're not suffering, and we won't as long as we're on a positive momentum."

"To just getting by, day by day?"

"What else do you need?"

"We get old. Security would be nice."

"If anyone has ever had reason to feel secure, it's you ... what was that look about, and don't tell me nothing just streamed behind your eyes?" she said, with disconcerting warmth.

"I have no idea what you're talking about," I said, honestly.

"It must be that you understood you will be all right, but you can't justify it, so you buried it." Laughing, she rhetorically said, "What I'd give to be present at that exhumation!"

Chapter Thirty-Three
Switching Focus

We finished lunch, washed the dishes and the corkscrew, then we went for a walk along the rocky beach where, on no apparent cue, Bonnie began recounting key phases in her life, as opposed to specific events or times. In and of themselves, there was nothing extraordinary about her experiences, maybe other than they spanned the gamut from potato soup poverty to caviar for twelve and back to mock chicken sandwich lunches for three.

In a nutshell, her parents had led her through a wandering adolescence, but in spite of many moves, Bonnie was a good student. When it came time to pony up, there was only enough money for her brother's university education and so went her dream of a career in marine biology. She subsequently survived a parade of small minds and petty tyrants at various jobs because she out-performed her peers before she married and became a successful client entertainer for her emotionally abusive husband. When their relationship ended, her adjustment back to the land of single living included date rape and the financial and social discrimination society bestows upon divorcees with children. These experiences included not qualifying for new car loan rates or quality rental properties, which in turn led to tradesman's theft for things like plumbing and auto repairs.

As she spoke her heart dispassionately, I had no doubt that she knew a lot about suffering, failure, and limbo-living between mans' sexually influenced decisions. I also believed that she had met some truly nasty people, and I better appreciated how children can be the source of one's deepest worries and greatest joys in the same moment. That said, the physical, mental, and emotional traumas she had suffered couldn't have been too bad because she had cracked wise about her life from day one. Or maybe she had somehow gotten even?

I felt the same way about her financial circumstances. Our mans' society had made earning a decent wage more difficult, but when she decided to become a writer, she had borrowed money from a long-time male friend and she was paying twenty percent of true rental value, courtesy of her looks. She also owned her five year old car, there was always food in the fridge, and her teenagers were clean, bright, and personable, as far as I could tell when they flashed by the doorway.

Overall, I viewed Bonnie's trials as distasteful necessities and unfortunate inevitabilities of learning self-reliance, just like the rest of us, neither of which had whizzed by her ear at 2300 feet per second or came with a distinctive smell that forced her to burn her clothing at the end of a particularly memorable day. This is not to say that her character wasn't stellar or that the well of courage from which she drew her dignity wasn't deeper than most people's. Then she told me that her decision to have an abortion had been agonizing, and it haunted her for a long time, but another child would have jeopardized the welfare of the first two.

Intellectually, I knew that making abortions illegal took away a woman's right to design their life in the same way that a man could, and that as neither science nor the courts could define life's moments of debut or demise, they had no business interfering, but religions and rights groups had forced the courts both ways. Bonnie's doctor had also declared that she couldn't become pregnant after he delivered Karl, which should have made me empathetic.

Maybe it was the memory of a "doll's" arm lying in the street before I saw the rest of her anatomically perfect parts blown apart that changed me in ways I still didn't realize. I can't say other than a sudden anger converted her trials into the admissions of a frightened woman liberating herself from guilt; her humour was evidence of wearing herself down to desperation: in an enlightened moment, I realised that creating Saa-ra's persona let her off the hook. Kha-lib and the others were camouflage, so deep and clever was her disguise.

"Who are we?" she said, cutting short my contemplation.

"Sounds like Saa-ra," I replied, in a neutral tone.

Saa-ra said, "It is time to examine your life for evidence of the unseen, for only in this way can you claim knowledge of our existence without frightening yourself beyond learning you are an open book to us."

"Where do I begin looking?" I said, scanning the sky wondering what I should do, or did my insight really change anything about writing a screenplay?

"Examine your so-called accidents and coincidences."

"I'll do that," I promised. A few seconds of silence passed. "You mean now?"

"Do you have a prior engagement?"

"Nope—how far back should I go?"

[311]

"Begin where your thoughts take you," she said as the thumping crack-roar of a motorcycle accelerating down Marine Drive filled the air.

"1971 it is," I said nonchalantly because any cue—hell, every cue could be attached to someone's experience. "The brakes failed on a borrowed motorcycle while I was going down a steep road that intersected a busy street. I tried to ditch it, but I ended up flying off a grassy slope and landed sideways."

"Tell her what was strange about the incident."

"My foot was crushed under the transmission, but there was no pain either in the moment or when they set the bones. Therapy was only uncomfortable." I caught on. "You're saying you had something to do with that?" I indulged Bonnie.

"Tell us about your other flying experiences."

"Commercial, private, or bush country?"

"He has walked away from them all and still believes nothing unusual has happened in his life," Saa-ra said to update Bonnie. "Begin with the private, if you please."

I told Bonnie I was finishing the last two hours of my solo training, practicing my approaches to a long runway at idle power with my angle of attack perfect for a text book sink into a ground-affect flare, when my Cessna 152 was suddenly thrust hard to the right. The stall warning screeched as it should, but I ran out of corrective rudder pedal with my nose pointing forty-five degrees off the runway. I glanced at Bonnie. "None of this is good."

"She can picture angular momentum," Saa-ra said.

"I knew I had time to punch on power and inch back to the centre line, which was my last thought before I was slammed sideways into the door. The next thing I remember is that I was sitting in the corn field at the side of the runway. There was no damage because a little Cessna lands slowly enough in normal conditions, but with a head wind, furrowed ground, and four feet of corn stalks in my way, I stopped on a dime. After I parked the plane, I learned that an eighty mile an hour ground sheer had blown through, evidenced by an expensive Apache Twin lying on its back at the fuel pumps. I was lucky."

"There was more to your luck than landing upright and unscathed," Saa-ra said.

Not surprised that she knew such details, because through my scotch affected haze during our first phone call I had given up a lot of experiences, I said, "My instructor said that an experienced pilot would

[312]

have gone to full power, edged up the nose, and done a go-around. He also said that going twenty miles an hour faster and fifty feet higher would have been fatal if the gust had gotten under a wing... like the one that drove me into the ground and flipped the Apache."

We entered our little manicured park where Bonnie led the way to an isolated bench. Using the table as a backrest, we sat side by side facing the community of Kitsilano across the water. Quietly gazing at nothing in particular, Saa-ra asked me to speak about the other air adventures that involved damage to the planes in which I was a passenger. I recalled two minor incidents, after which she said there was a fine distinction between minor and catastrophic when dealing with commercial aircraft traveling at high speeds on the ground. I agreed with her in principle but rightfully argued that by force of my physical presence, that distinction was moot.

"Mankind requires a great deal of convincing," Saa-ra said blandly. "Tell her of the times when your behaviour was unusual."

"She thinks that's most of the time."

"We are not referring to incidents you wish to forget or have dismissed as understandable under the circumstances. We are referring to the event-moments you have filed away hoping to understand them some day."

Her voice acted like a silky thread withdrawing memories from a rare sense of peace that had settled over me like a warm blanket. I pondered the sensation without worrying about it.

"In your Middle East," Saa-ra focused me.

I told her that our crew was interviewing a militia leader when the battery to my VCR died, and for the first and last time in my freelance career, I discovered that I had mixed my used batteries with the charged backups. I had to go back to our car which was parked on the perimeter of an area that was cordoned off, to protect buildings from car bombers, in plain sight of the guards who had searched us on the way in.

I had almost reached the car when a firefight broke out nearby, so I ran the last few steps to the rear of the vehicle. Crouching, I was trying to determine if I was at the right end of the car when a militiaman racing into the fray shouted at me, "*Sahafe!*" gesturing that I should scamper to the cover of a nearby building. My first thought was that running gathered attention while exposing me to the enemy of the hour. My next was that not all friendly fighters knew who I was, which led me to conclude that the chances of being eulogized as the *sahafe* who had single-handedly attacked Nabi Berri with a dead battery was

[313]

excellent if I moved at all. Logically, I decided to sit behind the right rear wheel to wait it out, occasionally waving at a soldier who persistently waved me toward him when things got noisier.

"Your normal reasoning was intact. Continue," Saa-ra said.

I told Bonnie that after the shooting stopped, I switched batteries and began walking down the middle of the street toward the apartment complex. From about thirty yards away, the same guard who had cleared me the first time, un-holstered his pistol, smiled, and levelled it at me. Groping for accurate wording, I said I felt a stutter in my thinking, and the moment split into two perceptions. One was of indifference, while the other understood that the guard was challenging my apparent bravery because I had sat with my back to the nearby action, waving at his friend. Within this perception, I understood that the guard wanted me to surrender or at least fake it for fun, and I slowed my pace to decide whether raising my hands or lying on the ground would please him more. At this point, the first perception over-wrote the latter, and I kept on walking as if I was starring in High Noon at the Abu K Coral."

Playing along, I looked for Saa-ra to confirm that this was the type of experience she was after. She nodded for me to continue.

"Maybe fifteen paces away," I said, "he pointed his gun at my crotch. At about ten, he aimed at my foot. At five, the muscles in his forearm tensed and at two he squeezed the trigger. Click."

"He laughed as if this was the funniest thing he had ever done, which I thought was likely as I moved to step around him, and he patted me on the shoulder, shrugged and said, 'Maalesh.' Roughly, this means it doesn't matter, but it's a versatile word. In my circumstance, I believed it was an apology with grudging respect to which I responded by dipping my head and solemnly saying 'Scheisskopf.' He nodded back as if I had said, 'And God be with you.'"

"You were feeling like your old self," Saa-ra said.

"Correct, so what was the split about?"

"The sensation of duality was a more definitive extension of what you often experienced at the times when you felt you should turn back. Aloofness was also a large part of her early experiences when we interceded in her ways. When we are finished here, ask her about these times. Continue."

I had nothing more to say until the word "aloofness" snagged an incident from my memory about the run up to the Falkland's war. Still feeling peaceful, I said, "In Argentina, the pressure of three authorities changing the rules caused Tony and Ski..."

"From the beginning, please."

I told her that we flew from Buenos Aries to Comodoro Rivadavia for a one day look at the Argentine military preparing for war, rented hotel rooms in case we had to stay the night, then drove to the media centre to see what venues were available to us. A freelance cameraman I knew from El Salvador came out of the door as we arrived, so Manny and I chatted while Ski, Ricardo our interpreter, and our producer Tony did their thing.

Zooming through superficial pleasantries, I asked Manny about the official rules versus unofficial practicalities of working in the area, and he said we had wasted our time. We could shoot nothing without permission, and the only permission any crew had ever received was to take pictures of the town itself. If there was anything military in that picture, "Even a boot," he warned me, it was a criminal offence.

"No cheating?" I said wryly.

"Not here, man," Manny said gravely. "I think you'd go missing faster than in Salvador." Lowering his voice, he looked around furtively and said, "Bin that way for a long time before the war, and they're good at it. You seen the mothers at the Casa Rosada in B.A.?"

I explained to Bonnie that "the mothers" of the missing, as they were known nationally, although regularly taunted by twenty something patriot idiots dancing around them, demonstrated in front of the pink palace in Buenos Aires every Thursday. The public was too scared to support them and the women too courageous to care that they stood alone.

I said to Manny, "Ya, we seen—saw them. You're not pulling my pisser on this because you're with NBC, are you?"

I knew better than to play the competition card, but I had to ask because Manny had taken huge risks in shooting wars - stories I had borrowed in the Cellar Tavern—and so far this war was just political crap leading up to a national election. Throwing a couple of foreign press in jail wouldn't matter much one way or the other.

Crossing his heart, he said, "No games, my man. Tell your people straight up, this is dangerous shit."

"So why are you here?" I grinned.

"NBC can afford shit," he said, with a shrug.

We chatted for a short while, then in compliance with a safety practice he had introduced me to in the Camino Real bar a year earlier, I told him where we were staying and that we might be back for lunch. If not, we agreed to meet for dinner, and Manny went off to wherever he spent his time while I went inside the building to tell Tony what I had learned. I first emphasized that I knew Manny from Salvador where credibility was a life and death matter: unofficially and never spoken of, we had all shared information to keep everyone safe, and it didn't go unnoticed back home. Network desk producers regularly complained to their correspondents that all stories from El Salvador looked the same, and they pushed for exclusive material. They didn't understand that they were asking clever people to quadruple the odds of them being killed, so it was customary for crews to share bodies first thing in the morning, while reporters coordinated potential stories before heading out. Gang journalism also made it more likely that truly representative scenes would get past the censors, if only by desensitizing them to the horrors.

We left the press building to discuss the situation, ultimately deciding to look for a battalion stationed on the outskirts of town in the hope that their commander would unilaterally agree to us taking pictures. Leaving a trail of legitimate directional inquiries behind us, we became lost in the rural outback to finally emerge on a mesa overlooking a maze of oil rigs. Planes were landing in the distance.

Ski and Tony had a terse discussion about the risk of taking pictures of the distant airport, during which Tony insinuated that it was ludicrous to think much could come of it when Ski reminded him that we had been ordered to lower our shades when we had landed two hours earlier. Our interpreter, Ricardo, when dragged into the fray, said it was unwise to test the Argentine authorities. Tony interpreted this as a warning born of a long-established fear from the soft spoken and gentle man, while my silence constituted consent.

Reluctantly, Ski was tracking the slow progression of a light plane on final approach when he noticed three vehicles racing into frame right on the empty highway, heading in our direction.

"Shit," he said quietly.

"Keep rolling," Tony said.

The cars turned onto the dirt road we were on.

"Fuck," Ski said.

"Keep rolling," Tony replied.

Moments later, two black and one grey 1966 Ford Falcons slid to dusty halts in front of us, and half a dozen soldiers scrambled out to form a semicircle of rifles levelled at our chests.

"There was more cause for fear than your story makes clear," Saa-ra said. "The vehicles?"

"Of the thousands of people who disappeared during the mid-seventies," I told Bonnie, "Most of them were last seen being put into grey or black 1966 Falcons."

"Carry on."

I told Bonnie that the soldiers drove us to the airfield where they had a facility to screen our footage and that we played catch with a ball of gaffer's tape for an hour before a small platoon led by a young officer came out of a nearby building. Our six guards dutifully pointed their weapons at us, and we stopped playing, waiting to be scolded. Instead, the officer asked us if we had spoken to anyone since our arrival. Other than the hotel clerk, we lied, we said we had spoken to no one.

Without explanation, the soldiers placed us in a bus with tinted windows and took us back to town where we were taken one at a time to the front desk clerk who gave our records of registry to the officer. Soldiers then took us to our rooms where we repacked what little we had unpacked before they swept the rooms clean of anything we might have left behind. In my case, this included a gum wrapper in the wastepaper basket and replacing a bar of soap.

Back on the bus, soldiers sat us one man per seat on alternate sides, three rows apart. Each of us was guarded by a soldier sitting one seat behind us, all of whom amused themselves by tapping Latin rhythms on the back of our heads with machine pistols as we headed back to the airport. Along the way, I understood the guards to say that our names were going to be removed from the passenger manifest of the morning flight from Buenos Aires, as well. We subsequently parked in front of the civilian terminal for fifteen minutes before being taken to the military side of the airport where we were told we were going to be placed on a military aircraft going back to Buenos Aires.

"At this point," I told Bonnie, "their practice of disposing of the missing over the Atlantic from military transport planes caused us some trepidation before something happened to change everything. For over an hour, we watched our young officer stomp from building to building becoming increasingly agitated over not getting whatever it was he wanted, which we figured could only be good for us. We didn't know this at the time, but Manny had gone to our hotel to see if we had returned for lunch. When the clerk denied that we had ever checked in, Manny ran with Salvador rule number one and made a phone call that generated a flood of communications between a military junta not used to explaining their actions to foreign diplomats and the local military garrison in Comodoro Rivadavia.

[317]

I turned to face Bonnie. "The host country is supposed to inform the embassy of a foreign country whenever they arrest one of their citizens. They hadn't done that, so I figured our lieutenant was having a hard time saving his ass."

"Which is what he believed was at stake," Bonnie/Saa-ra said.

"It would only be fair," I said. "Anyway, we spent the night in a city jail being interrogated by federal police who photographed us shirtless to prove they hadn't beaten us, before they locked us in military barracks around seven in the morning. Around noon, we were put under house arrest at a mom and pop hotel, the only place that would take us, and we were assigned a local attorney. Dr. Hector Viñales was his name."

"Why do you remember this?" Saa-ra said evenly.

"Because he took us on, and I'm here talking to you."

Saa-ra said, "She understands that you considered his representation key in a dire circumstance. Continue."

"His safety was an issue, as well. Anyway, after we gave him our depositions, we were repeatedly summoned back to his office to explain discrepancies between what we had individually told the police and our military interrogators. Hector told Ricardo that he expected some mistranslation, intentional and otherwise, but key parts of our stories didn't match. We had all agreed not to mention our conversation about taking pictures of the airport," I explained, "but their interrogators were good, and by morning they knew that we knew what we were doing wasn't kosher. It didn't help that we had obviously lied about talking to people, so they never stopped trying to make us slip up."

"Do you think they seriously considered you to be spies?"

"I think hiding us was designed to keep other news cowboys riding side-saddle, but Manny blew their cover at the point when it looked like they were going to make us disappear in their tradition sense. Because of this poor timing for them, the military, local, and federal police all wanted jurisdiction over our case."

"To what end?"

"To appear fair, to control the outcome, maybe to unmask more of our lies to hide theirs," I shrugged, "to pass the buck."

"Carry on."

"There was good news about this internal battle in that three bureaucracies, racing to circle their wagons, left gaps that made it clear none of them were being completely honest, if only about little things like threatening us. The bad news was that soon after our arrest, the

[318]

British attacked the Malvinas Islands, (Falklands, if you're not in Argentina) and they were threatening to blockade the mainland. This caused various authorities to amend the terms of our house arrest to insinuate control over the case. At the same time, Hector said that even a minor change in wording, times three versions of any event, would have a big affect in court; he had to note all of the changes and our omissions before he submitted our interrogation documents and depositions to the judge. As a result, our days dragged on in clarification meetings until the morning when everyone except me went to see Hector about boundary phone calls: as our travel restrictions were amended by another authority, sometimes only minutes apart and always to a smaller area, we were finally restricted to an area that precluded us from seeing Hector. Royally pissed off, Tony, Ski, and Ricardo went to see him while I stayed behind to take phone calls from the free world.

Shortly after they left the hotel, three closely cropped young men came into the quaint main floor cafe. Seeing me sitting alone in the empty room, they exchanged smiles, ordered coffee, then walked over and politely asked if they could join me as they sat down. I nodded as if my permission mattered, and continued reading a local newspaper.

"You read Spanish?" one of them said with mild surprise, meaning, "You never mentioned that in your interviews."

"Mostly just numbers and directions," I said, seeing no benefit in telling him that I could understand more words than I knew how to use. "I'm looking at pictures to learn more of your language."

He translated this for his friends, all of whom laughed heartily when one of them said I would have two to eight years to learn their language.

Returning his attention to me, the young leader seriously said, "It is very dangerous on the streets at night, no?"

I turned over the paper to look at the page he could see, and asked him to show me the article he was talking about. Shaking his head, he told his friends that I was not smart, to which one of them commented that this suited the disguise of a foreign correspondent. They all laughed again.

I must have twitched a sign of understanding because, as one, they suddenly stopped to stare at me. My stomach was in a steep dive, but I managed to casually ask him if the danger was specific to a local area of town, or was it everywhere because people were now more afraid.

"I think if you were to stay in the hotel, this would be safest. I am just trying to be friendly in these unfriendly times, no?"

[319]

I thanked him for his concern, as a foreign correspondent would, and they left the hotel probably wondering whether I had gotten the point.

I told Tony about this meeting when he came back, and he had Ricardo call Hector, who said he would look into it right away. Later that day, the British sunk the General Belgrano battleship.

The next day, authorities ordered the press corps out of Comodoro Rivadavia. The day after that, the same three visitors came back with the same message under identical circumstances. Tony was so pissed when I told him about this that he demanded of Hector that he complain directly to the federal judge. Hector did this, and the judge permanently established generous boundaries of our house arrest which still didn't stop some young patriot from telephoning a threat to me the next morning.

Two weeks into this bullshit, we pushed our arrest limits by fifty feet to go to a restaurant on the outskirts of town. This is when things fell apart. The dislike Ski and Tony had for one another, rooted in an argument they had while covering the revolution that had renamed Rhodesia, resurfaced, and each of them blamed the other for our predicament. As the argument got louder and nastier, Ricardo intervened to sternly explain that it was poor form in his culture for grown men to act like juveniles in public. Tony and Ski quieted, but both of them wanted the last word. When Tony's barb topped Ski's dart, Ski stormed out of the restaurant.

Thinking it was a good time to shoot an escaping spy, I went after him.

Catching up quickly, but with no idea what to say, I put my arm around his shoulder to buy time. This action caused Ski to slow his pace because a "born and bred" Midwest heterosexual male didn't like being touched by men, other than hand to hand or hand to jaw. Removing my gesture of reassurance, I felt increasingly detached as I began to talk about the benefits of sharing fear without caving into it, and saying that everyone was doubly sensitive to each other's moods because we were dependent on each other in unspoken ways. I needed his support to get through this because I was scared shitless—that moment notwithstanding, I told Bonnie. I also admitted to Ski that I stayed back to take calls from Toronto because Sally's pleasantly satirical manner was a transfusion of hope. I left it up to Wizichinski to figure out that I was too scared to step outside.

"You did not judge, nor give him permission to continue his tantrum," Saa-ra said as a statement.

"I guess. Anyway, he turned around."

[320]

"Later, your colleague asked you what happened."

"I couldn't remember it clearly, so I said 'not much.'"

"What do you recall about the transaction?" Saa-ra said.

"I was far more intimate than I cared to be, and I didn't realize I had made my point until I ran out of words. Still, it would have been a waste of time if Ski's mental toughness hadn't kicked back in," I shrugged. "We all get tired."

"You were all justifiably afraid. We will discuss situations such as these in your next phase, and your unconscious attempts to disguise them as something else. It is a fatal flaw of mankind's. Now," Saa-ra said, dealing with her original point, "she has often spontaneously told others what they needed to hear, unaware of the effects of her casually precise psychological bombing."

Paradoxically disturbed by the ridiculous implication that I had been invaded by Spirit, and annoyed that Saa-ra's comments caused me to remember yet another event, I said, "That's good for her friends."

Saa-ra studied the sky as if it was about to change into something else; I couldn't help but take a peek. It felt like forever, but was probably less than thirty seconds, before I realised Bonnie would sit there until we were staring at the moon, waiting to hear what had come to my mind.

"I know you're looking for every experience the audience might possibly relate to, but I can guarantee this isn't one of them."

"Guarantee with what?"

"I need a break for the can," I said standing.

"You can tell her on the way back," Saa-ra said.

Chapter Thirty-four
Patterns of Intent

A few steps later I said, "My ex-wife called after two years without any contact, and rambled about her life being over because she had herpes, then she made references about making sure her life was over. I had no idea what I was going to say, but I told her to come over, things had happened since we'd last seen each other. I still had nothing definite to say when she arrived, but my mood changed from concern to such a feeling of indifference that when I found a barely related incident I ran with it."

"What it was, specifically."

"That's the thing, it wasn't specific."

Saa-ra said nothing to interrupt the sounds of our footfalls.

Clearing my throat, I said, "I told Lynda that in Salvador the army had started killing people in a small village because they had allegedly helped the guerrillas, and that if it was true, the villagers wouldn't have had a choice but to help. Nearby neighbours grabbed whatever they could carry and ran into the jungle. Soldiers had been tracking a couple of families for three or four days when we came across them—first the soldiers and then a few minutes ahead, the families."

Abruptly awash in a wave of sticky vertigo, I reached for Bonnie's arm to steady myself. Cold and baffled, I took a few breaths before I said, "We told them they were really close to being caught, but they chose to stay. It meant certain death, but it didn't matter to them."

"What did your wife think about your story?"

"She calmed down, which surprised the hell out of me because I barely got the gist of the story myself."

"What was the point of your narrative?"

"Other people had worse things to deal with than controllable infections."

"She heard a story about self-pity killing her, and she needed to move on."

I stutter-stepped with the realization that Saa-ra's version had hit the mark—it had been in Lynda's eyes, but at the time I wasn't about to screw around with success by questioning why she seemed to feel better.

"We have more," Saa-ra carried on as if she was adding to an order through a takeout speaker. "Your interpretation of stunned amazement suited the moment in Ethiopia when you exclaimed, 'This cannot be.' In reality, Phillip was stating his intentions through you and for you. Also, knowing about your father's imminent return to us was an omen of your raw abilities and evidence of our benevolence because disappointment cripples you." She paused. "It is time to tell her."

"Tell her…" I was about to ask, but suddenly knew what she meant, and "what?" uselessly dribbled out of my mouth.

Saa-ra bowed out, saying, "If you have no questions, we will leave you for now. We love you."

"Uh-huh."

Bonnie's upper body movements became less stiff, and her gate more fluid as we walked toward her home. And walked, and walked.

Finally, I cleared my throat from a false start then I told her that in Ethiopia we were on our way to tape the distribution of Canadian wheat when we came across a withered old man lying on the side of the road. One toothpick thin arm was folded under his bald head to keep it off the cold, stony ground. The other, shaking under minimal weight, begged us for his life.

We took footage of him from three angles before going on our way.

I half expected Bonnie to do the same thing with me, as we left the park. Instead, with a delicate breath she said, "Thank you."

I had nothing to say.

Drawing upon a recent Kha-lib topic, in her normal tone, she said, "Our First Attention establishes perceptual absolutes that organize our inventory to seamlessly reason a world that suits the existence we experience. I mean that literally; we'll come back to how that is. In our version of here and now, a brick won't ever feel like a marshmallow; throw a ball and it will always curve down to the ground."

"By reason, this time you're talking about what's tangible or recordable according to our laws of physics?" I said, relieved to have left the body behind.

"I am. Reasoning is wired to perception, and our perceptions provide only descriptions about our reality. In the Second Attention, we can manipulate physically related assumptions without embracing them as anything more than representations borrowed from the First Attention. In other words, the ball can make a ninety-degree turn or hang in midair if we want it to because rules based on descriptions don't apply.

[323]

This," she said, with a sweeping gesture, "is a grand illusion, but it has a vital reality of its own."

"What's the point? I mean, if the Second Attention knows the First Attention is fabricated, why bother to throw the ball?"

"What we see and believe serve as vital reference points. Basically, the First Attention is like learning the alphabet before we can research in the library of the Second Attention. Kha-lib also said the First Attention uses all of the average person's energy to maintain descriptions—which is our reason—within a vast and ever-changing story line until we examine the repetitive acts that hold us back. The examination should be based on this simple assumption: we act and react to a description. If our emotions tell us to be angry, it is unhealthy not to express this until you remember you are angry at a description of events made personal by your self-image. In other words, you're letting your ego make you safe from a circumstance that doesn't exist; you just believe it does. With me?"

"I'm trying to connect to something you said a while back." Then I did. "This is like hating war, but not warriors; it's faulty reasoning that we misrepresent as a condemnation of others when it's their beliefs that piss us off."

"It's also a condemnation of ourselves when it's our beliefs that are making us pissed."

"Got it."

"The better the conclusions we act upon, the more energy we save by refining our acting skills. Simplistically, in time we become aware that we are acting almost all of the time, and we can thereafter choose how we will play a role as opposed to reacting to other characters."

We turned down the short driveway.

"The beginning point of intentional self-development is as simple and difficult as learning not to react. It's simple because not reacting saves enough energy for us to begin to see ourselves, and knowing why we reacted in one circumstance can free us from that reaction in another. It's difficult because the more we see, the more we might not want to see because it's extremely difficult to not offend the ego."

"The better we get, the easier it is to get better, even at two steps forward and one step back," I said, opening the side door for her.

"True, our potential increases, but our focus always determines how far and how fast we will go. Discovering one unflattering aspect doesn't reveal all of them, and we begin to set up barriers to self-discovery."

"But we're still ahead of the game."

[324]

"That focus is a barrier to creating a rolling momentum," she said, topping the stairs and turning into the living room. "If you don't make a consistent effort to find and connect the flaws, they'll draw you back to your old ways." She sat on the couch. "In effect, you're bargaining for an in-between stage where you can say, 'This is good enough,' like a thief feeling better because he's cutting back. The bottom line," she said as I made myself comfortable in the overstuffed chair, "Is that it takes less energy to dedicate yourself to a task because you're not constantly fighting the inertia of complacency or updating your excuses. Moreover, you begin to include Second Attention perceptions as you gain easier access to them. At first these arrive as unexpected gifts, like helpful coincidences, or visions and insights as a by-product of the commitment itself which adds to your commitment."

"Okay, I'm with you on all of that, but why are we talking about it?"

"The idea of channelling our friends frightened you, so I'm explaining the fundamentals of a process that can set aside your First Attention without giving you a heart attack. One more thing for today. The assumptions of your dreaming reality include spontaneous cause and effect, weightlessness, and fluidity, whereas the continuity of your waking reality rests on the concepts of linear time, gravity, and solidity. It follows that in the former state of awareness you should never become physically tired. Correct?"

"I guess."

"You can commit to an answer."

"Yes."

"It also follows that objects like beds should make no practical sense within the continuity of a dream, but it represents a place to rest, and the dream makes sense as a metaphor for that aspect of your waking life."

"Got it."

"Now, there's a huge difference in the scope of information available to us in each Attention. Think of it like a photographer using a wide-angle lens. Technological considerations aside, the lens is objective; it's the photographer's assumptions that contrive the focal point for people who view his prints through the same assumptions, adding whatever personal twists they might infer."

"All of them are drawing from the well of the First Attention, sure."

"Good," Bonnie nodded. "Phillip views events like a lens. From his point of view, an average looking, middle-aged, white man wearing sweats and a T-shirt, standing at the edge of frame is as detailed as the beautiful black woman dressed in a red coat, centre frame, standing a hundred feet closer. The pebble under the toe of his sneaker is a diamond ring, the distance between the couple is the back-story, and the woman taking a step toward the camera makes it her decision to leave. The backdrop of office buildings and a sports stadium could speak to their disparate lifestyles...you can stop me anytime."

"I get it. Phillip sees everything at once."

"It's more than that. He sees the entire nature of what is to you a single moment, plus he sees the timeless associations of all objects in his focus because objects are events when you have no artificial focal points to detract from the simultaneous whole. The ring is a piece of inventory, but what it signifies, where it lies, and how distant it is from centre frame tells the story."

"Ahhhh, got it," I said, beginning to see a bigger picture. Kind of.

Bonnie leaned forward. "From his vision of your life, he chose to relay an intimate experience that would help your ex-wife work through her problem. From your point of view, you thought you were talking about beds when Lynda was hearing a story about a place to rest."

"I get your point, but I don't remember it well enough to say one way or another."

"That's normal because you weren't focused exclusively in the First Attention. Phillip had to set aside the self-image aspects of your story." Chuckling, she said, "I don't know what you said to Lynda before she left for the day, but calling the guard in Beirut a shithead pinpointed the return of your First Attention in that case."

She waited for me to respond... to no avail.

"Yes or no," she then said patiently, "throughout your life, you've caught people off guard by uttering insights without thinking?"

"Everyone does that."

"Not everyone says things they couldn't know."

I struggled with the insinuation.

"Accessing other Attentions," she continued, "can be a spontaneous reaction to survival situations or a gift that occurs at the behest of Spirit, like when you formalized your despair and said humanitarian acts could have been rendered by the victors."

I worked my mouth like a child on a new wad of gum. Bonnie leaked a snicker through her nose, a snort then gave rise to a choking laugh which she struggled to stop as she said, "Rendering humanitarian acts instead of simply saying 'not helping people?'"

"I am capable of communicating well."

[326]

"I used to think I was naturally wise, as well." Her contained mirth broke into a giggle as she said, "No one can convince anyone of anything they don't want to believe, so there's no point in discussing this further." She got off the couch and headed for the kitchen.

"What would a real student do with this information?" I said to her back.

Turning around at the kitchen doorway, she said. "By this time in their relationship, a student would suspend their disbelief and look for a pattern of the Universe's presence in their life because they'd understand there's no place left to turn, other than reverting to their former ignorant state." She disappeared into kitchen.

"Didn't we just do that?"

"I'm talking about a pattern so large that you'd be embarrassed to have missed it; the events we discussed are clues that there is a pattern. Your travels had to have been portentous or symbolic," she said, to the sounds of filling the kettle.

"I could trace my jobs on a map and see if they form the letter omega?" I joked.

"That's an excellent idea. Let me know how it goes." Her voice floated innocently from the kitchen, but I knew in the days to come she would ask me what I had found. "If you would like to bring more of your work to help your search—no criticism from me because I know you're not finished—I'm up for that. Coffee or tea?" she said.

On the way home that afternoon, I bought a two by three foot map of the world and set aside time to plot my travels with pins and thread. Hours later, I discovered that dropping a basketball net would have accomplished the same thing in two seconds, which is what I told Bonnie the next day at Nolan's.

"Try plotting the nature of the events you covered instead of tracking every little town," she said, thoughtfully. "You could use different coloured thread for categories, like red for war and green for environmental calamities."

"Sowing a flag?"

"Maybe that's it!"

"Maybe," I said, handing her two short chapters for later consideration, then we discussed how her characters would deal with common personal conflicts, to help me understand the concept of an impeccable act. I still struggled with that, and how to assess event-natures.

When our day was done, and I was back at home, I exchanged black threads for other colours as she had suggested. It was tedious and I welcomed the distraction of a beer call from Ed.

[327]

Off and on for three afternoons, two colour reconfigurations caused me to realize there wasn't going to be a flag, a letter, or a symbol in the strands that had begun to evoke equally linear memories of those events. For example, when Salvador became a red line, it was easier to consult my day diary and old newspaper clippings for incidents in the hope of fleshing something out other than my emotions. They were flat by this time.

The police in Soyapango wounding Joaquin Zuniga, a cleverly disguised leftist sleeper guerrilla posing for many years as an accomplished photographer from the Associated Press, added a fanciful dimension as did George Thurlow's wounding, a far more conspicuous subversive from the Daily Democrat in Woodland California because of his Zapata moustache. The third red line pulled my tongue out of my cheek: it represented a local hire, Gregorio Moran, whose threat to the future of El Salvador seemed to have been that he could speak English. He was killed by *equivocación*-mistake. I moved on to incidents in the barrios of Suchitoto and Santa Anita, no longer thinking about people but focused on looking for something abstract portending to a purpose.

On the fourth day of finding no pattern, I awoke with an indistinct sense of loss. By that afternoon, it was frustration, and by nightfall, it had flashed into despair, and I quit searching for patterns that clearly weren't there.

The next day, walking back to Bonnie's from lunch at a West Van Sprout House, she asked me how it was going, and I simply said, "Went."

"Terrific! What did you discover?" she said, enthusiastically misinterpreting my comment.

"I discovered that not every event can be slotted into a niche. If there is a trail of something more in my travels, I need special glasses."

"What couldn't you place?"

"Ethiopia was about the famine, but there was also a civil war, both of which were related to political corruption and gross environmental mismanagement. I tried different colours and doubled up on the ones that fit." I shrugged. "That's how I figured out you set me up again."

"How did I do that?"

"The symbolism I was looking for was actually what I was doing; I was literally looking between the lines to see whatever I might be hiding from myself without emotional interference."

Bonnie stopped in the middle of a side street and said, "I would never have thought of that. Your mind is becoming agile. Unfortunately," she said, moving again, "you focused too closely, eventually

[328]

on me as the source of your frustration and not the underlying omens and metaphors in your travels. You need to assess your entire journey as if it had purpose," Bonnie threw her arms open wide, "as an omen of biblical proportions!" she shouted into the bay.

"I've gotten away with some things I shouldn't have, but who hasn't?" I stopped in my tracks. "So that's what you're researching— push hard enough, and I'll begin to see proof of Spirit in… fuck, you're manufacturing consent! Excellent. I didn't see that coming."

Bonnie waved her hand as if I had passed gas in the still air. Walking up the side stairs to her house, she said, "I didn't manufacture the long day in the mountains when you knew it was time to quit."

"That was a logical deduction, but a clever manipulation on your part."

"There was nothing logical about deducing you would be safe while people were still firing at you. All you could do was arrange the facts to suit an ill-defined trust in luck, along with an intellect so highly developed that you thought it reasonable that you could out-manoeuvre shrapnel. The fact is a wiser part of you recognized the entire experience as an omen, which made it a self-fulfilling prophecy."

With a pit stop in the kitchen, we headed out to the balcony with a bottle of wine and two plastic cups.

"We agreed that it's logical for every action to be a consequence of another action, not that everything is cosmically orchestrated," I said.

"We agreed that there is an underlying order to all events because nothing comes from nothing. It was you who designed a destiny that aligned you with consequences that sometimes didn't happen; the only logical explanation is that you had help."

"Goodbye damn-near killed me!"

"Damned near is still a miss," Bonnie said tranquilly. "Remember that your screenplay story just filled your head, and that you just knew your father would not live to come home? Same help."

"A real apprentice, and our audience, might see your claim as an example of how faith bends facts," I said logically, "which reinforces the idea that teachers are manufacturing their student's consent."

We sat down in the aluminum chairs.

Bonnie consulted the horizon, then turning her head so that the sun reflected off her glasses as pinpoints of light, she said, "A teacher would recognize this as one of those crossroads moments and ask the student to review the incident in detail. Hopefully, the apprentice's lessons to date would allow them to set aside self-interest long enough

[329]

for an omen to jump out at them." She brushed hair away from her forehead, took a sip of wine, and watched the waters of English Bay.

With occasional prompting for details, I told her the full story.

Chapter Thirty-five
The Omen of Goodbye

I had finished six weeks of an open-ended contract when Sean gave his notice to our bureau chief, Lucy. Four weeks was understood to be a fair freelance stint, but most of our friends were there, so the extra time wasn't a big deal to me. Sean said I should go home with him because he always missed the big trouble by only a day or two; six months earlier, his regular soundman had stayed behind and was badly wounded, which created the job opening for me. I was considering leaving with him when Sammi's soundman was hit, so Lucy sent Sean home early and shifted me over to work with Sammi.

"We thought Sean's plane coming under fire was something that would be over by noon," I said, "but his flight turned out to be the last to lift off for months. That night," I explained the lead-up events, "some of us were intimidated at the Hamra-Skeller restaurant, not that threats were unusual, but these guys knew where we had gone to school, where our parents lived—things like that. The next morning, all hell broke loose."

"What were the threats about?"

I looked into her eyes to see if she was kidding. Apparently not. "They suggested it would be wise to ignore a faction's activities?"

"Right—got it," she nodded.

"Shelling from the east fell downtown, and there was heavy fighting around the Green Line which meant they weren't just trying to pick each other off; someone intended to cross it. There was no fighting around the Corniche, so the touring crews decided to wait out the shelling, but when a sniper ruined that idea, we knew something big was happening—no one ever shot at us from the north."

"Us, as in you?"

I nodded. "By lunchtime, all crews had made it back to the hotel, except the Death Watch teams at the airport stayed put while Moslem factions shelled the Christian-held west all day and night, which drove us all into a the crawl space beneath the hotel. Around eight the next morning, Allan Pizzey from CBS asked for volunteers to see who was

[331]

winning the free-for-all, and Alain, a freelancer working for NBC, and I did the shoot." I took a breath, a short sip, then a longer second one of each, as that memory seemed to require.

"He had a habit of poking his lens around corners. Not that I blame him, but imagine what soldiers thought they saw, and you can appreciate why both sides tried to nail us within fifty yards of the hotel. Anyway, the next weeks were full of skirmishes and so many broken ceasefires that we had T-shirts printed that read, 'I survived cease-fire number five, six, seven, and so on' written in crossed out Roman numerals. Mine was at seventeen when Peter, the senior producer in the east, asked for volunteers. Half of the country was on fire or under fire by then, so the job was a bring-your-own-toilet paper type of deal, but you wouldn't need a lot of it because you probably wouldn't be eating. I had nothing to prove, but going with him pretty much guaranteed that CBS would put me on speed dial." I shrugged. "I didn't think it could be much different from working ceasefires, anyway."

"Hang on: you were working in the Christian held west, which became the losing side to Moslem factions, so you moved east?"

"Sammi was Christian Lebanese, so when the Moslem factions retook the west he was considered an enemy. It was something CBS hadn't thought through, and Sam didn't mention it until we came to our first Moslem road block and soldiers dragged him away to be shot. When we got back from that, Lucy moved us to the Alexander."

"How did he get away?"

"I don't know."

"What did he tell you?"

"He said they were insulting him when a soldier raised a pistol to his head, hesitated, and changed his mind."

"What did you do when they took him away?"

Agitated by her probing, I kept my temper in check as I said, "I argued that Sam had worked for CBS for years, everyone knew where we were and that we knew how to conduct ourselves, so we would never be mistaken for anything else. That kind of stuff."

"Argued?" she grinned.

"I might have had a small fit, like pointing at their heads like they were crazy. Things like that."

"What other things?"

"Nothing else."

"What did you think of doing and not do?" she said, hitting the nail on the head.

What the fuck. "I thought of grabbing my balls and motioning that they didn't have any to have taken a defenceless man away to be killed."

"Maybe your rant was enough to save him."

"No one left our group. Anyway, ceasefires were a bitch because…"

"Your voice had to have carried or maybe a radio?"

"Trust me," I said peevishly, "the only way I could have influenced anything was maybe trying to run away to distract them, which they wouldn't have cared about because if they wanted to shoot me, I would have been with Sam."

Bonnie studied my face as if she was retouching a photograph.

"What's the big deal?" I said. "Every earthquake has a ten-day survivor."

"You covered an earthquake?"

"I'm saying every conflict has strange moments when the inevitable is suspended, and there's no accounting for it. Shit happens." In the next moment, an involuntary shiver followed by an ozone smelling flashback riding a wave of vertigo caused me to tilt backwards: ape-like upright, skin rose and grey, trembling uncontrollably within an incendiary mist, tortured breaths wheezed from seared lungs.

I struggled for breath.

Bonnie's expression was of expectation, not concern, and when I appeared to be in control again she said, "What memory of shit happens did you just have?"

Still shaken, I said, "There was a pink guy standing stark naked in the middle of the street. Bodies—pieces of bodies, cars, and buildings were all around him. His clothes had been blown off."

"You must've been close," she whispered.

"What?"

"I said you must've been close when the bomb went off."

"No—not really. It was the eight-fifteen bomb taking out ambulance attendants." I cracked a sly grin. "Sean and I were still on our way to the eight o'clock bombing."

"You're camouflaging the fear, again," Bonnie said, shaking her head. "I just wanted to make the point. Carry on."

It took me a few seconds to gather my composure.

"Anyway, ceasefires made the risks in the east the same as the west until a breakaway faction tried to extort protection money by sniping at the Alexander lobby. When one of them was caught and sent back to his people," I paused, "on consecutive days, his brethren set off a car in the parking lot. The next day, everybody was shooting at everybody south of Beirut, and we had to stop traveling for more than a block or two. Couple of days after that, one of our spooks said a Moslem town had been taken by an alliance between the Christian Phalange and the Lebanese army then the Phalange had turned on their cohorts and taken their weapons, including a state of the art American tank. This is when Peter asked for volunteers."

"Because of the tank, the double cross, or something else?"

It took me a moment to line up my ducks. Essentially, I then explained that America backed the Israelis, who officially backed the Lebanese Army, who had just been screwed over by the Christian Phalange, who were regular army units until they split away for political reasons. Unofficially, but not a secret, the Israelis also trained the Phalange because the accredited army was not officially at odds with them. They just operated separately. It followed that Americans were de facto allies of both factions, neither of which should have a top-of-the-line American-made Israeli army tank. Questions would be asked, conditions of sale and end user declarations investigated, and Israeli /American relations would take another hit.

"What kind of footage could you get? The deed was done," Bonnie said.

"Pictures of the Phalange firing the tank could become historical stuff—a metaphor for more than the end of their alliance. We would also get voice clips to find out what the hell they were thinking." I stretched my legs. "Until that day, the Phalange were borderline large enough to be represented in whatever government emerged from the war, which is probably why they were inspired to convert a secondary military roll into a bigger political act."

"Did it?"

"Not like they planned. I'll get to that."

I told Bonnie there was no way to drive through contested territory, so we had to slip across the Green Line to the harbour, where we boarded two hundred feet of rust kept afloat by the faith of fifty weekend warriors—students on their way to battle.

"Slipped across a deadly zone?"

"Our driver paid for part of the way."

She took a considered breath as I said, "We stayed apart from them while we waited for the sun to go down—the inner harbour was a sniper's paradise by day—because students tended to turn every little thing into a crisis, and we were more likely to be hit by their retaliation than by a sniper's rounds. Conversely, the students politely shunned us because our job was to chronicle their deaths.

[334]

"Steaming south at ten knots," I said as Bonnie whispered under her breath 'snipers', "with a bad bootleg copy from the bazaar of the Moody Blues in my Walkman, I became mesmerized by the blazing towns that stretched for miles. Time passed quickly for me until the captain throttled back outside of a thick fog bank around one AM. With our engines at idle, a lazy beam sea soon caused a boy to puke, which set off a stampede to the aft leeward rail. Half an hour of choir retching ensued before two twenty-foot fishing boats found their way through thick mists eerily crowned by the gossamer glow of distant flames.

In turns of two, soldiers stood outboard of the lifelines with one leg dangling until the small crafts rose on the back of a swell, and the students stepped across and into the hands of their companions. This seemingly simple move could not be tentative because straddling bobbing gunwales meant falling between vessels and either sinking like a stone or having your head crushed between the hulls.

Everybody made it, our crew boarding with the last load of troops around three AM, then we blindly thump-thumped through the incandescent shroud under the power of an ancient one-lung diesel engine. Ten minutes passed before the water flattened into a pane of glass. Maybe a minute later, we crossed the thermal threshold where a vertical scythe of radiant heat from the shore cleaved the fog as if it were a snow bank to reveal a vivid vista of a narrow bay. Our skipper hastily shut down the engine, then pointing to a nearby promontory whispered with the tension of a tormented steam valve, "There is the enemy. No more talking!"

Peter and I exchanged comedic glances because, inexplicably, our guy seemed not to appreciate how far and clearly sound travels over flat water in the cool air of a still night. Not that it mattered because our students were smoking like a Kamikaze signals class practicing SHOOT-THE-GLOW as we rowed into an inlet less than a hundred yards from the aforementioned point.

We disembarked under the battle-weary stares of grimy fighters who led us to a dirt road where they mimed hunching over for us to scamper across. Soldiers on the other side then took us to a large house where we were led up a steep flight of wooden stairs into a black and barren room on the third floor. Leaving us with interesting smelling blankets, two candles, and a warning to avoid the windows, he said we would meet his commander in the morning. It was four thirty-five when I closed my eyes against the glow of false dawn merging with the blush of a nearby town's embers.

[335]

"Morning" arrived at five-thirty when a soldier came to take us to have coffee with a sullen colonel, and his second in command. During the consumption of two thick, high-test cups, Peter was circumspect in suggesting that tactics were the essence of victory, as the small faction of Phalange had recently demonstrated. The colonel acknowledged that resourceful manoeuvring had served them well, but he said there were times when trading blows was all one could do; brute force capability was essential.

I explained to Bonnie that Peter and the colonel were establishing boundaries, such as having Peter translate generalizations to mean the issue was not to be explored further. Conversely, Peter wanted the colonel to interpret apparently innocent words as challenges to his intellect, for example "detailed execution" would mean, "Did you think about this by yourself?" and "complex" to mean, "Do you know how to use it?" It was understood that the word "front" could include military, social, political, and international ramifications, depending on how deep one decided to acknowledge the term. What was left unsaid was deemed not pertinent, out of bounds, or otherwise rude to explore. You gotta love the Middle East.

Their dance of communication formally underway, with British understatement Peter continued to stroke inspired thinking over superior firepower to which the colonel philosophically acknowledged that illumination rarely penetrated far into the fog of war, but when it did, it was more powerful than bombs. Humility then compelled him to offer us a tour of his military might, which clandestinely underscored the rarity of illumination that had been his good fortune to author.

At sunrise, Peter, the colonel, and a driver took the lead in one jeep while Sammi and I were driven in their wake of fine dust.

On the way to view an Israeli armoured personnel carrier, our driver twice let them get too far ahead, stopped to put on his helmet, then hunched to look through the spokes of the steering wheel as he raced through a thickening cloud for what I imagined would be two feet too far. Both times we slid to a halt on the bumper of the lead jeep, and our driver turned to grin at us. His attention span problem finally ended when the roadbed disintegrated into ruts: the roadsides were mined, so it was with cracking teeth, bitten tongues, and pummelled kidneys making asphyxiation a welcome possibility that we finally turned onto the warming sands of a roaming stretch of beach.

Stopping behind a large dune, the colonel cautioned us to stay low because we were only fifty meters from the front. We should also follow his footprints along the midline slope of the dunes because

[336]

mines tended to gravitate into the troughs of sand waves before the wind blew them into flat plains. Ten minutes later, when the A.P.C. crew tired of performing for our camera, we took our real footage, then carefully retraced our steps before driving back into the foothills. This time, upon stopping at a signal from the lead driver who raced ahead, I asked our driver what was going on. Putting on his helmet, he said we were about to drive through Sniper Alley; we were staggering our passage and varying our speeds to make it more difficult to anticipate aim.

Annoyed that he had presumed my fate should befall me un-announced, I asked him why he hadn't said anything to us the first time through. In a fluid motion, practiced by males from the cradle to the grave in his world, he cocked his head like he had a crick in his neck, clicked his tongue, shrugged, and said, "*Maalesh*," as we lurched into the dissipating cloud of suffocating camouflage.

"Mined roads, mined beaches, fifty yards from the enemy, snipers again.... Christ, John!"

"That's why they're called volunteer shoots. Anyway, I wanted to smack him because he was too young to have evolved piss-yourself fear into the sophisticated expressions of irony I enjoyed from the mature of his culture. Instead, I crunched myself into a less con-spicuous target than Sammi, who sat ramrod straight for an extremely long minute before we slowed down."

Forty more minutes later, I told Bonnie, our polite enthusiasm over a substantial mobile arsenal of arms prompted our commander to reveal that his forces had acquired a state of the art tank, which was by itself holding the perimeter of their mountainous southern front. With keen interest, Peter asked the colonel to speculate on how acquiring a single, intricate killing machine might ultimately impact the Phalange's future.

Their exchange was pricelessly subtle, like the timing of a tongue click and accompanying shrug were a study in finesse: tilt to the left, click and shrug, and you had the moving sentiment of, "Mankind's idiocy is beyond words. I'm sorry about the death of your brother." Tilt to the right and click, pause for a hundredth of a second, shrug, and it meant "Mankind has no words to describe what an idiot your brother was."

In part, Peter had asked the colonel if he had plans for after the war because somewhere down the shell-holed road, elements of the Israeli army, and possibly the Americans by default, would find themselves positioned next to or between the Phalange and the regular army. Be it

[337]

through an actual communications problem, or a well-constructed misunderstanding, the day would come when someone would quietly abandon their position and the Christian Phalange Army would accidentally go the way of disco, only one of them being a tragedy.

Appropriately, the colonel heard a challenge to the long-term wisdom of his tactic for a short-term gain, but he first addressed an additional aspect to demonstrate he had thought more about the circumstance than Peter had contemplated.

"We are not enemies of America because we outwitted their ally," he assured Peter. "Come—you must see our equipment," the colonel said, reinforcing his original position about having firepower which supported his inspired tactical decision.

Sammi and I had no trouble keeping a straight face because sweat had caked the cement dust into that position.

An hour later, we found the tank nestled behind one of two earthen-covered houses that protected it from the Druze artillery across the valley. Between these bunkers was twenty yards of flat, open road.

Grimy, hot, and tired, Peter may have been a trifle curt when he asked the colonel if his men were comfortable with the new acquisition because the Colonel responded by ordering the crew into action. Moments later, the tank engine roared into life, and without a wasted manoeuvre the crew reversed the machine out of the niche and into firing position so quickly that I had to pull Sammi out of the way. Exposing only a small section of turret above the horizon, the cannon fired, our ears popped, the earth jumped beneath our feet, and a pulse of dust rolled from beneath the superstructure as the machine lurched behind cover as if it were on a taught spring. The steel ballet was so precise that Sammi didn't have time to reposition and capture the exploding earth plume erupting in the still air across the valley.

At this point, as curious soldiers ambled out of the house-bunkers, Sammi told the colonel that his crew was so good that he didn't have time to do their work justice. If they could just repeat everything as closely as possible, he now knew where to stand to complete the tight sequence that would make the Phalange appear as efficient as they really were. The colonel gave the order, and the crew replicated the show so precisely that there was only one set of tracks in the cracked earth. Equally exacting, Sammi centre-framed the arcing circle of crimson until it erupted into a greyish brown plume on the crown of the next hill.

We were all so pleased for our own reasons that no one saw a puff of white emerge from a point near the impact of our first round, and in a sharp moment, the crack-whack of an air-burst mortar round shrouded our crest in a rouge-grey mist of shrapnel and roofing tile. The prickly blast knocked Sammi and I to our knees.

Dazed, deafened, and not yet feeling supremely stupid for not asking if we were firing at anyone, we hobble-helped each other into the house bunker to our left, entering behind two fighters who were caring a wounded soldier. Sitting in the cool dimness as occasional rounds burst overhead, we checked ourselves for wet spots while the colonel expertly attended to the boy's injured leg. This is when we learned that the colonel was a physician and teacher at the American University, and our drivers were medical students.

During a reloading interval, Peter shouted across the gap to determine if we were okay; soldiers had bundled him into the house on the right side of the open ground after he had seen us "falter."

You gotta love the Brits.

I shouted back that we were "functional". I saw no point in mentioning the prickling I was feeling in my shoulder and shins, notwithstanding that Sammi wouldn't have mentioned a missing limb if the spurting didn't interfere with him taking pictures.

Unnecessarily, because everyone knew these exchanges never lasted long, Peter shouted that we should stay put and that should have been the end of it. However, when the commander finished bandaging his soldier student, he coldly said we were going back to the safety of the valley. Sammi and I looked at each other to question whether we were missing something, then as one we shrugged, meaning of course we would do that as soon as it was over. Our inadvertent insolence prompted the colonel to take out his pistol, aim it at Sammi's chest, and tell him to make a run for it after the next bang. All I could come up with to explain this bazaar moment was that Peter's shout had given the doctor the idea that the Phalange would get poorer press because we had been inconvenienced, or no press at all if we were killed, and tension had taken over the moment.

"Tending to the wounded," Bonnie said, "may have lifted the fog enough for him to realize that you guys had played him, and caused a casualty. What happened next?"

"I shouted that we were coming out," I belatedly said because her speculation resolved years of bafflement over that moment for me, "a blast interrupted his objection, then Sammi and I limped across the open ground. Peter was standing at the door of his bunker, poised to conduct a symphony of invectives over our carelessness until he saw the gun in the colonel's hand."

[339]

I told Bonnie that the Druze clearly had more experience targeting dust trails rising above the ridgeline than our driver had experience underneath them. Not that anything came closer than a hit seventy or eighty yards ahead of us, but our guy over-steered long before we came into the debris cloud, and we began sliding sideways down the narrow mountain road. Sammi shouted for him to ease off the steering while our front seat guard maniacally gestured for him to take his feet off the pedals. These actions took care of everything I might have done, and without thinking, I sat ramrod straight to watch the landscape pass by a couple thousand feet below us.

The scene was a classic action movie tease.

The jeep fish-tailed onto the precipice, inches away the tires dug in and swung us hard toward the vertical rock face on the other side of the road. Our driver wrenched the wheel taking us back to a wobbling purchase on the edge where the tires spun furiously on gravel.

Finding grip for a second time, we were catapulted across the road through a rare opening in the uphill side, crashing sideways into a four-foot high pile of sand that some befuddled fool had brought up the mountain to begin rebuilding his home.

"Did you come to terms with your impending death?" Bonnie said, cocking her head to imply that the Universe was in the construction business.

"A sudden calm didn't descend into a profound moment of intro-spection if that's what you mean." I snickered. "I did have a moment to think about how ridiculous it was to be killed rolling down a mountain, considering everything else that could have happened."

Bonnie raised a brow to underscore how many other things could have happened, which I acknowledged with a nod as I added more possibilities.

I was catapulted through the half-door simultaneous to our guard riding the front seat forward out of my way. Sammi smacked forward into the driver's seat, careened up and through the canvas roof, and landed upside down across the top of the windscreen facing our bloody, unconscious driver. In a short while, soldiers came from a nearby house to carry us to a shelter where the colonel called on a walkie-talkie to find out where we were. He subsequently sent an A.P.C. to pick us up, and sporadic shelling followed us to the bottom of the mountain. That was it.

"How did you get back to the hotel?"

"We were taken south to an Israeli medevac station, where as luck would have it, we joined about sixty armoured vehicles heading into East Beirut. I went home the next day."

"So you crossed the contested area you had to bypass by sea on the way in?"

"Sixty armoured vehicles?" I said, eliminating her point of danger.

"You said the airport was closed."

"It was."

"How did you get out of there?"

"I'm not sure."

Bonnie waited for me to explain why that was.

With a shrug, I said, "You'd think I would remember an overnight sail on the Junieh ferry or a long road trip to Tel Aviv, but a helicopter landing in the Sun Hall Hotel parking lot rings a hazy bell. That would've taken some kind of special wrangling between Lucy and the Marines, but if they somehow thought I was a wounded American journalist..." I shrugged. "She was like that."

"You really don't remember?"

"I had a bunch of drinks the night before, some kind of medication, and I had slept about fifty minutes out of the last thirty-six hours." I shook my head. "My passport stamp says I came into Cyprus through Larnaca, which is where the ferry comes in right across from the Sun Hall." I shrugged. "One thing led to another—no omens in sight."

"You should be dead a couple times over!" Bonnie said, shaking her head in disbelief.

"I think we covered that the first day we met."

"You weren't as educated in the ways of the unseen as you are now."

"After all I've told you about combat, you've got to know I'm not being trite when I say, again, that shit happens. Sometimes you end up in Cyprus."

Staring at a spot between us, Bonnie nodded at a private thought then she said as a statement, "You believe omens are knee-bending revelations bestowed only upon the worthy, whereas you have not embraced the words Kha-lib said to you: "You didn't kill him. Any of them, for that matter." She refocused. "All of your other objections to the existence of Spirit as a loving, guiding force are based on your never-ending suspicion that I am doling out religious propaganda. That's your focus, not mine."

"I was peppered with metal alloys that turned my shin into a barometer, and squashed through a closed half-door that still allows my hip to register changes in humidity. Logically, I'm either destined to become a meteorologist or the omen is that I'm on my own."

Looking disoriented, as if she had awakened in a stranger's apartment, she said, "You were *told* you would be safe!"

"Sure, by you."

Bonnie opened her palms toward the ceiling, sighed with eternal weariness, then with papal appeal precluding any doubt that a monumental moment had just passed me by, she pleaded into the ether, "Please, not the long way."

"There's a longer way?" I chuckled, sarcastically.

Puffing her cheeks in an exasperated pant, she said, "Maybe you would be more willing to recognize the presence of Spirit in your life if I used a term that appealed to your irreverence for all things unseen." Bonnie leaned back, crossed one arm below her breasts then rested an elbow in one cupped hand and her chin in the other. She remained motionless for half of an uncomfortable minute, for me, other than a tiny nibble on her lower lip challenging me to believe that she was browsing through sophisticated abstractions. The minute mark crawled by as I fought the ghost of giddy to try to believe she was giving her all to help me. Thirty more seconds and shallow breaths began to betray my anticipation of hearing the single word that might change my life. Ten more seconds and the wisdom of the ages seemed to clarify behind Bonnie's suddenly wide eyes.

I leaned forward to receive this vital knowledge a millisecond sooner.

"You can call them Smurfs," she said seriously. "Maybe that'll get you past religion to see how momentum doesn't distinguish between targets and bystanders, except for you."

Apparently not.

Chapter Thirty-six
Designs of Intent

Bonnie gathered her thoughts, and said, "Maybe it'll help to approach the issue from a more mundane perspective." She then offered me an overview of Universal presence she had discovered in the books Kha-lib had suggested I read.

She said that from the First World War to the end of the second, Edgar Cayce introduced western cultures to the concept of channelling. From the early 1960's through the mid 1980's, Jane Roberts further established the Universe's presence, intentions, and teaching of bona fides through her Seth channels. At the same time, the dexterity of human consciousness was being chronicled by Lynn V. Andrews and Carlos Castaneda in separate apprenticeships, from the male and female perspectives.

"In our time," Bonnie said, "there are growing waves of artists, writers, environmentalists, and healers moving away from traditional practices to form a bigger picture of a Universal intercession underway. Their role is to contribute to the collective unconscious and add momentum to a changing world."

"Without knowing Spirit directly, like ordinary people in your book represent our audience?" I said.

"Yes. Not everyone has access to a teaching entity," she explained, "but they can attract one by making a conscious and consistent effort to do the right thing. To that end, Carlos recorded how on Juan said Spirit makes its presence known so people can recognize the contact if it happens," Bonnie said.

"So your audience can participate; good idea. How do they do that?" I asked, dutifully.

"Spirit reveals prospective students to the seer through coincidences and omens, which don Juan called The Manifestation of Spirit. The next step is called The Knock of Spirit, which is essentially the same as a manifestation, but it is seen by the prospect."

"The person still doesn't know?" I said.

"Not a clue," Bonnie said good-naturedly. "Spirit next resorts to trickery by arranging unusual events or manipulating a person's awareness to bring the inexplicable into their field of vision." Rocking forward, she stopped to perch on her toes. "Trickery frees a person's attention from their compacted world view. However, personal fears and the elastics of social conditioning cause them to ignore or reason the experience away." Bonnie released her toehold and rocked back. "They think the less doubtful existence of an unseen force wouldn't have practical value, and telling anyone about the event would only label them."

"Like you've proven?"

Nodding, in the affirmative, she said, "The teacher participates at this point so that the prospect knows they're not alone." She rocked back and forth then stopped. "The final stage is an irrevocable act called The Descent of the Spirit. This event shatters the individual's view of reality in some way because it can only be attributed to the direct intervention of an abstract force. So!" she said loudly. "Let's start our search for Intent in your life with your dabbling in the mystical realm; I know you've done this."

Playing her game as best I could, I said, "I had two psychic readings twenty-one years apart. When I was a technical producer for a radio talk show, a guest speaker offered me information during a commercial break, and he finished his thoughts on air before taking more calls; he said I would be leaving radio for television, but I wouldn't end up there and that I would write a book when I was forty-two years old. The second was at a psychic fair—I don't remember it." Anticipating the next question, I said, "I became a community programmer at a rural cable station a few months later. After a year and a half, I moved into real broadcasting because switching jobs is how you work your way up to the big shows. I was twenty-four at the time and sitting at the console of a light bulb wattage radio station, so the psychic wasn't taking a big risk. As for the book, I'm thirty-five now and I can't imagine taking another seven years to finish it."

"You were introduced to the mystical realm earlier in life but not so early that you would bother to struggle with it," Bonnie said. "The psychic didn't say the book would be your first or last, just that you'd write one at age forty-two?"

"Conveniently."

"I told you months ago, there is nothing convenient about dealing with Spirit. That man tapped into the probability that you would become an author at the point in time when it had become inevitable."

[344]

She stretched her legs as she said, "The teaching scheme is designed to prod a student's assumptions with the language of probability and set up lessons that will eventually change these assumptions." She shrugged a miniscule effort. "That's it?"

"That's all."

"All physical events are spiritual at their core, so let's look at an overview of your life."

"My whole life?"

"Do you know someone else's better?"

I cleared my throat and said, "I'm from middle class parents who gave me a carefree upbringing. When my father died, I left high school and joined the Navy. A few years later..."

"Explore that time," she said.

My cooperative spirit took a blow with her ungrateful command, so I focused on the most insipid thing I could think of as a warning for her not to push me.

"In the navy, I developed an accidental interest in dusters—Zane Grey and Louis Lamour westerns—because they were everywhere on board. Asimov and Heinlein sci-fi came after that, then spy novels."

Bonnie stared as if I was taking a leak in the planter, so I made the connection to her world. "I also read books about the mysteries of the pyramids, the Bermuda triangle, runways on top of a mountain in Peru, and one Edgar Cacey book."

"Any other accidents?"

"That's a leap."

"It was your leap," Bonnie said cheerfully. "Accidental interest?"

Technically, my experiences in aircraft were all incidents not accidents, so I bypassed them for a tale about a minor scrape in a car that had a far greater potential for disaster when the on-ramp lane merged with traffic.

Bonnie claimed to have experienced the identical conundrum, of whether to boot it or stand on the brakes, then she led me by saying, "You told me you had an accident in the Navy, when we first talked?"

I told her that winter weather can quickly turn ugly in the Bay of Biscay, a half-moon Atlantic bay that acts like a washing machine for the hundreds of kilometres that it stretches across the northern borders of Spain and France, which is what it was doing while my destroyer, HMCS Nipigon, was conducting a Replenishment At Sea operation with the support ship HMCS Provider.

The wind, initially a gusty fifteen knots, created a sea state that was borderline safe for a R.A.S., but we were seriously short of fuel at the

[345]

conclusion of a NATO exercise. When the breeze freshened to a sustained twenty knots, we had no choice but to terminate the procedure that required us to keep station 150 feet abeam of Provider, doing twelve knots because it didn't take much of a helm mistake, or rogue wave, to suddenly cover that distance.

When the Chief Boson's Mate confirmed for the Deck Officer that all hoses, communications wires, and transfer lines between vessels were clear, the captain ordered Nipigon to full speed with port helm to take us away from Provider.

George and I were stowing the last of the jackstay lines down the forward hatch when the ship falling into a trough, as it turned to weather, caused our heels to leave the deck. We knelt to finish the job as Nipigon punched into the top third of a breaking roller, shuddered as if she was stuck in mud, and then threw us face down on the deck. Recovering, we slammed the hatch shut and lay flat, hanging onto the spindle wheel as the bow twenty feet ahead of us yawed mightily to starboard, cutting a deep groove in the quarter face of the next monster swell. Our 365 foot ship motored as far on the slant as physics allowed before the stern slid off the rolling mass, and we backed into another trough. The unusual angles of momentum and relative motion combined to point the bow toward the sky while twisting the ship broadsides to what had then become howling winds. A huge smack followed, a disconcerting wobble-shudder raced through the superstructure, and Nipigon yawed dramatically toward Provider with our starboard midships scuppers under water. Our helmsman wheeled full opposite rudder, and we began to climb an elongated fluorescent green wall.

Between the ship's buoyancy stored beneath the gunwales and twin screws chewing up huge chunks of ocean on full power, Nipigon rose like a reluctant rocket to punch through a breaking crest, only to plunge like a broken elevator off the back of a square wave. The main deck was awash as we hit bottom dead centre of the trough.

Looking up with round-eyed wonder at the moment of change in our momentum, all we could see was the froth rimmed, curling face of frigid Atlantic effervescence about to sweep us from the world. Anticipating the captain sending my mother a telegram, I clenched my sphincter muscle in a walnut-crushing strain and hoped my grip was just as strong.

It wasn't.

The rush of water tore both of our grasps free, then played pinball with our bodies between bollards on the non-skid deck before depositing George beneath the port side cannon-well breakwater, a three foot high inverted V, and me in a mirror position to starboard. In time, I don't know how much, George got up, didn't see me, and went to report me overboard.

Regaining my senses, I opened my eyes to see a pair of legs draped over the lifelines, realised they were mine, but I couldn't move them. A couple of drenching elevator rides into the bay convinced me this wasn't the worst thing that could happen, and I managed to hoist myself over the breakwater, flopping into the safety of the cannon-well where a lookout eventually spotted me from the bridge. Two days later, the storm subsided enough for a helicopter to take me to Provider, also a hospital ship, where I received my first real medical attention.

I told Bonnie that a radar mast about a hundred feet off calm water line was damaged. I was fifteen feet from the normal water line, so I granted her the miracle that a greeny didn't wash me overboard.

"Nobody had looked for me topside until the ship's interior had been searched," I added, "so I probably should've been swept overboard before I got over the breakwater as well. But I don't see what was so great about tearing my elbow to the bone, cracking three ribs, fracturing my skull, and turning eighty percent of my body the colour of crushed plums."

"In the grander scheme of things there are no accidents," Phillip said, Bonnie having taken a break, I guess.

"In part, you chose this adventure in treacherous waters to experience the inept casualness with which the bridge officers would treat your life. Did you not feel this way?"

"The thought occurred to me while I was congealing on deck like a popsicle."

"You were also less enthusiastic about pursuing that career because you received what you believed to be indifferent medical treatment and no special considerations afterwards. Is this not so?"

"The medic didn't bother to wash me after I had been drenched in salt water. I shook for hours, was itchy all over for days, and any voluntary movement I could make, which wasn't much because I was one big charley horse, registered like a hammer. I've never been hurt like that. A pill would've been nice. A pillow over my face would've been better. Anyway, I asked to be compensated for a broken watch. They said it wasn't required for the job, and they refused."

"Thereby failing to acknowledge your suffering," Phillip said. "Less dangerous events followed, and at levels of awareness unencumbered by self-involvement, you knew that the Navy had served its purpose, so you requested and received an early release."

[347]

I hadn't thought of it that way, but it fit.

"*Now*," the Phillip persona said, with emphasis, "other miracles also took place. Your shipmate escaped unscathed because his purpose was to ensure you would be found. There was also a disruption to your energy field which offered us the opportunity to insert a pulse of energy that we subsequently used to educate you about the dangers that lay ahead. This type of event occurs when there is an agreement between the individual and their Source for it creates a point of change in their evolutionary momentum. There are many stories of individuals becoming psychically aware through apparently accidental means."

"Why use a monster wave when a brick to the head would have done it, and left the rest of me alone?" I said.

"We did not choose to be on that deck."

"From what Bonnie has explained to me about your abilities, you must have known it was coming because you used it for your own purposes instead of influencing things so that I wouldn't have been there."

"Were we so arrogant as to interfere with the essence of personal evolution, neglect our responsibilities, or so cruel as to punish ignorance you would not have survived many incidents. Yet, you are still here, all be it little wiser for your experiences, but that too will change."

Chapter Thirty-seven
Life Strategy

Feeling combatant, I said, "I had an allergic reaction to a cat that drove me from a building into incoming shelling, and I've been saturated, dehydrated, and frozen. Am I missing any more signs of Intent?"

"You chose your own path. View your experiences in this way, and you'll find purpose unfolding with the dawn of each day."

"We stray so often..."

"The design you choose unfolds according to the nature of your beliefs. It follows that even a conscious effort to avoid challenges will bring you face to face with them." Phillip scanned my face, "We realize it is difficult to accept how clever you are," he said cheerfully.

"If my strategy is so good, why do I need your help?"

"The scope of your beliefs is too limited for the time you have left to broaden them on your own. However, to identify the boundaries of your personal attention is the first step to identifying responsibilities from which you need not repeat what has befallen you. Continue to trace the steps that led you to this meeting, and you might see how your strategy was as flexible as free will, and so precise as to have made your arrival inevitable."

"They weren't necessarily mine or thought through for that matter."

"To recall one's journey is the first step in transforming your apparent errors and successes into an encompassing empathy for the efforts of everyone's journey. From this place, recognition of the awesome forces at your command converts the formerly unremarkable into acts of creation. What will you create today?"

Bonnie twisted her neck, implying the Phillip persona was gone, but the unnatural positioning of her hands resting in her lap—upturned, with fingers splayed like a doctor waiting for a drying towel—told me another persona was on stand-by.

I began explaining why I moved from Toronto, but Bonnie interrupted me to say that I had to go further back. I restarted with my move from England, but she stopped me again. A final false start brought me to where Phillip had left off...

"A year after I left the Navy, I was working in a northern Manitoba construction camp with Ed when it burned down, and we transferred to a site where I worked twelve sevens at night. It wasn't long before I figured out that watching generator dials wasn't my calling, so I wrote to colleges in Manitoba and Ontario to see what they had to offer. Radio and television courses caught my attention, and I got an interview in Toronto for the September seventy-four class."

"Where you were supposed to be," Bonnie said.

"My academic history and the communication's director's assessment of my personality would determine if I would be accepted. I didn't meet the first standard because my grade twelve math teacher had told me to leave class until I was ready to learn, and I spent six months in the pool hall waiting for that moment. My father died the day before the final exam, so after I made that point to the director, I was going to imply that I had a genetic predisposition for the course. My mother had written over twenty children's books, and my father had been in radio and print journalism."

"Genetics are the physical manifestation of ideas. You are predisposed," Bonnie said.

I next explained that I had traipsed through a maze of vacant summer corridors until coming upon two men standing in an office doorway where I introduced myself as Mr. Gunkle's one o'clock interview. Gunkle identified himself by grimacing at his subordinate, who immediately offered to do the interview. Michael Monty introduced himself as we passed through a hole in the wall that contained a desk and two chairs; motioning for me to sit, he began reading the short story I was required to prepare as a demonstration of my raw talent. Too soon, he set it aside to read my résumé.

Flicking through pages as if he were reading a teenager's phone bill, I thought I had come a thousand miles to be imposed on a man who couldn't see the top of his desk through the pile of audio and video tapes that would have been filed in a closet had we not been sitting in it. Until his face lit up.

"You're well-traveled," he said, giving me hope.

At the age of twenty-two, I may not have been as mature as parents hope their children will be, but I wasn't stupid. Michael was tanned, and I had overheard Gunkle talking about vacations when I first approached the duo, so I translated Michael's remark to mean, "Have you been to...?"

[350]

I said the Navy had taken me to more places than most young people get to see, then I rattled off my ports of call, adding logical stops in the hope of finding common ground.

"Ah Spain," he said wistfully. "I just came back from there." Which was good but not as good as Portugal would have been; I imported an infamous strip of bars from Lisbon to Malaga.

At this point, Mike leaned forward to talk to John, not his boss's one o'clock, and I risked mentioning a particularly active attraction for seafaring men that I had heard much about. Apparently, one house stood out from the mass of green and rose pastels because it was painted in distinctive Navy grey.

Gently closing a predominantly unread packet of altered truths, a scholastically sombre Michael said he hadn't seen it himself, but he could imagine that the wear path in the cobblestones would make it easy to find. Taking a solemn breath, he then said my experiences and perspectives were suited to a life in the media, a judgement I confirmed by taking him for a beer.

My professional grades were adequate before I jobbed out to a radio station, shortly after which I went to cable TV as a programmer. A year later, a former classmate hired me at a local television station, and a year after that the Canadian Broadcasting Corporation advertised for editors experienced in the new electronic systems. Two weeks passed before I was turned down for that job, but a department head asked me if I'd be interested in becoming a soundman. It was my experience with new technology they were after. Three years later, Doug quit to free-lance in London. I was subsequently resting there between back to back assignments in India and Pakistan when he and a barrel of Guinness got me thinking about freelancing. For want of something to do, the next day I hopped a train to the East Croydon Immigration Office, explained my circumstances then left the decision in the hands of a petite immigration official. To my surprise, she issued me a work visa on the spot.

"Why did you even consider working in England?" Bonnie said.

"I loved London. Different stories."

"Carry on."

"I finished the job in India, came home and quit, sold my sailboat, motorcycle, and sports car to friends, and three weeks later I moved to London."

"Fast and smooth," Bonnie noted.

"I sold cheap. Anyway, I was about to lie down in a Knightsbridge hotel when the I.R.A. car bombed Harrods half a block down the road.

[351]

I was looking out my window at the billowing smoke when CBS phoned. Twenty minutes later, I was working my first freelance job with Sean Bobbit. At seven the next morning, we were on our way to Beirut. After that job, I worked as nonstop as I wanted to work, including all kinds of cushy jobs like touring Scotland's scotch industry, snooker and darts tournaments, rugby—all kinds of fluff stories."

"Hard life," she said dryly.

"It got better. I took time off in the south of France and sailing the Greek Islands. The only crappy thing that happened was that my allergies kicked in big time."

I next explained that my visa would expire while I was out of England, so I got an extension at the airport before leaving for Africa. When I came back, Immigration asked me about the recent date on the stamp, and I told them what I had done. They next asked me how I had obtained my original visa, a story that revealed a problem. Apparently, I should've applied for it from outside the U.K. for it to be valid.

I explained that the issuing officer must have considered me out of the country, in the sense that I was leaving England to quit my job before I would come back to live, but it was a moot point; I had a visa. We argued that point back to the details of my original application, which revealed that I didn't qualify for a work visa—the issuing officer had made a mistake. Maybe so, I said, but I already lived in their country, to which an officer blandly replied, "This is no longer the case."

Another official said it was the responsibility of the air carrier to take illegals back to their point of embarkation, so I was going to be to put on the plane I had just got off and returned to Johannesburg. I explained that I was one of many journalists who had been banned from entering South Africa and that our crew had chartered a plane from Mozambique to catch the SAA connection without going through South African Immigration. In other words, the Republic would send me to Mozambique where my entry visa had expired. I was returning from six weeks covering the famine in Eritrea and Ethiopia and working around another civil war in Mozambique. I was emotionally drained, fatigued from twelve hours on a plane, and stunned at hearing I was a vagrant. I asked them to have a heart.

"We're British," an officer replied as a fourth official arrived at our counter accompanied by a SAA representative. He said that considering where I had come from, South African Airways would be pleased to fly me anywhere in the world. I said nine pounds sterling didn't go far anywhere in the world. I needed access to my bank. This prompted a short conference between the representative and immigration officials who agreed to send me to Canada where the value of my money would more than double: I would have cab fare to a homeless shelter.

The absurdity of suddenly being a penniless refugee had me babbling about my work not taking bread off British tables, when a fifth immigration officer appeared from the Arrivals Concourse escorting my British girlfriend. Realizing I was in some kind of shit because Barbara had greeted the rest of our crew hours earlier, she had approached officials and asked where her fiancé might have gotten lost. Upon hearing this, the first official I had dealt with pointedly asked me why I hadn't mentioned my impending nuptials. I truthfully told him that it had not occurred to me.

The growing gang of officials apparently decided that my oversight was logical for a fellow who believed he was legal, and they grudgingly granted me temporarily permission to enter England. I had to surrender my passport and return the next day for voluntary deportation to wherever I wanted to begin the process of re-entering their country legally.

"That didn't work out, so I went back to Toronto—"

"The design is in the details," Bonnie said.

"The next day, I called or visited everyone I thought could help me, but none of the networks would part with a visa they used to import real employees. Between phone calls and meetings in the West End, I ran into Phillipe, the cameraman I had just worked with in Africa, and he told me that a mutual friend from our Lebanon gigs knew someone who could help me. He gave Maria a call. Half an hour later, Maria had talked to her father, who agreed to arrange a meeting between his friend and me in Paris the next day."

Bonnie held up a hand. "The man you were meeting was a friend of a friend's father, and he agreed to help you?"

"That's it."

"Why?"

"He was Maria's godfather."

"Which doesn't answer the question, but how could he help you?"

"He was the Columbian Ambassador to France. Anyway, I called Ski in Toronto to ask him if I could stay at his place if things didn't work out, and he said it wouldn't be a problem. The next morning, I bought a ticket to Paris before surrendering to British authorities who handcuffed me; their procedures included making a show of handing my passport to the flight crew before removing the cuffs in full view of the other passengers."

"The Ambassador?" Bonnie prompted me.

"Right. He greeted me as if we knew each other, asked about the health of our mutual friends and made nonstop small talk while he drove to a hotel near his embassy. Dropping me off, he said he would pick me up at eleven-thirty the next morning to see the British Ambassador, which he did. Walking into that Ambassador's office, my newest best buddy threw his arm around my shoulder and said, "Nice of you to see us on such short notice, Francis."

"That's quite all—"

"My dear friend has run into the most unfortunate circumstance."

"Well, shall we see what—"

"It's one great misunderstanding!"

"We were done in ten minutes, including obligatory social pleasantries such as, 'Nice country, Canada. Really.'"

"When we left the British embassy, my visa literally looked to be in the diplomatic bag, but the paperwork would take a week to process. Ten days later, my buddy said things would take a little longer. Paris is an expensive place to loiter, so Barbara called travel agencies and found a vacation package in the Canary Islands that would be cheaper. I flew to Tenerife. When I got back, my ambassador buddy said things would take a little longer, which is when I flew here to check out the freelance market."

"The pilot...your screenplay?" Bonnie interjected.

Backtracking, I said that while flying out of Amsterdam, I sat next to a burly, bearded man with a quick wit who successfully feigned interest in my slim-line electronic typewriter. I told him that I was writing a book, gave him some background information, and brought him up to speed on my uncertain situation. When it was his turn, Paul said he was an industrial helicopter pilot—logging, fire-fighting, and construction work—so he knew all about uncertainty. I asked him if he flew with two engines, implying that he had a second chance in his line of work.

"One engine," he said casually, "has exactly enough power to fly you to the scene of the crash."

We drank our way across the Atlantic, then wishing each other well with our uncertain lives at the Vancouver airport, we got on with them.

"While I was checking out the freelance market here, Tom planted the idea of writing a screenplay. When I got back to Europe, and the ambassador diplomatically asked me to pay him for his efforts, I knew it was the end of the line: we both knew I would have given him every-

[354]

thing I had for a work visa. Not long afterwards, I flew to Toronto with about a thousand dollars. It took me six months to get re-established, so I screwed up my credit."

"All of these circumstances," Bonnie said, "pointed to your destiny lying in London until you had the experiences essential to your quest. After that, there was no force on Earth that was going to allow you to stay. You had appointments elsewhere. What next?"

I told her that I built my client base by working steadily for Scarlet Productions, and I lectured at Seneca College whenever Michael felt his students' idealism needed a thrashing. After those sessions, we'd go for a beer to catch up on industry gossip, note how well our ex-wives were doing without us, and discuss our respective novels-in-progress. My lectures seemed to work, so Michael asked me to put together a four-part technical course. I would teach the sound aspect and take care of the personnel requirements of the other three. After that, I landed a cushy job working for the Ontario government, documenting the Spruce Budworm infestation. It was easy because most of the time we worked out of aircraft, and our hours were long. We started at four in the morning, did interviews at midday, then shot another round of flying footage until nine p.m.. We also went to a lot of different sites, three of which became important later on.

"At one of them," I said, "our pilot was a gorgeous blond woman who was a free spirit beneath her professional mask. At another, there was an impossibly straight company man who cracked us up by taking flippant comments seriously: we flew so low that at the right moment I switched on my intercom and said, 'There's an extra fiver in it if you miss that tree.' This guy said he wasn't allowed to take gratuities."

"The other locations?" Bonnie prompted me, again.

"Paul recognized my typewriter case before I remembered him. He was a skim-the-river-at-a-hundred knots kind of guy." I paused. "I paid him about fifty bucks."

"When I was back in the city with serious cash in my jeans and I told Michael that I was frustrated with my book, he encouraged me to write something short to inspire myself, and maybe clear out the crap. I might even get some money and an ego fix from entering a short story contest. Shortly after this, a client told me about a grant process for new screenwriters, and I submitted a proposal for that based on the antics of three helicopter pilots.

"A few months later, I came in the money in the contest, which made me think I was a writer at a time when my relationship with Scarlet was shaky. The company was expanding operations which created a cash flow problem, so I offered to do some unpaid work in exchange for profit sharing when they began hiring new staff. When that time came, the boss reneged, and he refused to pay me for past work. I was still pissed at him when a CBC producer casually asked me how my freelance career was going, and I told him the writing on my last job was soft. He repeated this to one of the professionals Scarlet was wooing, who relayed my remark to the boss with the added spin of a potential employee's angst, and I felt the consequences right away. Scarlet didn't hire me to service a client I had brought to them.

That next day, Michael offered me the possibility of a job that would make freelancing a secondary source of income. The college wanted to start a professional credit, television sound course, the forerunner to which I had already created as an English option. We both believed I was a shoe-in for the position, but I didn't want to burn my still smouldering bridge, so I called Scarlet to apologize, saying that I suspected my remark had been relayed with the momentum of an old acquaintance protecting a friend. Coldly, the boss repeated a distorted version of what had become sinister remarks that could ruin his company's reputation before he blatantly threatened to facilitate my professional demise, if I said anything about his personal behaviour on the road. This is when I clued into the full source of his vitriol: I knew things that could screw him worse than a single comment made in anger, and he was afraid I would leverage that knowledge against his promise. I knew him well enough to not doubt that he would do this. That he had already started undermining me with other clients, if only to make me dependent on him, hadn't crossed my mind.

In a final salvage effort, I went back to the producer and repeated what the boss said I had said, making it clear that I was in a tenuous situation. Admittedly, I had been indiscreet, and already lost work because of it, but the exaggerations had to be put straight.

"Instant justice," Bonnie said.

"The producer looked shocked," I said, "and claimed that he had simply repeated my comments in passing to someone we both knew wasn't prone to exaggerations. I asked him to call Scarlet anyway, which he agreed to do. The next day, I contacted the boss and received a frosty, 'Scripts are in development.' I understood this meant we would never work together, but he wouldn't poison my well if I didn't shit in his backyard. Forfeiting my back pay was his pound of flesh. Soon afterwards, a call from a fellow freelancer made it clear that I was already tainted and that it had been the boss who had created the exaggerations he then spread to friends in the business."

[356]

I told Bonnie that, later that week, the dean of communications offered me the position of the staffer they had hired to teach the course I had designed. The upside of this surprise was that I had an opportunity to regroup, and it didn't matter that I knew nothing about the quad format video tape system I was supposed to teach because it was obsolete. The technological boom was on, digital frame-storers were changing history from 'as it happened,' to emphasizing how it happened one thirtieth of a second at a time. Simple back-timers, slow motion, fades, and wipes were suddenly at a single editor's finger tips, which screamed there would be no need for a quad teacher next year. Another irking circumstance was that the other fellow had never worked in my field. In addition, I was unexpectedly angered that the first year students I had recently taught were going to learn nothing useful from me, at least not from the curriculum, and less than what they should learn from the other fellow.

For the first time, I seriously contemplated Ed's regular telephone offer of a free place to stay in Vancouver. I could help financially when I took on freelance work, he always said, otherwise I was not to worry if my income was zero. I called him to see if the offer was still good.

"When's your flight?" was all he said.

I went out for a couple of beers to decide whether I wanted to teach, or chuck everything to become a writer, and I came home swaying toward teaching as I opened my mail to discover that I had been awarded the grant. Without consulting Michael, who assumed I would accept the teaching position, I wrote a letter to the dean of communications in which I said I didn't understand what the school was doing, but I wouldn't be a part of screwing the students.

"That's it. I flew here, and Tom set up our meeting."

"Not until after your screenplay problem," Bonnie corrected me.

I told her more about the problem with my plot, which Tom resolved by suggesting that I contact a helicopter service to find out the lifting capacity of their biggest machine. The company secretary told me their Sikorski was the second largest civilian helicopter in the world, and that it could place a massive electrical transmission tower on a dime or lift ten tons of trees at the end of a cable in a dangerously exacting technique called long-lining. You had to be nuts to do it.

This was good stuff, but the pieces didn't come together in my mind until she said the Skycrane flew from one job to another carrying a complete modular apartment beneath it. I envisioned the great machine lifting a broken Jet Ranger out of a fire, being held back by the downwash of hundred foot rotor blades.

[357]

"The secretary said the pilots would be in at noon the next day. If I wanted to see their machine to research my work, I could ask them. Paul walked in the room just after twelve."

"Can't you feel a sense of being in all of this?" Bonnie said.

"It was a long road—like this story."

"Look at the pivot points: Ed, Michael, the East Croydon immigration officer, Paul, Tom, your friend in Argentina?" she paused.

"Manny."

"All of them opened and closed chapters to either keep you safe, sane, or push you to your next appointed experience, and the one possession to survive this journey was an omen of your path—the typewriter led you to me."

"I'll give you all of the manifestations of Spirit you like because by definition that applies to everyone at some point in their lives, but I don't see where that Knock thing comes into it. Doesn't a teacher have to know about it?"

"When we left the hotel, you walked straight to my car."

"As opposed to crookedly?"

"Why was I late?"

"A newspaper blew onto your windshield."

"Specifically, a page that pictured a car accident, so I changed my route to avoid the possibility of having one, and I didn't stop until it felt right." Focusing on my confused expression, she said, "Leading us to my car was no accident. You thought you had options, just like you did when the rolling force of Phillip's intentions brought you to Vancouver." She leaned back. "Telling you to take charge was Saa-ra's idea and an act of faith for me to trust that things would work out."

"Uh-huh," I said, appreciating the cleverness with which Bonnie had clad the simple coincidence. She breathed deeply, and seemed to be content to let the sleeping dog lie.

Chapter Thirty-eight
The Truth

Days later, I turned into Bonnie's driveway to pick her up for a rare dinner out, a gift from a client we had both worked with, when the evening view across the inlet between her house and her neighbour's shrubbery reminded me of a particularly beautiful part of Lebanon, possibly because it wasn't on fire. The incongruity of those remarkably hospitable people turning their nation into rubble saturated my mind like repressed sorrow cresting the dam of denial, disturbing quandaries that had rippled beneath my peace of mind for months. Not the least of these was her general state of sanity, a thought prompted by why an otherwise intelligent person would continue to view Josh as a potential partner. Nothing personal, just that the incongruity was staggering. Somehow, this did not apply to me.

I tapped on the side door and let myself in, forcing a jaunty, "Ready to go?"

"Ready," Bonnie said, over the sound of bi-fold doors sliding through metal tracks. "Kha-lib just..."

"Hold on—it's normal time," I interrupted her as I climbed the stairs.

"Pardon me?" Her voice floated hollow out of the hallway closet.

"We fed the brain all morning. It's time to digest things, literally," I said, reaching the top landing as Bonnie came out from behind the door with one sleeve stalled halfway up her arm. Misinterpreting her stance, I stepped forward to help her on with her coat, but she froze her pose leaving me holding one shoulder of the garment as if I was dressing a mannequin.

"You use love as a weapon to manipulate people according to your moods," she said, flatly, "I'll survive without your affection if need be, but I have no intention of changing who I am for anyone."

"Sorry if it came out wrong," I said, letting go and taking a step back. "You know diplomacy isn't my strong suit." I grinned crookedly.

"That's because you never stayed long enough to develop it with anyone who disagreed with you, and there was nothing inadvertent about your remark. It was calculated to see if I care more about keeping your company than I do about speaking my mind."

"We've established that I'm not a strategic thinker." I cocked my head.

"Thinking has nothing to do with it," Bonnie said, continuing her serene assault. "Your predisposition is to manipulate social exchanges so that you can tell people how to act while establishing the terms of a treaty before a hostile word is even spoken."

Caught in the undertow of whatever was really on her mind, I thought the only safe escape was to go with the flow until I could edge my way out of her current focus. Giving her comment a moment's thought, I said, "I think that's how everyone negotiates relationships. Our tone and facial expressions are essentially saying, 'This is what I'm like. If you don't like it, we can each move on. If you do, we can take the next step.'"

"Personal peace can't be negotiated. It requires that one confronts their flaws, like yours of baiting mini battles to establish a right-of-way through people's hearts."

I was about to call her on the feint of shifting from peaceful relationships to personal peace but I realised this would probably make her misery about me, when her tranquil savaging of my innocent comment had to be about Josh. So it would remain.

"I'll throw myself down the stairs as punishment if that will help."

"Not even if the issue was about forgiveness," she said coolly.

"Notwithstanding that I have apologized—almost twice?" I said, with a boyish grin.

"Your rough charm and contrived sincerity doesn't fool me. You not only avoided taking responsibility for your comment, you shuffled it back on me."

"How about this," I said as I took a step down, "I won't be charming, so you won't be concerned about being fooled, and neither of us will feel like we have to change anything while we eat? Let's go."

"Or you'll go without me?"

"What?"

"You don't realize how you telegraph your intentions because you're so entrenched in self-defence that even trivial circumstances become negotiations over who is in charge."

"Because I took a step closer to the restaurant?"

"Because you can't just like someone: you are always confirming your status with me and testing your position in ways you don't realize, like every time you stamp your approval by saying, 'Done' instead of,

[360]

'That sounds like a good idea,' or, 'Thanks Bonnie, I'll try that.'"
Dragging her coat, Bonnie closed the physical gap between us. "Somewhere along the way, you saw yourself as a product of a world you
abhor, which is why you use words as weapons whenever anyone
threatens your moral hideout by suggesting you're one of them."

"One of them, who?"

"Them is everyone who has been tricked into doing the unspeakable
because they are told from the cradle that it is necessary, then they are
betrayed by realizing their actions became necessary only because they
agreed to participate. This is why trick and betray are synonymous to
you."

"How was I tricked?"

"You covered stories that could only add fuel to the fire, while your
industry made huge profits under an altruistic banner that personal
events in Argentina ripped to shreds. That's when you realised it wasn't
your job to educate people. Your focus on financial retribution hid the
fact that you were playing the same game at a higher level, and you
kept going back to reclaim your losses."

"I didn't lose anything. To the contrary." I said no more.

"You discovered you were up to a task that few people are willing to
do, and fewer can do well, but you had to suppress the price you paid
to feed your accomplice; acknowledging that you enjoyed it."

"Maybe a rush now and then…."

She held up her hand. "There are no maybes in an essential act. You
accumulated cars and boats based on other people's misery and death,
and you enjoyed your work."

"I didn't create their circumstance, and the things I bought came
from the possibility of joining them," I said, not believing I was
hearing this.

"By your own words, you didn't believe it could happen to you
when you began covering wars, and by the time you quit, you didn't
care if it did kill you, so where was the risk?" Bonnie suddenly looked
concerned. "I'm sure your sniper kills LeBlanc because he's a metaphor for the spiritual death of all people of good heart who are tricked
into going to war. That metaphor worries me."

"I really don't know what you're getting at or how we got here," I
said plaintively.

"I'm getting at what you are like and why you are like this."
Looking at her hands as if they held crib notes, Bonnie quoted me
without inflection. "They chose to stay. It meant certain death, and it

[361]

didn't matter to them." The angle of her gaze and short distance between us were awkward, so I took two steps down as she continued.

"It was too painful to recall something your mind had tucked away,
but your body remembered everything about that moment; you recalled
the families begging you to protect them. They didn't know about your
dead colleagues or that the most dangerous place to be was in the
jungle." She leaned against the staircase. "The echoes of those shots
manifest in your every waking diatribe and nightmare that questioned
whether you could have saved anyone; or maybe you think you should
have died in the attempt. Either way, you carried that guilt with you,
adding to it with every encounter that fed your sense of impotence.
What Kha-lib wanted you to know when you first arrived tonight, was
that we all volunteer for events for our own reasons. When and where
everyone stood their ground, lay down, or were put to rest, was a
choice. You can stop being a casualty of conscience by assessing
events in a new light. It might help you to know that your personal
killing blow came in Makelle."

"No one who wasn't there knows anything about Makelle," I
snapped icily.

"And no one who wasn't in Vietnam," Bonnie said, with a dismissive wave, "and no one who wasn't at Normandy, said the fathers
who repeated their grandfather's words about the war to end all wars."

"You claimed my experiences were unique." I guffawed.

"I said they are unique by virtue of what their totality represents, and
you have yet to explore what that is. Instead, you've spent enormous
energy on quandary then anger, when I've done nothing more than
show you how to turn a missed shot into a positive lesson."

Too late to retreat with dignity, my mind whirled in search of the
illusive reason that would explain her overall grand effort, fancifully
fearful claims, sudden personal attacks, and multiple impersonations: I
knew beyond an intellectual grasp that we all give ourselves away,
which had to include Bonnie.

Far from the first time when I felt critically pressed, my mind began
to unwind reasons like a slinky going downstairs, culminating on her
key manipulation. She had coerced me into accepting metaphysical
concoctions by treating them as facts that had suffocated my common
sense and blinded me to what was really going on: Her endless casual
tirades were not about distancing herself vertically from an inferior
world, they were about conquering it to make it safe. Bonnie had been
making herself ready to reveal a secret to herself, about herself, from

[362]

the moment she labelled me the bad guy, by having her personas defeat my representative beliefs.

"Anytime," she said.

I swallowed once from reluctance, and once from embarrassment, then I stepped beyond the edge of our relationship. "You haven't written your ending because you've been counting on me to free you from a secret. The psychological bombshell you think you're leading me to is about learning why you are the way you are, not how I became the way I am. We already know that."

"And?" She tilted her head patiently.

"You said the human experience is not complicated because outside of our core drives, everything we do is a clue to seeing ourselves as we really are. This is why we design the lives we do and why you said my book reveals why I think the way I do. So does yours. Later, you told me about moving a lot when you were a kid, you also had a liberal attitude toward sex, in your adolescence at least, and you've had thousands of comfort dreams with super-powerful friends."

I waited for her to catch on, like she had so often done with me, but she didn't.

"Look between the lines of your work. Your male characters are all hard-ass masters of something, your women pretend to be timid when they're actually manipulating men for their own safety, and your teachers have unusual bonds with children in a culture conformed to secrecy."

Bonnie's amused expression dropped into a canyon, trapping a protest in her throat; it was time to leap to the truth she had been so meticulous at setting up for herself.

"The memory game you played on me was a ruse you were playing on yourself. If I found a red flag that revealed something terrible had happened to me, you had permission to surface what happened to Aleena, Jehaneh, and every other aspect of your personality that was set adrift by shattering childhood experiences. 'Not becoming a casualty of their internal disputes,'" I quoted her. "The townies punishing kids, ready to be played by cruel men, they would be empty without fear." The definitive quote poured into my mind. "'I can write about Aleena's life changes as a victim of men.'"

I made the final leap.

"The world's insanity is a metaphor for men's cruelty in general, and your dad's barbarity specifically, which brought about the conditional death of your childhood. Everything you said I'm blind to reflects your desperation to trust anyone, and you're trying to reclaim the loss of not

[363]

fitting in by exalting trees and clouds as a kind of litmus test for people's level of caring or malice. Your meta-double talk is about assessing your core assumptions in order to surface knowledge silenced by shame and the judgements of your neighbours because you acted out the disgrace that happened to you with their children in the sand box. I also think you refused to explain some things early on, not because it wasn't time for me to hear them, but because the explanation was still a hazardous place to go; you hadn't beaten the crap out of me to make yourself feel safe in the world you're trying to re-join. Shit," I said as another piece of the puzzle found its place. "That's when you embraced miracles."

"Which were?" Bonnie said, finding her voice.

"A little girl becoming old enough to remember despicable things meets a messenger from God. He says the world will get worse before it gets better, but he'll be there for her. She believes him in her retreat to a place without sensations, where fear is out-dated, and she has faith in her rescue because the ultimate master is benevolent with servants who explore Universes with him. As she gets older, she has to adjust the metaphor; the stars that surrounded her become a disco ball that can explain everyone's actions, except it can't protect her. It can only warn her about people, so she starts speaking with guardian angels about parking spaces."

"Why would she do that?"

"You know you're safe when God cares where you park."

"Do you have more?" she said, with a disconcerting calm.

"Just that all of the time you spent trying to convince me the world is coming to an end was about you coming to terms with the secret that would put an end to your cultural conformation as a child. In the meantime, being on a mission from God gave meaning to what happened to the chosen one, who had suffered for salvation. Your journey is unique by virtue of what its totality represents because the rescue mission isn't just about you; you designed and executed it to find yourself." I took a deep breath. "It's an amazing thing you have done and not just a little bit scary by using me to identify the source of the fears you had to neuter," I admitted.

"You are a truly amazing man," she said sincerely. "I can't begin to imagine how much effort you spent gathering those pieces."

"Your defence is that you have a limited imagination?" I took another step down, shifted my weight to my good hip, and waited to hear her interpretation of our interactions. I owed her that much.

[364]

"I have nothing to defend." Bonnie closed her eyes and speaking in a disinterested tone said, "As usual, you have got it backwards: I scratched *your* mirror of self-reflection by asking for intimate details of your decision making process and the stories you used to describe yourself. You regularly hid from this knowledge and punished me through threats like, 'I still don't know that coming here was the best thing to do', and by taking shots at my premises to repair the damage you think I had done to you. Your retaliations had no effect, so the next time I injured one of your beliefs you made up an excuse to leave, but truth is relentless, so I didn't have to try to stop you. You next made sure I understood the grave risk I was taking by ignoring me for days, and when I didn't fall to my knees when you came back, you quad-rupled the threat by vanishing after Kha-lib's first channel. You did all of this to maintain the illusion that you knew better than a middle-aged divorcee, which forced you to bend reasons, crush facts, and throw away whatever didn't fit to come up with your magnificent concoction, all to keep your own secret safe from you."

"I took a sabbatical when there was a lot to think about," was all I could argue.

"Without an explanation to a friend you've been seeing every day?"

"Without your parting words influencing what I'm trying to figure out."

"That would fly if we both didn't know the mindset that creates a problem can't solve it, and your mindset of running away is your historical focus." She counted on her fingers before I could protest. "You ran into the navy when your father died, you quit when they wouldn't acknowledge you almost died with as little as a replacement watch, you escaped to England after your fiancée dumped you, then you came here after your error in judgement in Toronto. You've also been testing me like you tested your mother ever since we met. 'If you love me, you'll let me get my way.' If I don't buy it, you take a sabbatical."

"My moves were always a financial or professional step forward."

"All the better to conceal the underlying act of moving to new territory, where you recreated the circumstances you left behind because you didn't deal with them properly. And how do you benefit when you pick up your pace on our walks?"

"How fast I walk is a personal failing?" I sneered.

"Distancing yourself implies that you're willing to keep on going unless your friends recognize the threat of losing what was destined to be fleeting relationships, anyway."

[365]

"Being alone is my destiny?"

"You created that cycle." Bonnie shifted her feet. "You fictionalized critical events to make things clearer to me and the women before me, knowing that only the experience could provide their true context. Your secret goal was to trap our intrigue between innocence and revulsion, to make us feel vulnerable. If that moment arrived in our eyes, the predacious aspect of seeking relief from your experiences would pounce to comfort us both. But somewhere along the way, you discovered that enhancing events made them less real to you, and your practice became a Band-Aid fix on a gaping wound because you knew that sharing a stark peek at the unthinkable was light years from it peering into their souls. Your relationships had to end with confrontations because you didn't know the true source of your pain, and you never looked back to see yourself through other people's eyes to try to find it."

"Come on. A lot of people just want to have a little fun and forget it." I said, without thinking.

"When did this happen?" she said, challenging my diversion.

"When I was sailing in the Med," I said as if this was my only transgression.

"You were a social privateer plundering favours from a willing tourist trade," she said without pausing. "You did not see yourself as a thief of a lethargic heart when a yarn captivated a wayward waif. You were a free spirit spending grand adventures on intense comfort while, with corresponding brevity, banishing a stranger's boredom to her own illusions. It looked like a no-harm no-foul circumstance, but the reckless pursuit of compliant prey is an extension of how you maintain your sense of superiority."

"Shit, I stole apples when I was a kid," I snapped. "How does that rank in the grand scheme of extra-terrestrial crimes?" I said, immediately feeling like I had launched sneeze-spittle toward a first date's wine glass.

Calmly, Bonnie took a step down to my eye level and tapped me lightly on my chest. "Sarcasm may be the most damaging of your manipulations because it's purposefully aimed at the heart of the unwary for no reason other than to punish them for offending you. Trust me," she said, leaning so close that the word "trust" thrust a fog on my glasses, "you don't want emotional blackmail coming back to you." She leaned back millimetres. "It leads to complications that can take lifetimes to resolve, and your next few are already booked. If you can't help yourself, at least try to limit your insecurities to the transparent condescension of small-minded men so that the harm you intended is laughable." Finally noticing her indecorous state, Bonnie slid her arm out of the sleeve and made a peace offering of her coat. I took it from her and stepped sideways to create room to hold the garment open.

Leaving me posing like a matador, she said, "As is your custom, you've bled our relationship dry of comfort, and the pressure of maintaining even cordial contact with me will soon force you to run. You need to know that you've got nowhere to go that won't become the same old circumstance, and I'm afraid for what you might do when you discover that."

Lowering the coat, I huffed and said, "Me bleed you dry? I've told you all I know about screenwriting, and I've been your guinea pig long enough to know you can finish it on your own if I can!" Defiantly, "Shit, that's what this is about…you're trying to break our deal and scoop the whole grant!"

Gawking with injured surprise, the underlying truth melted through Bonnie's face, and my smugness withered with the sharing of another intimate moment. She knew.

I felt like throwing up.

Pursing quivering lips, Bonnie stepped down to our final engagement distance of a single tread and riser, where I unblinking awaited the parting shot I deserved. At least it would all be over.

Confusing me to the marrow, Bonnie placed her hands on my shoulders for balance, and leaning forward kissed me gently on the forehead. Pushing away lightly, she said, "You can accept whatever the night may bring in the same way that I've accepted who you are without conditions, or you can call the evening off… to consider what I've just said, of course."

"Let's go," I said, with as much dignity as I could fake.

"Done!" she joked.

Mechanically, I walked down the stairs to the landing where I realised I had to chose between opening the door or holding open her coat. Handing her the garment, I said, "Fool me once."

"Once?" she chortled, stepping into the cool evening air.

Chapter Thirty-nine
The End of the Beginning

On the way to the restaurant, I told Bonnie that I cared for her just the way she was, and she said she cared for me beyond words, literally. Nevertheless, it was a subdued drive for me, the meal but a diversion from the awkwardness I continued to feel over my intended betrayal, as we compared the challenges and rewards of having cats or dogs as pets.

It was not until we were looking over the dessert cart with our server hovering, that Bonnie turned her attention to personal matters. Even then, it was as a whimsical refrain that she said, "Your experiences with me should have opened your mind to Intent's propositions by now," she grinned slyly, "considering that we've talked about the core events of your life."

Surprising me no more, this idea had just been displaced by darker thoughts of me having lived a mean, if not meaningless life, so I wasn't peeved to realize that Bonnie had carefully cajoled me into a Teyo-like recapitulation of key events to have me see a bigger picture. It didn't work, anyway.

Sombrely, I said, "I think the path was too intense. I guess I'm not up for anymore adventures, except maybe that raspberry thingy that looks like a coronary threat." I nodded at Evelyn.

"That's understandable," Bonnie said, pointing at a lemon tart topped with a strawberry hat, seated in meringue. "Seeing everything you came here to see came at a high price."

Prudently, Evelyn served us without comment, withdrew a step, and wheeled the cart away.

"Months ago," Bonnie said, focusing on my plate, "Kha-lib told me that your quest was personally expensive, but I didn't fully appreciate it until tonight on the stairs." Taking a small bite, she said, "Umm," pointing her fork at my plate.

"You know, it's not that I don't want to believe you, especially since I've had more strange stuff happen than I've told you about," I spoke the most honest words I had probably said since our first meeting, "but

I can't get past the idea that you're manufacturing a Universe to suit your story, and maybe some experiences, no different than you claim I've done with mine—notwithstanding that billions of people would believe my version. No offence."

Carefully setting her fork down, Bonnie patted the corners of her mouth delicately with a vermilion cloth, then placing it aside, reached across the table to cover my hand with hers. I studied her cheerless expression for signs of mischief but found only empathy as she softly said, "When we first met, you delivered your stories with an undertow designed to drag me into acknowledging your intellect and to conjure courage out of ill-conceived exploits, then you played down your role to luck while pummelling me with jabs of horror. That only made sense if you were defending secrets you held about yourself by placing experiences I haven't had in the way of my reasoning."

"I'm not arguing, but why would I want to defend something I don't know about?"

"But you do know, and you gave it away the first time we met: you used death as a job opportunity in the first story you wrote." She raised her brow.

I couldn't muster a cogent rebuttal.

Bonnie continued making her point.

"I showed you chapters that were about you, beginning with Aleena counting on her smarts to keep her safe, and Tartuu immediately leading her intellect down the garden path of shallow praise to demonstrate the folly of her ploy. You didn't get it, so I showed you more directly applicable chapters like the stranger at the harvest celebration. When you didn't see yourself in his glib remarks, I gave you the second part which foreshadowed what was coming your way with me. This was around the time you began having more vivid experiences in your mental meanderings, which were gifts from Spirit to help loosen your compressed views and see your reflection in my story. Even with the direct energy injections that you experienced as sudden fatigue, you remained blind to anything personally relevant, so all I could do was make sense of your experiences directly. There is no easy way to face ourselves, so you thought I was being a bitch for reasons you eventually conformed to suit your explanation tonight, and you became derisive to the point of scorning the concept of decency itself. This is something you wouldn't have done unless you believed you had lost yours, which you first confirmed when I prodded your conscience about Sammi. Anyone else would have conceded that making noise may have helped him, but you became angry because you think you acted cowardly from the moment they didn't take you away with him, no different than how key events in El Salvador made you feel." She leaned back to give me room to comment, but I saw no point in complaining about a headache at a beheading, so I waited for the axe to fall.

"An hour ago," she said, "you jokingly gave yourself away by offering to sacrifice the very thing you chose to challenge in me by throwing yourself down the stairs, your integrity. You wouldn't have done that if you thought you had any, not even in jest." She drew a controlled breath; I understood we were standing on my ledge now.

"You're ravaged by a relentless conscience conformed by aberrant ideas, and the jagged emotions generated from daring to learn all there is to know about malice and the encompassing senses of helplessness, guilt, and shame these experiences brought. You are a warrior who came to believe he was a coward, and to defend yourself from this judgement, you lashed out at everyone who came too close to seeing you. The price you paid to claim mankind's most destructive secrets as personal knowledge is that you loathe yourself." She squeezed back tears. "And you've still not given up."

"You think so?" I said as a prelude to giving up.

"I know so. The focus of your arguments has changed from defending your ideas to trying to understand mine, which is doing the right thing for the right reason as an act of faith that voluntarily sets your ego aside. Doing this opened the door to Spirit shifting your perceptions to a new level of learning that most people would have dismissed as mental tricks, or tried to run from, but you embraced them as valid experiences, regardless that you couldn't explain them." She held up a hand to stifle my protest. "What you thought you were doing doesn't matter. You acted as if these were signs of awakening knowledge, and at the risk of your life as you know it, you've been gathering energy to assess your inventory: every day for months I've presented you with the piffling dares and resulting brutality of men's bravado, and you're still here. This is an extraordinary achievement at the end of a crushing journey." She smiled as though at an injured puppy.

"You have no idea how often or how close I came to leaving, and you really can't believe I'll quit writing my story my way. It's all I have."

Bonnie's look of mystification reminded me of the Canadian ambassador's wife at an embassy dinner in Brasilia, when LeBlanc farted at a pitch that betrayed a hundred percent humidity as he asked her to pass the bread.

[370]

"Quit?" she said, when she remembered to breath. "It's key."

"To what?"

"Yes or no," she said, inspecting me for signs self-awareness, "you've covered flood, famine, drought, earthquake, pestilence, and war?"

"I guess."

"There's no guessing about it, you've seen the end unfolding." A ribbon grin momentarily crimped her lips. "Picture your string map; flood, famine, drought," she said, using her fork as a conductor's baton to move my thoughts through the signs of the apocalypse.

"Getting fucked up made me special?" I said as that deception warmed my face.

"Those experiences encompass how we create and react to circumstances that ultimately contribute to humankind's most extreme behaviours. In a profound way, you're a crowd that has been conformed to embrace apocalyptic beliefs."

"What do beliefs have to do with earthquakes?" I said, groping for a sense of balance—of reason.

"Unrestrained nuclear testing, sapping the earth of its tectonic lubricant, levelling forests that clean the air and keep the earth in place, draining marshlands that filter water. Shall I go on?"

"Why choose me?" I tried to say as a demand, but it warbled.

"Give me a moment. Saa-ra is here."

I had time enough only to wet my dry mouth with ice water before Bonnie's eerie gaze of fire and steel welded my ass to the chair.

"Unrecognized and unchecked," she said, flatly, "generations of mankind have condensed and assimilated their capacity for malice and horror to the degree that even a man born in the grace of infinite love and raised with boundless clemency blithely participated in the madness. You chose this path to become a great grandchild of the Somme, a grandson of Normandy, and a child of Vietnam to maul your beautiful spirit in the chaos of your times. You have seen the end, and you have become it. Now, as your nations lead their children down the path of ruin, the momentum of their egomaniacal focus is methodically killing every relationship they have in and to your world, just as you do. A crucial lesson you all must, and will soon embrace as your own knowledge, is that fear is not a consequence of warfare, it is its *source*." She dredged the last word like a bucket of toxic waste from the bottom of an industrial harbour. Most harbours, I suppose.

"So tell us young warrior, who weeps bittersweet acrimony over the threads of his humanity, who better to explain the source of mankind's dire circumstances than the archetype aberrant man seeking himself under the brilliant light of his own demise?"

"Explain to who? Are you saying I'm supposed to write about the screwed up world in Bonnie's imagination?" I scoffed.

"Your purpose is to find yourself amid the madness."

"Hers, you mean."

"It is a quest that will soon pass a point of change," Saa-ra said, ignoring my comment. "We love you."

"Maybe we should just be friends." I stood to go to the men's room.

When I came back, Bonnie had put a twenty-dollar tip under the vase, so I gave her a ten without comment and pulled out the chair for her. The short drive back was quiet but not awkward for me because everything that could be said was out there. No secrets, no angst. Nothing left, really.

Getting out of her car in the driveway, I declined her offer of a decaf coffee because I had a legitimate job in the morning. "A bird guy is speaking about fences screwing up the migratory crawl of bugs which screws up the food supply," I said.

"Ornithologist," Bonnie said as I straddled and started my 550cc machine.

"You just can't help it, can you?"

"It seems that neither of us can," she said, ending our confrontation scene.

Chapter Forty
The Descent of Spirit

L ying restlessly on my futon, the evening's conversation circled annoyingly around my mind until a cascading mixture of ire and helplessness modeled a revelation framed in humiliation. I so deeply resented Bonnie's deceptions that I had no interest in continuing a relationship in any form. In spite of inexplicable events apparently 'stalking' me, as Bonnie described it, I simply didn't have an act of faith left in me, and within the freedom of again having no expectations in life, I rolled over and fell into a deep sleep.

Around half past three, I awakened from a dream that was lost as soon as I realised I was dreaming, but it left behind a mental itch I could not scratch. I passed time by rehearsing how I was going to tell Bonnie I was finished without creating a scene; her efforts and my experiences made it almost impossible for me to just run.

The alarm went off while I was staring at it.

I showered, then met Matt and a local producer, who did the interview with the bird guy, after which we walked around the park taking generic cover footage because there were no bugs of this particularly sensitive species to be found. My day was over in three hours, so I picked up a couple bottles of wine on the way home, jogged, showered again, and called Bonnie. She said she was parched. Twenty minutes later, I led her to commenting on her client's interests, to open the door through which I intended to make my escape.

"I'm not surprised that she didn't accept what you said," I commented. "My world still makes more sense to me, the contradictions you've chipped away at notwithstanding."

"Chipped away?" Bonnie exclaimed as if I had plugged her finger into a 220V outlet. "I've blasted all reason out of them, but you won't let go!"

"Actually, I have thought about…"

"Do you ever wonder what it would be like to just write? Where would you go if you could do that?"

"Some place warm, I guess. I've thought about…"

[373]

"There wouldn't be any guessing about it for me."

Exuberantly, Bonnie filled out her fantasy before apologizing for monopolizing our time, then she asked me about my ideal living conditions in excruciating detail, thereby monopolizing our time.

We explored another wish, and then another, as the afternoon became an evening that passed in a gentle blur until my body called it quits around ten. I was home in bed by a quarter to eleven and asleep soon afterwards, only to again awaken with the feeling there was something I should know. Glancing at the digital clock, I saw that it was three twenty-seven, exactly the same time I had looked at the clock the night before. The feeling passed, and I went to sleep.

In passing the next morning, I told Bonnie about the coincidence, and she said Phillip was delivering a message, "How was my morning writing session?" "Isn't it a gorgeous day?" etc., leaving me no opportunity to tell her this was our last gorgeous day together... except there was little reason to rush things, because Bonnie was a hoot to be with when she left her elves in the forest.

At three twenty-seven the next morning, I awoke with an over-powering sense that I should know something. For lack of a better idea, and no one would ever know, I imagined sending a messenger into the cosmos, then I watched the tree shadows cast from a street lamp dance on my wall while waiting for the postal fairy to return.

In a short while, an old joke nestled into my thoughts and wouldn't leave me alone: East Berlin guards at Checkpoint Charlie suspected that a man, who crossed from the west every morning, was smuggling something, so they regularly stripped his shiny CCM bicycle, but they never found anything hidden in the frame. Neither did the night shift when they checked his dilapidated Russian built pedal machine.

This ruse cycled in my head until I realised my messenger had returned; the obvious was the answer—I was being awakened.

The itch was scratched, I went back to sleep, and in the morning I said nothing to Bonnie about this experience, lest I interrupt another great day of wine and wishful thinking. To test my supposition that night, I decided that if I again awakened early, which I did, I would allow a few minutes to pass before I looked at the clock, which I did at exactly three twenty-seven.

Six hours later, Bonnie was enjoying herself like a parolee revelling in the freedom passers-by no longer appreciate, and although I was curious about my early morning awakenings, I didn't risk breaking her spell by talking about them. My decision to remain quiet subsequently caused me to realize that the ambiance of pending conflict, which had reigned over our meetings since she had first interrogated me at the English Bay Café, was gone. In fact, it had been for days. Again, we shared a carefree day, reluctantly parting company in the late afternoon as if it was Christmas Eve and we were going home to wrap ourselves for each other.

At three twenty-seven the next morning, I rolled over and said to the ceiling, "If you guys are here, move my hand." It was the first thing that came to my mind.

A digital minute passed before, feeling sillier by the second, I assumed my usual sleeping position on my right side with my arm under my head. Wiggling my hip into a non-prognosticating position, I was falling into shallow breathing when my right arm shot out from beneath the pillow, striking the wall so hard that I didn't think I had dreamed it. Rolling over to face the ceiling, I said, "Was that you?" not caring if Ed could hear me from his room.

I waited for something to happen for minutes, before deciding the event was a trick of my mind, as the time between my request and its manifestation logically suggested. Rolling onto my stomach, I had just placed my hands flat on either side of me for a hip shift when a blunt force struck me heavily between the shoulder blades knocking me breathless while pushing my face deep into the pillow. Instantly outraged, I rolled onto my back and challenged the ceiling, "If you're really here, do something undeniable, and let's be done with this shit!"

Of course, I was stuck for what this deed might be because I didn't consider recent events undeniable. Then it came to me. "Pick me up," I demanded obstinately, "and I won't ever question you again, or fuck off, and get out of my life!"

My challenge and shallow promise warbled into a pleading, "Put me down! Put me down!" as I rose toward the light fixture and then gently back down.

Sucking air as if the atmosphere had sprung a leak, I asked infantile questions of myself to establish that what I thought happened really had. Did I have the ability to awaken myself at the same time every morning? Did I want to break my fist on a wall? Was I secretly so depressed over quitting that I would try to smother myself? Had I been oxygen deprived, and made up my flight? All of the answers literally left me staring at the most irrational, but inescapable conclusion, and time passed like gelatine through a straw while I pondered my curiously puny life.

I phoned Bonnie as soon as the seven blinked on the clock.

"You're early," she said, answering on the first ring.

[375]

"Are you interested in adjoining rooms at whatever institution we're heading for?"

"We?" she said, tittering, which soon became undulating snickering as I told her about the Universe's attempts to reach me, and finally howling laughter through which she managed a choking, "Put me down! Put me down!" until she banged her head on the backboard of her bed.

I knew that sound—not her bed—but not until that moment did I realize how much humour it contained.

When my own gasping eventually transitioned into a weary panting, Bonnie brought me to my knees by role-playing a solo conversation with my admitting psychiatrist.

"Und zo, how long have you been levitating?" she said, in an Inspector Clouseau imitation.

"First time, Doc, but the broad in the next room worked for months to make me ready for it," she imitated my blasé manner.

"Zee one who hears voices?"

"Actually, it's telepathy. That's a common thing for mothers who…"

"Yes, yes, und do you hear these voices?"

"She says I will."

"Ziss does not trouble you?"

"Fuck, try flying!"

There was more, all of it lost to me struggling to tell her to stop before I asphyxiated—the irony of which, after all we had been through, revved both of us into ragged sobs accented by cackle-gurgles, like masochists joyfully garrotting each other with piano wire. Already challenging the limits of human physiology, this quasi-obscene theatre escalated when Bonnie abruptly inhaled what must have been an agonizing double snort for a 130lb woman, and the second funniest sound I had ever heard dropped me to the floor in convulsions.

I can only speculate, but the complexity of my sobbing seizure must have been the funniest sound Bonnie had ever heard; I have no idea how long we writhed in our respective states of euphoria, but both of my hands cramped from squeezing my penis. Saying this did nothing to resolve matters.

Rivers of pain rippling through tributaries of ecstasy emanating from body parts not designed for either activity finally created a simul-taneous, double-huffing moment of exquisitely strained anticipation into which Bonnie said, "And you thought *I* was crazy."

[376]

Her emphasis evoked the encompassing perception that telling anyone what I now knew to be true would require explaining everything. And not even then.

The ludicrousness of *me* being trapped by the truth was an unbearable delight to my every corpuscle; I dropped the phone and began crawling across the fine pile carpet toward the bathroom, like a slug through my spittle and mucus, because I didn't want Ed to find me lying in my own waste, face grotesquely contorted in what a puzzled coroner would eventually call 'mirthicide'.

***

We met outside of Nolan's fifty minutes later and exchanged nods while visibly stifling impulses as if we each had a soot ring around one eye. Entering the restaurant together, taking undue care not to trip over the pattern imbedded in the tile floor, we took our usual seats by the window just as they became available.

Uncertain about what drug we were on so early in the day, Bréta suggested an odd breakfast concoction that Bonnie declined with the unsolicited explanation, "You had be there. The usual, please."

Bréta shrugged, leaving us in that peculiar space of not knowing what to say after everything and nothing had changed. After one false start each, Bonnie cleared her throat and took the lead.

"Every direct experience I've had with Intent brought ramifications that transcended their immediate effects. Being yanked out of your body to glimpse our timeless existence, for example, proved that Spirit is real, and their quest is underway, but it also took your recovery past the point of change where it has now become inevitable."

"*My* recovery?"

"You are the first to be rescued."

"From what?"

"You believe in nothing and trust no one," she said warmly. "You would be empty without fear and suspicion; the journey has exhausted you. You are on the cusp of becoming a permanent prisoner of yourself, so you were sent to me."

"But... but all of the lessons..." I stammered.

"...were preliminary," Bonnie finished my thought. "They were about having you accept that you need them. Even then you needed a push; a rise, actually," she grinned.

"I'm just beginning?" I said, incredulously.

"Think about it. What have you really learned?"

[377]

"I can list all of the lessons," I said, without hesitation. Then I realised my error. "But that's not what you mean."

"Tell me what I mean."

Working my tongue around unformed thoughts, I said, "You demonstrated how our thinking is dangerously skewed, how we constantly confuse ourselves, and I experienced enough moments of true clarity to know how and why we're like this." I raised my brow.

"You're this close," she said, holding her thumb and forefinger together. "What was the essence of our chat on the stairs?"

My joyful, but stunned, state of mind allowed me to envision our last confrontation impersonally; I saw it as the student's journey being a message that represented the ways of the masses who would fight to the last of their reason to remain as they were. There would be resistance and many would be casualties of free will, but it could be no other way because as a species we are quite mad.

"Shhhhit," I said, exhaling a whisper as I realised I had barely skimmed the surface of...anything. I was an idiot, just a little less dangerous after the Universe … crap.

"Who, who are you?" I stammered.

"I think you know who I am," she said evenly.

"I guess the question is, what are you?" I said, finding courage to voice this thought.

"I guess it is," Kha-li's messenger deadpanned.

Epilogue

"Simplistically," Bonnie said with a casualness I had never before seen, "there are three phases to your journey. Phase one represented mankind's reactions to their perceptions of the world they created. Specifically, fear forced you to focus inwardly so that self-absorption became the shield that further blinded you to all that was not about you, while self-importance demanded that you compete against the contradiction of hiding your secrets while ensuring the accomplishments that created them were acknowledged. As you appeared to win battles in social and professional circumstances, self-interest demanded that you distance yourself from the carnage both of these encounters generated and the world you perceived became increasingly naïve. As a self-anointed monarch stranded on an island of his buried secrets, you used blunt force denial and razor sarcasm to defend against perceived intruders, and you balanced these unwinnable conflicts by conquering unsuspecting women to allay your true sense of powerlessness."

"Thanks."

"I choose to accept your words as spoken, and I say that it has been my profound honour to have been gifted with you as my first student, this time around. You are not only welcome, but cherished, so it is I who thank you."

"You're welcome," I mumbled.

Bonnie continued speaking with the casual air of what I then interpreted as comprehensive relief. "Phase one represented the unavoidable self-stalking lessons created by the average man's choices. The second phase of your journey is not based on my acts of subterfuge, just yours, nor is it otherwise average by any measure. It is about consciously being stalked into recognizing instances of aberrant behaviour, and categorizing these so that you can learn to stop them. Theoretically, you could make this an intellectual endeavour aimed at defeating the addictions of personality that uphold your self-image, and I will offer you many lessons in this way. However, I know of no instances where a student was able to do this, because they consider their behaviours to be who they are, not how they feel about an interpretation of themselves." She inhaled deeply. "In reality, every-thing I say will be an observation, but you will be unable to interpret my remarks in any other way but criticism. It is because my every comment will sound like a challenge for you to choose between continuing or quitting, phase two is the single most difficult physical evolutionary event you, and everyone else, will ever face, while its reward is the most important achievement an individual can make. This is claiming as their own knowledge what they are really like. Without this knowledge, your evolutionary journey all but stalls because access to true power depends upon it. I say all but stalls because, of necessity, you will know more than enough to harm yourself before you reach this stage."

"All of this," I interjected to voice a troubling thought, "means becoming like you - a loner, I mean?"

"Until there are others of like mind and similar training, yes." She softened her tone. "You are free to communicate anything to anyone, but know that if you speak about your training and unusual experiences the people who know you will think you have cracked under the strain of post-traumatic stress, which does apply but isn't the point. And those who don't know you won't want to know a crazy man any more than you wanted to know me, in other than the biblical sense. That said," she grinned, "There's a certain elegance in the irony."

I chuckled at the memory of the comment that almost killed me: 'And you thought *I* was crazy.' Now there were two of us.

"Right now," Bonnie said seriously, "leaving the world of the average man might seem like an arrogant, fanciful, and fearful task, but you've already left your feet—literally this time—so all you can logically do is face your destiny head on. As you noted, it would be stupid not to."

"I guess I'm feeling—you know, like it's all too much to take in, and I still don't understand why me. I mean, I get that I volunteered but there has to have been a lot of candidates?"

"Kha-lib will tell you about your evolutionary history in terms of why you were chosen." She shifted in her seat, moving closer to me. "Your success in this training is still a probability, not an inevitability, so I want you to hold onto these words until the day you die, because they might be the reason you choose not to, at least on that day: You're not grasping the significance of what's on offer. There are many events to come that will overwhelm your sense and senses because they are designed to lead you into another cognition entirely, where it is

[380]

possible to access knowledge directly, thereby making life as you now know it antiquated."

I didn't have to ask.

"I'll keep it simple for today, but don't for a second underestimate the potential of what I'm telling you: this other cognition is based on knowledge handed down for millennia by seers, shamans, and mystics by any other name who learned that we literally assemble our view of the physical world energetically. They also deduced the processes responsible for awareness, and realized that we all fall under the umbrella of the cognition of the average person; it is the evolutionary starting point of all physical journeys and there are no exceptions. To believe you are not average by force of any ability, liability, accomplishments, or lack thereof, is to pinpoint lessons yet to faced in your journey."

She paused and I said, "So far, so good."

Bonnie continued. "To get out from under that umbrella, one must have the evolutionary energy or an extremely rare Will to change. This is because seeing ourselves is so difficult that it requires the aid of a relentless teacher who understands the moods and modes of man so well as to become an overt perpetrator of their freedom. Maybe predator is a more accurate term," she said, briefly closing her eyes, "but I'll deal with that tomorrow. To fully embrace this knowledge as one's own is to live in the cognition of a stalker, which is your natural bent. This cognition will someday include the clarity you frequently experienced, and Intending to Know as assumptions of your energetic reality."

"Are you saying my brushes with clarity will become a way of thinking, and that what I don't understand I can Intend to Know, according to the rules of energy, that is?"

"This is inevitable, although maybe not this time around. It's up to you." She leaned closer. "To help you grasp the enormity of that evolutionary step, personal experiences of merely standing on the doorstep of a stalker's cognition occurred when we shared assumptions in our snappy conversations and when you simply understood the back-story of Rachel's and Meaghan's tales. These experiences were not even a function of Knowing, but a consequence of enhancing your general awareness through practicing clarity for only a few weeks. Beginning to get the big picture?"

"Better."

She nodded. "My actions, viewed from within the cognition of stalking you into seeing yourself, will be based on a coherent system of regulations that I will explain as aspects of it become appropriate to reveal, but because you stand outside of this system I will appear to be many things at odd times, sometimes simply crazy, then suddenly what you consider to be normal."

"Like your merchants... like you've sometimes been."

"From the stalker's standpoint, these events are reversed."

"So I'm nuts," I said as a spontaneous statement I couldn't fully appreciate.

"Annnd?" she said, enticing me to conquer another intellectual hill with her anticipation.

"Annnd... shit," I said crisply, like the last word most often heard on scorched cockpit recorders. "We really are, I mean, this place *is* an asylum!"

Nodding with sad satisfaction, Bonnie said, "There will come a stark moment, when you are momentarily standing outside the cognition of the average person, that you will embrace this recognition in its totality, and you will literally need something to hang onto."

Apparently satisfied with my limited comprehension of my circumstance, she said impersonally, "To help you get you over yourself and enter into a new cognition, I will use every resource I can to stalk your beliefs into plain sight. Everything you say, think, and do is fair game, including your dreams because I will either know about them, or be in them to propel you along. It is irrelevant if you think you are hallucinating, or that I am lying about anything; the sooner you fully embrace the fact that Spirit has manifest on your behest, and that I can know whatever I need to know to teach you the better off you will be."

"Be in my dreams?"

"You know the dreamer and the dreamed are reversed, so why not here *and* there?"

"It's a bit personal," I said.

"Nothing is personal. That's the entire point."

"What if I don't make it?"

"You have the same choices everyone has, to quit or continue; you will know enough to be able do that on your own," she added, but I wasn't reassured.

"What if I don't continue?"

"Life will become intolerable," she said evenly, and I understood her as best a man living inside the average person's cognition could: Ed had already noticed I was becoming impatient with our friend's casual conversations at the Avalon, although the visuals compensated....

"As you become ready for phase three," she said, interrupting my placating thoughts, "you will learn about, or experience, the magical arts that the returning emissaries will master, if only to know that their abilities are real. The transition between phase one and the beginning of your end starts tomorrow, when we will overtly stalk an average man into unmasking the truly nasty person that lies beneath his good intentions."

To my surprise, Bonnie stood up, smiled warmly, and with a jaunty wave toward Bréta, all but skipped toward the door.

"I'll get the tab," I joked.

She turned, smiled an unrecognizably youthful face, and said, "Our first lesson will be to dismember the illusion that you are a generous soul, that in fact you are cheap, and otherwise withhold personal resources like kindness and humour until you can get something for them. See you tomorrow at nine, my friend." She left Nolan's gleefully, and me with a bill plus a ten percent tip that took all of my cash to the penny.

Confused by her unwarranted accusation, annoyed that she had left me alone on this special day, and having to go to the bank again, I saw neither the irony nor the omen in the moment.

Not right away.

Excerpt from Volume Two:
Stalking The Bridge of Reason

On the way to the restaurant, Bonnie and Mattie repeated their offer to pick up my share of the tab, but I insisted on stopping at a cash machine to deposit my cheque and make a withdrawal. By insisted, I mean that I was driving, so I ignored them.

As I turned into a space in front of the bank, I discovered too late that the sidewalk was being modified for wheelchair access. Concrete forms and assorted construction debris extended two feet from the curb. I was pondering whether to leave Bonnie's car partially exposed to traffic, when we all noticed an elderly gentleman shuffle to a sudden halt next to us. His walker had become stuck in a crevice between the old cement and the wooden curb forms. In the instant of thinking that I should get out and help him, Bonnie, channelling Kha-lib in his distinctive accent, said, "Are you not going to help him?"

With flagrant emphasis on surprise, I said, "I was just going to do that!" Feeling foolish, I leapt out of the car to offer the man a hand, nearly losing Bonnie's door to oncoming traffic in the process. The man beamed without inhibition at my risky rush to his aid.

Holding him steady with one hand, I pulled his walker out of the crevice while, without complaint, he began an in-depth explanation of his plight. Recently released from a hospital, after a hip operation, he was taking his daily walk of therapy. He didn't dare lift his walker over the wooden forms, the foot deep hole on the other side of it notwithstanding. Looking at the six inch drop of the curb, he said, "I'll need help for that, anyway."

"And that," I said, pointing across the street at similar debris then I held his weight while he gingerly stepped down to road level.

Making our way across the broad intersection at a snail's pace, he continued his monologue like a child revealing a secret so precious that I thought we'd have to prick our fingers to seal a vow of silence before we parted company.

"My wife doesn't know how far I go," he said, conspiratorially. "She thinks I'm taking sun in front of our apartment, so my rapid recovery is an act of God to her." He looked sideways and winked at me. "I haven't told her about the help I've been giving God. She'd be frightened I might fall; that's why she isn't walking with me now."

His conniving charm might have suggested that his chuckles were of triumph, had his eyes not misted in appreciation for the love of a woman who had shared his life for fifty-one years, come October.

We made our way through the obstacles on the other side of the road, where I finally let him go. He thanked me, joking that he would have to find another route home, one also out of sight of his apartment window. Chuckling a last time for me, though I dare say not for the last of a day which he refused to measure a few painful inches at a time as he continued his journey. If someone else was lucky, I thought as I trotted back across the intersection, he would go home the same way.

I used the bank machine and returned to the car.

Barely seated, with my door still ajar, Kha-lib said, "How do you feel?"

"It was great to meet such a gentle man," I said, putting the key into the ignition.

"Do you regret helping him?"

"Of course not," I replied, so surprised at the question that I turned to face Bonnie in the back seat.

"Did he mind you helping him?" Kha-lib said.

"Not at all. It was a social occasion—he told me about his convalesc—"

"There are times when one needs help," Kha-lib cut me off. "If that man had acted as you do, he would have been embarrassed and slighted you. This would have robbed you of your joy in helping him, while cheating himself out of the very memories that now sustain him. This is what you do when others offer you their knowledge, friendship, and generosity."

I got the point—couldn't miss it, which left nothing more to be said on the matter.

We drove to the restaurant, where I struggled to offer the gift of my sparkling personality to our table of three. When lunch was over, I said I would be grateful if Bonnie and Mattie would allow me to construct some positive memories, as well. Bonnie shot me her sketch artist's look.

Though my tone had been forced, my level gaze told her that the last few days of lessons had drained me of sarcasm. My offer was a conscious attempt to change my ways, and to begin right away, as other lessons had made abundantly clear was the only way to challenge myself. Later wouldn't do.

Bonnie slid the tab over to me and said, "Give this some thought: what core difference existed between your attitude before you met that man and his attitude both before and after he met you?"

"Appreciation," I said right away.

"What guts appreciation?"

"I'll have to give that some thought."

[385]

John Axelson lives in the Kootenay Mountains of British Columbia, with Geri, Zoot, Vista, and Simon.

Made in the USA
Charleston, SC
16 November 2011